ZIGGY copyright 1991 ZIGGY AND FRIENDS, INC.
Dist. by UNIVERSAL PRESS SYNDICATE. Reprinted with permission. All rights reserved.

Looking for essential information about the 250 leading colleges that most students should consider?

---

320 helpful pages

150 important facts and figures

Set out in clear, concise form on each of 130 leading schools with average SATs over 1080

Student body - Academics - Admissions
Class Composition - Costs - Financial Aid
Housing - Alumni Support - Endowment, etc.

---

45 unique statistical tables
on
Guide book ratings - Average SATs -Minorities
Percent admitted - Transfer prospects
Graduation rate - Out of state students
Housing on campus
and other pertinent information

Handy location maps:
Northeast - Mid Atlantic - South - Midwest - West

Basic useful facts on 120 other colleges with average SATs over 1000

The College Comparison Guide

Kiliaen V. R. Townsend
Educational Consultant
Author of *The Boarding School Guide*

AGEE PUBLISHERS INC.
Athens, Georgia

All inquiries should be addressed to:
Kiliaen V. R. Townsend
56 Paces West Drive, N.W.
Atlanta, Georgia 30327
(404) 261-2682

Library of Congress Catalog Card No. 92-73762

Agee Publishers, Inc.
Athens, Georgia 30603

Printed in the United States of America

To my late father, who lived in the old days
when he could skip college altogether,
go to work in Wall Street as a teenager
and become a partner in a leading
brokerage firm at the ripe old age of 23.

Acknowledgments

The cover design and the assembly of the entire book on computer discs were the fine, patient work of Preston Rose and Roberta Granville of Preston Rose Printing Company in Atlanta.

Invaluable technical advice and proofreading were provided by Jane Agee of Agee Publishers, Inc. Athens, Georgia.

Some information, including 1992-1993 tuition, was obtained from the colleges themselves.

* Considerable data was also provided by College Research Group of Concord, MA. All data is copyright and all rights reserved.

* The National Association of College and University Business Officers, Washington, DC furnished the endowment information set out on pages 48-49 and is as of 1991.

* Council of Aid to Education, NYC, supplied the Alumni financial information on Pages 50-51 and is based on 1990 figures.

Last but not least, my wife, Rena, who was willing, ready and able to do whatever was not done otherwise.

* *The reader should bear in mind that much of this information is based on the 1991-92 school year. Tuition figures can be expected to increase 5 to 7% a year in most cases. Most other numbers remain relatively constant over at least a two or three year span.*

Contents

Introduction

With over 2000 four year colleges, it's very easy to be unaware of or overlook some that are entirely suitable as to location, size, academics, financial aid, etc.

In addition, many students believe or are advised that SATs below 1000 and certainly as far down as 900 eliminate as a possibility all the more selective colleges and particularly the well-known ones.

This is actually not the case. And this COLLEGE COMPARISON GUIDE furnishes the pertinent facts and figures on 187 selective colleges that afford a possible "reach" for students with SATs of 900 or higher. (See pages 18-23). At the same time, it includes all the very selective colleges for the better-than-average students.

Another 63 fine colleges, set out on pages 24-25, are possibilities for those with SATs as low as 800.

Another misconception is about actual cost. The financial aid offered, particularly by many of the more selective colleges with substantial endowments, levels the net outlay. Therefore, if one qualifies on a need basis, the awards will be such that the net cost of the more expensive colleges may often be approximately the same as the less expensive. And that includes matching the low cost of public universities in many instances. In short, nobody should fail to apply and determine the aid offered by any college or university that otherwise fits his or her needs and desires.

The various statistical tables provide all the essential information that can be obtained otherwise only by researching a number of voluminous college guides or catalogues.

As explained on pages 16-17, these, then, are all of the more selective colleges and universities from which many of the high school students should make their preliminary choices. And this COLLEGE COMPARISON GUIDE assembles all the necessary information between the covers of one book for the early elimination decision process.

Those who have already been through the laborious college search will recognize immediately the usefulness of this publication. And the students and parents about to start such an important task will find this COLLEGE COMPARISON GUIDE most helpful.

250 Leading Colleges (in 41 states)

130 with average SATs above 1080 and over 800 out-of-state undergraduates (shown in CAPS)

57 with average SATs above 1080 but less than 800 out-of-state undergraduates (shown in *italics*)

63 with average SATs from 1000 to 1080 and over 800 out-of-state undergraduates (shown in lower case)

63 Public (P) 8 Women (W) 3 Men (M)

Religious affiliation, if any, shown in parentheses

District of Columbia (4)

Florida (9)

Georgia (6)

Illinois (7)

Indiana (10)

Iowa (5)

Kentucky

Louisiana (2)

Maine (3)

Maryland (6)

Massachusetts (19)

Michigan (8)

Minnesota (6)

Missouri (3)

Nebraska

New Hampshire (2)

New Jersey (5)

New Mexico (2)

New York (34)

North Carolina (5)

Ohio (10)

Oklahoma

Oregon (4)

Pennsylvania (25)

Rhode Island (4)

South Carolina (3)

Tennessee (3)

Texas (9)

Utah

Vermont (3)

Virginia (9)

Washington (4)

West Virginia

Wisconsin (4)

Basis For Selection of the 250 Colleges

This guide's selection of 250, or 12.5% of the 2000 four year colleges, provides a broad choice for the exceptional student as well as the average student with SATs even as low as 800.

With so many colleges to choose from, it's essential to narrow the number to a few hundred for even the most preliminary exploration.

The institutions with an average freshman class SAT score above 1080 have been included. The institutions (130) with at least 800 out of state undergraduates are listed individually in considerable depth. (pages 18-21 and 58-217)

An additional 57 colleges that have average SATs over 1080 but less than 800 out of state undergraduates are shown with eight pertinent statistics. (pages 22-23)

These 187 more selective schools provide a broad cross section, namely, the 13 nationwide with average SATs over 1300 as well as a number in the 1100 range. The latter provide a "reach" for students with SATs as low as 900, since most of the colleges take some students as much as 200 points below their freshman class average SATs.

Also included are 63 schools that have average SATs above 1000 but below 1085 and also have at least 800 out of state undergraduates (pages 24-25). These afford an opportunity for students with SATs even in the 800 range, particularly if they are above average in some areas other than academics.

These 250 colleges and universities are among the 200 to 300 that are recognized as the more selective by other leading college guides that cover all the 2000 four year schools. And the highly regarded *Fiske Guide to Colleges* as well as the Yale Daily News *Inside Guide to Colleges* include most of these 250 in their selection of 300 outstanding colleges.

Pope's book, *Looking Beyond the Ivy League,* has almost all of the 250 in his chapter entitled "A Few Favorites and Two Hundred Worth Going To". And the 33 public colleges designated as highly selective by Nemko's *How to Get an Ivy League Education at a State University* are included in these 250.

U. S. News And World Report's Annual Survey of 1373 colleges places these 250 either in the top 50, or high in their regional selections or are listed, with few exceptions, in quartile one or two.

These 250 schools make up the great majority of the selective liberal arts colleges and leading research universities designated by the Carnegie Foundation for the Advancement of Teaching. Also 132, or over 80%, of the 160 institutions with endowments over 60 million dollars are among these 250. (Source: National Association of Colleges and University Business Officers).

In addition, this selective group of 250 institutions includes well over two thirds of the universities with the largest research libraries in the U. S. (Source: Association of Research Libraries), and three-fourths of the top ones in total research and spending. (Source: National Science Foundation).

In regard to the 187 colleges with average SATs over 1080 (pages 18-23), a numerical rating is listed in the column headed "Average Rating Guide Books." This is arrived at by averaging together the ratings given by five well-known college guidebooks. The rating categories follow:

"1" indicates "most selective."
"2" indicates "highly selective."
"3" indicates "very selective."
"4" indicates "selective."

It should be kept in mind that all of these 187 colleges are well above average among the 2000 four-year schools.

Moreover, the 63 other colleges included in this guide with SAT averages between 1000 and 1080 (pages 24-25) are relatively selective compared with most of the remaining 1750 institutions that are not included in this COLLEGE COMPARISON GUIDE.

Therefore, the 250 schools in this book are definitely the ones that many students should be seriously considering for their preliminary selections. They provide 41 states to choose as to location, a wide selection as to size and academics, a number of public as well as private colleges, and both "back-ups" and "reaches" for all students whose SATs are more than 800.

130 Leading Colleges

with average SATs over 1080
and
at least 800 out of State
Undergraduates
5 are for women only (W)

22 are Public Universities (P)

% In State Students	% Rtn. 2nd Yr.	Graduate after 4 Yrs.	Average Rating Guide Books	Ratings: 1 Most Selective, 2 Highly Selective, 3 Very Selective		No. of Undergrads	Graduate Students	% In Top 5th High Sch. Class	Average SAT or ACTS
10	88	57	2.6	American University	DC	4900	3800	57	1135
9	95	91	1	Amherst	MA	1600	0	95	1310
60	87	85	3	Babson	MA	1600	1400	50	1110
40	95	87	1.4	Barnard (W)	NY	2200	0	77	1250
13	98	88	1.8	Bates	ME	1500	0	80	1250
35	98	85	2	Boston College	MA	8700	4300	92	1200
30	85	65	2.2	Boston University	MA	14,000	9700	70	1145
17	93	90	1.2	Bowdoin	ME	1350	0	80	1300
30	90	75	1.8	Brandeis	MA	2900	850	75	1220
6	97	89	1	Brown	RI	5600	1500	90	1280
13	96	85	1.2	Bryn Mawr (W)	PA	1200	650	80	1260
29	95	86	2	Bucknell	PA	3400	200	70	1195
85	89	65	1.8	Calif. U of-Berkeley (P)	CA	21,500	9000	95	1195
95	94	60	2.2	Calif. U of-L.A. (P)	CA	24,000	12,000	NA	1125
25	95	77	1.6	Carleton	MN	1700	0	80	1290
38	90	70	2	Carnegie Mellon	PA	4100	2600	78	1230
69	90	69	2.2	Case Western	OH	2900	5500	87	1200
5	90	65	3	Catholic University	DC	3100	3300	36	1085
25	93	71	1	Chicago, University of	IL	3400	7400	90	1290
30	87	70	2.6	Clark	MA	2200	700	63	1090
12	95	81	2	Colby	ME	1700	0	60	1200
35	96	85	1.8	Colgate	NY	2700	0	83	1250
30	90	75	2	Colorado College	CO	1900	22	75	1160
65	82	55	3	Colorado, U of (P)	CO	20,000	4700	59	1085
20	98	92	1	Columbia	NY	3200	16,000	95	1270
20	98	85	2	Connecticut College	CT	1600	75	67	1225
47	95	80	1	Cornell University	NY	12,400	5500	96	1290
5	95	94	1	Dartmouth	NH	4300	1000	95	1300
30	98	90	1.8	Davidson	NC	1400	0	90	1240
43	87	50	3.2	Delaware, U of (P)	DE	13,000	2500	65	1085
25	90	77	3.2	Denison	OH	2000	0	48	1085
40	87	78	2.8	Depauw	IN	2300	0	65	1140

There are also 2 pages on each of the above colleges starting on page 58

130 Leading Colleges

with average SATs over 1080
and
at least 800 out of State
Undergraduates
5 are for women only (W)

22 are Public Universities (P)

% In State Students	% Rtn. 2nd Yr.	Graduate after 4 Yrs.	Average Rating Guide Books	Ratings: 1 Most Selective, 2 Highly Selective, 3 Very Selective		No. of Undergrads	Graduate Students	% In Top 5th High Sch. Class	Average SAT or ACTS
40	95	82	2.2	Dickinson College	PA	2050	0	76	1130
15	99	93	1	Duke	NC	5950	4400	97	1320
15	72	75	2.8	Earlham	IN	1150	0	55	1120
20	90	75	2	Emory University	GA	4600	4100	75	1210
35	91	84	2.4	Fairfield	CT	2900	800	57	1115
92	88	40	2.4	Florida, U of (P)	FL	23,000	7700	NA	1155
75	92	78	2.8	Fordham University	NY	5050	6500	60	1085
38	92	79	2	Franklin and Marshall	PA	1800	0	43	1180
35	95	75	2.4	Furman	SC	2450	400	80	1190
2	95	78	1.2	Georgetown	DC	5600	5600	85	1230
55	85	63	2.6	George Washington	DC	5900	8600	65	1130
65	86	66	2	Georgia Tech (P)	GA	8600	2750	88	1190
25	90	76	2.4	Gettysburg	PA	1900	0	75	1120
48	91	72	2.2	GMI Engineering	MI	2500	700	87	1150
25	95	78	1.8	Grinnell	IA	1250	0	78	1235
48	94	85	2	Hamilton College	NY	1650	0	78	1170
14	84	50	2.8	Hampshire College	MA	1250	0	27	1105
22	97	95	1	Harvard	MA	6600	11,200	98	1365
15	97	89	1	Haverford	PA	1150	0	94	1290
45	93	77	2.4	Hobart & William Smith	NY	1850	0	55	1110
35	99	87	2	Holy Cross	MA	2650	0	88	1210
94	95	72	1.8	Il., U of-Urbana (P)	IL	25,000	6200	82	1145
77	92	60	2.8	James Madison (P)	VA	9300	1400	64	1090
20	93	80	1	Johns Hopkins	MD	3000	1300	88	1290
25	90	80	2.2	Kenyon	OH	1550	0	70	1170
20	96	88	2	Lafayette	PA	2000	0	80	1200
29	95	85	2	Lehigh University	PA	4500	4500	71	1180
25	85	65	3.2	Lewis and Clark	OR	2000	700	53	1105
55	90	65	3.2	Loyola College	MD	3100	2800	50	1100
25	90	61	2	Macalester	MN	1750	0	78	1220
53	89	72	3.2	Marquette	WI	7850	3000	54	1085
10	97	87	1	MIT	MA	4400	5000	99	1355

There are also 2 pages on each of the above colleges starting on page 58

130 Leading Colleges

with average SATs over 1080
and
at least 800 out of State
Undergraduates
5 are for women only (W)

22 are Public Universities (P)

% In State Students	% Rtn. 2nd Yr.	Graduate after 4 Yrs.	Average Rating Guide Books	Ratings: 1 Most Selective, 2 Highly Selective, 3 Very Selective		No. of Undergrads	Graduate Students	% In Top 5th High Sch. Class	Average SAT or ACTS
77	93	68	2.6	Miami University (P)	OH	13,600	1600	69	1140
45		70	2.6	Miami, U of	FL	7750	5100	59	1100
70	90	75	1.8	Michigan, U of-Ann A(P)	MI	21,800	13,200	90	1190
5	85	91	1.6	Middlebury	VT	1950	0	86	1250
20	95	80	2	Mount Holyoke (W)	MA	1950	0	74	1160
34	90	85	2.6	Muhlenberg	PA	1600	0	63	1100
50	87	70	2.2	New York University	NY	14,500	14,000	45	1140
25	95	84	1.4	Northwestern	IL	7250	4000	89	1260
10	96	92	1.4	Notre Dame, U of	IN	7500	2200	95	1250
11	90	77	1.4	Oberlin	OH	2700	0	84	1250
54	92	75	2	Occidental	CA	1650	20	76	1170
47	85	71	2.8	Ohio Wesleyan	OH	2000	0	50	1100
83	84	35	2.6	Penn State-Park (P)	PA	30,000	6500	73	1095
20	96	90	1	Pennsylvania, U of	PA	9200	10,300	93	1270
52	81	80	2.8	Pepperdine	CA	2600	85	90	1085
40	99	85	1	Pomona	CA	1400	0	90	1320
14	97	95	1	Princeton	NJ	4500	1800	97	1350
15	96	87	2.8	Providence College	RI	3800	650	47	1085
20	90	57	1.6	Reed	OR	1250	20	93	1250
40	85	72	1.8	Rensselaer Polytech	NY	4400	2050	83	1230
34	87	70	2.2	Rhodes	TN	1350	0	75	1200
47	95	88	1	Rice	TX	2700	1300	75	1345
20	93	76	2.4	Richmond, U of	VA	2800	2000	59	1215
48	90	68	2	Rochester, U of	NY	4800	2300	59	1150
30	88	72	3	Rollins	FL	1500	600	53	1085
85	91	59	2.2	Rutgers, New Bruns. (P)	NJ	8000	0	83	1140
49	89	80	3.2	St. Lawrence University	NY	1925	129	50	1085
60	95	66	2	St. Olaf	MN	3000	0	68	1110
68	90	68	3.2	Santa Clara	CA	3650	3400	60	1085
31	91	75	2.4	Skidmore	NY	2150	0	38	1150
14	92	84	1.6	Smith (W)	MA	2550	100	83	1190
55	94	63	3.2	Sou. Calif., U of	CA	16,000	14,000	68	1085
52	86	69	3.2	Southern Methodist	TX	5000	3400	65	1085

There are also 2 pages on each of the above colleges starting on page 58

130 Leading Colleges

with average SATs over 1080
and
at least 800 out of State
Undergraduates
5 are for women only (W)

22 are Public Universities (P)

Ratings: 1 Most Selective
2 Highly Selective
3 Very Selective

% In State Students	% Rtn. 2nd Yr.	Graduate after 4 Yrs.	Average Rating Guide Books	College	State	No. of Undergrads	Graduate Students	% In Top 5th High Sch. Class	Average SAT or ACTS
37	97	91	1	Stanford	CA	6500	6850	96	1340
10	99	80	1	Swarthmore	PA	1300	0	80	1330
35	91	70	2.6	Syracuse University	NY	12,000	4500	63	1120
94	83	52	2.2	Texas, U of-Austin (P)	TX	37,000	12,000	78	1105
34	95	88	1.8	Trinity College	CT	1750	180	40	1180
60	90	69	2.2	Trinity University	TX	2250	200	83	1210
74	99	90	1.4	Tufts	MA	4700	3050	86	1250
19	90	75	2.4	Tulane	LA	5600	4000	57	1175
61	85	65	3	Tulsa, U of	OK	2600	1350	47	1100
55	94	76	2	Union	NY	2000	250	70	1170
2	83	74	2	US Air Force Acad. (P)	CO	4300	0	92	1220
13	85	76	1.4	US Military Academy (P)	NY	4400	0	86	1215
5	86	74	1.6	US Naval Academy (P)	MD	4300	0	81	1240
82	92	77	1.8	UNC-Chapel Hill (P)	NC	15,000	6200	93	1110
22	87	77	2.2	University of the South	TN	1051	75	75	1155
18	90	79	2.2	Vanderbilt	TN	5200	3800	54	1195
41	98	86	1.6	Vassar	NY	2450	0	76	1240
49	86	71	3	Vermont, U of (P)	VT	8500	1450	68	1085
30	91	82	2.6	Villanova	PA	6400	3000	51	1110
65	97	78	1.4	Virginia, U of (P)	VA	11,100	6200	68	1210
75	89	71	3	Virginia Polytech (P)	VA	18,200	4100	61	1100
39	92	72	2	Wake Forest	NC	3400	1950	85	1250
11	95	85	1.4	Washington and Lee	VA	1600	400	83	1250
15	92	84	1.8	Washington University	MO	5000	5300	87	1210
90	89	51	2.8	Washington, U of (P)	WA	20,000	9000	70	1090
16	98	84	1	Wellesley (W)	MA	2300	0	92	1250
10	97	92	1	Wesleyan University	CT	2650	150	89	1285
24	94	75	2.4	Wheaton College	IL	2200	300	77	1145
65	95	80	1.4	William and Mary	VA	5250	1600	91	1225
12	98	90	1	Williams College	MA	2050	50	91	1335
70	86	61	2.6	Wisconsin, U of (P)	WI	27,000	11,600	62	1090
11	89	65	2	Worcester Polytech	MA	2700	1000	85	1210
10	98	95	1	Yale	CT	5200	5600	95	1350

There are also 2 pages on each of the above colleges starting on page 58

57 Leading Colleges
with average SATs over 1080
but
fewer than 800 out of State
Undergraduates

% In State Students	% Rtn. 2nd Yr.	Graduate after 4 Yrs.	Average Rating Guide Books	3 Men only (M) 3 Women only (W) 17 Public Universities (P)		No. of Undergrads	Graduate Students	% In Top 4th High Sch. Class	Average SAT or ACTS
50	80	55	2.8	Agnes Scott (W)	GA	515	0	70	1085
85	85	65	3.2	Albion	MI	1700	0	60	1110
45	95	90	2.8	Albright	PA	1300	0	75	1120
75	80	65	3.2	Alfred	NY	2000	300	70	1085
95	85	65	3.2	Alma	MI	1200	0	80	1110
30	90	50	2.4	Bard	NY	900	110	70	1210
35	95	75	1	Cal Tech	CA	850	1000	100	1400
95	95	60	2.4	Ca., U of-San Diego (P)	CA	14,000	2100	100	1150
65	85	75	2.2	Centre	KY	850	0	82	1100
50	90	80	1.4	Claremont McKenna	CA	850	0	95	1260
75	90	90	2.6	Clarkson	NY	3000	400	80	1200
70	90	55	2.2	Co. S. of Mines (P)	CO	1500	800	90	1180
40	95	80	1	Columbia Engr.	NY	1000	1100	95	1290
75	85	85	1.4	Cooper Union	NY	950	50	90	1250
65	85	65	2.8	Dallas, U of	TX	1000	1700	70	1120
50	90	80	2.4	Drew	NJ	1400	850	80	1140
65	85	80	3	Grove City	PA	2100	0	90	1110
75	75	40	3	Hamline	MN	1500	800	75	1100
55	90	60	3	Hampden-Sydney (M)	VA	950	0	45	1095
50	95	85	1	Harvey Mudd	CA	540	0	100	1370
90	90	25	2.6	Illinois Wesleyan	IL	1700	0	65	1160
75	90	70	2.4	Kalamazoo	MI	1250	0	50	1130
40	85	75	2.4	Lawrence University	WI	1250	0	80	1130
75	90	65	3	Mary Washington (P)	VA	2800	75	70	1085
85	85	60	3	Mich. Tech (P)	MI	5600	500	75	1105
80	90	70	2	Mn., U of-Morris (P)	MN	2000	0	90	1130
80	80	50	3	Mo., U of-Rolla (P)	MO	3700	1200	75	1110
50	85	35	2	New Coll. of S. Fl. (P)	FL	520	0	70	1260
80	65	40	3	NM Inst. of Mining (P)	NM	700	200	60	1125

57 Leading Colleges

with average SATs over 1080
but
fewer than 800 out of State
Undergraduates

% In State Students	% Rtn. 2nd Yr.	Graduate after 4 Yrs.	Average Rating Guide Books	3 Men only (M) 3 Women only (W) 17 Public Universities (P)		No. of Undergrads	Graduate Students	% In Top 4th High Sch. Class	Average SAT or ACTS
60	75	85	2.4	Oglethorpe	GA	800	50	75	1100
45	90	70	2.6	Pitzer	CA	740	0	50	1110
95	90	65	3	Polytech University	NY	1300	2000	75	1140
75	80	55	2.6	Puget Sound, U of	WA	2900	125	75	1085
55	95	70	3	Ripon	WI	825	0	65	1190
60	85	80	2.2	Rose-Hulman (M)	IN	1300	100	95	1220
15	90	70	1.8	St. John's College	MD	450	50	70	1230
5	85	60	2	St. John's College	NM	370	50	50	1180
90	80	50	3	St. Mary's (P)	MD	1300	0	70	1120
20	90	80	2.6	Sarah Lawrence	NY	950	150	60	1085
45	85	70	2	Scripps (W)	CA	600	0	60	1110
65	85	70	3	Shepherd (P)	WV	2200	0	50	1100
20	85	25	2.6	Simon's Rock of Bard	MA	300	0	75	1140
85	85	65	2.4	Southwestern	TX	1150	0	80	1115
60	85	60	2.2	Stevens	NJ	1350	2000	95	1200
95	90	70	2.2	Suny-Albany (P)	NY	10,500	4600	75	1150
90	80	65	2.2	Suny-Binghampton (P)	NY	8000	2800	95	1155
95	85	45	2.2	Suny-Buffalo (P)	NY	14,000	8400	80	1110
95	90	65	2.2	Suny-Genesco (P)	NY	4800	400	95	1140
90	90	60	2.4	Trenton State (P)	NJ	4700	1000	95	1115
10	90	60	1.4	US Coast Guard (P)	CT	850	0	95	1190
10	85	75	2	US Mer. Marine (P)	NY	850	0	95	1190
60	85	70	3	Ursinus	PA	1200	0	75	1105
90	90	75	2.8	Wabash (M)	IN	1000	0	75	1150
60	85	85	3	Wells (W)	NY	450	0	80	1085
50	90	70	2.4	Whitman	WA	1250	0	80	1140
65	80	55	2.4	Yeshiva	NY	1600	1700	35	1170

63 Leading Colleges

with average SATs between
1000 and 1085
and with over 800
Out of State
Undergraduates

% In State Students	LD Program	% Rtn. 2nd Yr.	Graduate in 5 Yrs.	24 Public Universities (P)		No. of Undergrads	Graduate Students	% In Top 4th High Sch. Class	Average SAT or ACTS
50		90	70	Allegheny	PA	1900	10	70	1080
65	LD	80	60	Arizona, U of (P)	AZ	23,000	7500	75	1041
60	LD	85	55	Auburn (P)	AL	18,000	2400	60	1080
75		85	70	Baylor	TX	10,000	1400	70	1010
65		10	75	Bentley	MA	3950	1600	50	1020
80		90	60	Bradley	IL	4500	750	55	1070
30	LD	80	25	Brigham Young	UT	25,000	2100	70	1025
15		90	85	Bryant College	RI	3000	900	50	1030
55	LD	90	50	Calvin	MI	4000	150	45	1040
55		80	70	Citadel, The (P)	SC	2000	1200	45	1010
70		85	65	Clemson (P)	SC	12,000	3500	60	1025
85	LD	85	65	Connecticut, U of (P)	CT	12,000	4500	65	1050
30	LD	80	65	Cornell College	IA	1150	0	65	1025
45		80	60	Creighton	NE	3500	700	50	1023
60	LD	85	70	Dayton, U of	OH	6500	3500	40	1020
30		90	75	Denver, U of (P)	CO	2750	2800	55	1060
85	LD	80	50	DePaul	IL	6000	4400	65	1030
65	LD	85	65	Drake	IA	3500	3500	60	1005
65	LD	NA	NA	Drexel	PA	7000	3000	70	1055
30		80	70	Eckerd	FL	1350	0	60	1070
15		65	35	Embry-Riddle	FL	5000	100	NA	1025
60		95	90	Evansville, U of	IN	2300	300	65	1010
80	LD	85	45	Florida State (P)	FL	18,500	2500	NA	1080
40		80	55	Florida Tech	FL	2500	1100	75	1075
90		90	30	Florida, U of S. (P)	FL	13,000	4400	NA	1020
90		75	60	George Mason (P)	VA	9400	6400	45	1070
85	LD	80	60	Georgia, U of (P)	GA	19,000	6000	45	1045
35		75	65	Harding	AR	3000	125	55	1020
80	LD	85	60	Hofstra	NY	7100	3700	65	1035
70	LD	80	55	Indiana U-Bloom. (P)	IN	26,000	7000	70	1020
75	LD	80	55	Iowa, U of (P)	IA	17,000	8500	50	1024
55		85	65	Ithaca College	NY	6100	125	65	1060

63 Leading Colleges
with average SATs between
1000 and 1085
and with over 800
Out of State
Undergraduates

% In State Students	LD Program	% Rtn. 2nd. Yr.	Graduate in 5 Yrs.	24 Public Universities (P)		No. of Undergrads	Graduate Students	% In Top 4th High Sch. Class	Average SAT or ACTS
60		95	75	John Carroll	OH	3000	800	40	1040
70		90	90	La Salle	PA	3500	1250	35	1060
60		95	80	Luther College	IA	2200	0	70	1080
55		80	40	Loyola University	LA	2900	1200	45	1020
75	LD	85	50	Md., U of-Coll. Pk .(P)	MD	22,500	9000		1080
80	LD	85	55	Ma., U of-Amherst (P)	MA	18,000	6300	60	1020
50		85	60	Messiah	PA	2200	0	70	1055
90	LD	90	65	Michigan State (P)	MI	31,500	6500	65	1005
80		90	65	Mn., U of-Twin Cities (P)	MN	20,000	12,000	55	1030
60	LD	90	65	New Hampshire, U of (P)	NH	9700	1300	80	1075
75		80	50	NE Missouri State (P)	MO	5600	250	70	1025
83		90	55	N. Carolina State (P)	NC	15,800	4000	84	1055
75	LD	90	75	Ohio University (P)	OH	14,000	2100	50	1010
80		80	40	Oregon, U of (P)	OR	13,000	300	60	1014
60		80	60	Pacific Lutheran	WA	3000	500	70	1040
30		95	70	Parsons Sch. of Design	NY	1800	200	75	1030
90	LD	85		Pittsburgh, U of (P)	PA	13,500	9500	60	1025
70	LD	85	60	Purdue-W. Lafayette (P)	IN	27,000	6100	75	1025
10		70	75	Rhode I. Sch. of Design	RI	1800	100	60	1050
65	LD	85	55	Rochester Institute	NY	8500	1500	50	1030
60		95	75	St. Joseph's	PA	2600	2300	55	1045
15		90	75	Saint Michael's	VT	1700	400	60	1040
55		90	75	San Diego, U of	CA	3500	2200		1035
25		65	60	Savannah Coll. of Art	GA	1400	125	65	1020
55		95	85	Scranton, U of	PA	3850	750	70	1075
35		95	79	Taylor University	IN	1700	0	65	1015
95	LD	80	60	Texas A&M (P)	TX	30,500	7500	80	1040
70		80	55	Texas Christian	TX	5000	1050	55	1025
65		95	70	Valparaiso	IN	3000	550	70	1080
50		90	75	Widener	PA	2650	1900	65	1020
45		85	70	Wittenberg	OH	2300	0	60	1050

Basis for Selection of the 130 Colleges and Universities

The 2000 four-year colleges are narrowed down to 130, or just 6.5% of the total, by selecting the ones that have average SATs over 1080 as well as more than 800 out of state undergraduates.

This "over 800 out of state" provision is an effort to feature the schools that have a student body with considerable geographical diversity and, therefore, are of interest to the vast majority.

As a consequence, this produces a broad cross section of colleges that have better than average academics as well as a "national" or at least an extensive "regional" appeal as contrasted with primarily a "local" or "in state" interest.

This, of course, excludes some very fine small colleges that also enjoy a "national" ranking for academics. With relatively few students, it necessarily results in their having only several hundred out of state undergraduates.

Six notable examples are Cal Tech (CA), Claremont McKenna (CA), Columbia Engineering (NY), Cooper Union (NY), Harvey Mudd (CA) and St. John's (MD).

These 6 and 51 other colleges with SATs also over 1080 but less than 800 out of state undergraduates are set out on pages 22-23.

These 130 institutions listed on pages 18-21 are covered in considerable detail throughout the rest of this book, starting with the 45 comparison tables on pages 30 through 57.

There are two pages on each of the 130 schools (pages 58-317). They are arranged alphabetically, with 150 facts and figures on each one.

It should be pointed out that these 130 colleges and universities provide at least a "reach" for students with SATs of 900 or higher, for many schools accept 200 points lower than their average SATs. And some of the "most selective" colleges with averages of 1300 or more take a few otherwise exceptional applicants with SATs of 1000 or even less.

13 have average SATs of 1300 or more.
49 have average SATs from 1200 to 1300.
49 have average SATs from 1100 to 1200.
19 have average SATs between 1085 and 1100.

18 graduate 90% or more after 4 years.
36 graduate 80% or more after 4 years.
45 graduate 70% or more after 4 years.
23 graduate 60% or more after 4 years.

38 have 2000 undergraduates or less.
35 have 2000 to 4000 undergraduates.
23 have 4000 to 6000 undergraduates.
13 have 6000 to 10,000 undergraduates.
13 have 10,000 to 20,000 undergraduates.
8 have over 20,000 undergraduates.

37 have no graduate students.
27 have under 1000 graduate students.
29 have 1000 to 4000 graduate students.
22 have 4000 to 7000 graduate students.
6 have 7000 to 10,000 graduate students.
10 have over 10,000 graduate students

46 have 25% or less "in-state" undergraduates.
48 have 25% to 50% "in-state" undergraduates.
23 have 50% to 75% "in-state" undergraduates.
13 have over 74% "in-state" undergraduates..

28 have over 95% return 2nd year.
46 have over 90% return 2nd year.
41 have over 85% return 2nd year.
15 have over 80% return 2nd year.

64 of these 130 are colleges with no graduate students or less than 1000.

66 are universities with graduate students from 1000 to as many as 35,000.

130 LEADING COLLEGES — 50 IN MID-ATLANTIC AND SOUTH

WITH SAT AVERAGES OVER 1080 AND AT LEAST 800 OUT OF STATE UNDERGRADUATES

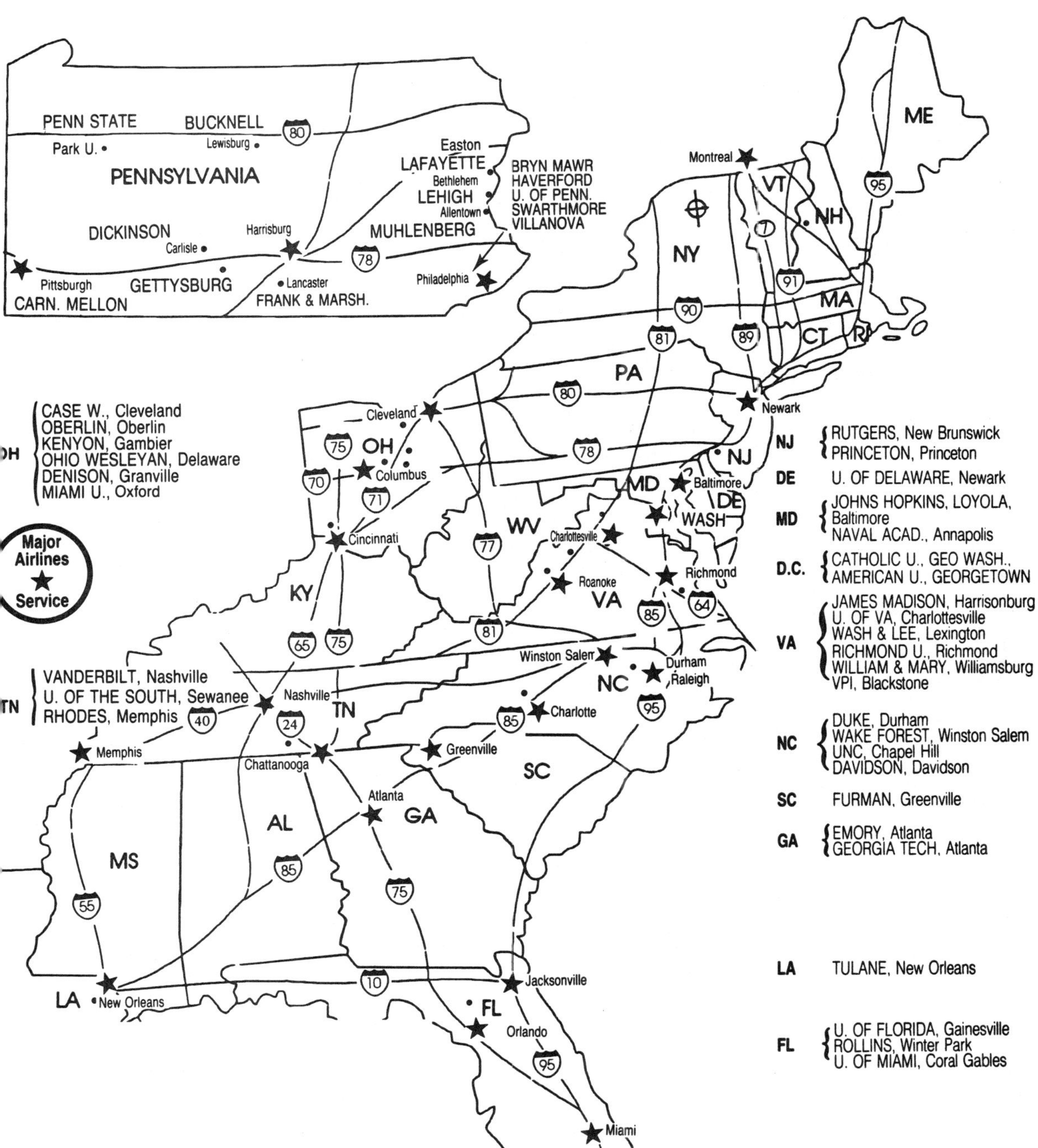

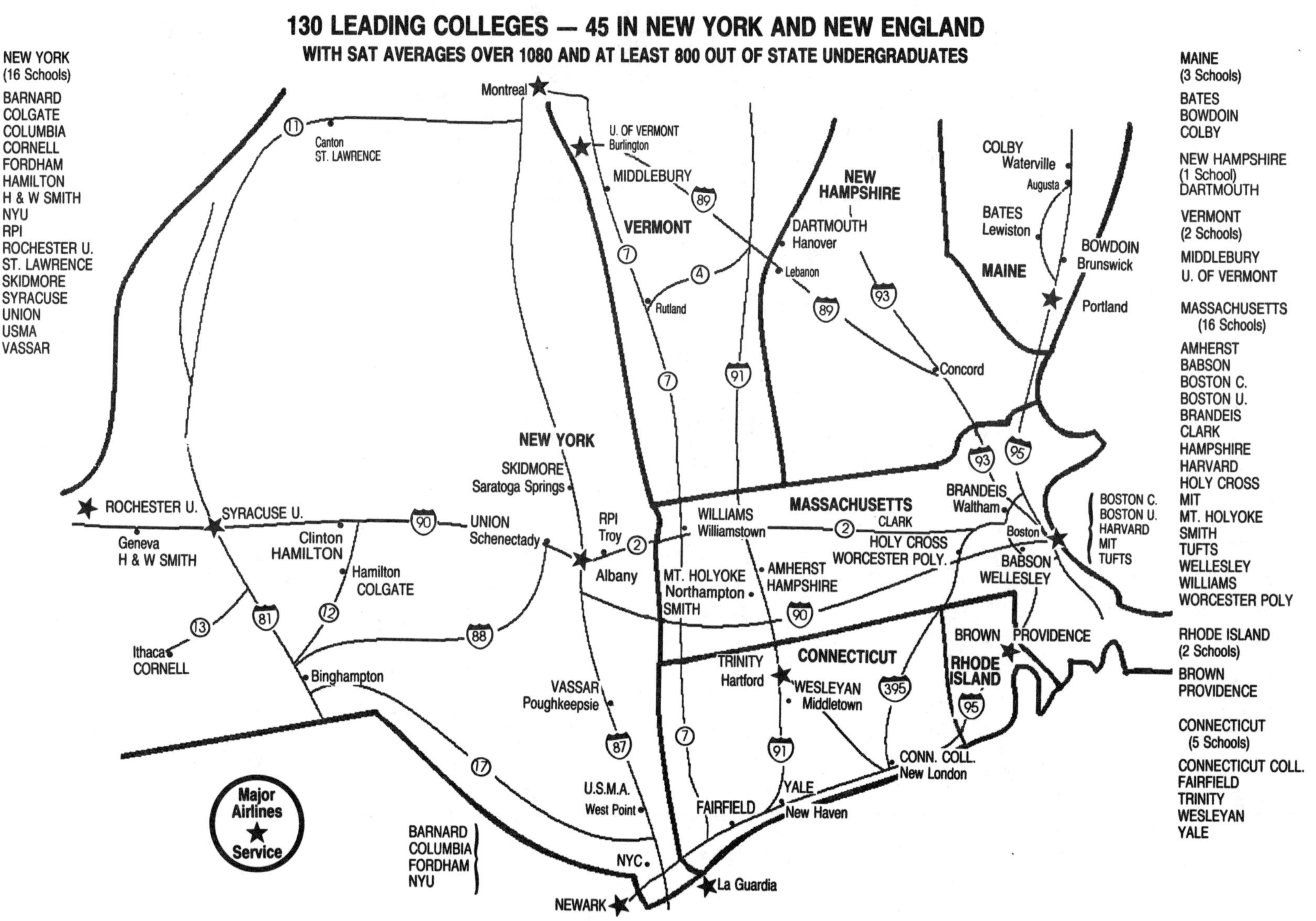
130 LEADING COLLEGES — 45 IN NEW YORK AND NEW ENGLAND
WITH SAT AVERAGES OVER 1080 AND AT LEAST 800 OUT OF STATE UNDERGRADUATES
NEW YORK
(16 Schools)
BARNARD
COLGATE
COLUMBIA
CORNELL
FORDHAM
HAMILTON
H & W SMITH
NYU
RPI
ROCHESTER U.
ST. LAWRENCE
SKIDMORE
SYRACUSE
UNION
USMA
VASSAR
MAINE
(3 Schools)
BATES
BOWDOIN
COLBY
NEW HAMPSHIRE
(1 School)
DARTMOUTH
VERMONT
(2 Schools)
MIDDLEBURY
U. OF VERMONT
MASSACHUSETTS
(16 Schools)
AMHERST
BABSON
BOSTON C.
BOSTON U.
BRANDEIS
CLARK
HAMPSHIRE
HARVARD
HOLY CROSS
MIT
MT. HOLYOKE
SMITH
TUFTS
WELLESLEY
WILLIAMS
WORCESTER POLY
RHODE ISLAND
(2 Schools)
BROWN
PROVIDENCE
CONNECTICUT
(5 Schools)
CONNECTICUT COLL.
FAIRFIELD
TRINITY
WESLEYAN
YALE
Montreal
Canton
ST. LAWRENCE
U. OF VERMONT
Burlington
MIDDLEBURY
VERMONT
Rutland
NEW HAMPSHIRE
DARTMOUTH
Hanover
Lebanon
Concord
COLBY
Waterville
Augusta
BATES
Lewiston
MAINE
BOWDOIN
Brunswick
Portland
NEW YORK
SKIDMORE
Saratoga Springs
ROCHESTER U.
SYRACUSE U.
Geneva
H & W SMITH
Clinton
HAMILTON
Hamilton
COLGATE
UNION
Schenectady
RPI
Troy
Albany
WILLIAMS
Williamstown
MASSACHUSETTS
CLARK
HOLY CROSS
WORCESTER POLY.
BRANDEIS
Waltham
Boston
BABSON
WELLESLEY
BOSTON C.
BOSTON U.
HARVARD
MIT
TUFTS
MT. HOLYOKE
Northampton
SMITH
AMHERST
HAMPSHIRE
Ithaca
CORNELL
Binghampton
TRINITY
Hartford
CONNECTICUT
WESLEYAN
Middletown
BROWN
PROVIDENCE
RHODE ISLAND
VASSAR
Poughkeepsie
CONN. COLL.
New London
U.S.M.A.
West Point
FAIRFIELD
YALE
New Haven
NYC.
La Guardia
NEWARK
BARNARD
COLUMBIA
FORDHAM
NYU
Major Airlines Service
11
89
7
4
93
91
95
90
2
12
13
81
88
87
17
395

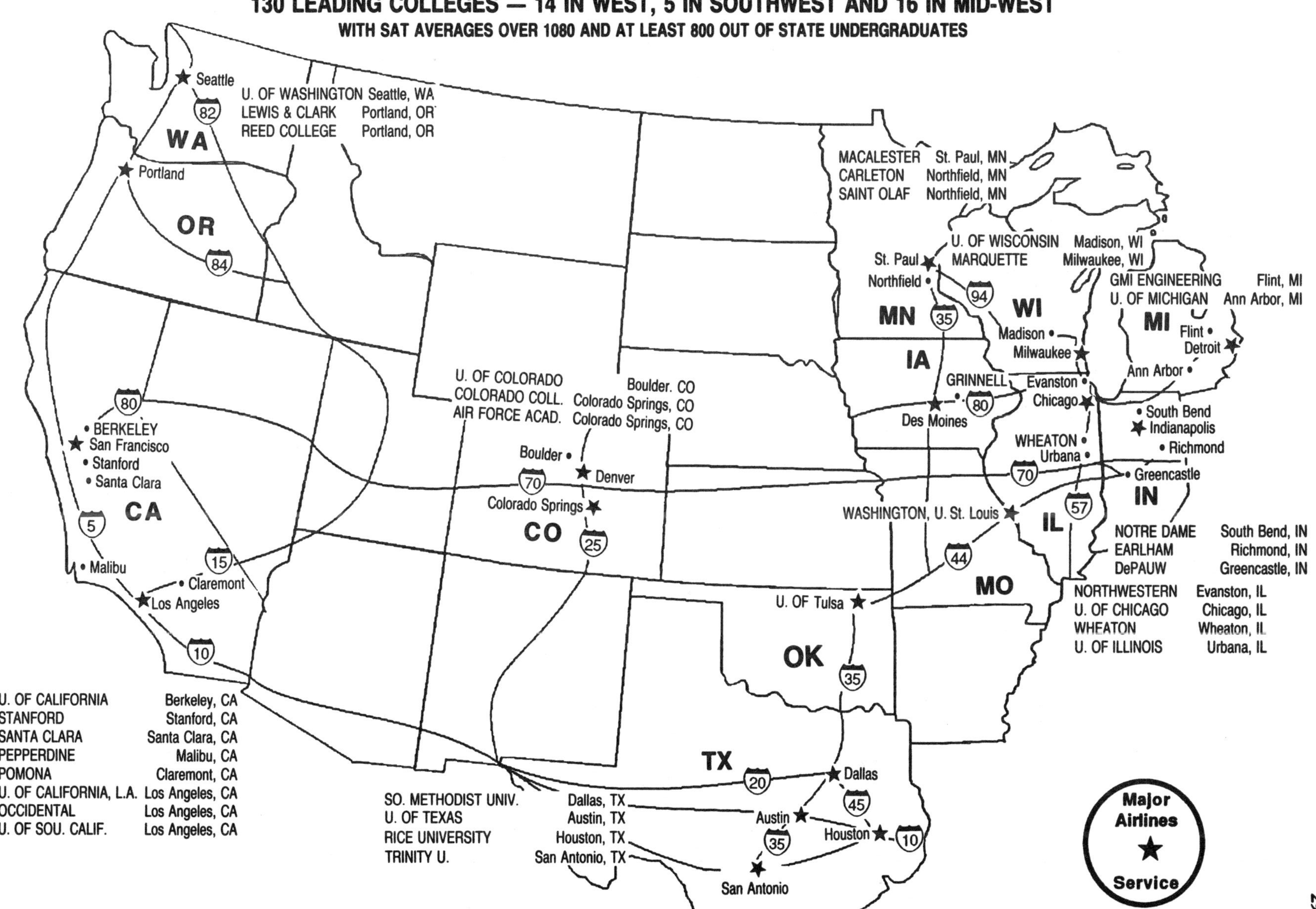
130 LEADING COLLEGES — 14 IN WEST, 5 IN SOUTHWEST AND 16 IN MID-WEST
WITH SAT AVERAGES OVER 1080 AND AT LEAST 800 OUT OF STATE UNDERGRADUATES
U. OF WASHINGTON Seattle, WA
LEWIS & CLARK Portland, OR
REED COLLEGE Portland, OR
U. OF CALIFORNIA Berkeley, CA
STANFORD Stanford, CA
SANTA CLARA Santa Clara, CA
PEPPERDINE Malibu, CA
POMONA Claremont, CA
U. OF CALIFORNIA, L.A. Los Angeles, CA
OCCIDENTAL Los Angeles, CA
U. OF SOU. CALIF. Los Angeles, CA
U. OF COLORADO Boulder. CO
COLORADO COLL. Colorado Springs, CO
AIR FORCE ACAD. Colorado Springs, CO
SO. METHODIST UNIV. Dallas, TX
U. OF TEXAS Austin, TX
RICE UNIVERSITY Houston, TX
TRINITY U. San Antonio, TX
MACALESTER St. Paul, MN
CARLETON Northfield, MN
SAINT OLAF Northfield, MN
U. OF WISCONSIN Madison, WI
MARQUETTE Milwaukee, WI
GMI ENGINEERING Flint, MI
U. OF MICHIGAN Ann Arbor, MI
NOTRE DAME South Bend, IN
EARLHAM Richmond, IN
DePAUW Greencastle, IN
NORTHWESTERN Evanston, IL
U. OF CHICAGO Chicago, IL
WHEATON Wheaton, IL
U. OF ILLINOIS Urbana, IL
GRINNELL
WASHINGTON, U. St. Louis
U. OF Tulsa
WA
OR
CA
CO
TX
OK
MO
IA
MN
WI
MI
IL
IN
Seattle
Portland
BERKELEY
San Francisco
Stanford
Santa Clara
Malibu
Claremont
Los Angeles
Boulder
Denver
Colorado Springs
St. Paul
Northfield
Madison
Milwaukee
Des Moines
Evanston
Chicago
WHEATON
Urbana
Flint
Detroit
Ann Arbor
South Bend
Indianapolis
Richmond
Greencastle
Dallas
Austin
Houston
San Antonio
82
84
80
5
15
10
70
25
94
35
57
44
20
45
Major Airlines Service

Index
45 Statistical Tables on these 130 Selective Colleges

Combined Ratings of 5 Prominent College Guides

Based on "1" to "4" -- "1" indicates Most Competitive or Selective -- "2" is Highly Selective -- "3" is Very -- "4" is Selective

21 Colleges with a "1" Average (Combined Total of 5)

College	State	College	State	College	State
Amherst	MA	Harvard	MA	Pennsylvania, U of	PA
Brown	RI	Haverford	PA	Stanford	CA
Chicago, U of	IL	Johns Hopkins	MD	Swarthmore	PA
Columbia University	NY	MIT	MA	Wellesley	MA
Cornell University	NY	Pomona	CA	Wesleyan	CT
Dartmouth	NH	Princeton	NJ	Williams	MA
Duke	NC	Rice	TX	Yale	CT

13 Colleges with an Average Better Than "1.5" (Combined Total of 6 or 7)

College	State	College	State	College	State
Barnard	NY	Notre Dame	IN	US Naval Academy	MD
Bowdoin	ME	Oberlin	OH	Virginia, U of	VA
Bryn Mawr	PA	Tufts	MA	Washington and Lee	VA
Georgetown	DC	US Military Academy	NY	William and Mary	VA
Northwestern	IL				

18 Colleges with an Average Better Than "2" (Combined Total of 8 or 9)

College	State	College	State	College	State
Bates	ME	Grinnell	IA	Smith	MA
Brandeis	MA	Il., U of-Urbana	IL	Trinity College	CT
Calif.-Berkeley, U of	CA	Michigan, U of	MI	US Air Force Academy	CO
Carleton	MN	Middlebury	VT	UNC-Chapel Hill	NC
Colgate	NY	Reed	OR	Vassar	NY
Davidson	NC	RPI	NY	Washington University	MO

42 Colleges with an Average Better Than "2.5" (Combined Total of 10, 11 or 12)

College	State	College	State	College	State
Boston College	MA	Georgia Tech	GA	Richmond	VA
Boston University	MA	Gettysburg	PA	Rochester, U of	NY
Bucknell	PA	GMI Engineering	MI	Rutgers-New Brunswick	NJ
Calif.-L.A., U of	CA	Hamilton	NY	St. Olaf	MN
Carnegie Mellon	PA	Horbart and W Smith	NY	Skidmore	NY
Case Western	OH	Holy Cross	MA	Texas, U of	TX
Colby	ME	Kenyon	OH	Trinity University	TX
Colorado College	CO	Lafayette	PA	Tulane	LA
Connecticut College	CT	Lehigh	PA	Union	NY
Dickinson	PA	Macalester	MN	University of the South	TN
Emory University	GA	Mount Holyoke	MA	Vanderbilt	TN
Fairfield	CT	NYU	NY	Wake Forest	NC
Franklin and Marshall	PA	Occidental	CA	Wheaton	IL
Furman	SC	Rhodes	TN	Worcester Polytech	MA

36 Colleges with an Average of "2.5" to "3" (Combined Total of 13, 14 or 15)

College	State	College	State	College	State
American University	DC	Hampshire College	MA	Rollins	FL
Babson	MA	James Madison	VA	St. Lawrence	NY
Catholic University	DC	Lewis and Clark	OR	Santa Clara	CA
Clark	MA	Loyola College	MD	Sou. Calif., U of	CA
Colorado, U of	CO	Marquette	WI	SMU	TX
Delaware, U of	DE	Miami, U of	FL	Syracuse University	NY
Denison	OH	Miami University	OH	Tulsa, U of	OK
Depauw	IN	Muhlenberg	PA	Vermont, U of	VT
Earlham	IN	Ohio Wesleyan	OH	Villanova	PA
Florida, U of	FL	Penn State	PA	VPI	VA
Fordham	NY	Pepperdine	CA	Washington, U of	WA
George Washington	DC	Providence	RI	Wisconsin, U of	WI

Number of Undergraduates and Graduate Students

(Full-Time Graduate Students Shown in Parentheses)

12 Colleges with Less than 1500 Undergraduates

Bowdoin	1300	0
Bryn Mawr	1200	(550)
Davidson	1400	0
Earlham	1200	0
Grinnell	1300	0
Hampshire College	1250	0
Haverford	1150	0
Pomona	1400	0
Reed	1250	(25)
Rhodes	1350	0
Swarthmore	1300	0
University of the South	1050	(75)

26 Colleges with 1500 to 2000 Undergraduates

Amherst	1600	0
Babson	1600	(1400)
Bates	1500	0
Carleton	1700	0
Colby	1700	0
Colorado College	1950	(25)
Connecticut College	1600	(75)
Dickinson	2000	0
Franklin & Marshall	1800	0
Gettysburg	1950	0
Hamilton	1650	0
Hobart & W Smith	2000	0
Kenyon	1550	0
Lafayette	2000	0
Lewis & Clark	2000	(700)
Macalester	1750	0
Middlebury	1950	0
Mount Holyoke	1950	0
Muhlenberg	1600	0
Occidental	1650	0
Ohio Wesleyan	2000	0
Rollins	1500	(600)
St. Lawrence	2000	(100)
Trinity College	1750	(150)
Washington & Lee	1650	(350)
Williams	2000	(50)

27 Colleges with 2000 to 3000 Undergraduates

Barnard	2200	0
Brandeis	2900	(800)
Case Western	2500	(5500)
Clark	2200	(700)
Colgate	2700	0
Denison	2050	0
Depauw	2300	0
Fairfield	2900	(800)
Furman	2500	(400)
GMI Engineering	2500	(700)
Holy Cross	2650	0
Johns Hopkins	2900	(1300)
Oberlin	2700	0
Pepperdine	2600	(85)
Rice	2700	(1300)
Richmond	2800	(2000)
St. Olaf	3000	0
Skidmore	2150	0
Smith	2550	(250)
Trinity U	2250	(200)
Tulsa U	2600	(1350)
Union	2100	(100)
Vassar	2400	0
Wellesley	2300	0
Wesleyan	2650	(150)
Wheaton	2200	(250)
Worcester Poly	2650	(1000)

Number of Undergraduates and Graduate Students

(Full-Time Graduate Students Shown in Parentheses)

20 Colleges with 3000 to 5000 Undergraduates

Bucknell	3400	(200)	Princeton	4500	(1800)
Carnegie Mellon	4100	(2600)	Providence	3800	(650)
Catholic U	3100	(3300)	Rensselaer Poly	4450	(2000)
Chicago U	3400	(7400)	Rochester U	4800	(2300)
Columbia University	3200	(16,000)	Santa Clara	3650	(3400)
Dartmouth	4300	(1050)	Tufts	4700	(3000)
Emory U	4600	(4100)	US Air Force Academy	4300	0
Lehigh	4500	(4500)	US Military Academy	4300	0
Loyola	3100	(2800)	US Naval Academy	4500	0
MIT	4400	(5000)	Wake Forest	3400	(1750)

24 Colleges with 5000 to 10,000 Undergraduates

American U	5000	(3800)	Northwestern	7250	(4000)
Boston College	8700	(4300)	Notre Dame	7500	(2200)
Brown	5600	(1500)	Pennsylvania U	9200	(10,300)
Duke	5950	(4400)	SMU	5000	(3300)
Fordham	5050	(6500)	Stanford	6500	(6850)
Georgetown	5600	(5600)	Tulane	5600	(4000)
George Washington	5900	(8500)	Vanderbilt	5150	(160)
Georgia Tech	8600	(2750)	Vermont	7000	(1150)
Harvard	6600	(11,200)	Villanova	6400	(2300)
James Madison	9300	(400)	Washington U	5000	(5050)
Miami, U of	7750	(5100)	William & Mary	8500	(1660)
Marquette	8750	(3000)	Yale	5200	(5600)

13 Colleges with 10,000 to 20,000 Undergraduates

Boston U	14,000	(9700)	Sou. Calif.	16,000	(14,000)
Colorado U	19,500	(5000)	Syracuse	12,500	(4500)
Cornell U	12,700	(5500)	UNC	16,000	(6200)
Delaware, U of	13,000	(2500)	Virginia	11,000	(6200)
Miami U	13,000	(1700)	VPI	17,950	(4000)
NYU	14,500	(14,000)	Washington, U of	19,500	(8600)
Rutgers	10,000	(35,000)			

8 Colleges with over 20,000 Undergraduates

Calif.-Berkeley	22,000	(9000)	Michigan, U of	23,000	(13,000)
Calif.-L.A.	24,000	(12,000)	Penn State	30,000	(6000)
Florida U	23,000	(7500)	Texas U	37,000	(12,000)
Il.,U of	25,000	(6200)	Wisconsin U	27,000	(11,400)

Percent of Out of State Undergraduates

31 Colleges with Over 85% Out-of-State

American U	DC	90%	George Wash.	DC	94%	Swarthmore	PA	90%
Amherst	MA	90	Hampshire Coll.	MA	85	US Air Force	CO	98
Bates	ME	85	Haverford	PA	85	US Mil. Acad.	NY	85
Brown	RI	95	MIT	MA	90	US Naval Acad.	MD	95
Bryn Mawr	PA	85	Middlebury	VT	95	Wash. & Lee	VA	90
Catholic U	DC	85	Notre Dame	IN	90	Washington U	MO	85
Colby	ME	90	Oberlin	OH	90	Wesleyan	CT	85
Dartmouth	NH	95	Princeton	NJ	85	Williams	MA	90
Duke	NC	85	Providence	RI	85	Worcester Poly	MA	90
Earlham	IN	85	Smith	MA	85	Yale	CT	90
Georgetown	DC	98						

34 Colleges with 70% to 85% Out-of-State

Boston U	MA	70%	Emory U	GA	80%	Northwestern	IL	75%
Bowdoin	ME	83	Gettysburg	PA	75	U of the South	TN	80
Brandeis	MA	70	Grinnell	IA	75	Pennsylvania	PA	80
Bucknell	PA	70	Harvard	MA	80	Reed	OR	80
Carleton	MN	75	Johns Hopkins	MD	80	Richmond	VA	80
Chicago, U of	IL	75	Kenyon	OH	75	Rollins	FL	70
Clark	MA	70	Lafayette	PA	80	Tufts	MA	75
Colorado Coll.	CO	70	Lehigh	PA	70	Tulane	LA	80
Columbia	NY	80	Lewis & Clark	OR	75	Vanderbilt	TN	80
Connecticut Coll.	CT	80	Macalester	MN	75	Wellesley	MA	84
Davidson	NC	70	Mt. Holyoke	MA	80	Wheaton	IL	75
Denison	OH	75						

32 Colleges with 50% to 70% Out-of-State

Barnard	NY	60%	Hamilton	NY	52%	Rice	TX	55%
Boston Coll.	MA	65	GMI Engineering	MI	52	St. Lawrence	NY	51
Carnegie Mellon	PA	60	H & W Smith	NY	55	Skidmore	NY	69
Colgate	NY	65	Holy Cross	MA	65	Stanford	CA	63
Cornell U	NY	55	Muhlenberg	PA	65	Syracuse	NY	65
Delaware, U of	DE	55	NYU	NY	50	Trinity Coll.	CT	55
Depauw	IN	60	Ohio Wesleyan	OH	55	Vassar	NY	60
Dickinson	PA	60	Pomona	CA	60	Vermont	VT	51
Fairfield	CT	65	Rensselaer Poly	NY	60	Villanova	PA	68
Franklin & Marsh.	PA	60	Rhodes	TN	65	Wake Forest	NC	60
Furman	SC	65	Rochester, U of	NY	52			

20 Colleges with 30% to 50% Out-of-State

Babson	MA	40%	Michigan, U of	MI	30%	Trinity U	TX	40%
Case Western	OH	40	Occidental	CA	45	Tulsa, U of	OK	40
Colorado, U of	CO	35	Pepperdine	CA	48	Union	NY	45
Georgia Tech	GA	35	St. Olaf	MN	40	Virginia, U of	VA	35
Loyola Coll.	MD	45	Santa Clara	CA	32	William & Mary	VA	35
Marquette	MN	45	Sou. Calif., U of	CA	45	Wisconsin, U of	WI	30
Miami, U of	FL	45	SMU	TX	48			

13 Colleges with Less Than 30% Out-of-State

Calif.-Berkeley	CA	15%	Miami U	OH	23%	Texas, U of	TX	6%
Calif.-L.A.	CA	5	Fordham	NY	25	UNC-Chapel Hill	NC	18
Florida, U of	FL	8	Penn State	PA	17	VPI	VA	25
Il., U of-Urbana	IL	6	Rutgers-New B.	NJ	15	Washington, U of	WA	10
James Madison	VA	23						

Percent of Minority Freshmen

(Percent of Blacks Shown in Parentheses) and Number of Students from Foreign Countries

27 Colleges with under 10% Minorities

	%	No.		%	No.		%	No.
Babson	6 (2)	190	Gettysburg	9 (3)	NA	St. Lawrence	6 (3)	60
Bucknell	6 (2)	60	Holy Cross	8 (4)	20	St. Olaf	5 (1)	60
Colby	8 (2)	40	Lehigh	8 (2)	140	Skidmore	8 (3)	40
Davidson	8 (4)	70	Loyola Coll.	7 (2)	NA	U. of the South	3 (1)	20
Delaware, U of	7 (4)	130	Miami U (OH)	5 (2)	NA	Vermont, U of	5 (1)	90
Denison	9 (5)	40	Muhlenberg	9 (2)	30	Villanova	8 (2)	130
Dickinson	6 (1)	20	Providence	6 (2)	40	Wash. & Lee	7 (4)	20
Fairfield	8 (1)	30	Rhodes	8 (4)	30	Wheaton (IL)	8 (1)	20
Furman	6 (4)	70	Richmond, U of	6 (3)	30	Worcester Poly	8 (1)	140

26 Colleges with 10% to 15% Minorities

	%	No.		%	No.		%	No.
Bates	12 (2)	30	Hampshire Coll.	12 (3)	40	Smith	13 (4)	150
Bowdoin	12 (4)	40	H & W Smith	10 (4)	40	Union	12 (3)	40
Brandeis	12 (3)	70	James Madison	13 (9)	100	UNC	14(10)	NA
Carleton	13 (3)	20	Kenyon	10 (4)	NA	Vanderbilt	10 (4)	110
Colorado, U of	13 (2)	200	Lewis & Clark	12 (2)	100	VPI	13 (5)	180
Connecticut Col.	13 (5)	80	Marquette	11 (4)	NA	Wake Forest	10 (7)	70
Depauw	12 (6)	60	Middlebury	10 (3)	180	William & Mary	12 (6)	110
Frank. & Marsh.	11 (3)	90	Mount Holyoke	14 (4)	160	Wisconsin, U of	10 (2)	800
Hamilton	14 (3)	80	Rollins	12 (4)	60			

26 Colleges with 15% to 20% Minorities

	%	No.		%	No.		%	No.
Boston Coll.	18 (3)	170	Grinnell	18 (5)	100	Syracuse U	17 (5)	240
Boston U	19 (4)	900	Haverford	18 (5)	60	Trinity Coll.	19 (7)	50
Colgate	16 (5)	110	Lafayette	17 (7)	200	Trinity U	19 (1)	30
Colorado Coll.	18 (1)	80	Michigan, U of	16 (6)	440	Tulane	16 (8)	NA
Dartmouth	18 (6)	210	Notre Dame	15 (40	150	Tulsa, U of	19 (5)	260
Duke	15 (6)	120	Ohio Wesleyan	16 (4)	180	US Air Force A.	15 (6)	40
Earlham	15 (8)	40	Penn State	19 (3)	300	US Military A.	17 (7)	40
Emory U	18 (7)	220	Reed	16 (1)	20	US Naval A.	18 (6)	40
Geo. Wash.	18 (6)	800	SMU	15 (4)	100			

35 Colleges with 20% to 30% Minorities

	%	No.		%	No.		%	No.
American U	22 (7)	600	GMI Engineer.	23 (6)	170	Rochester, U of	22 (6)	190
Brown	23 (7)	550	Il.,U of-Urbana	23 (7)	250	Sou. Cal., U of	29 (5)	1400
Bryn Mawr	27 (5)	130	Johns Hopkins	27 (6)	150	Swarthmore	20 (8)	130
Case Western	25 (7)	250	Macalester	21 (4)	180	Texas, U of	29 (4)	1700
Catholic U	23 (5)	270	Northwestern	24 (8)	150	Tufts	21 (4)	270
Chicago, U of	22 (4)	80	Oberlin	20 (8)	110	Vassar	21 (8)	160
Clark U	26 (3)	200	Occidental	29 (4)	60	Virginia, U of	21(11)	200
Columbia U	29 (7)	100	Pennsylvania U	25 (7)	600	Washington U	20 (6)	700
Cornell U	27 (5)	500	Pepperdine	27 (2)	260	Wesleyan	26 (8)	50
Florida, U of	21 (6)	1100	Princeton	25 (7)	230	Williams	22 (8)	60
Georgetown	27 (8)	550	RPI	22 (3)	130	Yale	26 (8)	210
Georgia Tech	22 (7)	170	Rice	22 (6)	40			

16 Colleges with 30% or More Minorities

	%	No.		%	No.		%	No.
Amherst	30 (7)	50	Harvard	35 (8)	410	Rutgers U	32 (8)	160
Barnard	30 (5)	180	MIT	37 (7)	400	Santa Clara	31 (2)	300
Calif.-Berkeley	58 (7)	630	Miami U (FL)	39 (7)	700	Stanford	40 (8)	200
Calif.-L.A.	53 (7)	480	NYU	48 (7)	700	Wash. U (WA)	36 (4)	400
Carnegie Mellon	31 (6)	300	Pomona	35 (4)	40	Wellesley	31 (7)	120
Fordham	34(10)	100						

67 Colleges that Accept the Common Application

American University	DC	Hamilton	NY	St. Lawrence	NY
Bates	ME	Hampshire College	MA	St. Olaf	MN
Boston University	MA	Haverford	PA	Skidmore	NY
Brandeis	MA	Kenyon	OH	Smith	MA
Bryn Mawr	PA	Lafayette	PA	University of the South	TN
Bucknell	PA	Lehigh	PA	Sou. Calif., U of	CA
Carleton	MN	Lewis and Clark	OR	SMU	TX
Case Western	OH	Macalester	MN	Swarthmore	PA
Clark University	MA	Mount Holyoke	MA	Trinity College	CT
Colgate	NY	Muhlenberg	MA	Trinity University	TX
Colorado College	CO	NYU	NY	Tulane	LA
Connecticut College	CT	Oberlin	OH	Tulsa, U of	OK
Denison	OH	Occidental	CA	Union	NY
Depauw	IN	Ohio Wesleyan	OH	Vanderbilt	TN
Dickinson College	PA	Pomona	CA	Vassar	NY
Duke	NC	Reed	OR	Wake Forest	NC
Earlham	IN	Rensselaer Polytech	NY	George Washington	DC
Emory University	GA	Rhodes	TN	Washington and Lee	VA
Fairfield	CT	Rice	TX	Wesleyan	CT
Fordham	NY	Richmond	VA	Hobart and W Smith	NY
Franklin and Marshall	PA	Rochester, U of	NY	Williams	MA
Gettysburg	PA	Rollins	FL	Worcester Polytech	MA
Grinnell	IA				

88 Colleges that Have Early Decision

American University	DC	Furman	SC	Richmond	VA
Amherst	MA	George Washington	DC	Rochester, U of	NY
Babson	MA	Gettysburg	PA	Rollins	FL
Barnard	NY	Grinnell	IA	St. Lawrence	NY
Bates	ME	Hamilton	NY	St. Olaf	MN
Boston University	MA	Hampshire College	MA	Smith	MA
Bowdoin	ME	Harvard	MA	SMU	TX
Brandeis	MA	Haverford	PA	Swarthmore	PA
Bryn Mawr	PA	Horbart and W Smith	NY	Syracuse	NY
Bucknell	PA	Holy Cross	MA	Trinity University	TX
Carleton	MN	Johns Hopkins	MD	Tufts	MA
Carnegie Mellon	PA	Kenyon	OH	Union	NY
Case Western	OH	Lafayette	PA	US Air Force Academy	CO
Clark	MA	Lehigh	PA	US Military Academy	NY
Colby	ME	Macalaster	MN	UNC	NC
Colgate	NY	Miami University	OH	University of the South	TN
Columbia	NY	Middlebury	VT	Vanderbilt	TN
Connecticut College	CT	Muhlenberg	PA	Vassar	NY
Cornell University	NY	Mount Holyoke	MA	Vermont, U of	VT
Dartmouth	NH	NYU	NY	Virginia, U of	VA
Davidson	NC	Oberlin	OH	VPI	VA
Denison	OH	Ohio Wesleyan	OH	Wake Forest	NC
Dickinson	PA	Pennsylvania	PA	Washington and Lee	VA
Duke	NC	Pepperdine	CA	Washington University	MO
Earlham	IN	Pomona	CA	Wellesley	MA
Emory University	GA	Reed	OR	Wesleyan	CT
Fairfield	CT	Rensselaer Polytech	NY	William and Mary	VA
Florida, U of	FL	Rhodes	TN	Williams	MA
Fordham	NY	Rice	TX	Worcester Polytech	MA
Franklin and Marshall	PA				

Application Closing Dates

November

California-Berkeley	30
California-L.A.	30
Illinois, U of	11/15
Penn State	15

December

Stanford	15
Yale	31

January

Amherst	1
Boston University	15
Bowdoin	15
Brown	1
Bryn Mawr	15
Bucknell	1
Chicago, U of	15
Colby College	15
Colgate	15
Columbia	15
Connecticut College	15
Cornell University	1
Dartmouth	1
Duke	1
Georgetown	10
Hamilton	15
Harvard	1
Haverford	15
Johns Hopkins	1
MIT	1
Miami University (OH)	31
Middlebury	15
Northwestern (IL)	1
Notre Dame, U of	10
Oberlin	15
Pennsylvania, U of	1
Pomona	15
Princeton	2
RPI	15
Rice	2
Rochester, U of	15
Rutgers-New Brunswick	15
Smith	15
Trinity College	15
Tufts	1
Tulane	15
UNC-Chapel Hill	15
U S Air Force Academy	31
Vanderbilt	15
Vassar	15
Villanova	15
Virginia, U of	2
William and Mary	15
Williams College	1
Wake Forest	15
Wesleyan University	15

February

American University	1
Babson	1
Barnard	1
Bates	1
Boston College	1
Brandeis	1
Carleton	1
Carnegie Mellon	1
Catholic University	15
Clark University (MA)	15
Colorado College	1
Colorado, U of	15
Davidson College	1
Denison	1
Depauw	15
Earlham	15
Emory University	15
Florida, U of	1
Fordham University	1
Franklin and Marshall	10
Furman	1
GMI	1
George Washington	1
Georgia Tech	1
Gettysburg	15
Grinnell	1
Hampshire College	1
Hobart and W Smith	15
Holy Cross (MA)	1
James Madison	1
Kenyon	15
Lafayette College	1
Lehigh University	31
Lewis and Clark	15
Loyola College	1
Macalester	1
Michigan, U of	1
Mt. Holyoke	1
Muhlenberg	15
NYU	1
Occidental	1
Pepperdine	1
Providence College	1
Reed	1
Rhodes	1
Richmond, U of	1
Rollins	15
St. Lawrence	1
St. Olaf	15
Santa Clara	1
Skidmore	1
Swarthmore	1
Syracuse University	1
Trinity University	1
Union College (NY)	1
University of the South	1
Vermont, U of	1

February (Continued)

VPI	1
Washington University	1
Washington & Lee	1
Wellesley	1
Wheaton College (IL)	15
Wisconsin, U of	1
Worcester Polytech	1

March

Delaware, U of	1
Miami, U of (FL)	1
Ohio Wesleyan	1
Sou California, U of	1
Texas, U of	1
US Military Academy	1
US Naval Academy	1
Washington, U of	

April 1

Fairfield	1
SMU	1

Rolling

Case Western
Marquette
Penn State-Park
Tulsa, U of

Percent of Freshmen in Top 20% of Their High School Class

28 Colleges with 90% or More in Top 5th

College	State	College	State	College	State
Amherst	MA	Harvard	MA	Reed	OR
Boston College	MA	Haverford	PA	Stanford	CA
Brown	RI	Michigan, U of	MI	Swarthmore	PA
Calif.-Berkeley	CA	MIT	MA	US Air Force Academy	CO
Chicago, U of	IL	Notre Dame	IN	UNC	NC
Columbia University	NY	Pennsylvania, U of	PA	Wellesley	MA
Cornell University	NY	Pepperdine	CA	William and Mary	VA
Dartmouth	NH	Pomona	CA	Williams	MA
Davidson	NC	Princeton	NJ	Yale	CT
Duke	NC				

28 Colleges with 80% to 90% in Top 5th

College	State	College	State	College	State
Bates	ME	Holy Cross	MA	Trinity University	TX
Bowdoin	ME	Il. U.-Urbana	IL	Tufts	MA
Bryn Mawr	PA	Johns Hopkins	MD	US Military Academy	NY
Carleton	MN	Middlebury	VT	US Naval Academy	MD
Case Western	OH	Northwestern	IL	Wake Forest	NC
Colgate	NY	Oberlin	OH	Washington and Lee	VA
Furman	SC	RPI	NY	Washington University	MO
Georgetown	DC	Rutgers-New Brunswick	NJ	Wesleyan	CT
Georgia Tech	GA	Smith	MA	Worcester Polytech	MA
GMI Engineering	MI				

26 Colleges with 70% to 80% in Top 5th

College	State	College	State	College	State
Barnard	NY	Gettysburg	PA	Rhodes	TN
Boston University	MA	Grinnell	IA	Rice	TX
Brandeis	MA	Hamilton	NY	Texas, U of	TX
Bucknell	PA	Kenyon	OH	Union	NY
Carnegie Mellon	PA	Lehigh	PA	University of the South	TN
Colorado College	CO	Macalester	MN	Vassar	NY
Colorado, U of	CO	Mount Holyoke	MA	Washington, U of	WA
Dickinson	PA	Occidental	CA	Wheaton	IL
Emory University	GA	Penn State	PA		

20 Colleges with 60% to 70% in Top 5th

College	State	College	State	College	State
Clark	MA	James Madison	VA	SMU	TX
Colby	ME	Lafayette	PA	Syracuse	TX
Connecticut College	CT	Miami, U of	FL	Vermont University	VT
Delaware, U of	DE	Muhlenberg	PA	Virginia	VA
Depauw	IN	St. Olaf	MN	VPI	VA
Fordham	NY	Santa Clara	CA	Wisconsin University	WI
George Washington	DC	Sou. Calif., U of	CA		

26 Colleges with less than 60% in Top 5th

College	State	College	State	College	State
American University	DC	Lewis and Clark	OR	Rollins	FL
Babson	MA	Loyola College	MD	St. Lawrence	NY
Catholic University	DC	Marquette	WI	Skidmore	NY
Denison	OH	Miami University	OH	Trinity College	CT
Earlham	IN	NYU	NY	Tulane	LA
Fairfield	CT	Ohio Wesleyan	OH	Tulsa	OK
Franklin and Marshall	PA	Providence	RI	Vanderbilt	TN
Hampshire College	MA	Richmond	VA	Villanova	PA
Hobart and W Smith	NY	Rochester, U of	NY		

Figures not available: University of California in Los Angeles and University of Florida

Average SAT Scores of Freshmen (Fall 1990)
In These 130 Leading Colleges

13 Colleges with Average SATs above 1300

Amherst	MA	Harvard	MA	Princeton	NJ	Swarthmore	PA
Bowdoin	ME	MIT	MA	Rice	TX	Williams	MA
Dartmouth	NH	Pomona	CA	Stanford	CA	Yale	CT
Duke	NC						

22 Colleges with Average SATs between 1250 and 1300

Barnard	NY	Colgate	NY	Northwestern	IL	Tufts	MA
Bates	MA	Columbia U	NY	Notre Dame	IN	Wake Forest	NC
Brown	RI	Cornell U	NY	Oberlin	OH	Wash. & Lee	VA
Bryn Mawr	PA	Haverford	PA	Pennsylvania	PA	Wellesley	MA
Carleton	MN	Johns Hopkins	MD	Reed	OR	Wesleyan	CT
Chicago, U of	IL	Middlebury	VT				

27 Colleges with Average SATs between 1200 and 1250

Boston Coll.	MA	Emory U	GA	Mt. Holyoke	MA	US Naval A.	MD
Brandeis	MA	Georgetown	DC	RPI	NY	Vassar	NY
Carnegie Mellon	PA	Georgia Tech	GA	Rhodes	TN	Virginia, U of	VA
Case Western	OH	Grinnell	IA	Richmond	VA	Washington U	MO
Colby	ME	Holy Cross	MA	Trinity U	TX	William & Mary	VA
Connecticut Coll.	CT	Lafayette	PA	US Air Force A.	CO	Worcester Poly	MA
Davidson	NC	Macalester	MN	US Military A.	NY		

20 Colleges with Average SATs between 1150 and 1200

Bucknell	PA	Furman	SC	Michigan, U of	MI	Trinity Coll.	CT
Calif.-Berkeley	CA	GMI Engineering	MI	Occidental	CA	Tulane	LA
Colorado Coll.	CO	Hamilton	NY	Rochester, U of	NY	Union	NY
Florida, U of	FL	Kenyon	OH	Smith	MA	Univ. of the South	TN
Frank.& Marsh.	PA	Lehigh	PA	Skidmore	NY	Vanderbilt	TN

29 Colleges with Average SATs between 1100 and 1150

American U	DC	Fairfield	CT	Loyola Coll.	MD	Syracuse	NY
Babson	MA	George Washi.	DC	Miami, U of	FL	Texas, U of	TX
Boston U	MA	Gettysburg	PA	Miami U	OH	Tulsa, U of	OK
Calif.-L.A.	CA	Hampshire Coll.	MA	Muhlenberg	PA	UNC	NC
Clark U	MA	Hobart & W Smith	NY	NYU	NY	Villanova	PA
Depauw	IN	Il., U of-Urbana	IL	Rutgers	NJ	VPI	VA
Dickinson	PA	Lewis & Clark	OK	St. Olaf	MN	Wheaton	IL
Earlham	IN						

19 Colleges with Average SATs between 1085 and 1100

Catholic U	DC	James Madison	VA	Providence	RI	SMU	TX
Colorado, U of	CO	Marquette	WI	Rollins	FL	Washington, U of	WA
Delaware, U of	DE	Ohio Wesleyan	OH	St. Lawrence	NY	Vermont, U of	VT
Denison	OH	Penn State	PA	Santa Clara	CA	Wisconsin, U of	WI
Fordham	NY	Pepperdine	CA	Sou. Cal., U of	CA		

Percent of Applicants Admitted and Number Applying

17 Colleges Admitting Under 30% of Applicants

Amherst	4600	Georgetown	9400	US Mil Academy	12,700
Bowdoin	3200	Harvard	12,200	US Naval Academy	12,475
Brown	12,000	Princeton	12,650	William & Mary	9500
Columbia U	6500	Rice	5300	Williams	4350
Dartmouth	8000	Stanford	12,950	Yale	11,920
Duke	13,400	US Air Force Acad.	12,700		

37 Colleges Admitting 30% to 50% of Applicants

Bates	3180	Hamilton	3800	Richmond, U of	5500
Boston	12,400	Haverford	2150	Rutgers	14,300
Calif.-Berkeley	19,000	Holy Cross	3870	Skidmore	5000
Calif.-L.A.	22,000	James Madison	11,200	Swarthmore	3250
Carleton	2800	Lafayette	41,500	Tufts	7200
Chicago, U of	5500	MIT	6400	UNC	15,200
Colby	3200	Middlebury	3700	Vassar	3975
Colgate	5200	Northwestern	10,800	Virginia, U of	12,850
Connecticut Coll.	3300	Notre Dame	9100	Wake Forest	5430
Cornell U	20,000	Occidental	2500	Washington & Lee	3050
Davidson	2100	Pennsylvania, U of	10,650	Wellesley	2600
Furman	2970	Pomona	2850	Wesleyan U	4830
Gettysburg	3800				

44 Colleges Admitting 50% to 70% of Applicants

Babson	1450	Grinnell	1600	Rochester, U of	2100
Barnard	1200	Hampshire	1450	Rollins	2350
Boston U	18,800	Hobart & W Smith	1700	Smith	2250
Brandeis	3900	Johns Hopkins	5250	SMU	4400
Bryn Mawr	1400	Kenyon	2500	Syracuse	13,500
Bucknell	5940	Loyola	4400	Texas, U of	16,000
Colorado Coll.	2770	Macalester	2330	Trinity Coll.	2900
Dickinson	3600	Michigan, U of	17,500	Union	2750
Emory U	5900	Mount Holyoke	2000	Univ. of the South	1124
Fairfield	4980	Muhlenberg	2420	Vanderbilt	7050
Florida, U of	10,900	NYU	10,600	Vermont, U of	5800
Fordham	4750	Oberlin	3500	Villanova	8000
Franklin & Marshall	3150	Penn State	22,500	VPI	15,160
Georgia Tech	5850	Providence	4700	Washington U	8000
GMI Engineering	2200	Reed	1970		

32 Colleges Admitting 70% or More of Applicants

American U	4900	Il., U of-Urbana	14,750	St. Olaf	2175
Carnegie Mellon	6100	Lehigh	5200	Santa Clara	3400
Case Western	2100	Lewis & Clark	2370	Sou. Calif., U of	12,500
Catholic U	2000	Marquette	6300	Trinity U	2240
Clark U	3000	Miami, U of (FL)	8400	Tulane	6900
Colorado, U of	13,000	Miami U (OH)	9300	Tulsa, U of	1630
Delaware, U of	12,800	Ohio Wesleyan	2560	Washington, U of	10,000
Denison	3300	Pepperdine	2630	Wheaton (IL)	1185
Depauw	1900	RPI	4600	Wisconsin, U of	14,200
Earlham	1240	Rhodes	1950	Worcester Poly	2700
George Washington	6100	St. Lawrence	2550		

Percent of Applicants Admitted and Percent of Those That Matriculated

	% Admitted	% Matric-ulated
American University (DC)	75	31
Amherst	22	41
Babson	69	42
Barnard	57	51
Bates	42	33
Boston College	45	38
Boston University	66	28
Bowdoin	27	47
Brandeis	67	27
Brown	23	50
Bryn Mawr	57	41
Bucknell	55	27
Cal-Berkeley	38	41
Cal-L.A. (UCLA)	43	37
Carleton	47	35
Carnegie Mellon	72	26
Case Western	86	35
Catholic University (DC)	85	34
Chicago, U of	46	37
Clark University	71	21
Colby	41	32
Colgate	43	30
Colorado College	50	36
Colorado, U of	74	39
Columbia University	28	43
Connecticut College	45	30
Cornell University (NY)	30	49
Dartmouth	25	52
Davidson	40	35
Delaware, U of	70	33
Denison	70	24
Depauw	84	38
Dickinson	66	23
Duke	25	44
Earlham	74	36
Emory University (GA)	66	29
Fairfield	54	28
Florida, U of	66	40
Fordham	67	40
Franklin and Marshall	59	27
Furman	43	47
Georgetown	29	50
George Washington (DC)	81	24
Georgia Tech	69	40
Gettysburg	45	28
GMI Engineering	67	43
Grinnell	69	31
Hamilton	43	27
Hampshire College	61	35
Harvard	18	73
Haverford	40	34
Hobart and W Smith	64	22
Holy Cross	43	38
Il., U of-Urbana	77	53
James Madison	43	39
Johns Hopkins	55	29
Kenyon	55	35
Lafayette	44	28
Lehigh	72	31
Lewis and Clark	79	25
Loyola College	55	30
Macalester	56	33
Marquette	80	32
MIT	32	54
Miami, U of (FL)	74	32
Miami University (OH)	78	48
Michigan, U of	60	44
Middlebury	40	36
Mount Holyoke	60	42
Muhlenberg	60	29
NYU	54	44
Northwestern	47	35
Notre Dame, U of	37	53
Oberlin	54	30
Occidental	49	33
Ohio Wesleyan	74	30
Penn State	50	40
Pennsylvania, U of	42	49
Pepperdine	74	35
Pomona	37	35
Princeton	17	55
Providence (RI)	62	32
Reed	62	24
Rensselaer Polytech	77	28
Rhodes	72	28
Rice	25	47
Richmond, U of	37	34
Rochester, U of	68	24
Rollins	56	31
Rutgers-New Brunswick	44	26
St. Lawrence	70	30
St. Olaf	77	50
Santa Clara (CA)	71	38
Skidmore	44	27
Smith	63	44
Sou. Calif., U of	75	30
SMU	60	30
Stanford	22	56
Swarthmore	31	36
Syracuse University	64	32
Texas, U of (Austin)	63	58
Trinity College (CT)	50	29
Trinity University (TX)	75	36
Tufts	46	34
Tulane	72	27
Tulsa, U of	92	48
Union	52	31
US Air Force Academy	15	74
US Military Academy	14	74
US Naval Academy	12	83
UNC-Chapel Hill	32	67
University of the South (Sewanee)	69	37
Vanderbilt	59	34
Vassar	43	33
Vermont, U of	55	40
Villanova	65	31
Virginia, U of	38	52
VPI	68	41
Wake Forest	37	43
Washington and Lee	31	41
Washington University (MO)	58	26
Washington, U of (WA)	75	48
Wellesley	49	46
Wesleyan University	40	37
Wheaton College (IL)	77	56
William and Mary	27	50
Williams College	28	41
Wisconsin, U of-Madison	72	46
Worcester Polytech	79	33
Yale	20	58

Number and % of Transfer Applications Accepted

	Accepted No.	Accepted %
American University (DC)	700	75
Amherst	27	12
Babson	106	48
Barnard	167	35
Bates	66	33
Boston College	537	33
Boston University	1305	60
Bowdoin	10	11
Brandeis	137	6
Brown	173	22
Bryn Mawr	32	40
Bucknell	102	60
Cal-Berkeley	2800	38
Cal-L.A. (UCLA)	3300	45
Carleton	28	27
Carnegie Mellon	229	65
Case Western	219	60
Catholic University (DC)	300	75
Chicago, U of	191	22
Clark University	206	70
Colby	41	20
Colgate	74	35
Colorado College	160	35
Colorado, U of	3000	65
Columbia University	126	17
Connecticut College	76	45
Cornell University (NY)	603	24
Dartmouth	198	11
Davidson	20	NA
Delaware, U of	1440	66
Denison	102	45
Depauw	40	78
Dickinson	87	55
Duke	32	7
Earlham	42	55
Emory University (GA)	200	65
Fairfield	84	26
Florida, U of	4400	48
Fordham	NA	NA
Franklin and Marshall	30	NA
Furman	23	16
Georgetown	417	33
George Washington (DC)	1060	70
Georgia Tech	431	43
Gettysburg	25	NA
GMI Engineering	135	55
Grinnell	153	50
Hamilton	34	32
Hampshire College	102	62
Harvard	136	13
Haverford	4	3
Hobart and W Smith	26	49
Holy Cross	44	NA
Il., U of-Urbana	1025	33
James Madison	882	55
Johns Hopkins	136	50
Kenyon	NA	NA
Lafayette	84	52
Lehigh	153	55
Lewis and Clark	207	6
Loyola College	190	NA
Macalester	87	41
Marquette	519	55
MIT	80	NA
Miami, U of (FL)	1180	70
Miami University (OH)	250	30
Michigan, U of	1050	50
Middlebury	81	38
Mount Holyoke	45	NA
Muhlenberg	74	80
NYU	1900	63
Northwestern	289	44
Notre Dame, U of	250	33
Oberlin	126	38
Occidental	NA	NA
Ohio Wesleyan	84	70
Penn State	696	35
Pennsylvania, U of	436	32
Pepperdine	248	60
Pomona	48	18
Princeton	5	1
Providence (RI)	160	50
Reed	132	52
Rensselaer Polytech	407	80
Rhodes	41	33
Rice	70	14
Richmond, U of	62	22
Rochester, U of	546	53
Rollins	118	50
Rutgers-New Brunswick	3800	27
St. Lawrence	66	65
St. Olaf	101	65
Santa Clara (CA)	277	53
Skidmore	65	28
Smith	153	40
Sou. Calif., U of	1500	NA
SMU	NA	NA
Stanford	167	14
Swarthmore	20	7
Syracuse University	960	60
Texas, U of (Austin)	2790	50
Trinity College (CT)	95	53
Trinity University (TX)	40	30
Tufts	142	28
Tulane	NA	NA
Tulsa, U of	452	78
Union	73	70
US Air Force Academy	0	0
US Military Academy	0	0
US Naval Academy	0	0
UNC-Chapel Hill	NA	NA
University of the South (Sewanee)	35	60
Vanderbilt	170	50
Vassar	112	49
Vermont, U of	344	35
Villanova	252	60
Virginia, U of	805	40
VPI	1215	50
Wake Forest	202	60
Washington and Lee	13	10
Washington University (MO)	382	63
Washington, U of (WA)	3080	75
Wellesley	48	35
Wesleyan University	100	20
Wheaton College (IL)	150	60
William and Mary	179	35
Williams College	32	17
Wisconsin, U of-Madison	2600	55
Worcester Polytech	113	70
Yale	23	3

% of all New Students Who Were Transfers into all Classes and Minimum GPA or Grade Accepted

	%	GPA
American University (DC)	10	2.0
Amherst	5	3.0
Babson	11	3.1
Barnard	18	3.0
Bates	4	3.0
Boston College	14	2.5
Boston University	15	C
Bowdoin	1	3.0
Brandeis	8	3.0
Brown	8	NA
Bryn Mawr	6	C
Bucknell	5	2.5
Cal-Berkeley	31	2.8
Cal-L.A. (UCLA)	35	D
Carleton	3	3.0
Carnegie Mellon	11	3.0
Case Western	15	3.0
Catholic University (DC)	33	3.0
Chicago, U of	11	3.0
Clark University	19	2.8
Colby	3	3.0
Colgate	5	3.0
Colorado College	11	3.0
Colorado, U of	9	2.5
Columbia University	NA	3.0
Connecticut College	2	3.0
Cornell University (NY)	15	3.0
Dartmouth	3	3.0
Davidson	NA	B
Delaware, U of	21	3.0
Denison	2	2.5
Depauw	5	3.0
Dickinson	5	NA
Duke	1	NA
Earlham	7	2.8
Emory University (GA)	8	3.0
Fairfield	2	2.8
Florida, U of	42	2.0
Fordham	10	3.0
Franklin and Marshall	5	NA
Furman	5	3.0
Georgetown	NA	3.0
George Washington (DC)	NA	3.0
Georgia Tech	12	3.0
Gettysburg	3	NA
GMI Engineering	10	3.0
Grinnell	11	3.0
Hamilton	4	3.0
Hampshire College	16	B-
Harvard	5	C-
Haverford	1	3.0
Hobart and W Smith	1	3.0
Holy Cross	1	2.0
Il., U of-Urbana	4	3.25
James Madison	21	C
Johns Hopkins	8	3.0
Kenyon	4	NA
Lafayette	7	2.0
Lehigh	5	3.0
Lewis and Clark	22	3.0
Loyola College	5	NA
Macalester	10	3.0
Marquette	13	2.0
MIT	2	3.0
Miami, U of (FL)	7	2.5
Miami University (OH)	6	3.0
Michigan, U of	9	3.0
Middlebury	2	B
Mount Holyoke	NA	NA
Muhlenberg	8	2.5
NYU	39	2.5
Northwestern	6	NA
Notre Dame, U of	5	3.5
Oberlin	7	3.0
Occidental	14	3.0
Ohio Wesleyan	7	3.0
Penn State	9	2.0
Pennsylvania, U of	14	3.2
Pepperdine	19	2.7
Pomona	5	C-
Princeton	1	3.5
Providence (RI)	8	3.0
Reed	NA	C
Rensselaer Polytech	19	3.0
Rhodes	9	C
Rice	7	3.2
Richmond, U of	4	C
Rochester, U of	16	C-
Rollins	14	2.7
Rutgers-New Brunswick	23	C
St. Lawrence	7	3.0
St. Olaf	7	3.0
Santa Clara (CA)	17	3.0
Skidmore	4	3.0
Smith	12	C
Sou. Calif., U of	9	NA
SMU	8	2.5
Stanford	8	NA
Swarthmore	5	3.0
Syracuse University	16	2.5
Texas, U of (Austin)	30	3.0
Trinity College (CT)	9	3.2
Trinity University (TX)	2	2.0
Tufts	6	C
Tulane	7	3.0
Tulsa, U of	28	2.3
Union	11	3.0
US Air Force Academy		
US Military Academy		
US Naval Academy	8	
UNC-Chapel Hill	22	3.0
University of the South (Sewanee)	7	3.0
Vanderbilt	5	C
Vassar	10	3.0
Vermont, U of	11	3.0
Villanova	9	3.0
Virginia, U of	18	C
VPI	4	2.0
Wake Forest	3	2.0
Washington and Lee	1	2.0
Washington University (MO)	13	3.0
Washington, U of (WA)	33	2.0
Wellesley	6	C
Wesleyan University	9	3.5
Wheaton College (IL)	15	3.0
William and Mary	7	3.0
Williams College	1	NA
Wisconsin, U of-Madison	27	3.0
Worcester Polytech	3	C
Yale	2	NA

Percent of Freshmen Who Graduate After 4 Years And Percent Who Go on to Graduate School Within 3 to 5 Years

(Shown in Parentheses. * Means within One Year -- ** 2 Years)

18 Colleges Graduated 90% or More After 4 Years

Amherst	MA	*(28)	Duke	NC	NA	Princeton	NJ	NA
Bowdoin	ME	(70)	Harvard	MA	(33)	Stanford	CA	NA
Brown	RI	(60)	Haverford	PA	(80)	Tufts	MA	NA
Columbia	NY	(90)	Middlebury	VT	(40)	Wesleyan	CT	(75)
Dartmouth	NH	(75)	Notre Dame	IN	*(45)	Williams	MA	NA
Davidson	NC	NA	Pennslyvania, U of	PA	*(23)	Yale	CT	*(28)

36 Colleges Graduated 80% to 90% After 4 Years

Babson	MA	(9)	Hamilton	NY	(50)	Providence	RI	NA
Barnard	NY	(40)	Holy Cross	MA	(30)	Rice	TX	*(45)
Bates	ME	NA	Johns Hopkins	MD	NA	St. Lawrence	NY	*(33)
Boston Coll.	MA	(22)	Kenyon	OH	(60)	Smith	MA	(35)
Bryn Mawr	PA	(50)	Lafayette	PA	*(24)	Swarthmore	PA	(40)
Bucknell	PA	(50)	Lehigh	PA	(15)	Trinity Coll.	CT	(60)
Colby	ME	(65)	MIT	MA	*(52)	Vassar	NY	(85)
Colgate	NY	*(30)	Mount Holyoke	MA	(70)	Villanova	PA	(25)
Connecticut Coll.	CT	*(20)	Muhlenberg	PA	*(35)	Wash. & Lee	VA	NA
Cornell U	NY	*(26)	Northwestern	IL	(50)	Washington U	MO	(61)
Dickinson	PA	(50)	Pepperdine	CA	NA	Wellesley	MA	(35)
Fairfield	CT	(15)	Pomona	CA	NA	William & Mary	VA	NA

45 Colleges Graduated 70% to 80% After 4 Years

Brandeis	MA	*(39)	GMI Engineering	MI	(55)	Skidmore	NY	(36)
Carleton	MN	(75)	Grinnell	IA	NA	Syracuse	NY	*(30)
Chicago, U of	IL	(80)	H & W Smith	NY	(60)	Tulane	LA	(80)
Clark U	MA	(70)	Il., U of-Urbana	IL	NA	Union	NY	*(35)
Colorado Coll.	CO	(55)	Marquette	WI	(75)	US Air Force A.	CO	NA
Denison	OH	(40)	Miami, U of	FL	NA	US Military A.	NY	(90)
Depauw	IN	(50)	Michigan, U of	MI	NA	US Naval A.	MD	NA
Earlham	IN	NA	NYU	NY	(65)	UNC-Chapel Hill	NC	(16)
Emory U	GA	(65)	Oberlin	OH	**(75)	Univ. of the South	TN	*(37)
Fordham	NY	(60)	Occidental	CA	(46)	Vanderbilt	TN	**(46)
Franklin & Marshall	PA	(36)	Ohio Wesleyan	OH	(55)	Vermont, U of	VT	NA
Carnegie Mellon	PA	(50)	RPI	NY	NA	UVA	VA	(64)
Furman	SC	(70)	Rhodes	TN	(45)	VPI	VA	*(15)
Georgetown	DC	*(26)	Richmond	VA	NA	Wake Forest	NC	*(29)
Gettysburg	PA	(40)	Rollins	FL	(30)	Wheaton	IL	NA

23 Colleges Graduated 60% to 70% After 4 Years

Boston U	MA	NA	James Madison	VA	NA	Santa Clara	CA	(680)
Calif.-Berkeley	CA	(30)	Lewis & Clark	OR	(60)	Sou. Calif., U of	CA	NA
Calif.-L.A.	CA	*(60)	Loyola Coll.	MD	NA	SMU	TX	NA
Case Western	OH	*(33)	Macalester	MN	NA	Trinity U	TX	(60)
Catholic U	DC	(50)	Miami U	OH	NA	Tulsa, U of	OK	(35)
Geo. Washington	DC	NA	Rochester, U of	NY	(73)	Wisconsin, U of	WI	NA
Georgia Tech	GA	(20)	Rutgers	NJ	NA	Worcester Poly	MA	*(12)
Colorado, U of	CO	(38)	St. Olaf	MN	*(23)			

8 Colleges Graduated Up to 60% After 4 Years

American U	DC	NA	Hampshire Coll.	MA	(54)	Texas, U of	TX	NA
Delaware, U of	DE	*(17)	Penn State-Park	PA	NA	Washington, U of	WA	NA
Florida, U of	FL	NA	Reed	OR	(65)			

% Receiving Aid and Average Total of Scholarships and Grants

(Note: College and government loans are not included)

	%	Avg $
American University (DC)	60	$ 4,800
Amherst	40	15,700
Babson	33	12,100
Barnard	53	14,600
Bates	40	12,300
Boston College	70	6,400
Boston University	50	9,800
Bowdoin	60	11,000
Brandeis	40	15,400
Brown	32	9,500
Bryn Mawr	43	11,000
Bucknell	32	10,400
Cal-Berkeley	50	2,600
Cal-L.A. (UCLA)	52	2,000
Carleton	55	5,700
Carnegie Mellon	65	9,800
Case Western	70	11,800
Catholic University (DC)	40	5,500
Chicago, U of	70	9,000
Clark University	43	13,100
Colby	42	13,400
Colgate	32	12,100
Colorado College	52	10,900
Colorado, U of	28	1,750
Columbia University	70	8,000
Connecticut College	42	10,400
Cornell University (NY)	31	7,100
Dartmouth	34	8,800
Davidson	30	8,200
Delaware, U of	35	2,100
Denison	35	8,300
Depauw	49	7,900
Dickinson	49	13,400
Duke	NA	NA
Earlham	44	6,350
Emory University (GA)	37	9,750
Fairfield	48	5,260
Florida, U of	20	2,500
Fordham	75	3,500
Franklin and Marshall	47	11,900
Furman	60	1,600
Georgetown	45	8,000
George Washington (DC)	36	9,000
Georgia Tech	36	750
Gettysburg	40	8,500
GMI Engineering	48	2,500
Grinnell	69	6,700
Hamilton	42	10,000
Hampshire College	47	14,400
Harvard	41	8,500
Haverford	55	9,600
Hobart and W Smith	40	13,500
Holy Cross	40	12,500
Il., U of-Urbana	NA	NA
James Madison	50	1,000
Johns Hopkins	32	9,100
Kenyon	30	7,400
Lafayette	40	10,800
Lehigh	38	8,500
Lewis and Clark	60	7,500
Loyola College	60	5,700
Macalester	60	7,400
Marquette	60	4,100
MIT	60	10,700
Miami, U of (FL)	32	3,100

	%	Avg $
Miami University (OH)	NA	NA
Michigan, U of	40	3,000
Middlebury	33	11,400
Mount Holyoke	60	1,000
Muhlenberg	50	7,500
NYU	60	7,500
Northwestern	50	8,900
Notre Dame, U of	25	6,000
Oberlin	NA	9,200
Occidental	60	NA
Ohio Wesleyan	60	12,000
Penn State	57	2,350
Pennsylvania, U of	40	10,600
Pepperdine	65	NA
Pomona	55	10,400
Princeton	39	10,500
Providence (RI)	45	5,000
Reed	48	6,100
Rensselaer Polytech	68	9,200
Rhodes	47	7,800
Rice	NA	4,500
Richmond, U of	52	4,600
Rochester, U of	75	11,400
Rollins	30	6,400
Rutgers-New Brunswick	58	1,460
St. Lawrence	40	10,400
St. Olaf	6	9,100
Santa Clara (CA)	76	9,700
Skidmore	25	8,500
Smith	45	14,000
Sou. Calif., U of	55	NA
SMU	55	NA
Stanford	60	7,600
Swarthmore	60	9,500
Syracuse University	49	NA
Texas, U of (Austin)	33	3,900
Trinity College (CT)	38	14,300
Trinity University (TX)	69	8,100
Tufts	31	9,900
Tulane	48	10,000
Tulsa, U of	60	3,500
Union	37	8,800
US Air Force Academy	100	
US Military Academy	100	
US Naval Academy	100	
UNC-Chapel Hill	NA	2,200
University of the South (Sewanee)	45	11,900
Vanderbilt	39	7,600
Vassar	60	9,300
Vermont, U of	35	4,500
Villanova	38	7,600
Virginia, U of	28	3,500
VPI	45	1,000
Wake Forest	55	5,000
Washington and Lee	24	6,750
Washington University (MO)	54	9,000
Washington, U of (WA)	NA	2,300
Wellesley	43	10,200
Wesleyan University	35	10,400
Wheaton College (IL)	7	4,800
William and Mary	21	NA
Williams College	36	13,900
Wisconsin, U of-Madison	NA	1,880
Worcester Polytech	63	6,350
Yale	31	9,300

% of Students Working on Campus and Rating of Off-Campus Work Opportunities

E - Excellent G - Good F - Fair P - Poor

	% Work on Campus	Off Campus
American University (DC)	NA	E
Amherst	NA	F
Babson	45	E
Barnard	60	E
Bates	40	F
Boston College	24	G
Boston University	35	E
Bowdoin	65	F
Brandeis	45	G
Brown	65	G
Bryn Mawr	70	G
Bucknell	60	F
Cal-Berkeley	30	E
Cal-L.A. (UCLA)	42	E
Carleton	80	F
Carnegie Mellon	65	G
Case Western	80	G
Catholic University (DC)	15	E
Chicago, U of	80	E
Clark University	36	E
Colby	65	F
Colgate	60	P
Colorado College	38	G
Colorado, U of	70	E
Columbia University	60	G
Connecticut College	51	G
Cornell University (NY)	41	F
Dartmouth	50	G
Davidson	22	P
Delaware, U of	12	F
Denison	45	F
Depauw	25	G
Dickinson	49	G
Duke	26	E
Earlham	40	F
Emory University (GA)	40	G
Fairfield	15	G
Florida, U of	22	F
Fordham	40	E
Franklin and Marshall	49	G
Furman	20	G
Georgetown	47	E
George Washington (DC)	NA	E
Georgia Tech	25	E
Gettysburg	35	G
GMI Engineering	17	E
Grinnell	50	F
Hamilton	30	F
Hampshire College	85	G
Harvard	67	E
Haverford		G
Hobart and W Smith	23	F
Holy Cross	34	F
Il., U of-Urbana	40	G
James Madison	26	G
Johns Hopkins	50	G
Kenyon	85	P
Lafayette	5	G
Lehigh	16	G
Lewis and Clark	60	E
Loyola College	NA	NA
Macalester	50	E
Marquette	33	E
MIT	55	E
Miami, U of (FL)	38	G
Miami University (OH)	34	G
Michigan, U of	56	E
Middlebury	60	G
Mount Holyoke	85	F
Muhlenberg	32	F
NYU	27	E
Northwestern	70	E
Notre Dame, U of	40	G
Oberlin	55	G
Occidental	NA	G
Ohio Wesleyan	38	E
Penn State	27	G
Pennsylvania, U of	27	G
Pepperdine	65	E
Pomona	65	G
Princeton	60	E
Providence (RI)	35	E
Reed	55	G
Rensselaer Polytech	NA	F
Rhodes	38	G
Rice	20	G
Richmond, U of	25	E
Rochester, U of	48	G
Rollins	8	E
Rutgers-New Brunswick	31	F
St. Lawrence	45	F
St. Olaf	65	F
Santa Clara (CA)	24	G
Skidmore	40	G
Smith	60	E
Sou. Calif., U of	NA	G
SMU	NA	G
Stanford	40	E
Swarthmore	75	F
Syracuse University	53	G
Texas, U of (Austin)	20	G
Trinity College (CT)	30	E
Trinity University (TX)	10	G
Tufts	46	E
Tulane	25	G
Tulsa, U of	35	E
Union	30	G
US Air Force Academy		
US Military Academy		
US Naval Academy		
UNC-Chapel Hill	30	G
University of the South (Sewanee)	43	F
Vanderbilt	55	E
Vassar	62	F
Vermont, U of	14	E
Villanova	25	G
Virginia, U of	27	G
VPI	25	G
Wake Forest	31	G
Washington and Lee	15	P
Washington University (MO)	24	E
Washington, U of (WA)	NA	G
Wellesley	46	E
Wesleyan University	64	G
Wheaton College (IL)	43	G
William and Mary	30	E
Williams College	32	F
Wisconsin, U of-Madison	50	E
Worcester Polytech	31	E
Yale	60	G

99 Colleges having ROTC and/or AFROTC and/or NROTC

All 3 Services

American U*	DC	Georgetown	DC	Skidmore*	NY
Boston Coll.*	MA	George Washington U	DC	Sou. Calif., U of	CA
Boston U	MA	Georgia Tech	GA	Stanford*	CA
Bryn Mawr*	PA	Harvard*	MA	Texas, U of	TX
Calif.-Berkeley	CA	Holy Cross	NH	Tufts*	MA
Calif.-L.A.	CA	Il., U of-Urbana	IL	Tulane	LA
Catholic U*	DC	Marquette	WI	UNC	NC
Chicago, U of *	IL	MIT	MA	Vanderbilt*	TN
Clark U*	MA	Michigan, U of	MI	Virginia, U of	VA
Colorado Coll.	CO	Notre Dame	IN	VPI	VA
Colorado, U of	CO	Penn State	PA	Washington, U of	WA
Cornell U	NY	Pennslyvania, U of	PA	Wellesley*	MA
Duke	NC	Rensselaer Poly	NY	Wisconsin, U of	WI
Florida, U of	FL	Santa Clara	CA	Worcester Poly	MA

AFROTC and ROTC

Amherst*	MA	Loyola	MD	Rutgers	NJ
Brandeis*	MA	Miami, U of	FL	St. Lawrence	NY
Case Western*	OH	Mount Holyoke*	MA	Smith*	MA
Colby*	ME	Muhlenberg*	PA	SMU*	TX
Columbia*	NY	NYU	NY	Syracuse	NY
Davidson	NC	Occidental	CA	Trinity U	TX
Delaware, U of	DE	Pepperdine*	CA	Vermont	VT
Depauw*	IN	Pomona*	CA	VPI	VA
Johns Hopkins	MD	Princeton	NJ	Washington U	MO
Lafayette	PA	Rhodes*	TN	Yale*	CT
Lehigh	PA				

ROTC

Bowdoin*	MA	Hamilton*	NY	Trinity Coll.	CT
Brown*	RI	Furman	SC	Tulsa, U of	OK
Bucknell	PA	James Madison	VA	Wake Forest	NC
Colorado Coll.*	CO	Providence	RI	Washington & Lee	VA
Fordham	NY	Richmond	VA	William & Mary	VA
Gettysburg	PA				

ROTC and NROTC

Loyola Coll.	MD

NROTC

Northwestern	IL	Rochester, U of	NY
Rice	TX	Villanova	PA

AROTC

Hampshire Coll.*	MA	Macalester*	MN
Lewis & Clark*	OR	Ohio Wesleyan*	OH

AFROTC and NROTC

Carnegie Mellon	PA

* Available only on another nearby campus

Endowment

Total and per Student (including graduate students)

7 Colleges with over $200,000 per Student

Grinnell	292 mil	$230,000	Rice	1.14 bil	$290,000
Harvard	4.7 bil	300,000	Swarthmore	342 mil	260,000
Pomona	316 mil	220,000	Yale	2.6 bil	210,000
Princeton	2.6 bil	400,000			

6 Colleges with $150,000 to $200,000 per Student

Amherst	269 mil	$170,000	Stanford	2 bil	$150,000
Macalester	390 mil	180,000	Wellesley	388 mil	170,000
MIT	1.4 bil	150,000	Williams	315 mil	160,000

14 Colleges with $100,000 to $150,000 per Student

Bowdoin	161 mil	$120,000	Lafayette	206 mil	$110,000
Chicago U	1.1 bil	100,000	Middlebury	209 mil	105,000
Carleton	174 mil	100,000	Smith	343 mil	135,000
Dartmouth	595 mil	120,000	Trinity U	307 mil	125,000
Earlham	130 bil	110,000	Vassar	243 mil	105,000
Emory U	1.3 bil	145,000	Washington U	1.4 bil	140,000
Johns Hopkins	561 mil	145,000	Wesleyan	271 mil	100,000

12 Colleges with $75,000 to $100,000 per Student

Bryn Mawr	153 mil	$80,000	Occidental	147 mil	$85,000
Columbia U	1.5 bil	90,000	Oberlin	245 mil	85,000
Hamilton	115 mil	80,000	Rochester	588 mil	80,000
Haverford	84 mil	75,000	Trinity College	144 mil	75,000
Mount Holyoke	180 bil	90,000	Tulsa, U of	319 mil	75,000
Northwestern	1.2 bil	90,000	University of the South	96 mil	90,000

16 Colleges with $50,000 to $75,000 per Student

Brown	431 mil	$60,000	Notre Dame	637 mil	$65,000
Case Western	443 mil	70,000	Reed	98 mil	70,000
Colgate	147 mil	55,000	Rhodes	84 mil	70,000
Colorado College	144 mil	65,000	Richmond	297 mil	65,000
Cornell U	954 mil	50,000	Texas, U of	3.3 bil	65,000
Davidson	93 mil	65,000	Vanderbilt	604 mil	65,000
Duke	527 mil	50,000	Wake Forest	336 mil	65,000
Franklin & Marshall	105 mil	55,000	Washington & Lee	114 mil	55,000

Source: National Association of College and University Business Officers
The latest figures available are 1991

Endowment

Total and per Student (including graduate students)

22 Colleges with $25,000 to $50,000 per Student

Bates	69 mil	$45,000	Lehigh	262 mil	$30,000
Brandeis	161 mil	45,000	Pennsylvania	826 mil	40,000
Bucknell	109 mil	30,000	Pepperdine	80 mil	30,000
Carnegie Mellon	313 mil	45,000	Providence	18 mil	40,000
Colby	78 mil	45,000	Rensselaer	240 mil	35,000
Connecticut College	43 mil	27,000	St. Lawrence	86 mil	40,000
Denison	86 mil	40,000	SMU	367 mil	40,000
Depauw	99 mil	40,000	Union	106 mil	45,000
Dickinson	61 mil	30,000	Virginia, U of	507 mil	30,000
Furman	88 mil	31,000	Wheaton (IL)	85 mil	35,000
Holy Cross	88 mil	35,000	Worcester Poly	106 mil	40,000

27 Colleges with $10,000 to $25,000 per Student

Babson	33 mil	$11,000	Michigan, U of	500 mil	$14,000
Barnard	48 mil	23,000	Muhlenberg	29 mil	18,000
Boston College	312 mil	21,000	NYU	582 mil	21,000
Clark U	50 mil	18,000	Ohio Wesleyan	41 mil	22,000
Delaware, U of	390 mil	22,000	Rollins	32 mil	16,000
Georgetown	262 mil	24,000	St. Olaf	47 mil	16,000
George Washington	305 mil	21,000	Santa Clara	115 mil	17,000
Georgia Tech	223 mil	19,000	Skidmore	39 mil	16,000
Gettysburg	45 mil	24,000	Sou. Calif., U of	523 mil	19,000
Hobart & W Smith	37.5 mil	19,000	Syracuse	176 mil	10,000
Kenyon	35 mil	23,000	Tufts	168 mil	20,000
Lewis & Clark	35 mil	17,000	Tulane	234 mil	24,000
Loyola College	42 mil	13,000	William & Mary	94 mil	12,000
Miami, U of	196 mil	13,000			

20 Colleges with up to $10,000 per Student

American U	23 mil	$ 3,300	Marquette	95 mil	$8,000
Boston U	167 mil	7,000	Miami U (OH)	31 mil	2,400
Calif.-L.A.	304 mil	8,000	Penn State	208 mil	5,500
Colorado, U of	68 mil	2,600	Rutgers	126 mil	2,900
Fairfield	25 mil	7,000	UNC	181 mil	9,000
Florida, U of	225 mil	7,000	Vermont, U of	75 mil	9,500
Fordham	73 mil	6,500	Villanova	28 mil	3,500
GMI Engineering	10 mil	3,300	VPI	130 mil	5,500
Hampshire College	10 mil	8,000	Washington, U of	179 mil	6,500
James Madison	9 mil	900	Wisconsin, U of	218 mil	5,500

Source: National Association of College and University Business Officers
The latest figures available are 1991

Total Number of Living Alumni

Percent of Solicited that Contributed and Average Amount Contributed

Over 100,000 Alumni (22 Colleges)

College	%	Amount	College	%	Amount	College	%	Amount
Boston U	20%	$160	Harvard	27%	$1100	Syracuse	19%	$400
Calif.--Berkeley	NA	700	Northwestern	26%	500	Texas, U of	11%	250
Calif.-L.A.	NA	400	Pennsylvania	45%	700	UNC	23%	550
Chicago, U of	35%	480	Penn State-Park	22%	250	Virginia, U of	35%	400
Columbia U	25%	850	Rutgers	19%	130	VPI	24%	180
Cornell U	60%	1200	Sou. Calif.,U of	NA	400	Washington, U of	NA	550
Florida, U of	20%	330	Stanford	21%	2200	Wisconsin, U of	NA	NA
Geo. Washington	37%	190						

60,000 to 100,000 Alumni (18 Colleges)

College	%	Amount	College	%	Amount	College	%	Amount
Boston Coll.	28%	$ 350	Johns Hopkins	41%	$1400	Princeton	47%	$1200
Brown	38%	1100	Marquette	23%	380	SMU	20%	410
Case Western	35%	350	MIT	38%	1200	Tufts	42%	870
Duke	52%	500	Miami U	30%	220	Tulane	23%	570
Georgia Tech	34%	600	Miami, U of	17%	420	Washington U	32%	600
Georgetown	29%	550	Notre Dame	50%	670	Vanderbilt	28%	450

40,000 to 60,000 Alumni (11 Colleges)

College	%	Amount	College	%	Amount	College	%	Amount
American U	NA	$ 470	Lehigh	45%	210	Vermont, U of	29%	$210
Carnegie Mellon	37%	570	Rensselaer Poly	25%	650	Villanova	23%	250
Dartmouth	60%	1050	Rochester	29%	480	William & Mary	22%	700
Emory U	NA	290	Smith	45%	1300			

20,000 to 40,000 Alumni (29 Colleges)

College	%	Amount	College	%	Amount	College	%	Amount
Barnard	30%	$500	Holy Cross	55%	$400	Rochester U	29%	$480
Brandeis	42%	210	James Madison	30%	445	St. Olaf	31%	570
Bucknell	37%	600	Loyola Coll.	28%	120	Santa Clara	24%	250
Colgate	51%	500	Mount Holyoke	60%	800	Tulsa, U of	12%	450
Denison	38%	600	Oberlin	52%	440	Vassar	55%	700
Depauw	41%	700	Ohio Wesleyan	39%	700	Wake Forest	31%	410
Fairfield	31%	300	Pepperdine	6%	210	Wellesley	55%	1400
Furman	35%	550	Providence	29%	280	Wesleyan	40%	800
Gettysburg	34%	400	Rice	42%	420	Wheaton	33%	380
GMI Engineering	23%	130	Richmond, U of	30%	1200			

10,000 to 20,000 Alumni (32 Colleges)

College	%	Amount	College	%	Amount	College	%	Amount
Amherst	65%	$ 800	Grinnell	48%	$550	Rollins	29%	$900
Bates	48%	450	Hamilton	63%	600	Skidmore	42%	470
Bowdoin	63%	1200	H & W Smith	44%	300	St. Lawrence	45%	300
Bryn Mawr	38%	3000	Kenyon	45%	400	Swarthmore	61%	1200
Carleton	48%	500	Lewis & Clark	28%	70	Trinity Coll.	45%	600
Colby	46%	400	Macalester	31%	400	Trinity U	24%	100
Colorado Coll.	40%	250	Middlebury	51%	650	Union	60%	500
Connecticut Coll.	40%	700	Muhlenberg	35%	220	U. of the South	53%	280
Davidson	51%	900	Occidental	27%	190	Wash. & Lee	37%	1200
Earlham	32%	360	Pomona	42%	1450	Williams	62%	1050
Franklin & Marsh.	29%	380	Rhodes	44%	550			

Under 10,000 Alumni (3 Colleges)

College	%	Amount	College	%	Amount	College	%	Amount
Hampshire	31%	$120	Haverford	58%	$450	Reed	41%	$400

Note: Colleges omitted where information unavailable

Source: Council for Aid to Education

Annual Alumni Support

$5000 and Larger per Student (16 Colleges)

College	Total	Per Student
Amherst	8.1 mil	$ 5100
Bowdoin	9.8 mil	7100
Bryn Mawr	16.4 mil	8900
Columbia U	32 mil	10,000
Dartmouth	24.4 mil	5000
Johns Hopkins	31.6 mil	10,000
Lafayette	11 mil	$5500
MIT	34 mil	8000
Mt. Holyoke	10.7 mil	5400
Pomona	11.4 mil	8200
Princeton	31.7 mil	5000
Stanford	68 mil	$ 5200
Smith	25 mil	10,200
Swarthmore	11.5 mil	8800
Wellesley	23 mil	10,400
Williams	12.7 mil	6000

$2500 to $5000 per Student (16 Colleges)

College	Total	Per Student
Brown	22.6 mil	$3000
Carleton	4.5 mil	2600
Connecticut Col.	4.5 mil	2600
Cornell U	57 mil	3200
Davidson	6 mil	4400
Dennison	5.6 mil	2800
Grinnell	4.1 mil	$3300
Harvard	71 mil	4000
Middlebury	6.3 mil	3100
Ohio Wesleyan	6 mil	3100
Pennsylvania	52 mil	2700
Richmond, U of	9.3 mil	$2600
Vassar	9 mil	4000
Wash. & Lee	8 mil	4000
Wesleyan	8.2 mil	3000
Yale	50 mil	4600

$1000 to $2500 per Student (42 Colleges)

College	Total	Per Student
Barnard	3 mil	$2300
Bates	3 mil	2000
Bucknell	6.3 mil	1900
Carn. Mellon	8.1 mil	1200
Case Western	9.1 mil	1100
Chicago, U of	14.7 mil	1700
Colby	2.8 mil	1700
Colgate	5.8 mil	2000
Depauw	5.4 mil	2300
Duke	21.5 mil	2000
Earlham	1.5 mil	1300
Frank. & Marsh.	2 mil	1050
Furman	3.5 mil	1200
Georgia Tech	11.6 mil	1000
Gettysburg	2.9 mil	$1500
Hamilton	4 mil	2400
Haverford	1.9mil	1600
H & W Smith	1.9 mil	1000
Holy Cross	5.3 mil	2000
Kenyon	1.8 mil	1200
Lehigh	14 mil	2100
Macalester	2.2 mil	1250
Northwestern	16.3 mil	1300
Notre Dame	24mil	2200
Oberlin	6.2 mil	2200
Reed	1.5 mil	1200
Rensselaer	7.6 mil	1200
Rhodes	2.5 mil	1900
Rice	5.2 mil	$1200
Rochester, U of	8.3 mil	1100
St. Lawrence	2.2 mil	1000
St. Olaf	4 mil	1300
Skidmore	3.5 mil	1400
Stanford	68 mil	2200
Trinity Coll.	4.5 mil	2400
Tufts	14.3 mil	2000
Union	4.9 mil	2300
U of the South	1.5 mil	1300
Vanderbilt	13 mil	1400
Washington U	13 mil	1300
Wheaton	3.7 mil	1500
William & Mary	7.6 mil	1000

$500 to $1000 per Student (23 Colleges)

College	Total	Per Student
American U	1.3 mil	$400
Boston Coll.	8.5mil	650
Clark U	2 mil	700
Colorado Coll.	1.6 mil	800
Dickinson	1.9 mil	950
Emory U	4.5 mil	500
Georgetown	10 mil	800
Marquette	6 mil	550
Michigan ,U of	32 mil	$950
Muhlenberg	1 mil	700
NYU	14 mil	600
Occidental	900,000	550
Providence	2.8 mil	700
Rollins	1.8 mil	800
Rutgers	4.3 mil	500
SMU	5 mil	600
Sou. Calif.	22.5 mil	$550
Syracuse	9.5 mil	550
Tulane	8.2 mil	850
UNC	19 mil	900
Virginia, U of	14.8 mil	800
Wake Forest	4.8 mil	950
Worcester Poly	3.4 mil	950

Under $500 per Student (23 Colleges)

College	Total	Per Student
Babson	1.3 mil	$400
Boston U	5.7 mil	250
Brandeis	1.2 mil	300
Colorado, U of	5.2 mil	250
Fairfield	1.7 mil	400
Florida, U of	10.1 mil	350
George Wash.	3.1 mil	210
GMI Eng.	500,000	170
Hampshire Col.	157,000	$120
James Madison	460,000	45
Lewis & Clark	270,000	100
Loyola Coll.	850,000	140
Miami U	5.6 mil	250
Miami, U of	5.2 mil	400
Penn State	12.2 mil	350
Pepperdine	500,000	200
Santa Clara	2 mil	$300
Texas, U of	6.2 mil	120
Trinity U	450,000	180
Tulsa, U of	1.5 mil	400
Vermont, U of	2.8 mil	350
Villanova	3.4 mil	250
Washington, U of	12.8 mil	400

Note: Colleges omitted where information unavailable

Source: Council for Aid to Education

54 Colleges Offering Services for Learning Disabled

College	State	College	State	College	State
American University	DC	Florida, U of	FL	Princeton	NJ
Barnard	NY	Georgetown	DC	Providence	RI
Bates	ME	George Washington	DC	Rutgers, N. Brunswick	NJ
Boston College	MA	Georgia Tech	GA	St. Lawrence	NY
Boston University	MA	Harvard	MA	St. Olaf	MN
Carnegie Mellon	PA	Haverford	PA	Smith	MA
Case Western	OH	Illinois U of-Urbana	IL	Southern California, U of	CA
Catholic University	DC	James Madison	VA	Stanford	CA
Clark University	MA	Johns Hopkins	MD	Syracuse University	NY
Colorado College	CO	Lewis and Clark	OR	Texas, U of	TX
Columbia University	NY	Miami University	OH	UNC-Chapel Hill	NC
Cornell University	NY	Michigan, U of	MI	Vanderbilt	TN
Dartmouth	NH	Mount Holyoke	MA	Vermont, U of	VT
Delaware, U of	DE	Muhlenberg	MA	Virginia, U of	VA
Dickinson College	PA	NYU	NY	VPI	VA
Duke	NC	Oberlin	OH	Washington University	MO
Earlham	IN	Ohio Wesleyan	OH	Wellesley	MA
Emory University	GA	Pennsylvania, U of	PA	Wisconsin, U of	WI
				Yale	CT

27 Colleges with Work-Study CO-OP Programs

College	State	College	State	College	State
American University	DC	Illinois, U of	IL	SMU	TX
Carnegie Mellon	PA	Marquette	WI	Syracuse University	NY
Case Western	OH	Miami, U of	FL	Texas, U of	TX
Colorado, U of	CO	Michigan, U of	MI	Vermont, U of	VT
Cornell University	NY	Northwestern	IL	VPI	VA
Florida, U of	FL	Penn State	PA	Washington University	MO
George Washington	DC	RPI	NY	Washington, U of	WA
Georgia Tech	GA	Santa Clara	CA	Wisconsin, U of	WI
GMI Engineering	MI	Southern Calif, U of	CA	Worcester Poly	MA

Colleges Accepting Freshmen in Terms other than Fall and Percent of Freshman Entering other than Fall

College	State	%	College	State	%	College	State	%
American University	DC	5	Georgia Tech	GA	15	Rhodes	TN	1
Babson	MA	3	Gettysburg	PA	1	Rochester, U of	NY	1
Barnard	NY	1	GMI Enginering	MI	1	Rollins	FL	1
Boston College	MA	1	Hampshire College	MA	3	St. Lawrence	NY	1
Boston University	MA	2	Holy Cross	MA	1	St. Olaf	MN	NA
Brandeis	MA	NA	Illinois, U of	IL	2	Santa Clara	CA	1
Brown University	RI	2	Lafayette College	PA	NA	Sou. Calif., U of	CA	1
Bryn Mawr	PA	1	Lehigh	PA	1	SMU	TX	1
Case Western	OH	4	Lewis and Clark	OR	1	Syracuse University	NY	1
Catholic University	DC	1	Macalester	MN	1	Texas, U of	TX	20
Clark University	MA	1	Marquette	WI	2	Trinity University	TX	1
Colby College	ME	7	Miami, U of	FL	4	Tulane	LA	NA
Colgate	NY	NA	Miami U	OH	2	Tulsa, U of	OK	2
Colorado, U of	CO	NA	Michigan, U of	MI	NA	Univ. of the South	TN	NA
Cornell University	NY	3	Middlebury	VT	NA	Vanderbilt	TN	1
Delaware, U of	DE	2	Mount Holyoke	MA	11	Vermont, U of	VT	2
Denison	OH	1	Muhlenberg	PA	1	Villanova	PA	1
Depauw	IN	NA	NYU	NY	8	VPI	VA	5
Duke	NC	1	Northwestern	IL	1	Wake Forest	NC	3
Earlham	IN	1	Oberlin	OH	NA	Washington U	MO	1
Emory University	GA	NA	Ohio Wesleyan	OH	1	Wesleyan University	CT	5
Florida, U of	FL	30	Penn State	PA	24	Wheaton College	IL	2
Fordham University	NY	3	Pepperdine	CA	NA	William and Mary	VA	1
Franklin and Marshall	PA	1	Reed	OR	NA	Wisconsin, U of	WI	2
George Washington	DC	5	RPI	NY	1	Worcester Poly	MA	2

Students Living on Campus and Percent Staying on Weekends - in Parentheses

95% or More Living on Campus (24)

School	Living on Campus	Weekends
Amherst	99	(95)
Barnard	95	NA
Bryn Mawr	95	NA
Carleton	95	(95)
Connecticut Coll.	98	(95)
Denison	97	(85)
Depauw	96	(95)
Hamilton	99	(95)
Harvard	99	NA
Haverford	99	(90)
Kenyon	100	(95)
MIT	95	(80)
Middlebury	98	(85)
Mt. Holyoke	97	(75)
Muhlenberg	96	(80)
Pomona	97	NA
Princeton	98	(75)
Richmond	95	(80)
Smith	95	(90)
US Air Force A.	100	NA
US Mil. Acad.	100	NA
US Naval Acad.	100	NA
Vassar	95	(90)
Williams	98	(95)

90% to 95% Living on Campus (18)

School	Living on Campus	Weekends
Bates	90	(65)
Brandeis	91	NA
Bucknell	92	(90)
Colby	93	NA
Columbia U	92	(90)
Dickinson	92	(95)
Duke	91	(95)
Lafayette	90	(85)
Ohio Wesleyan	91	NA
St. Lawrence	92	(90)
Stanford	91	(90)
Swarthmore	92	(90)
Trinity Coll.	90	(80)
U. of the South	93	(96)
Vanderbilt	91	(90)
Wellesley	92	(90)
Wesleyan	92	NA
Yale	90	(85)

80% to 90% Living on Campus (26)

School	Living on Campus	Weekends
Babson	80	(70)
Brown	85	(95)
Carnegie Mellon	80	(95)
Case Western	85	(85)
Catholic U	80	(80)
Dartmouth	88	NA
Davidson	89	(90)
Earlham	80	(90)
Fairfield	80	(70)
Georgetown	80	NA
Gettysburg	88	(85)
Grinnell	86	(90)
Hampshire Coll.	87	(75)
H & W Smith	85	(80)
Holy Cross	80	(80)
Northwestern	80	(60)
Notre Dame	85	(75)
Rhodes	82	(80)
Rochester, U of	89	(90)
Rollins	80	(85)
St. Olaf	86	(85)
Skidmore	83	(80)
Tufts	80	(95)
Wake Forest	84	(80)
Wheaton	85	NA
William & Mary	80	(95)

65% to 80% Living on Campus (21)

School	Living on Campus	Weekends
Boston Coll.	67	(85)
Bowdoin	71	(95)
Chicago, U of	67	(90)
Clark U	67	(90)
Colgate	65	(90)
Colorado Coll.	67	NA
Emory	75	(95)
Franklin & Marsh.	71	(90)
Lehigh	75	NA
Loyola Coll.	65	(80)
Macalester	70	(95)
Marquette	65	(95)
Oberlin	71	(95)
Occidental	75	(75)
Providence	65	(90)
RPI	70	(70)
Rice	70	(75)
Syracuse	75	(75)
Trinity U	75	(75)
Union	76	NA
Wash. & Lee	67	(80)

50% to 65% Living on Campus (23)

School	Living on Campus	Weekends
American U	60	NA
Boston U	55	(80)
Delaware, U of	55	NA
Fordham	50	(65)
Furman	60	(85)
Geo. Washington	50	NA
James Madison	51	NA
Johns Hopkins	50	(90)
Lewis & Clark	53	(80)
Miami, U of (FL)	50	(70)
Miami U (OH)	60	NA
Michigan, U of	52	NA
Pennsylvania	63	(80)
Pepperdine	62	(35)
Reed	50	NA
Rutgers	59	NA
Santa Clara	50	(75)
Tulane	50	NA
Tulsa	51	NA
Villanova	50	(90)
Virginia, U of	51	(80)
Washington U	60	(80)
Worcester Poly	50	(85)

Under 50 % Living on Campus (18)

School	Living on Campus	Weekends
Calif.-Berkeley	25	NA
Calif.-L.A.	26	NA
Colorado U	25	(70)
Cornell U	43	NA
Florida, U of	25	NA
Georgia Tech	36	(75)
GMI Engineering	32	(80)
Il., U of-Urbana	33	NA
NYU	48	(60)
Penn State	40	(40)
Sou. Calif., U of	31	NA
SMU	38	(800)
Texas, U of	13	NA
UNC	40	NA
Vermont, U of	46	NA
VPI	45	(90)
Wash., U (WA)	15	NA
Wisconsin, U of	24	NA

% of Students in Fraternities / Sororities and Students with Cars on Campus

(* Indicates no chapter houses)

	%F %S	% Cars
American University (DC)	11-7	30
Amherst	None	NA
Babson	10*-4*	30
Barnard	1	1
Bates	None	NA
Boston College	None	9
Boston University	11-12	NA
Bowdoin	37-37	30
Brandeis	None	NA
Brown	11-1	NA
Bryn Mawr	None	NA
Bucknell	55-50*	54
Cal-Berkeley	7-7	26
Cal-L.A. (UCLA)	16*-17*	NA
Carleton	None	NA
Carnegie Mellon	33-29	5
Case Western	36-18*	NA
Catholic University (DC)	3-2*	20
Chicago, U of	8-2*	NA
Clark University	None	NA
Colby	None	50
Colgate	37-32	42
Colorado College	33-33	38
Colorado, U of	15-15	NA
Columbia University	15-15*	1
Connecticut College	None	50
Cornell University (NY)	37-32	NA
Dartmouth	60-60	20
Davidson	50-0	60
Delaware, U of	17-17	NA
Denison	58-62	34
Depauw	80-80	42
Dickinson	34*-42*	30
Duke	40-35	40
Earlham	None	5
Emory University (GA)	40-45	75
Fairfield	None	40
Florida, U of	18*-14*	55
Fordham	None	NA
Franklin and Marshall	40-30	NA
Furman	35*-30*	50
Georgetown	None	8
George Washington (DC)	26-18*	10
Georgia Tech	26-23	60
Gettysburg	60-45*	35
GMI Engineering	60-60	80
Grinnell	None	10
Hamilton	45*-10*	30
Hampshire College	None	60
Harvard	None	3
Haverford	None	NA
Hobart and W Smith	35-0	23
Holy Cross	None	26
Il., U of-Urbana	25-29	NA
James Madison	19-16	25
Johns Hopkins	25-30*	None
Kenyon	55*-0	22
Lafayette	53-46	35
Lehigh	51-45	80
Lewis and Clark	1*-0	25
Loyola College	None	NA
Macalester	None	NA
Marquette	2*-1*	NA
MIT	55-18*	30
Miami, U of (FL)	18-11*	NA
Miami University (OH)	38-42*	NA
Michigan, U of	15*-20*	NA
Middlebury	None	33
Mount Holyoke	None	32
Muhlenberg	50-40	35
NYU	8-8	2
Northwestern	36-39	NA
Notre Dame, U of	None	50
Oberlin	None	NA
Occidental	18-18	50
Ohio Wesleyan	58-53	27
Penn State	14-14*	NA
Pennsylvania, U of	35-35	NA
Pepperdine	15*-10*	45
Pomona	10*-5*	30
Princeton	None	10
Providence (RI)	None	NA
Reed	None	40
Rensselaer Polytech	35*-35	35
Rhodes	56-62	79
Rice	None	75
Richmond, U of	55-60*	50
Rochester, U of	26-18	NA
Rollins	24-30	NA
Rutgers-New Brunswick	6-4*	NA
St. Lawrence	45-45	50
St. Olaf	None	23
Santa Clara (CA)	17-15	30
Skidmore	None	45
Smith	None	1
Sou. Calif., U of	22-20	NA
SMU	45-50	NA
Stanford	10-10*	NA
Swarthmore	15-0	10
Syracuse University	20-28	NA
Texas, U of (Austin)	14-14	50
Trinity College (CT)	20*-10*	NA
Trinity University (TX)	29*-29*	50
Tufts	15-4	30
Tulane	34*-38*	NA
Tulsa, U of	21-22	60
Union	45-25	27
US Air Force Academy	None	40
US Military Academy	None	NA
US Naval Academy	None	23
UNC-Chapel Hill	20-20	NA
University of the South (Sewanee)	70-74*	75
Vanderbilt	47-51	NA
Vassar	None	22
Vermont, U of	15-7	20
Villanova	30*-30*	30
Virginia, U of	28-30	26
VPI	17-18	65
Wake Forest	40*-44*	63
Washington and Lee	70-53*	33
Washington University (MO)	32-35*	36
Washington, U of (WA)	18-16	4
Wellesley	None	23
Wesleyan University	10-2*	30
Wheaton College (IL)	None	35
William and Mary	35-35	48
Williams College	None	28
Wisconsin, U of-Madison	14-14	9
Worcester Polytech	40-40	25
Yale	None	NA

Percent Participating in Intramural Sports

(Intercollegiate percent participation shown in parentheses)

	%	%
American University (DC)	58	(5)
Amherst	30	(30)
Babson	75	(20)
Barnard	40	(20)
Bates	55	(40)
Boston College	40	(7)
Boston University	50	(10)
Bowdoin	55	(20)
Brandeis	70	(35)
Brown University	60	(40)
Bryn Mawr	30	(20)
Bucknell	75	(25)
Calif., U of-Berkeley	20	(2)
Calif., U of-L. A.	75	(25)
Carleton	60	(35)
Carnegie Mellon	90	(15)
Case Western	60	(30)
Catholic University	35	(15)
Chicago, U of	75	(15)
Clark University	40	(15)
Colby College	65	(5)
Colgate	35	(15)
Colorado College	70	(15)
Colorado, University of	35	(2)
Columbia University	50	(15)
Connecticut College	80	(70)
Cornell University	85	(10)
Dartmouth	60	(40)
Davidson College	75	(25)
Delaware, U of	60	(5)
Denison College	40	(35)
Depauw	65	(15)
Dickinson College	55	(40)
Duke	60	(10)
Earlham	50	(35)
Emory University	80	(15)
Fairfield	65	(20)
Florida, U of	10	(5)
Fordham University	15	(10)
Franklin and Marshall	35	(30)
Furman	50	(25)
Georgetown	50	(15)
George Washington	75	(5)
Georgia Tech	60	(10)
Gettysburg	70	(25)
GMI Engineering	40	(1)
Grinnell	50	(25)
Hamilton College	65	(35)
Hampshire College	65	(35)
Harvard	70	(20)
Haverford	60	(50)
Hobart & W. Smith	60	(50)
Holy Cross (MA)	45	(25)
Illinois, U of-Urbana	15	(1)
James Madison	65	(10)
Johns Hopkins	30	(25)
Kenyon	75	(50)
Lafayette	70	(25)
Lehigh University	60	(25)
Lewis and Clark	60	(25)
Loyola College	80	(25)
Macalester	50	(20)
Marquette	50	(2)
MIT	70	(40)
Miami, U of (FL)	50	(35)

	%	%
Miami University (OH)	90	(3)
Michigan, U of-A. Arbor	90	(3)
Middlebury	60	(35)
Mount Holyoke	20	(10)
Muhlenberg	60	(25)
New York University	5	(3)
Northwestern (IL)	80	(65)
Notre Dame, U of	90	(15)
Oberlin	50	(15)
Occidental	30	(75)
Ohio Wesleyan	80	(40)
Penn State-Park	80	(15)
Pennsylvania, U of	80	(25)
Pepperdine	75	NA
Pomona	65	(45)
Princeton	40	(40)
Providence College	65	(10)
Reed	25	(15)
Rensselaer Polytech	70	(15)
Rhodes	45	(25)
Rice	100	(10)
Richmond, U of	15	(15)
Rochester, U of	60	(15)
Rollins	90	(20)
Rutgers-N. Bruns.	NA	(5)
St. Lawrence	50	(25)
St. Olaf	50	(25)
Santa Clara	50	(25)
Skidmore	80	(25)
Smith	20	(20)
Southern Calif., U of	40	(5)
Southern Methodist	40	(5)
Stanford	50	(10)
Swarthmore	55	(35)
Syracuse University	50	(5)
Texas, U of-Austin	75	(1)
Trinity College (CT)	50	(40)
Trinity University	75	(10)
Tufts	75	(20)
Tulane	85	(10)
Tulsa, University of	30	(50)
Union (NY)	70	(40)
U S Air Force Academy	65	(35)
U S Military Academy	100	(25)
U S Naval Academy	100	NA
UNC-Chapel Hill	50	(5)
University of the South	80	(40)
Vanderbilt	15	(5)
Vassar	50	(25)
Vermont, U of	20	(10)
Villanova	70	(10)
Virginia, U of	85	(50)
Virginia Polytech	NA	NA
Wake Forest	55	(10)
Washington & Lee	75	(40)
Washington University	75	(15)
Washington, U of(WA)	NA	NA
Wellesley	20	(10)
Wesleyan University	50	(40)
Wheaton College (IL)	50	(20)
William and Mary	80	(15)
Williams College	50	(50)
Wisconsin, U of-Madison	NA	(4)
Worcester Polytech	50	(40)
Yale	50	(30)

Availability of Ten Additional Distinctive Sports

Crew (89)	Ice Hockey (87)	Lacrosse (117)	Rugby (106)	Sailing (84)		Squash (90)	Ultimate Frisbee (80)	Water Polo (96)	Wrestling (77)	Skiing (84)
			Xm		American University (DC)	X			Xm	
X	X	X	X	X	Amherst	X		X	Xm	X
	Xm	X	Xm	X	Babson	X	X	X		X
X					Barnard					
X	X	X	X	X	Bates	X	X	X		X
X	X	X	X	X	Boston College		X	Xm	Xm	X
X	Xm	X	X	X	Boston University		X	X	Xm	X
X	X	X	X	X	Bowdoin	X		X		X
X	X	Xm	X	X	Brandeis	X	X	X	Xm	X
X	X	X	X	X	Brown	X	X	Xm	Xm	X
	X	X	X	X	Bryn Mawr	X				
X	Xm	X	Xm	X	Bucknell	X	X	Xm	Xm	X
X	X	X	X	X	Cal-Berkeley	Xm	X	Xm		X
X	X	X	X	X	Cal-L.A. (UCLA)	X		Xm	Xm	X
	Xm	X	X		Carleton		X	X	Xm	X
X	Xm	X	X		Carnegie Mellon		X	X	Xm	X
	X	Xm			Case Western	X		X	Xm	
		X	Xm		Catholic University (DC)			X	Xm	
X	Xm	X	X	X	Chicago, U of	X	X		Xm	
X		X			Clark University	X	X	X		
X	X	X	X	X	Colby College	X	X	Xm		X
X	Xm	X	X	X	Colgate	X	X			X
	Xm	X			Colorado College	X	X			X
	Xm	X	X		Colorado, U of		X	X		X
X	X	Xm	Xm	X	Columbia University	X	X	Xm	Xm	X
X	X	X	X	X	Connecticut College	X	X	X		X
X	X	X	X	X	Cornell University (NY)	X	X	X	Xm	X
X	X	X	X	X	Dartmouth	X	X	X	Xm	X
X		Xm	Xm	X	Davidson	X	X		Xm	X
	X	X			Delaware, U of	X	X	X	Xm	
	Xm	X	X	X	Denison	Xm	X	Xm	X	X
X		Xm		X	Depauw				Xm	
	X	X	X		Dickinson	X			X	X
X	X	X	X	X	Duke	X	X	Xm	Xm	X
		X		X	Earlham	X	X	Xw		X
X	Xm	Xm	X	X	Emory University (GA)		X	Xm		
	Xm	X	Xm	X	Fairfield			X		X
					Florida, U of		X			
X	X	X	X		Fordham	X		Xm	X	X
X	X	Xm	X	X	Franklin and Marshall	X		X	Xm	
X		X	X	X	Furman		X	X	Xm	X
X		X		X	Georgetown	X				
X		Xm	X	X	George Washington (DC)	Xm		Xm		X
X	X	Xm	X	X	Georgia Tech	X		X	Xm	
	Xm	X	Xm		Gettysburg				Xm	
	Xm			X	GMI Engineering					X
					Grinnell	X	X			
X	Xm	X	X	X	Hamilton	X		X		X
					Hampshire College		X	X		X
X	X	X	X	X	Harvard	X	X	X	Xm	X
	X	X	X	X	Haverford	X	X	X	Xm	
X	X	X	X	X	Hobart and W Smith	Xm	X			X
X	Xm	X	X	X	Holy Cross	X				
	X		Xm	X	Il., U of-Urbana	X	X	X	Xm	X
		X	X		James Madison			X	Xm	X
X	Xm	X	X	X	Johns Hopkins	X	X	X	Xm	
Xm	Xm	X	X	X	Kenyon	X	X	X	X	X
X	Xm	Xm	X		Lafayette	X	X	X		
X	X	X	X	X	Lehigh	X	Xm	Xm	Xm	X
X		X	X	X	Lewis and Clark	X	X	X		X
X		X	X	X	Loyola College	X		X		
X		X	X		Macalester	X	X	X		
	X	X	X	X	Marquette	X		X	Xm	X
X	X	X	X	X	MIT	X	X	X	Xm	X
X		X	X	X	Miami, U of (FL)			X	Xm	

Note: "m" indicates male only

Availability of Ten Additional Distinctive Sports

Crew (89)	Ice Hockey (87)	Lacrosse (117)	Rugby (106)	Sailing (84)		Squash (90)	Ultimate Frisbee (80)	Water Polo (96)	Wrestling (77)	Skiing (84)
	Xm	X	X	X	Miami University (OH)	Xm	X	X	Xm	X
X	Xm	X	X	X	Michigan, U of-A. Arbor	X		X	Xm	X
	X	X	X		Middlebury	X	X	Xm		X
X		X	X		Mount Holyoke	X		X		X
	X	X	X		Muhlenberg			X	Xm	
X	X	X			New York University			X	Xm	
X	Xm	X		X	Northwestern		X	X	Xm	X
X	Xm	Xm	Xm	X	Notre Dame, U of			Xm	Xm	X
	Xm	X	X		Oberlin	X	X			
		X	Xm		Occidental		X	X		X
	Xm	X	Xm	X	Ohio Wesleyan	X				
	X	X	Xm	X	Penn State-Park	X		X	Xm	X
X	X	X	Xm	X	Pennsylvania	X	X	Xm	Xm	X
X		Xm	X	X	Pepperdine			X		X
		X	X		Pomona	X	X	X	Xm	X
X	X	X	X	X	Princeton	X	X	Xm	Xm	X
	X	Xm	X	X	Providence (RI)	X	X	X	X	X
X			X	X	Reed	X	X	X	Xm	X
X	X	X	X	X	Rensselaer Polytech	X		X		
		X	X		Rhodes			X		
X		X	X	X	Rice	X	X	X		
Xm		X	Xm		Richmond, U of	X		Xm		
X	Xm	X	Xm	X	Rochester, U of	X	X	X		X
X				X	Rollins		X			
X		X			Rutgers-New Brunswick				Xm	
	X	X			St. Lawrence	X			Xm	X
	Xm				St. Olaf		X	X	Xm	X
X		X	X		Santa Clara (CA)			X		
X	X	X			Skidmore	X				X
X		X	X	X	Smith	X	X	X		X
X		Xm	Xm	X	Sou. Calif., U of	X		Xm		X
X	Xm	X	X	X	SMU					
X	X	X	X	X	Stanford	X	X	Xm	Xm	X
	X	X	Xm	X	Swarthmore	X	X		Xm	
X	X	Xm	X		Syracuse University	X			Xm	X
X		X		X	Texas, U of (Austin)	X	X	X	Xm	X
X	Xm	X	X		Trinity College (CT)	X		X	Xm	X
					Trinity University (TX)		X	X	Xm	
X	Xm	X	X	X	Tufts	X	X		Xm	X
X		X	X	X	Tulane		X		Xm	
					Tulsa, U of	X	X	X		
X	X	X	X	X	Union	X	X	X		X
	X	X	X		US Air Force Academy	X	X	Xm	Xm	X
X	X	X	Xm	X	US Military Academy	X		X	Xm	X
X	Xm	Xm	Xm	X	US Naval Academy	X	X	Xm	Xm	
X		X	Xm	X	UNC-Chapel Hill		X	X	Xm	X
X		X	X		University of the South		X			X
X		X	X	X	Vanderbilt	X				
X		X	X	X	Vassar	X	X	X		X
X	X	X	X		Vermont, U of	X	X		Xm	X
X	Xm	Xm	Xm	X	Villanova			Xm		
X		X	X	X	Virginia, U of	X	X	X	Xm	X
		Xm	X		VPI		X	X	Xm	
		X			Wake Forest		X	X		
		X	X		Washington and Lee	X		Xm	Xm	X
X	X	X	X		Washington University (MO)		X		Xm	
X	X	X	X	X	Washington, U of (WA)	X	X	X	X	X
X	X	X	X	X	Wellesley	X		X		X
X	X	X	X	X	Wesleyan University	X	X	X	Xm	
X	Xm	Xm			Wheaton College (IL)				Xm	
Xm		Xm	X		William and Mary				Xm	
X	X	X	X	X	Williams College	X	X	X	Xm	X
X	X		X	X	Wisconsin, U of-Madison				Xm	
X	X	X	X	X	Worcester Polytech		X	X	Xm	X
X	X	X	X	X	Yale	X	X	X	Xm	X

Note: "m" indicates male only

THE AMERICAN UNIVERSITY (Private)

4400 Massachusetts Avenue
Washington, DC 20016-8001

VERY SELECTIVE
(Composite rating of guide books)

Main tel.: 202-885-1000
Admissions tel.: 202-885-6000
Financial aid tel.: 202-885-6107
Scheduled Airline Service: Washington
Miles to airport: 5

Founded: 1891
Nickname: Eagles
Religious affiliation: Methodist
(Coed since 1891)

Student Body

Undergraduates: 4,900 **Men:** 42% **Women:** 58 %
Graduate students: 3,800 **Freshman class:** 1,140

Academics

SAT Averages: 1135 **Verbal:** 548 **Math:** 587 **(Taking SATs:** 90 %**)**
700-800: V 2 % M 5 % **500-600:** V 48 % M 47 %
600-700: V 24 % M 40 % **400-500:** V 23 % M 7 % **300-400:** V NA% M NA%
High school class rank: Top fifth 57 % **2nd fifth** 29 % **3rd fifth** 10 %

Admissions

Applied: 4,970 **Accepted:** 75 % **Matriculated:** 31 %
Deadline: Feb. 1 **Accept common application:** Yes
Interview recommended: NA **Off-campus interview available:** No
Evaluative: No **Informational only:** Yes **LD program:** Yes
Night in dorm provided: Yes **Non-refundable application fee:** $35
Early decision program: Yes **Applied:** 227 **Accepted:** 80 % **Deadline:** Nov. 15
Freshmen accepted other than Fall term: 5 % **SAT/FAF Code #** 5007

Transfers

Applied: 900 **Accepted:** 77 % **Application deadline for Fall:** June 1 **Spring:** Dec.1
Minimum grades recommended: 2.0 **All new students who were transfers into all classes:** 10 %

Class Experience

Return 2nd year: 88 % **Graduate after 4 years:** 57 % **To graduate school within 5 years:** NA %

Cost

Tuition deposit: $200 **Total cost (Including school's estimate on fees and books):** $22,000
Tuition: $15,385 **(In state:** $ **)** **Room and board:** $5,900
Annual giving by parents: $290,000 **Average per student:** $33

Financial Aid

Average total package per student: $7,600 **Number receiving aid:** 68 %
Average scholarships and grants: $4,800 **Average loans:** $2,800 **Work-study program:** Yes
Undergraduates working on campus: NA % **Average earnings:** $1,500
Non-need scholarships 35% **Athletic scholarships:** NA **FAF deadline:** March 1
Off-campus part-time employment: Excellent **CO-OP program:** Yes
ROTC: at Georgetown **NROTC:** at Geo. Wash. **AFROTC:** at Howard

Endowment

Total: $23 Million **Per student (including graduate students):** $3,300

Location

Acres: 80 **Setting:** NW Washington **Miles from town center:** 3 (Pop. 700,000)
Miles from (Pop.) **Miles from** (Pop.)

Class Composition

Asian: 3 % **Black:** 7 % **Hispanic:** 4 % **White:** 78 % **Other:** 8 %
Total minority : 22 % **Foreign countries:** 12 % (1000 students)
From public schools: 80 % **Students from in state:** 10 %

Housing (on campus)

Freshmen required to live on campus: No **Guaranteed for:** 1 year
Available for all students: 60 % **Fraternity / Sorority housing:** Yes / No
On-campus married student housing: No **Women-only dorms available:** No

Campus Life

Students living on campus: 60 % **Remain weekends:** NA % **Handicap access:** 90 %
Car regulations: None on campus for freshman and sophomore
Number with cars: 30 % **Adequacy of on-campus parking:** Poor
Number of fraternities: 7 **Chapter houses:** 3 **Number of sororities:** 7 **Chapter houses:** 0
Students belonging to fraternities: 11 % **Students belonging to sororities:** 7 %

Libraries and Computers

Books: 500,000 **Periodicals:** 2,700 **Microform items:** 500,000
Microcomputers available: 150 **Microcomputers networked:**

Classes

Faculty / Student Ratio: 1/15 **Classes taught by teacher assistants:** 15 %
Most popular majors: Communications, International Studies **Classes begin:** Aug. & Jan.
Baccalaureate degrees offered: BA, BFA, BOS, B. MUS, BS, BSBA, BA Tech Mgmt

Sports

Division: I **Except:** **Physical ed requirements:** None
Students participating in intercollegiate sports: 5 % **In intramural sports:** 58 %
Additional intercollegiate and/or intramural sports: (not found at all colleges)

Crew: No	**Ice Hockey:** No	**Lacrosse:** No	**Wrestling:** Yes/M
Rugby: Yes/M	**Sailing:** No	**Skiing:** No	
Squash: Yes	**Ultimate Frisbee:** No	**Water Polo:** No	

Alumni

Number living: 50,000 **Annual giving:** $2.9 million **Participation:** 13 %
Average annual gift: $470 **Average per student:** $320

3-2 Programs (2 degrees in 5 years)

Engineering: U of Maryland & Washington U

Observation and Opinion of:

Undergraduates and graduates ______________________________

____

College counselor ______________________________

____

AMHERST COLLEGE (Private)

Amherst, MA 01002

MOST SELECTIVE
(Composite rating of guide books)

Main tel.: 413-542-2000
Admissions tel.: 413-542-2328
Financial aid tel.: 413-542-2296
Scheduled Airline Service: Hartford
Miles to airport: 45

Founded: 1821
Nickname: Lord Jeffs
Religious affiliation: None
(Coed since 1975)

Student Body

Undergraduates: 1,600 **Men:** 55% **Women:** 45 %
Graduate students: None **Freshman class:** 400

Academics

SAT Averages: 1310 **Verbal:** 640 **Math:** 670 **(Taking SATs:** 95 %**)**
700-800: V 2 % **M** 51 % **500-600: V** 21 % **M** 13 %
600-700: V 46 % **M** 34 % **400-500: V** 4 % **M** 2 % **300-400: V** NA % **M** NA%
High school class rank: Top fifth 95 % **2nd fifth** 100 % **3rd fifth** %

Admissions

Applied: 4,600 **Accepted:** 22 % **Matriculated:** 41 %
Deadline: Jan. 1 **Accept common application:** No
Interview recommended: No **Off-campus interview available:** Yes
Evaluative: No **Informational only:** Yes **LD program:** No
Night in dorm provided: Yes **Non-refundable application fee:** $45
Early decision program: Yes **Applied:** 357 **Accepted:** 30 % **Deadline:** Nov. 15
Freshmen accepted other than Fall term: 0 % **SAT/FAF Code #** 3003

Transfers

Applied: 208 **Accepted:** 12 % **Application deadline for Fall:** Feb. 1 **Spring:** Nov. 1
Minimum grades recommended: 3.0 **All new students who were transfers into all classes:** 5 %

Class Experience

Return 2nd year: 95 % **Graduate after 4 years:** 91 % **To graduate school within 1 year:** 28 %

Cost

Tuition deposit: $200 **Total cost (Including school's estimate on fees and books):** $23,200
Tuition: $17,900 **(In state:** $ **)** **Room and board:** $4,800
Annual giving by parents: $220,000 **Average per student:** $140

Financial Aid

Average total package per student: $17,900 **Number receiving aid:** 40 %
Average scholarships and grants: $15,700 **Average loans:** $2,200 **Work-study program:** Yes
Undergraduates working on campus: NA % **Average earnings:** NA
Non-need scholarships 0 % **Athletic scholarships:** No **FAF deadline:** Feb. 1
Off-campus part-time employment: Fair **CO-OP program:** No
ROTC: Off campus **NROTC:** No **AFROTC:** Off campus

Endowment

Total: $269 million **Per student (including graduate students):** $170,000

Location

Acres: 965 **Setting:** Rural **Miles from town center:** 0 (**Pop.** 36,000)
90 **Miles from** Boston (**Pop.** 600,000) 150 **Miles from** New York (**Pop.** 7 million)

Class Composition

Asian: 8 % **Black:** 6 % **Hispanic:** 6 % **White:** 76 % **Other:** NA %
Total minority : 24 % **Foreign countries:** 3 % (50 students)
From public schools: 58 % **Students from in state:** 9 %

Housing (on campus)

Freshmen required to live on campus: Yes **Guaranteed for:** 4 years
Available for all students: 100 % **Fraternity / Sorority housing:** No / No
On-campus married student housing: Off campus **Women-only dorms available:** No

Campus Life

Students living on campus: 99 % **Remain weekends:** 95 % **Handicap access:** 80 %
Car regulations: OK all 4 years
Number with cars: NA % **Adequacy of on-campus parking:** Fair
Number of fraternities: 0 **Chapter houses:** 0 **Number of sororities:** 0 **Chapter houses:** 0
Students belonging to fraternities: % **Students belonging to sororities:** %

Libraries and Computers

Books: 720,000 **Periodicals:** 2,300 **Microform items:** 330,000
Microcomputers available: 75 **Microcomputers networked:** Yes

Classes

Faculty / Student Ratio: 1/10 **Classes taught by teacher assistants:** 0 %
Most popular majors: English, Pol. Science, History **Classes begin:** Early Sept.
Baccalaureate degrees offered: BA

Sports

Division: III **Except:** **Physical ed requirements:** None
Students participating in intercollegiate sports: 30 % **In intramural sports:** 30 %
Additional intercollegiate and/or intramural sports: (not found at all colleges)

Crew: Yes **Ice Hockey:** Yes **Lacrosse:** Yes **Wrestling:** No
Rugby: Yes **Sailing:** Yes **Skiing:** Yes
Squash: Yes **Ultimate Frisbee:** No **Water Polo:** Yes

Alumni

Number living: 17,000 **Annual giving:** $8.1 million **Participation:** 65 %
Average annual gift: $800 **Average per student:** $5100

3-2 Programs (2 degrees in 5 years)

Cross registration with 4 other colleges
(Hampshire Coll., Mt. Holyoke, Smith and U of Mass.)

Observation and Opinion of:

Undergraduates and graduates ______________________________

____

College counselor ______________________________

____

BABSON COLLEGE (Private)

Babson Park
Wellesley, MA 02157-0901

SELECTIVE
(Composite rating of guide books)

Main tel.: 617-239-5522
Admissions tel.:
Financial aid tel.: 617-239-4001
Scheduled Airline Service: Boston
Miles to airport: 17

Founded: 1919
Nickname: Beaver
Religious affiliation: None
(Coed since 1968)

Student Body

Undergraduates: 1,600 **Men:** 65% **Women:** 35 %
Graduate students: 1,400 **Freshman class:** 422

Academics

SAT Averages: 1110 **Verbal:** NA **Math:** NA **(Taking SATs:** 99 %)
700-800: V 1 % **M** 6 % **500-600: V** 34 % **M** 44 %
600-700: V 4 % **M** 37 % **400-500: V** 47 % **M** 12 % **300-400: V** 14 % **M** 1 %
High school class rank: Top fifth 50 % **2nd fifth** 32 % **3rd fifth** 13 %

Admissions

Applied: 1,450 **Accepted:** 69 % **Matriculated:** 42 %
Deadline: Feb. 1 **Accept common application:** No
Interview recommended: Yes **Off-campus interview available:** Yes
Evaluative: No **Informational only:** Yes **LD program:** Yes
Night in dorm provided: Yes **Non-refundable application fee:** $40
Early decision program: Yes **Applied:** 100 **Accepted:** 64 % **Deadline:** Dec. 1
Freshmen accepted other than Fall term: 3 % **SAT/FAF Code #** 1780

Transfers

Applied: 227 **Accepted:** 45 % **Application deadline for Fall:** May 1 **Spring:** Nov. 1
Minimum grades recommended: 3.1 **All new students who were transfers into all classes:** 11 %

Class Experience

Return 2nd year: 87 % **Graduate after 4 years:** 85 % **To graduate school within 5 years:** 9 %

Cost

Tuition deposit: $100 **Total cost (Including school's estimate on fees and books):** $23,465
Tuition: $15,666 **(In state:**) **Room and board:** $6,350
Annual giving by parents: N/A **Average per student:** $33

Financial Aid

Average total package per student: NA **Number receiving aid:** 32 %
Average scholarships and grants: $12,200 **Average loans:** NA **Work-study program:** Yes
Undergraduates working on campus: 45 % **Average earnings:** $1,000
Non-need scholarships 0 % **Athletic scholarships:** 0 **FAF deadline:** Feb. 1
Off-campus part-time employment: Excellent **CO-OP program:** No
ROTC: None **NROTC:** None. **AFROTC:** None

Endowment

Total: $33 Million **Per student (including graduate students):** $11,000

Location

Acres: 450 **Setting:** Suburban
12 Miles from Boston **(Pop.** 600,000)
Miles from town center: 2 **(Pop.** 33,000)
Miles from **(Pop.**)

Class Composition

Asian: 2 % **Black:** 1 % **Hispanic:** 2 % **White:** 88 % **Other:** 8 %
Total minority : NA % **Foreign countries:** 12 % (180 students)
From public schools: 39 % **Students from in state:** 60 %

Housing (on campus)

Freshmen required to live on campus: No
Available for all students: 80 %
On-campus married student housing: No
Guaranteed for: 1 year
Fraternity / Sorority housing: 0 / 0
Women-only dorms available: No

Campus Life

Students living on campus: 80 % **Remain weekends:** 70 % **Handicap access:** NA%
Car regulations: Sticker required
Number with cars: 30 %
Adequacy of on-campus parking: Fair
Number of fraternities: 4 **Chapter houses:** 0
Number of sororities: 2 **Chapter houses:** 0
Students belonging to fraternities: 10 %
Students belonging to sororities: 4 %

Libraries and Computers

Books: 120,000 **Periodicals:** 1,450 **Microform items:** 313,000
Microcomputers available: Yes **Microcomputers networked:** Yes

Classes

Faculty / Student Ratio: 1/22 **Classes taught by teacher assistants:** 0 %
Most popular majors: Finance, Marketing, Accounting **Classes begin:** Mid-Sept.
Baccalaureate degrees offered: BS Management

Sports

Division: III **Except:** **Physical ed requirements:** 2 semesters
Students participating in intercollegiate sports: 20 % **In intramural sports:** 75 %
Additional intercollegiate and/or intramural sports: (not found at all colleges)

Crew: No **Ice Hockey:** Yes/M **Lacrosse:** Yes **Wrestling:** Yes/M
Rugby: Yes/M **Sailing:** Yes **Skiing:** Yes/M
Squash: Yes **Ultimate Frisbee:** Yes/M **Water Polo:** Yes

Alumni

Number living: NA **Annual giving:** $1.3 million **Participation:** NA %
Average annual gift: NA **Average per student:** $400

3-2 Programs (2 degrees in 5 years)

Cross registration with Brandeis, Pine Manor, Regis College and Wellesley College

Observation and Opinion of:

Undergraduates and graduates ______________________________

____

College counselor ______________________________

____

BARNARD COLLEGE (Private)

3009 Broadway
New York, NY 10027-6598

MOST SELECTIVE
(Composite rating of guide books)

Main tel.: 212-854-5262
Admissions tel.: 212-854-2014
Financial aid tel.:212-854-2154
Scheduled Airline Service: New York
Miles to airport: 10

Founded: 1889
Nickname: Bears
Religious affiliation: None
(Coed since NA **)**

Student Body

Undergraduates: 2,200 **Men:** 0 % **Women:** 100 %
Graduate students: 0 **Freshman class:** 530

Academics

SAT Averages: 1250 **Verbal:** 610 **Math:** 640 **(Taking SATs:** 100 %**)**
700-800: V 7 % **M** 0 % **500-600: V** 42 % **M** 33 %
600-700: V 44 % **M** 54 % **400-500: V** 7 % **M** 4 % **300-400: V** NA % **M** NA %
High school class rank: Top fifth 77 % **2nd fifth** 20 % **3rd fifth** 3%

Admissions

Applied: 1,820 **Accepted:** 57 % **Matriculated:** 51 %
Deadline: None **Accept common application:** No
Interview recommended: No **Off-campus interview available:** Yes
Evaluative: No **Informational only:** Yes **LD program:** Yes
Night in dorm provided: Yes **Non-refundable application fee:** $40
Early decision program: Yes **Applied:** 139 **Accepted:** 60 % **Deadline:** Nov. 15
Freshmen accepted other than Fall term: 1 % **SAT/FAF Code #** 2718

Transfers

Applied: 275 **Accepted:** 60 % **Application deadline for Fall:** May 1 **Spring:** Nov. 1
Minimum grades recommended: 3.0 **All new students who were transfers into all classes:** 18 %

Class Experience

Return 2nd year: 95 % **Graduate after 4 years:** 87 % **To graduate school within 5 years:** 40 %

Cost

Tuition deposit: $200 **Total cost (Including school's estimate on fees and books):** $24,500
Tuition: $16,228 **(In state:** $ **)** **Room and board:** $7,200
Annual giving by parents: $250,000 **Average per student:** $115

Financial Aid

Average total package per student: $14,600 **Number receiving aid:** 53 %
Average scholarships and grants: $4,800 **Average loans:** $2,800 **Work-study program:** Yes
Undergraduates working on campus: 60 % **Average earnings:** NA
Non-need scholarships 0 % **Athletic scholarships:** No **FAF deadline:** Feb. 1
Off-campus part-time employment: Excellent **CO-OP program:** No
ROTC: No **NROTC:** No. **AFROTC:** No

Endowment

Total: $48 Million **Per student (including graduate students):** $23,000

Location

Acres: 4 **Setting:** Next to Columbia **Miles from town center:** 0 **(Pop.** 7.5 Million**)**
Miles from **(Pop.** **)** **Miles from** **(Pop.** **)**

Class Composition

Asian: 19 **%** **Black:** 5 **%** **Hispanic:** 4 **%** **White:** 70 **%** **Other:** 8 **%**
Total minority : 30 **%** **Foreign countries:** 8 **%** (170 students)
From public schools: 60 **%** **Students from in state:** 40 **%**

Housing (on campus)

Freshmen required to live on campus: No **Guaranteed for:** 4 years
Available for all students: 100 **%** **Fraternity / Sorority housing:** No/No
On-campus married student housing: Yes **Women-only dorms available:** Yes

Campus Life

Students living on campus: 95 **%** **Remain weekends:** NA **%** **Handicap access** 100 **%**
Car regulations: No parking on campus
Number with cars: 1 **%** **Adequacy of on-campus parking:** None
Number of fraternities: **Chapter houses:** **Number of sororities:** 1 **Chapter houses:** 1
Students belonging to fraternities: NA **%** **Students belonging to sororities:** 0 **%**

Libraries and Computers

Books: 158,000 **Periodicals:** 750 **Microform items:** 13,000
Microcomputers available: Yes **Microcomputers networked:** NA

Classes

Faculty / Student Ratio: 1/12 **Classes taught by teacher assistants:** 0 **%**
Most popular majors: English, History, Political Science **Classes begin:** Aug.
Baccalaureate degrees offered: BA, BS

Sports

Division: I **Except:** **Physical ed requirements:** 2 semesters Phys/Ed
Students participating in intercollegiate sports: 20 **%** **In intramural sports:** 40 **%**
Additional intercollegiate and/or intramural sports: (not found at all colleges)

Crew: Yes **Ice Hockey:** No **Lacrosse:** No **Wrestling:** No
Rugby: No **Sailing:** No **Skiing:** No
Squash: No **Ultimate Frisbee:** No **Water Polo:** No

Alumni

Number living: 20,500 **Annual giving:** $2.9 million **Participation:** 30 **%**
Average annual gift: $500 **Average per student:** $2300

3-2 Programs (2 degrees in 5 years)

Engineering with Columbia U
Music with Julliard School of Music

Observation and Opinion of:

Undergraduates and graduates ________________________

College counselor ________________________

BATES COLLEGE (Private)

Lewiston, ME 04240

HIGHLY SELECTIVE
(Composite rating of guide books)

Main tel.: 207-786-6255
Admissions tel.: 207-786-6000
Financial aid tel.: 207-786-6060
Scheduled Airline Service: Portland
Miles to airport: 40

Founded: 1855
Nickname: Bobcats
Religious affiliation: None
(Coed since 1855)

Student Body

Undergraduates: 1,500 **Men:** 50 % **Women:** 50 %
Graduate students: 0 **Freshman class:** 440

Academics

SAT Averages: 1250 **Verbal:** 600 **Math:** 650 **(Taking SATs:** 75 %**)**
700-800: V 5 % **M** 17 % **500-600: V** 48 % **M** 25 %
600-700: V 41 % **M** 56 % **400-500: V** 6 % **M** 2 % **300-400: V** NA % **M** NA %
High school class rank: Top fifth 80 % **2nd fifth** 16 % **3rd fifth** 4 %

Admissions

Applied: 3,200 **Accepted:** 42 % **Matriculated:** 33 %
Deadline: Feb. 1 **Accept common application:** Yes
Interview recommended: Yes **Off-campus interview available:** Yes
Evaluative: Yes **Informational only:** No **LD program:** Yes
Night in dorm provided: Yes **Non-refundable application fee:** $40
Early decision program: Yes **Applied:** 204 **Accepted:** 55 % **Deadline:** Dec. 15
Freshmen accepted other than Fall term: 0 % **SAT/FAF Code #** 3076

Transfers

Applied: 212 **Accepted:** 34 % **Application deadline for Fall:** Mar. 1 **Spring:** Nov. 15
Minimum grades recommended: 3.0 **All new students who were transfers into all classes:** 4 %

Class Experience

Return 2nd year: 98 % **Graduate after 4 years:** 88 % **To graduate school within 5 years:** N/A %

Cost

Tuition deposit: $200 **Total cost (Including school's estimate on fees and books):** $22,850
Tuition: N/A **(In state:** $ **)** **Room and board:** N/A
Annual giving by parents: $163,000 **Average per student:** $110

Financial Aid

Average total package per student: $14,550 **Number receiving aid:** 36 %
Average scholarships and grants: $12,350 **Average loans:** $2,200 **Work-study program:** Yes
Undergraduates working on campus: 40 % **Average earnings:** $1,200
Non-need scholarships 0 % **Athletic scholarships:** No **FAF deadline:** Feb. 15
Off-campus part-time employment: Fair **CO-OP program:** No
ROTC: No **NROTC:** No **AFROTC:** No

Endowment

Total: $69 Million **Per student (including graduate students):** $45,000

Location

Acres: 125 **Setting:** Urban
Miles from town center: 2 **(Pop.** 80,000)
35 **Miles from** Portland **(Pop.** 80,000)
145 **Miles from Boston (Pop.** 600,000)

Class Composition

Asian: 4 % **Black:** 2 % **Hispanic:** 1 % **White:** 88 % **Other:** NA %
Total minority : 12 % **Foreign countries:** 2 % (30 students)
From public schools: 68 % **Students from in state:** 13 %

Housing (on campus)

Freshmen required to live on campus: Yes
Available for all students: 95 %
On-campus married student housing: No
Guaranteed for: 4 years
Fraternity / Sorority housing: 0 / 0
Women-only dorms available: Yes

Campus Life

Students living on campus: 90 % **Remain weekends:** 65 % **Handicap access:** 90 %
Car regulations: All may have cars
Number with cars: NA %
Adequacy of on-campus parking: Poor
Number of fraternities: 0 **Chapter houses:** 0
Students belonging to fraternities: 0 %
Number of sororities: 0 **Chapter houses:** 0
Students belonging to sororities: 0 %

Libraries and Computers

Books: 515,000 **Periodicals:** 1,760 **Microform items:** 220,000
Microcomputers available: 35 **Microcomputers networked:** NA

Classes

Faculty / Student Ratio: 1/12 **Classes taught by teacher assistants:** 0 %
Most popular majors: English, History, Pol. Science **Classes begin:** Early Sept.
Baccalaureate degrees offered: BA, BS

Sports

Division: III **Except:** Skiing I **Physical ed requirements:** One year
Students participating in intercollegiate sports: 40 % **In intramural sports:** 55 %
Additional intercollegiate and/or intramural sports: (not found at all colleges)

Crew: Yes **Ice Hockey:** Yes **Lacrosse:** Yes **Wrestling:** No
Rugby: Yes **Sailing:** Yes **Skiing:** Yes
Squash: Yes **Ultimate Frisbee:** Yes **Water Polo:** Yes

Alumni

Number living: 13,300 **Annual giving:** $3 Million **Participation:** 48 %
Average annual gift: $450 **Average per student:** $2,000

3-2 Programs (2 degrees in 5 years)

Engineering with Case Western, Columbia U, RPI

Observation and Opinion of:

Undergraduates and graduates ______________________________

____

College counselor ______________________________

____

BOSTON COLLEGE (Private)

Chestnut Hill, MA 02167

HIGHLY SELECTIVE
(Composite rating of guide books)

Main tel.: 617- 552-8000
Admissions tel.: 617- 552-3100
Financial aid tel.: 617-552-4946
Scheduled Airline Service: Boston
Miles to airport: 5

Founded: 1863
Nickname: Eagles
Religious affiliation: Catholic
(Coed since 1970)

Student Body

Undergraduates: 8,700 **Men:** 40 % **Women:** 60 %
Graduate students: 4,300 **Freshman class:** 2,100

Academics

SAT Averages: 1,200 **Verbal:** 570 **Math:** 630 (Taking SATs: 99 %)
700-800: V 3 % **M** 17 % **500-600: V** 50 % **M** 22 %
600-700: V 27 % **M** 56 % **400-500: V** 17 % **M** 5 % **300-400: V** 2 % **M** 0 %
High school class rank: Top fifth 92 % **2nd fifth** 8 % **3rd fifth** %

Admissions

Applied: 12,400 **Accepted:** 45 % **Matriculated:** 38 %
Deadline: Jan. 25 **Accept common application:**
Interview recommended: Yes **Off-campus interview available:** Yes
Evaluative: No **Informational only:** Yes **LD program:** Yes
Night in dorm provided: No **Non-refundable application fee:** $45
Early decision program: Yes **Applied:** 1,085 **Accepted:** 68 % **Deadline:** Nov. 15
Freshmen accepted other than Fall term: 1 % **SAT/FAF Code #** 1788

Transfers

Applied: 1,570 **Accepted:** 33 % **Application deadline for Fall:** May 1 **Spring:** Nov. 1
Minimum grades recommended: 2.5 **All new students who were transfers into all classes:** 14 %

Class Experience

Return 2nd year: 98 % **Graduate after 4 years:** 85 % **To graduate school within 5 years:** 22 %

Cost

Tuition deposit: $200 **Total cost (Including school's estimate on fees and books):** $22,000
Tuition: $14,580 **(In state:** $ **)** **Room and board:** $7,000
Annual giving by parents: $3.9 Million **Average per student:** $330

Financial Aid

Average total package per student: $9,100 **Number receiving aid:** 70 %
Average scholarships and grants: $6,400 **Average loans:** $2,700 **Work-study program:** Yes
Undergraduates working on campus: 24 % **Average earnings:** $2,000
Non-need scholarships 25 % **Athletic scholarships:** Yes **FAF deadline:** Feb. 1
Off-campus part-time employment: Good **CO-OP program:** No
ROTC: at Northeastern **NROTC:** at BU **AFROTC:** at BU

Endowment

Total: $312 Million **Per student (including graduate students):** $21,000

Location

Acres: 240 **Setting:** Surburban
Miles from town center: 0 **(Pop.** 83,000**)**
6 **Miles from** Boston **(Pop.** 600,000**)**
Miles from (Pop.)

Class Composition

Asian: 6 % **Black:** 3 % **Hispanic:** 5 % **White:** 82 % **Other:** NA %
Total minority : 18 % **Foreign countries:** 2 % (170 students)
From public schools: 56 % **Students from in state:** 35 %

Housing (on campus)

Freshmen required to live on campus: Yes
Available for all students: 70 %
On-campus married student housing: Yes
Guaranteed for: 1 year
Fraternity / Sorority housing: 0 / 0
Women-only dorms available: Yes

Campus Life

Students living on campus: 67 % **Remain weekends:** 85 % **Handicap access:** 100%
Car regulations: No freshmen or sophomores
Number with cars: 9 %
Adequacy of on-campus parking: Expensive
Number of fraternities: 0 **Chapter houses:**
Students belonging to fraternities: 0 %
Number of sororities: 0 **Chapter houses:**
Students belonging to sororities: 0%

Libraries and Computers

Books: 1.2 Million **Periodicals:** 13,500 **Microform items:** 2 Million
Microcomputers available: 250 **Microcomputers networked:** Yes

Classes

Faculty / Student Ratio: 1/15 **Classes taught by teacher assistants:** 30 %
Most popular majors: English, Finance, Economics **Classes begin:** Early Sept.
Baccalaureate degrees offered: AB, BS

Sports

Division: I **Except:** **Physical ed requirements:** None
Students participating in intercollegiate sports: 7 % **In intramural sports:** 40 %
Additional intercollegiate and/or intramural sports: (not found at all colleges)

Crew: Yes	**Ice Hockey:** Yes	**Lacrosse:** Yes	**Wrestling:** Yes/M
Rugby: Yes	**Sailing:** Yes	**Skiing:** Yes	
Squash: No	**Ultimate Frisbee:** Yes	**Water Polo:** Yes/M	

Alumni

Number living: 95,000 **Annual giving:** $8.5 million **Participation:** 78 %
Average annual gift: $350 **Average per student:** $650

3-2 Programs (2 degrees in 5 years)

Education: BA/MA, Social Work BA/MSW, Nursing: BS/MS, Arts & Sciences: BA/MA

Observation and Opinion of:

Undergraduates and graduates ______________________________

____

College counselor ______________________________

____

BOSTON UNIVERSITY (Private)

881 Commonwealth Avenue
Boston, MA 02215

HIGHLY SELECTIVE
(Composite rating of guide books)

Main tel.: 617-353-2000
Admissions tel.: 617-353-2300
Financial aid tel.: 617-353-2965
Scheduled Airline Service: Boston
Miles to airport: 2

Founded: 1839
Nickname: Terriers
Religious affiliation: None
(Coed since 1839)

Student Body

Undergraduates: 14,000 **Men:** 43 % **Women:** 57 %
Graduate students: 9,700 **Freshman class:** 3,500

Academics

SAT Averages: 1,145 **Verbal:** 546 **Math:** 599 (Taking SATs: NA %)
700-800: V 3 % **M** 32 % **500-600: V** 49 % **M** 41 %
600-700: V 27 % **M** 38 % **400-500: V** 20 % **M** 9 % **300-400: V** 1 % **M** 0 %
High school class rank: Top fifth 70 % **2nd fifth** 25 % **3rd fifth** 4 %

Admissions

Applied: 18,700 **Accepted:** 66 % **Matriculated:** 28 %
Deadline: Jan. 15 **Accept common application:** Yes
Interview recommended: No **Off-campus interview available:** Yes
Evaluative: No **Informational only:** Yes **LD program:** Yes
Night in dorm provided: No **Non-refundable application fee:** $40
Early decision program: Yes **Applied:** 325 **Accepted:** 38 % **Deadline:** Nov. 15
Freshmen accepted other than Fall term: 2 % **SAT/FAF Code #** 1794

Transfers

Applied: 2,100 **Accepted:** 60 % **Application deadline for Fall:** May 1 **Spring:** Nov. 15
Minimum grades recommended: C **All new students who were transfers into all classes:** 15 %

Class Experience

Return 2nd year: 85 % **Graduate after 4 years:** 65 % **To graduate school within 5 years:** %

Cost

Tuition deposit: $200 **Total cost (Including school's estimate on fees and books):** $22,700
Tuition: $16,590 **(In state:** $ **)** **Room and board:** $6,320
Annual giving by parents: $345,000 **Average per student:** $16

Financial Aid

Average total package per student: $12,700 **Number receiving aid:** 50 %
Average scholarships and grants: $9,800 **Average loans:** $2,900 **Work-study program:** Yes
Undergraduates working on campus: 35 % **Average earnings:** $1,800
Non-need scholarships Yes **Athletic scholarships:** Yes **FAF deadline:** March 1
Off-campus part-time employment: Excellent **CO-OP program:** Yes
ROTC: Yes **NROTC:** Yes **AFROTC:** Yes

Endowment

Total: $167 Million **Per student (including graduate students):** $7,000

Location

Acres: 99 **Setting:** City **Miles from town center:** 0 (Pop. 600,000)
Miles from (Pop.) **Miles from** (Pop.)

Class Composition

Asian: 10 % **Black:** 4 % **Hispanic:** 4 % **White:** 81 % **Other:** %
Total minority : 19 % **Foreign countries:** 6 % (780 students)
From public schools: 70 % **Students from in state:** 30 %

Housing (on campus)

Freshmen required to live on campus: Yes **Guaranteed for:** 1 year
Available for all students: 55 % **Fraternity / Sorority housing:** Yes / Yes
On-campus married student housing: Yes **Women-only dorms available:** Yes

Campus Life

Students living on campus: 55 % **Remain weekends:** 80 % **Handicap access:** 75 %
Car regulations: Strict city police
Number with cars: 10 % **Adequacy of on-campus parking:** None
Number of fraternities: 12 **Chapter houses:** 2 **Number of sororities:** 10 **Chapter houses:** 1
Students belonging to fraternities: 11 % **Students belonging to sororities:** 12 %

Libraries and Computers

Books: 1.7 Million **Periodicals:** 30,000 **Microform items:** 2.6 Million
Microcomputers available: Yes **Microcomputers networked:** Yes

Classes

Faculty / Student Ratio: 1/15 **Classes taught by teacher assistants:** 15 %
Most popular majors: **Classes begin:** Early Sept.
Baccalaureate degrees offered: BA, BAS, BFA, BLS, BS, BSBA, BS ED, MUS B

Sports

Division: I **Except:** **Physical ed requirements:**
Students participating in intercollegiate sports: 10 % **In intramural sports:** 50 %
Additional intercollegiate and/or intramural sports: (not found at all colleges)

Crew: Yes **Ice Hockey:** Yes/M **Lacrosse:** Yes **Wrestling:** Yes/M
Rugby: Yes **Sailing:** Yes **Skiing:** Yes
Squash: No **Ultimate Frisbee:** Yes **Water Polo:** Yes

Alumni

Number living: 181,000 **Annual giving:** $5.7 million **Participation:** 20 %
Average annual gift: $160 **Average per student:** $250

3-2 Programs (2 degrees in 5 years)

3-4 Program in Medicine & Dentistry, cross registration with Boston Coll, Brandeis, Hebrew U and Tufts

Observation and Opinion of:

Undergraduates and graduates ______________________________

____

College counselor ______________________________

____

BOWDOIN COLLEGE (Private)

Brunswick, ME 04011

MOST SELECTIVE
(Composite rating of guide books)

Main tel.: 207-725-3000
Admissions tel.: 207-725-3100
Financial aid tel.: 207-725-3273
Scheduled Airline Service: Portland
Miles to airport: 25

Founded: 1794
Nickname: Polar Bears
Religious affiliation: None
(Coed since 1970)

Student Body

Undergraduates: 1,350 **Men:** 60 % **Women:** 40 %
Graduate students: 0 **Freshman class:** 400

Academics

SAT Averages: 1300 **Verbal: Math: (Taking SATs:** 67 %)
700-800: V 7 % **M** 36 % **500-600: V** 28 % **M** 10 %
600-700: V 60 % **M** 50 % **400-500: V** 5 % **M** 4 % **300-400: V** NA % **M** NA %
High school class rank: Top fifth 79 % **2nd fifth** 1 % **3rd fifth** NA %

Admissions

Applied: 3,250 **Accepted:** 27 % **Matriculated:** 47 %
Deadline: Jan. 15 **Accept common application:** Yes
Interview recommended: No **Off-campus interview available:** No
Evaluative: Yes **Informational only:** No **LD program:** No
Night in dorm provided: Yes **Non-refundable application fee:** $40
Early decision program: Yes **Applied:** 370 **Accepted:** 35 % **Deadline:** Nov. 15
Freshmen accepted other than Fall term: 0 % **SAT/FAF Code #** 3089

Transfers

Applied: 94 **Accepted:** 27 % **Application deadline for Fall:** Apr. 15 **Spring:** Nov. 15
Minimum grades recommended: 3.0 **All new students who were transfers into all classes:** 1 %

Class Experience

Return 2nd year: 93 % **Graduate after 4 years:** 90 % **To graduate school within 5 years:** 70 %

Cost

Tuition deposit: $200 **Total cost (Including school's estimate on fees and books):** $23,210
Tuition: $17,035 **(In state:** $ **)** **Room and board:** $5,600
Annual giving by parents: $350,000 **Average per student:** $275

Financial Aid

Average total package per student: $13,745 **Number receiving aid:** 60 %
Average scholarships and grants: $10,975 **Average loans:** $2,750
Undergraduates working on campus: 65 %
Non-need scholarships 0 % **Athletic scholarships:** 0
Off-campus part-time employment: Fair
ROTC: U of Maine **NROTC:** No

Work-study program:
Average earnings: $400
FAF deadline:
CO-OP program: No
AFROTC: No

Endowment

Total: $161 Million **Per student (including graduate students):** $120,000

Location

Acres: 110 **Setting:** Urban **Miles from town center:** 1 (**Pop.** 20,500)
25 **Miles from** Portland (**Pop.** 80,000) 135 **Miles from** Boston (**Pop.** 600,000)

Class Composition

Asian: 3 % **Black:** 4 % **Hispanic:** 3 % **White:** 88 % **Other:** NA %
Total minority : 12 % **Foreign countries:** 3 % (40 students)
From public schools: 57 % **Students from in state:** 17 %

Housing (on campus)

Freshmen required to live on campus: Yes **Guaranteed for:** 1 year
Available for all students: 75 % **Fraternity / Sorority housing:** Yes / Yes
On-campus married student housing: Yes **Women-only dorms available:** No

Campus Life

Students living on campus: 71 % **Remain weekends:** 95 % **Handicap access:** 50 %
Car regulations: None
Number with cars: 30 % **Adequacy of on-campus parking:** Good
Number of fraternities: 8 **Chapter houses:** 8 **Number of sororities:** 8 **Chapter houses:** 8
Students belonging to fraternities: 37 % **Students belonging to sororities:** 37 %

Libraries and Computers

Books: 750,000 **Periodicals:** 2,100 **Microform items:** 260,000
Microcomputers available: 90 **Microcomputers networked:**

Classes

Faculty / Student Ratio: 1/10 **Classes taught by teacher assistants:** 0 %
Most popular majors: Government, Legal Studies, History **Classes begin:** Late August
Baccalaureate degrees offered: AB

Sports

Division: III **Except:** **Physical ed requirements:** None
Students participating in intercollegiate sports: 53 % **In intramural sports:** 20 %
Additional intercollegiate and/or intramural sports: (not found at all colleges)

Crew: Yes **Ice Hockey:** Yes **Lacrosse:** Yes **Wrestling:** No
Rugby: Yes **Sailing:** Yes **Skiing:** Yes
Squash: Yes **Ultimate Frisbee:** No **Water Polo:** Yes

Alumni

Number living: 14,000 **Annual giving:** $9.8 Million **Participation:** 63 %
Average annual gift: $1200 **Average per student:** $7100

3-2 Programs (2 degrees in 5 years)

Engineering with Cal Tech and Columbia U
Law with Columbia U

Observation and Opinion of:

Undergraduates and graduates ______________________

____

College counselor ______________________

____

BRANDEIS UNIVERSITY (Private)

415 South Street
Waltham, MA 02254-9110

Main tel.: 617-736-2000
Admissions tel.: 617-736-3500
Financial aid tel.: 800-622-0622
Scheduled Airline Service: Boston
Miles to airport: 10

HIGHLY SELECTIVE
(Composite rating of guide books)

Founded: 1948
Nickname: Judges
Religious affiliation: Jewish
(Coed since 1948)

Student Body

Undergraduates: 2,900 **Men:** 47 % **Women:** 53 %
Graduate students: 850 **Freshman class:** 715

Academics

SAT Averages: 1220 **Verbal:** 580 **Math:** 640 **(Taking SATs:** 1220 %)
700-800: V 10 % **M** 25 % **500-600:** V 40 % **M** 25 %
600-700: V 40 % **M** 45 % **400-500:** V 10 % **M** 5 % **300-400:** V NA % **M** NA %
High school class rank: Top fifth 75 % **2nd fifth** 23 % **3rd fifth** 2 %

Admissions

Applied: 3,900 **Accepted:** 67 % **Matriculated:** 27 %
Deadline: Feb. 1 **Accept common application:** Yes
Interview recommended: No **Off-campus interview available:** Yes
Evaluative: No **Informational only:** Yes **LD program:** 40
Night in dorm provided: Yes **Non-refundable application fee:** $40
Early decision program: Yes **Applied:** 188 **Accepted:** 55 % **Deadline:** Jan. 1
Freshmen accepted other than Fall term: Yes % **SAT/FAF Code #** 1802

Transfers

Applied: 209 **Accepted:** 68 % **Application deadline for Fall:** Apr. 1 **Spring:** Dec. 1
Minimum grades recommended: 3.0 **All new students who were transfers into all classes:** 8 %

Class Experience

Return 2nd year: 90 % **Graduate after 4 years:** 75 % **To graduate school within 1 year:** 39 %

Cost

Tuition deposit: $300 **Total cost (Including school's estimate on fees and books):** $24,287
Tuition: $17,320 **(In state:** $ **)** **Room and board:** $6,300
Annual giving by parents: $2.9 Million **Average per student:** $1,000

Financial Aid

Average total package per student: $18,400 **Number receiving aid:** 40 %
Average scholarships and grants: $15,400 **Average loans:** $3,000 **Work-study program:** Yes
Undergraduates working on campus: 45 % **Average earnings:** $1,500
Non-need scholarships 8 % **Athletic scholarships:** No **FAF deadline:** Feb. 1
Off-campus part-time employment: Good **CO-OP program:** Yes
ROTC: at BU **NROTC:** No **AFROTC:** at BU

Endowment

Total: $150 Million **Per student (including graduate students):** $46,000

Location

Acres: 250 **Setting:** Surburban
Miles from town center: 1 **(Pop.** 58,000**)**
9 **Miles from** Boston **(Pop.** 600,000 **)**
Miles from **(Pop.** **)**

Class Composition

Asian: 6 % **Black:** 3 % **Hispanic:** 3 % **White:** 88 % **Other:** NA %
Total minority : 12 % **Foreign countries:** 4 % (115 students)
From public schools: 74 % **Students from in state:** 30 %

Housing (on campus)

Freshmen required to live on campus: No
Available for all students: 91 %
On-campus married student housing: Yes
Guaranteed for: 1 year
Fraternity / Sorority housing: 0 / 0
Women-only dorms available: No

Campus Life

Students living on campus: 91 % **Remain weekends:** NA % **Handicap access:** %
Car regulations: No restrictions
Number with cars: 30 %
Adequacy of on-campus parking: OK
Number of fraternities: 0 **Chapter houses:** 0
Students belonging to fraternities: 0 %
Number of sororities: 0 **Chapter houses:** 0
Students belonging to sororities: 0 %

Libraries and Computers

Books: 900,000 **Periodicals:** 7,700 **Microform items:** 730,000
Microcomputers available: 87 **Microcomputers networked:** 59

Classes

Faculty / Student Ratio: 1/8 **Classes taught by teacher assistants:** 15 %
Most popular majors: Psychology, Politics, Economics **Classes begin:** Late Aug.
Baccalaureate degrees offered: BA

Sports

Division: III **Except:** **Physical ed requirements:** 2 semesters
Students participating in intercollegiate sports: 35 % **In intramural sports:** 70 %
Additional intercollegiate and/or intramural sports: (not found at all colleges)

Crew: Yes
Ice Hockey: Yes/M
Lacrosse: Yes
Wrestling: Yes/M
Rugby: Yes
Sailing: Yes
Skiing: Yes
Squash: Yes
Ultimate Frisbee: Yes
Water Polo: Yes

Alumni

Number living: 23,000 **Annual giving:** $1.2 Million **Participation:** 26 %
Average annual gift: $210 **Average per student:** $410

3-2 Programs (2 degrees in 5 years)

BA/MA in International Economics and Finance
Cross registration with Boston Coll, Boston U, Tufts and Wellesley

Observation and Opinion of:

Undergraduates and graduates ______________________________

____

College counselor ______________________________

____

BROWN UNIVERSITY (Private)

45 Prospect Street
Providence, RI 02912

MOST SELECTIVE
(Composite rating of guide books)

Main tel.: 401-863-1000
Admissions tel.: 401-863-2378
Financial aid tel.: 401-863-2721
Scheduled Airline Service: Providence
Miles to airport: 5

Founded: 1784
Nickname: Bears
Religious affiliation: None
(Coed since 1971)

Student Body

Undergraduates: 5,600 **Men:** 51 % **Women:** 49 %
Graduate students: 1,500 **Freshman class:** 1,400

Academics

SAT Averages: 1280 **Verbal:** 610 **Math:** 670 **(Taking SATs: 89 %)**
700-800: V NA % **M** NA % **500-600: V** NA % **M** NA %
600-700: V NA % **M** NA % **400-500: V** NA % **M** NA % **300-400: V** NA % **M** NA %
High school class rank: Top fifth 90 % **2nd fifth** 95 % **3rd fifth** 100 %

Admissions

Applied: 12,000 **Accepted:** 23 % **Matriculated:** 50 %
Deadline: Jan. 1 **Accept common application:** No
Interview recommended: No **Off-campus interview available:** Yes
Evaluative: Yes **Informational only:** No **LD program:** No
Night in dorm provided: Yes **Non-refundable application fee:** $55
Early decision program: Yes **Applied:** 1,960 **Accepted:** 25 % **Deadline:** Jan. 1
Freshmen accepted other than Fall term: 2 % **SAT/FAF Code #** 3094

Transfers

Applied: 727 **Accepted:** 25 % **Application deadline for Fall:** Apr. 1 **Spring:** NA
Minimum grades recommended: 8 % **All new students who were transfers into all classes:** 8%

Class Experience

Return 2nd year: 97 % **Graduate after 4 years:** 89 % **To graduate school within 5 years:** 60 %

Cost

Tuition deposit: N/A **Total cost (Including school's estimate on fees and books):** $21,543
Tuition: $17,384 **(In state: $)** **Room and board:** $5,488
Annual giving by parents: $26 Million **Average per student:** $420

Financial Aid

Average total package per student: $12,400 **Number receiving aid:** 32 %
Average scholarships and grants: $9,500 **Average loans:** $2,900 **Work-study program:** Yes
Undergraduates working on campus: NA % **Average earnings:** $1,500
Non-need scholarships NA % **Athletic scholarships:** 0 **FAF deadline:** NA
Off-campus part-time employment: Good **CO-OP program:** No
ROTC: at Providence **NROTC:** No **AFROTC:** No

Endowment

Total: $441 Million **Per student (including graduate students):** $60,000

Location

Acres: 146 **Setting:** Urban
Miles from town center: 2 (**Pop.** 165,000)
45 **Miles from** Boston (**Pop.** 600,000)
Miles from (**Pop.**)

Class Composition

Asian: 11 % **Black:** 7 % **Hispanic:** 4 % **White:** 77 % **Other:** NA %
Total minority : 23 % **Foreign countries:** 10 % (560 students)
From public schools: 80 % **Students from in state:** 6 %

Housing (on campus)

Freshmen required to live on campus: Yes
Guaranteed for: 2 years
Available for all students: 55 %
Fraternity / Sorority housing: Yes / Yes
On-campus married student housing: Yes
Women-only dorms available: No

Campus Life

Students living on campus: 85 % **Remain weekends:** 95 % **Handicap access:** 50 %
Car regulations: No freshmen
Number with cars: NA %
Adequacy of on-campus parking: NA
Number of fraternities: 10 **Chapter houses:** 10
Number of sororities: 1 **Chapter houses:** 1
Students belonging to fraternities: 11 %
Students belonging to sororities: 1 %

Libraries and Computers

Books: 2.1 Million **Periodicals:** 15,000 **Microform items:** 1 Million
Microcomputers available: 300 **Microcomputers networked:**

Classes

Faculty / Student Ratio: 1/9 **Classes taught by teacher assistants:** 20 %
Most popular majors: History, International Relations **Classes begin:** Early Sept.
Baccalaureate degrees offered: AB, ScB

Sports

Division: I **Except:** **Physical ed requirements:** None
Students participating in intercollegiate sports: 40 % **In intramural sports:** 60 %
Additional intercollegiate and/or intramural sports: (not found at all colleges)

Crew: Yes	**Ice Hockey:** Yes	**Lacrosse:** Yes	**Wrestling:** Yes
Rugby: Yes	**Sailing:** Yes	**Skiing:** Yes	
Squash: Yes	**Ultimate Frisbee:** Yes	**Water Polo:** Yes	

Alumni

Number living: 60,000 **Annual giving:** $23 Million **Participation:** 38 %
Average annual gift: $1,100 **Average per student:** $3,000

3-2 Programs (2 degrees in 5 years)

AB/MA and ScB/MS
Exchange programs with R.I. School of Design and Dartmouth Medical School

Observation and Opinion of:

Undergraduates and graduates ______________________________

____

College counselor ______________________________

____

BRYN MAWR (Private)

Bryn Mawr, PA 19010

MOST SELECTIVE
(Composite rating of guide books)

Main tel.: 215-526-5000
Admissions tel.: 215-526-5152
Financial aid tel.: 215-526-5245
Scheduled Airline Service: Philadelphia
Miles to airport: 10

Founded: 1885
Nickname: Mawrters
Religious affiliation: None
(Coed since NA **)**

Student Body

Undergraduates: 1,200 **Men:** 0 % **Women:** 100 %
Graduate students: 650 **Freshman class:** 327

Academics

SAT Averages: 1260 **Verbal:** 630 **Math:** 630 **(Taking SATs: 99 %)**
700-800: V 15 % **M** 14 % **500-600: V** 30 % **M** 30 %
600-700: V 42 % **M** 47 % **400-500: V** 13 % **M** 9 % **300-400: V** NA % **M** NA %
High school class rank: Top fifth 80 % **2nd fifth** 15 % **3rd fifth** 4 %

Admissions

Applied: 1,400 **Accepted:** 57 % **Matriculated:** 41 %
Deadline: Jan. 1 **Accept common application:** Yes
Interview recommended: Yes **Off-campus interview available:** Yes
Evaluative: Yes **Informational only:** No **LD program:** No
Night in dorm provided: Yes **Non-refundable application fee:** $40
Early decision program: Yes **Applied:** 137 **Accepted:** 60 % **Deadline:** Nov. 15
Freshmen accepted other than Fall term: 1 % **SAT/FAF Code #** 2049

Transfers

Applied: 77 **Accepted:** 40 % **Application deadline for Fall:** Mar. 15 **Spring:** Nov. 1
Minimum grades recommended: C **All new students who were transfers into all classes:** 6 %

Class Experience

Return 2nd year: 96 % **Graduate after 4 years:** 85 % **To graduate school within 5 years:** 50 %

Cost

Tuition deposit: $200 **Total cost (Including school's estimate on fees and books):** $22,800
Tuition: $16,160 **(In state:** $ **)** **Room and board:** $6,150
Annual giving by parents: $330,000 **Average per student:** $180

Financial Aid

Average total package per student: $13,300 **Number receiving aid:** 43 %
Average scholarships and grants: $10,900 **Average loans:** $2,400 **Work-study program:** Yes
Undergraduates working on campus: 70 % **Average earnings:** $1,150
Non-need scholarships 0 % **Athletic scholarships:** 0 **FAF deadline:** Jan. 1
Off-campus part-time employment: Good **CO-OP program:** No
ROTC: at U of PA **NROTC:** at St. Joe's **AFROTC:** at U of PA

Endowment

Total: $153 Million **Per student (including graduate students):** $80,000

Location

Acres: 135 **Setting:** Surburban **Miles from town center:** 0 **(Pop.** 9,000**)**
11 **Miles from** Phil. **(Pop.** 1.6 Mil. **)** 105 **Miles from** NYC **(Pop.** 7.5 Mil. **)**

Class Composition

Asian: 10 % **Black:** 5 % **Hispanic:** 2 % **White:** 73 % **Other:** 10 %
Total minority : 27 % **Foreign countries:** 11 % (220 students)
From public schools: 63 % **Students from in state:** 13 %

Housing (on campus)

Freshmen required to live on campus: Yes **Guaranteed for:** 1 year
Available for all students: NA % **Fraternity / Sorority housing:** No / No
On-campus married student housing: No **Women-only dorms available:** Yes

Campus Life

Students living on campus: 95 % **Remain weekends:** NA % **Handicap access:** 60 %
Car regulations: No freshmen
Number with cars: NA % **Adequacy of on-campus parking:** Poor
Number of fraternities: **Chapter houses:** **Number of sororities:** 0 **Chapter houses:** 0
Students belonging to fraternities: % **Students belonging to sororities:** 0 %

Libraries and Computers

Books: 900,000 **Periodicals:** 2,500 **Microform items:** NA
Microcomputers available: 100 **Microcomputers networked:** NA

Classes

Faculty / Student Ratio: 1/9 **Classes taught by teacher assistants:** 10 %
Most popular majors: English, Economics, Chemistry **Classes begin:** Early Sept.
Baccalaureate degrees offered: AB

Sports

Division: III **Except:** **Physical ed requirements:** 4 semesters
Students participating in intercollegiate sports: 70 % **In intramural sports:** 30 %
Additional intercollegiate and/or intramural sports: (not found at all colleges)

Crew: No	**Ice Hockey:** Yes	**Lacrosse:** Yes	**Wrestling:** No
Rugby: Yes	**Sailing:** Yes	**Skiing:** No	
Squash: Yes	**Ultimate Frisbee:** Yes	**Water Polo:** No	

Alumni

Number living: 15,500 **Annual giving:** $16.4 million **Participation:** 38 %
Average annual gift: $3,000 **Average per student:** $8,000

3-2 Programs (2 degrees in 5 years)

Engineering: Cal Tech & U of Pennsylvania. Combined AB/MD at Medical Coll. of Penn.
Close social, academic and residential cooperation with Haverford

Observation and Opinion of:

Undergraduates and graduates ______________________________

____

College counselor ______________________________

____

BUCKNELL UNIVERSITY (Private)

Lewisburg, PA 17837

HIGHLY SELECTIVE
(Composite rating of guide books)

Main tel.: 717-523-1271
Admissions tel.: 717-524-1101
Financial aid tel.: 717-524-1331
Scheduled Airline Service: Harrisburg
Miles to airport: 55

Founded: 1846
Nickname: Bisons
Religious affiliation: None
(Coed since 1846)

Student Body

Undergraduates: 3,400 **Men:** 60 % **Women:** 40 %
Graduate students: 200 **Freshman class:** 880

Academics

SAT Averages: 1190 **Verbal:** 550 **Math:** 640 **(Taking SATs:** 99 %**)**
700-800: V 1 % **M** 17 % **500-600: V** 55 % **M** 27 %
600-700: V 22 % **M** 53 % **400-500: V** 21 % **M** 3 % **300-400: V** 1 % **M** 0 %
High school class rank: Top fifth 70 % **2nd fifth** 11 % **3rd fifth** 3 %

Admissions

Applied: 5,950 **Accepted:** 55 % **Matriculated:** 27 %
Deadline: Jan. 1 **Accept common application:** Yes
Interview recommended: No **Off-campus interview available:** Yes
Evaluative: Yes **Informational only:** No **LD program:**
Night in dorm provided: Yes **Non-refundable application fee:** $35
Early decision program: Yes **Applied:** 408 **Accepted:** 60 % **Deadline:** Dec. 15
Freshmen accepted other than Fall term: 0 % **SAT/FAF Code #** 3528

Transfers

Applied: 178 **Accepted:** 60 % **Application deadline for Fall:** Apr. 1 **Spring:** Dec.1
Minimum grades recommended: 2.5 **All new students who were transfers into all classes:** 5 %

Class Experience

Return 2nd year: 95 % **Graduate after 4 years:** 86 % **To graduate school within 5 years:** 52 %

Cost

Tuition deposit: $200 **Total cost (Including school's estimate on fees and books):** $21,400
Tuition: $16,560 **(In state:** $ **)** **Room and board:** $4,110
Annual giving by parents: $300,000 **Average per student:** $90

Financial Aid

Average total package per student: $12,900 **Number receiving aid:** 32 %
Average scholarships and grants: $10,400 **Average loans:** $2,500 **Work-study program:** Yes
Undergraduates working on campus: 60 % **Average earnings:** $1,200
Non-need scholarships 0 % **Athletic scholarships:** Yes **FAF deadline:** Feb. 15
Off-campus part-time employment: Fair **CO-OP program:** No
ROTC: Yes **NROTC:** No **AFROTC:** No

Endowment

Total: $109 Million **Per student (including graduate students):** $30,000

Location

Acres: 300 **Setting:** Rural **Miles from town center:** 0 **(Pop.** 8,500)
55 **Miles from** Harrisburg **(Pop.** 53,000) 135 **Miles from** Phil. **(Pop.** 1.6 Million)

Class Composition

Asian: 2 % **Black:** 2 % **Hispanic:** 1 % **White:** 94 % **Other:** NA %
Total minority : 6 % **Foreign countries:** 2 % (75 students)
From public schools: 72 % **Students from in state:** 30 %

Housing (on campus)

Freshmen required to live on campus: No **Guaranteed for:** 1 year
Available for all students: 92 % **Fraternity / Sorority housing:** Yes / No
On-campus married student housing: Yes **Women-only dorms available:** Yes

Campus Life

Students living on campus: 92 % **Remain weekends:** 90 % **Handicap access:** 85 %
Car regulations: No freshmen
Number with cars: 54 % **Adequacy of on-campus parking:** Poor
Number of fraternities: 12 **Chapter houses:** 12 **Number of sororities:** 10 **Chapter houses:** 0
Students belonging to fraternities: 55 % **Students belonging to sororities:** 50 %

Libraries and Computers

Books: 475,000 **Periodicals:** 2,600 **Microform items:** 10,000
Microcomputers available: 200 **Microcomputers networked:** 50

Classes

Faculty / Student Ratio: 1/13 **Classes taught by teacher assistants:** 0 %
Most popular majors: Bus. Adm., Economics, English **Classes begin:** Early Sept.
Baccalaureate degrees offered: BA, BMUS, BS, BSBA, BSE, BSED

Sports

Division: I **Except:** **Physical ed requirements:** None
Students participating in intercollegiate sports: 25 % **In intramural sports:** 75 %
Additional intercollegiate and/or intramural sports: (not found at all colleges)

Crew: Yes **Ice Hockey:** Yes/M **Lacrosse:** Yes **Wrestling:** Yes/M
Rugby: Yes/M **Sailing:** Yes **Skiing:** Cross Country
Squash: Yes **Ultimate Frisbee:** Yes **Water Polo:** Yes/M

Alumni

Number living: 37,000 **Annual giving:** $6.3 Million **Participation:** 37 %
Average annual gift: $600 **Average per student:** $1,900

3-2 Programs (2 degrees in 5 years)

Engineering BS/BA Program at Bucknell

Observation and Opinion of:

Undergraduates and graduates ______________________________

____

College counselor ______________________________

____

UNIVERSITY OF CALIFORNIA AT BERKELEY (Public)

Berkeley, CA 94720

HIGHLY SELECTIVE
(Composite rating of guide books)

Main tel.: 510-642-6000
Admissions tel.: 510-642-3175
Financial aid tel.: 510-642-6442
Scheduled Airline Service: S.F. & Oakland
Miles to airport: 20

Founded: 1868
Nickname: Bears
Religious affiliation: None
(Coed since 1886)

Student Body

Undergraduates: 21,500 **Men:** 55 % **Women:** 45 %
Graduate students: 9,000 **Freshman class:** 3,130

Academics

SAT Averages: 1195 **Verbal:** 555 **Math:** 640 **(Taking SATs:** NA **%)**
700-800: V 6 % **M** 38 % **500-600: V** 35 % **M** 18 %
600-700: V 33 % **M** 34 % **400-500: V** 19 % **M** 8 % **300-400: V** 6 % **M** 2 %
High school class rank: Top fifth 95 % **2nd fifth** NA % **3rd fifth** NA %

Admissions

Applied: 19,995 **Accepted:** 38 % **Matriculated:** 41 %
Deadline: Nov. 30 **Accept common application:** No
Interview recommended: No **Off-campus interview available:** Yes
Evaluative: No **Informational only:** Yes **LD program:** NA
Night in dorm provided: No **Non-refundable application fee:** $40
Early decision program: No **Applied:** NA **Accepted:** NA % **Deadline:** NA
Freshmen accepted other than Fall term: 0 % **SAT/FAF Code #** 4833

Transfers

Applied: 7,600 **Accepted:** 33 % **Application deadline for Fall:** Nov. 30 **Spring:** July 30
Minimum grades recommended: 2.8 **All new students who were transfers into all classes:** 31 %

Class Experience

Return 2nd year: 89 % **Graduate after 4 years:** 65 % **To graduate school within 5 years:** 30 %

Cost

Tuition deposit: $100 **Total cost (Including school's estimate on fees and books):** $19,500
Tuition: $11,000 **(In state:** $ 3,250**)** **Room and board:** $5,800
Annual giving by parents: 0 **Average per student:**

Financial Aid

Average total package per student: $5,500 **Number receiving aid:** 60 %
Average scholarships and grants: $2,600 **Average loans:** $2,000 **Work-study program:** Yes
Undergraduates working on campus: 30 % **Average earnings:** $2,000
Non-need scholarships 5 % **Athletic scholarships:** Yes **FAF deadline:** March 2
Off-campus part-time employment: Excellent **CO-OP program:** No
ROTC: Yes **NROTC:** Yes **AFROTC:** Yes

Endowment

Total: N/A **Per student (including graduate students):** NA

Location

Acres: 1,200 **Setting:** City
10 **Miles from** San Fran. **(Pop.** 680,000 **)**
Miles from town center: 1 **(Pop.** 100,000**)**
Miles from **(Pop.** **)**

Class Composition

Asian: 29 % **Black:** 7 % **Hispanic:** 14 % **White:** 42 % **Other:** 7 %
Total minority : 58 % **Foreign countries:** 3 % (600 students)
From public schools: % **Students from in state:** 85 %

Housing (on campus)

Freshmen required to live on campus: No
Available for all students: 25 %
On-campus married student housing: No
Guaranteed for: NA
Fraternity / Sorority housing: Yes / Yes
Women-only dorms available: Yes

Campus Life

Students living on campus: 25 % **Remain weekends:** NA % **Handicap access:** 90 %
Car regulations: All may have (Fee)
Number with cars: 26 %
Number of fraternities: 39 **Chapter houses:** 25
Students belonging to fraternities: 7 %
Adequacy of on-campus parking: Fair
Number of sororities: 15 **Chapter houses:** 25
Students belonging to sororities: 7 %

Libraries and Computers

Books: 7.6 Million **Periodicals:** 103,000 **Microform items:** 4 Million
Microcomputers available: Yes **Microcomputers networked:** Yes

Classes

Faculty / Student Ratio: 1/12 **Classes taught by teacher assistants:** 30 %
Most popular majors: NA **Classes begin:** Late Aug.
Baccalaureate degrees offered: BA, BS

Sports

Division: I **Except:** **Physical ed requirements:** None
Students participating in intercollegiate sports: 2 % **In intramural sports:** 20 %
Additional intercollegiate and/or intramural sports: (not found at all colleges)

Crew: Yes	**Ice Hockey:** No	**Lacrosse:** Yes	**Wrestling:** No
Rugby: Yes	**Sailing:** No	**Skiing:** Yes	
Squash: Yes/M	**Ultimate Frisbee:** Yes	**Water Polo:** Yes	

Alumni

Number living: 325,000 **Annual giving:** NA **Participation:** NA %
Average annual gift: $ NA **Average per student:** $ NA

3-2 Programs (2 degrees in 5 years)

Exchange programs with Cal State U, Harvard, Mill's Coll and Stanford

Observation and Opinion of:

Undergraduates and graduates ______________________________

____

College counselor ______________________________

____

UNIVERSITY OF CALIFORNIA, LOS ANGELES (Public)

405 Hilgard Avenue
Los Angeles, CA 90024-1435

HIGHLY SELECTIVE
(Composite rating of guide books)

Main tel.: 213-825-4321
Admissions tel.: 213-825-3101
Financial aid tel.: 213-206-0400
Scheduled Airline Service: Los Angeles
Miles to airport: 10

Founded: 1919
Nickname: Bruins
Religious affiliation: None
(Coed since 1919)

Student Body

Undergraduates: 24,000 **Men:** 48 % **Women:** 52 %
Graduate students: 12,000 **Freshman class:** 3,600

Academics

SAT Averages: 1125 **Verbal:** 519 **Math:** 612 (Taking SATs: 98 %)
700-800: V 2 % M 22 % **500-600:** V 38 % M 28 %
600-700: V 21 % M 41 % **400-500:** V 25 % M 11 % **300-400:** V 11 % M 13 %
High school class rank: Top fifth % 2nd fifth % 3rd fifth %

Admissions

Applied: 22,600 **Accepted:** 43 % **Matriculated:** 37 %
Deadline: Nov. 30 **Accept common application:** No
Interview recommended: No **Off-campus interview available:** No
Evaluative: No **Informational only:** NA **LD program:** No
Night in dorm provided: No **Non-refundable application fee:** $40
Early decision program: No **Applied:** NA **Accepted:** NA % **Deadline:** NA
Freshmen accepted other than Fall term: 0 % **SAT/FAF Code #** 4837

Transfers

Applied: 2,300 **Accepted:** 45 % **Application deadline for Fall:** Nov. 30 **Spring:** Oct. 31
Minimum grades recommended: 3.0 **All new students who were transfers into all classes:** 35 %

Class Experience

Return 2nd year: 94 % **Graduate after 4 years:** 60 % **To graduate school within 5 years:** 60 %

Cost

Tuition deposit: $100 **Total cost (Including school's estimate on fees and books):** $17,500
Tuition: $11,000 (In state: $3,250) **Room and board:** $5,800
Annual giving by parents: NA **Average per student:** $NA

Financial Aid

Average total package per student: $NA **Number receiving aid:** NA %
Average scholarships and grants: $2,000 **Average loans:** $2,000 **Work-study program:** NA
Undergraduates working on campus: 42 % **Average earnings:** $2,000
Non-need scholarships 18 % **Athletic scholarships:** Yes **FAF deadline:** March 2
Off-campus part-time employment: Excellent **CO-OP program:** No
ROTC: Yes **NROTC:** Yes **AFROTC:** Yes

Endowment

Total: $304 Million **Per student (including graduate students):** $8,000

Location

Acres: 420 **Setting:** City **Miles from town center:** 1 **(Pop.** 3 Million**)**
Miles from **(Pop.** **)** **Miles from** **(Pop.** **)**

Class Composition

Asian: 28 **%** **Black:** 7 **%** **Hispanic:** 16 **%** **White:** 47 **%** **Other:** 1 **%**
Total minority : 53 **%** **Foreign countries:** 2 **%** (480 students)
From public schools: 79 **%** **Students from in state:** 95 **%**

Housing (on campus)

Freshmen required to live on campus: No **Guaranteed for:** 0 year
Available for all students: 26 **%** **Fraternity / Sorority housing:** 0 / 0
On-campus married student housing: NA **Women-only dorms available:** No

Campus Life

Students living on campus: 26 **%** **Remain weekends:** NA **%** **Handicap access:** 90 **%**
Car regulations: OK
Number with cars: NA **%** **Adequacy of on-campus parking:** Poor
Number of fraternities: 31 **Chapter houses:** 0 **Number of sororities:** 18 **Chapter houses:** 0
Students belonging to fraternities: 16 **%** **Students belonging to sororities:** 17 **%**

Libraries and Computers

Books: 6 Million **Periodicals:** 96,000 **Microform items:** 5.6 Million
Microcomputers available: Yes **Microcomputers networked:** Yes

Classes

Faculty / Student Ratio: 1/17 **Classes taught by teacher assistants:** 0 **%**
Most popular majors: Economics, Psychology, Poly Science **Classes begin:** Sept.
Baccalaureate degrees offered: BA, BS

Sports

Division: I **Except:** **Physical ed requirements:** None
Students participating in intercollegiate sports: 23 **%** **In intramural sports:** 75 **%**
Additional intercollegiate and/or intramural sports: (not found at all colleges)

Crew: Yes	**Ice Hockey:** Yes	**Lacrosse:** Yes	**Wrestling:** Yes
Rugby: Yes	**Sailing:** Yes	**Skiing:** Yes	
Squash: Yes	**Ultimate Frisbee:** No	**Water Polo:** Yes/M	

Alumni

Number living: 183,000 **Annual giving:** $8.5 million **Participation:** 12 **%**
Average annual gift: $400 **Average per student:** $270

3-2 Programs (2 degrees in 5 years)

Engineering U of Maryland & Washington U

Observation and Opinion of:

Undergraduates and graduates ______________________

____

College counselor ______________________

____

CARLETON COLLEGE (Private)

One North College Street
Northfield, MN 55057

HIGHLY SELECTIVE
(Composite rating of guide books)

Main tel.: 507-663-4000
Admissions tel.: 507-663-4190
Financial aid tel.: 507-663-4190
Scheduled Airline Service: Minneapolis-St. Paul
Miles to airport: 33

Founded: 1866
Nickname: Knights
Religious affiliation: None
(Coed since 1866)

Student Body

Undergraduates: 1,700 **Men:** 51 % **Women:** 49 %
Graduate students: 0 **Freshman class:** 465

Academics

SAT Averages: 1290 **Verbal:** 635 **Math:** 655 **(Taking SATs:** 55 %**)**
700-800: V 13 % M 37 % **500-600:** V 25 % M 17 %
600-700: V 57 % M 44 % **400-500:** V 5 % M 2 % **300-400:** V NA % M NA %
High school class rank: Top fifth 80 % 2nd fifth 6 % 3rd fifth NA %

Admissions

Applied: 2,840 **Accepted:** 47 % **Matriculated:** 35 %
Deadline: Feb. 1 **Accept common application:** Yes
Interview recommended: No **Off-campus interview available:** Yes
Evaluative: Yes **Informational only:** NA **LD program:** No
Night in dorm provided: Yes **Non-refundable application fee:** $35
Early decision program: Yes **Applied:** 325 **Accepted:** 33 % **Deadline:** Nov. 15
Freshmen accepted other than Fall term: 0 % **SAT/FAF Code #** 5081

Transfers

Applied: 107 **Accepted:** 25 % **Application deadline for Fall:** Apr. 15 **Spring:** Nov. 1
Minimum grades recommended: 3.0 **All new students who were transfers into all classes:** 3 %

Class Experience

Return 2nd year: 95 % **Graduate after 4 years:** 77 % **To graduate school within 5 years:** 75 %

Cost

Tuition deposit: $100 **Total cost (Including school's estimate on fees and books):** $20,900
Tuition: $16,700 **(In state:** $ **)** **Room and board:** $3,500
Annual giving by parents: $165,000 **Average per student:** $100

Financial Aid

Average total package per student: $8,000 **Number receiving aid:** 55 %
Average scholarships and grants: $5,700 **Average loans:** $2,300 **Work-study program:** Yes
Undergraduates working on campus: 80 % **Average earnings:** $1,375
Non-need scholarships 2 % **Athletic scholarships:** No **FAF deadline:** March 1
Off-campus part-time employment: Fair **CO-OP program:** No
ROTC: No **NROTC:** No **AFROTC:** No

Endowment

Total: $174 Million **Per student (including graduate students):** $100,000

Location

Acres: 950 **Setting:** Urban
35 **Miles from** St. Paul **(Pop.** 370,000 **)**
Miles from town center: 1 **(Pop.** 15,000**)**
Miles from **(Pop.** **)**

Class Composition

Asian: 6 % **Black:** 3 % **Hispanic:** 2 % **White:** 87 % **Other:** 1 %
Total minority : 13 % **Foreign countries:** 1 % (17 students)
From public schools: 75 % **Students from in state:** 25 %

Housing (on campus)

Freshmen required to live on campus: Yes
Available for all students: 100 %
On-campus married student housing: No
Guaranteed for: 2 years
Fraternity / Sorority housing: No/ No
Women-only dorms available: No

Campus Life

Students living on campus: 95 % **Remain weekends:** 95 % **Handicap access:** 50 %
Car regulations: Permission needed
Number with cars: NA %
Number of fraternities: 0 **Chapter houses:** 0
Students belonging to fraternities: 0 %
Adequacy of on-campus parking: Fair
Number of sororities: 0 **Chapter houses:** 0
Students belonging to sororities: 0 %

Libraries and Computers

Books: 450,000 **Periodicals:** 1,400 **Microform items:** 53,000
Microcomputers available: Yes **Microcomputers networked:** NA

Classes

Faculty / Student Ratio: 1/11 **Classes taught by teacher assistants:** 0 %
Most popular majors: English, Poly Science **Classes begin:** Sept.
Baccalaureate degrees offered: BA

Sports

Division: III **Except:** **Physical ed requirements:** 4 terms required
Students participating in intercollegiate sports: 35 % **In intramural sports:** 60 %
Additional intercollegiate and/or intramural sports: (not found at all colleges)

Crew: No	**Ice Hockey:** Yes	**Lacrosse:** Yes	**Wrestling:** Yes/M
Rugby: Yes	**Sailing:** No	**Skiing:** Yes	
Squash: Yes	**Ultimate Frisbee:** Yes	**Water Polo:** Yes	

Alumni

Number living: 19,300 **Annual giving:** $4.5 Million **Participation:** 48 %
Average annual gift: $500 **Average per student:** $2,600

3-2 Programs (2 degrees in 5 years)

Engineering with Columbia and Washington U Law with Columbia

Observation and Opinion of:

Undergraduates and graduates ____________________

____

College counselor ____________________

____

CARNEGIE MELLON UNIVERSITY (Private)

5000 Forbes Avenue
Pittsburgh, PA 15213

HIGHLY SELECTIVE
(Composite rating of guide books)

Main tel.: 412-268-2000
Admissions tel.: 412-268-2082
Financial aid tel.: 412-268-2068
Scheduled Airline Service: Pittsburgh
Miles to airport: 5

Founded: 1900
Nickname: Tartans
Religious affiliation: None
(Coed since 1900)

Student Body

Undergraduates: 4,200 **Men:** 70 % **Women:** 30 %
Graduate students: 2,600 **Freshman class:** 1,150

Academics

SAT Averages: 1230 **Verbal:** 580 **Math:** 650 (Taking SATs: 98 %)
700-800: V 3 % **M** 30 % **500-600: V** 45 % **M** 20 %
600-700: V 28 % **M** 45 % **400-500: V** 20 % **M** 5 % **300-400: V** NA %**M** NA %
High school class rank: Top fifth 78 % **2nd fifth** 16 % **3rd fifth** 6 %

Admissions

Applied: 6,150 **Accepted:** 72 % **Matriculated:** 26 %
Deadline: Feb. 1 **Accept common application:** No
Interview recommended: No **Off-campus interview available:** Yes
Evaluative: Yes **Informational only:** NA **LD program:** Yes
Night in dorm provided: Yes **Non-refundable application fee:** $40
Early decision program: Yes **Applied:** 345 **Accepted:** 55 % **Deadline:** Dec. 1
Freshmen accepted other than Fall term: 0 % **SAT/FAF Code #** 2074

Transfers

Applied: 455 **Accepted:** 40 % **Application deadline for Fall:** Nov. 1 **Spring:** Apr. 1
Minimum grades recommended: 3.0 **All new students who were transfers into all classes:** 11 %

Class Experience

Return 2nd year: 90 % **Graduate after 4 years:** 70 % **To graduate school within 5 years:** 50 %

Cost

Tuition deposit: $350 **Total cost (Including school's estimate on fees and books):** $23,010
Tuition: $16,000 (In state: $) **Room and board:** $5,460
Annual giving by parents: $122,000 **Average per student:** $17

Financial Aid

Average total package per student: $12,500 **Number receiving aid:** 53 %
Average scholarships and grants: $9,800 **Average loans:** $2,600 **Work-study program:** Yes
Undergraduates working on campus: 65 % **Average earnings:** $1,400
Non-need scholarships 10 % **Athletic scholarships:** NA **FAF deadline:** Feb. 13
Off-campus part-time employment: Good **CO-OP program:** Yes
ROTC: No **NROTC:** Yes **AFROTC:** Yes

Endowment

Total: $313 Million **Per student (including graduate students):** $45,000

Location

Acres: 105 **Setting:** Urban **Miles from town center:** 5 (**Pop.** 600,000)
Miles from (**Pop.**) **Miles from** (**Pop.**)

Class Composition

Asian: 21 % **Black:** 6 % **Hispanic:** 4 % **White:** 69 % **Other:** %
Total minority : 31 % **Foreign countries:** 7 % (290 students)
From public schools: 65 % **Students from in state:** 38 %

Housing (on campus)

Freshmen required to live on campus: Yes **Guaranteed for:** 4 years
Available for all students: 80 % **Fraternity / Sorority housing:** Yes / Yes
On-campus married student housing: Yes **Women-only dorms available:** Yes

Campus Life

Students living on campus: 80 % **Remain weekends:** 95 % **Handicap access:** 100 %
Car regulations: OK(with permit)
Number with cars: 5 % **Adequacy of on-campus parking:** Poor
Number of fraternities: 14 **Chapter houses:** 12 **Number of sororities:** 5 **Chapter houses:** 5
Students belonging to fraternities: 33 % **Students belonging to sororities:** 29 %

Libraries and Computers

Books: 750,000 **Periodicals:** 4,400 **Microform items:** 544,000
Microcomputers available: Yes **Microcomputers networked:** Yes

Classes

Faculty / Student Ratio: 1/9 **Classes taught by teacher assistants:** 10 %
Most popular majors: Electrical & Computer Engineering **Classes begin:** Late Aug.
Baccalaureate degrees offered: BA, B ARCH, BFA, BS

Sports

Division: III **Except:** **Physical ed requirements:**
Students participating in intercollegiate sports: 17 % **In intramural sports:** 91 %
Additional intercollegiate and/or intramural sports: (not found at all colleges)

Crew: Yes **Ice Hockey:** Yes/M **Lacrosse:** Yes **Wrestling:** Yes
Rugby: Yes **Sailing:** Yes **Skiing:** Yes
Squash: Yes **Ultimate Frisbee:** Yes **Water Polo:** Yes

Alumni

Number living: 45,000 **Annual giving:** $8.1 million **Participation:** 39 %
Average annual gift: $570 **Average per student:** $1200

3-2 Programs (2 degrees in 5 years)

Bachelor's/Master's Degree Programs in Social Science, Public Policy
BS/JD Program with Duquesne U

Observation and Opinion of:

Undergraduates and graduates __________

College counselor __________

CASE WESTERN RESERVE UNIVERSITY (Private)

University Circle
Cleveland, OH 44106

HIGHLY SELECTIVE
(Composite rating of guide books)

Main tel.: 800-321-6984
Admissions tel.: 216-368-4450
Financial aid tel.: 216-368-4530
Scheduled Airline Service: Cleveland
Miles to airport: 8

Founded: 1826
Nickname: Spartans
Religious affiliation: None
(Coed since 1967)

Student Body

Undergraduates: 2,500 **Men:** 63 % **Women:** 37 %
Graduate students: 5,500 **Freshman class:** 650

Academics

SAT Averages: 1200 **Verbal:** 548 **Math:** 587 **(Taking SATs: 90 %)**
700-800: V 4 % **M** 26 % **500-600: V** 40 % **M** 25 %
600-700: V 24 % **M** 44 % **400-500: V** 24 % **M** 5 % **300-400: V** 6 % **M** 0 %
High school class rank: Top fifth 87 % **2nd fifth** 5 % **3rd fifth** 5 %

Admissions

Applied: 2,160 **Accepted:** 86 % **Matriculated:** 35 %
Deadline: Mar. 1 **Accept common application:** Yes
Interview recommended: Yes **Off-campus interview available:** Yes
Evaluative: Yes **Informational only:** No **LD program:** Yes
Night in dorm provided: Yes **Non-refundable application fee:** $35
Early decision program: Yes **Applied:** 65 **Accepted:** 80 % **Deadline:** Jan. 15
Freshmen accepted other than Fall term: 4 % **SAT/FAF Code #** 3244

Transfers

Applied: 370 **Accepted:** 60 % **Application deadline for Fall:** June 30 **Spring:** Nov. 15
Minimum grades recommended: 3.0 **All new students who were transfers into all classes:** 15 %

Class Experience

Return 2nd year: 90 % **Graduate after 4 years:** 68 % **To graduate school within 5 years:** 33 %

Cost

Tuition deposit: $200 **Total cost (Including school's estimate on fees and books):** $20,300
Tuition: $14,500 **(In state:** $ **)** **Room and board:** $4,500
Annual giving by parents: $46,000 **Average per student:** $ 18

Financial Aid

Average total package per student: $16,600 **Number receiving aid:** 68 %
Average scholarships and grants: $4,800 **Average loans:** $11,800 **Work-study program:** Yes
Undergraduates working on campus: 80 % **Average earnings:** $1,100
Non-need scholarships 10 % **Athletic scholarships:** NA **FAF deadline:** Feb. 1
Off-campus part-time employment: Good **CO-OP program:** Yes
ROTC: at John Carrol **NROTC:** No **AFROTC:** at U of Akron

Endowment

Total: $443 Million **Per student (including graduate students):** $70,000

Location

Acres: 130 **Setting:** City **Miles from town center:** 4 (Pop. 875,000)
Miles from (Pop.) **Miles from** (Pop.)

Class Composition

Asian: 14 % **Black:** 7 % **Hispanic:** 1 % **White:** 75 % **Other:** 2 %
Total minority : 25 % **Foreign countries:** 10 % (250 students)
From public schools: 76 % **Students from in state:** 69 %

Housing (on campus)

Freshmen required to live on campus: Yes **Guaranteed for:** 4 years
Available for all students: 85 % **Fraternity / Sorority housing:** Yes/No
On-campus married student housing: NA **Women-only dorms available:** Yes

Campus Life

Students living on campus: 85 % **Remain weekends:** 85 % **Handicap access:** NA %
Car regulations: All students (permit - $180)
Number with cars: NA % **Adequacy of on-campus parking:** Poor
Number of fraternities: 16 **Chapter houses:** 15 **Number of sororities:** 4 **Chapter houses:** 0
Students belonging to fraternities: 36 % **Students belonging to sororities:** 18 %

Libraries and Computers

Books: 1.8 Million **Periodicals:** 12,500 **Microform items:** 1.7 Mil.
Microcomputers available: Yes **Microcomputers networked:** NA

Classes

Faculty / Student Ratio: 1/8 **Classes taught by teacher assistants:** 10 %
Most popular majors: Electrical & Mechanical Engineering **Classes begin:** Aug.
Baccalaureate degrees offered: BA, BS, BSN

Sports

Division: III **Except:** **Physical ed requirements:** 2 Semesters
Students participating in intercollegiate sports: 30 % **In intramural sports:** 60 %
Additional intercollegiate and/or intramural sports: (not found at all colleges)

Crew: No **Ice Hockey:** Yes **Lacrosse:** Yes/M **Wrestling:** Yes/M
Rugby: No **Sailing:** No **Skiing:** Yes
Squash: Yes **Ultimate Frisbee:** No **Water Polo:** Yes

Alumni

Number living: 78,000 **Annual giving:** $9.1 Million **Participation:** 34 %
Average annual gift: $350 **Average per student:** $1,100

3-2 Programs (2 degrees in 5 years)

Host university for Engineering, Nutrition and Medical Technology

Observation and Opinion of:

Undergraduates and graduates ______________________________

____

College counselor ______________________________

____

THE CATHOLIC UNIVERSITY OF AMERICA (Private)

620 Michigan Avenue
Washington, DC 20064

SELECTIVE
(Composite rating of guide books)

Main tel.: 202-319-5305
Admissions tel.: 202-319-5305
Financial aid tel.: 202-319-5307
Scheduled Airline Service: Washington
Miles to airport: 8

Founded: 1887
Nickname: Cardinals
Religious affiliation: Catholic
(Coed since 1925)

Student Body

Undergraduates: 3,100 **Men:** 40 % **Women:** 60 %
Graduate students: 3,300 **Freshman class:** 575

Academics

SAT Averages: 1085 **Verbal:** 530 **Math:** 555 **(Taking SATs:** NA %**)**
700-800: V 1 % **M** 1 % **500-600: V** 40 % **M** 47 %
600-700: V 14 % **M** 21 % **400-500: V** 28 % **M** 26 % **300-400: V** 8 % **M** 5 %
High school class rank: Top fifth 36 % **2nd fifth** 30 % **3rd fifth** 15 %

Admissions

Applied: 2,000 **Accepted:** 85 % **Matriculated:** 34 %
Deadline: Feb. 15 **Accept common application:** No
Interview recommended: Yes **Off-campus interview available:** No
Evaluative: No **Informational only:** Yes **LD program:** Yes
Night in dorm provided: Yes **Non-refundable application fee:** $20
Early decision program: Yes **Applied:** 105 **Accepted:** 80 % **Deadline:** Dec. 15
Freshmen accepted other than Fall term: 1 % **SAT/FAF Code #** 5104

Transfers

Applied: 400 **Accepted:** 25 % **Application deadline for Fall:** Feb. 1 **Spring:** NA
Minimum grades recommended: 3.0 **All new students who were transfers into all classes:** 33 %

Class Experience

Return 2nd year: 90 % **Graduate after 4 years:** 65 % **To graduate school within 5 years:** 50 %

Cost

Tuition deposit: $100 **Total cost (Including school's estimate on fees and books):** $19,000
Tuition: $12,556 **(In state:** $ **)** **Room and board:** $5,970
Annual giving by parents: NA **Average per student:** NA

Financial Aid

Average total package per student: $ NA **Number receiving aid:** 40 %
Average scholarships and grants: $5,500 **Average loans:** $ NA **Work-study program:** Yes
Undergraduates working on campus: 15 % **Average earnings:** $1,000
Non-need scholarships NA % **Athletic scholarships:** NA **FAF deadline:** Feb. 15
Off-campus part-time employment: Excellent **CO-OP program:** No
ROTC: at Georgetown **NROTC:** at Geo Wash **AFROTC:** at Howard U

Endowment

Total: $ NA **Per student (including graduate students):** $ NA

Location

Acres: 190 **Setting:** City **Miles from town center:** 5 (Pop. 700,000)
Miles from (Pop.) **Miles from** (Pop.)

Class Composition

Asian: 3 % **Black:** 5 % **Hispanic:** 5 % **White:** 77 % **Other:** 9 %
Total minority : 23 % **Foreign countries:** 9 % (270 students)
From public schools: NA % **Students from in state:** 5 %

Housing (on campus)

Freshmen required to live on campus: No **Guaranteed for:** 1 year
Available for all students: 80 % **Fraternity / Sorority housing:** No / No
On-campus married student housing: NA **Women-only dorms available:** Yes

Campus Life

Students living on campus: 80 % **Remain weekends:** 90 % **Handicap access:** 100 %
Car regulations: $120 annual sticker
Number with cars: 30 % **Adequacy of on-campus parking:** Fair
Number of fraternities: 1 **Chapter houses:** 1 **Number of sororities:** 1 **Chapter houses:** 0
Students belonging to fraternities: 3 % **Students belonging to sororities:** 2 %

Libraries and Computers

Books: 1.2 Million **Periodicals:** 7,000 **Microform items:** 580,000
Microcomputers available: Yes **Microcomputers networked:** NA

Classes

Faculty / Student Ratio: 1/11 **Classes taught by teacher assistants:** 15 %
Most popular majors: Poly Science, Business **Classes begin:** Early Sept.
Baccalaureate degrees offered: B.PH, BA, BCE, BEE, BFA, BME, B MUS, BS, BS ARCH, BSE, BSN, BSN ED

Sports

Division: III **Except:** **Physical ed requirements:** None
Students participating in intercollegiate sports: 15 % **In intramural sports:** 35 %
Additional intercollegiate and/or intramural sports: (not found at all colleges)

Crew: No **Ice Hockey:** No **Lacrosse:** Yes **Wrestling:** Yes/M
Rugby: Yes **Sailing:** No **Skiing:** No
Squash: No **Ultimate Frisbee:** No **Water Polo:** Yes

Alumni

Number living: NA **Annual giving:** $ NA **Participation:** NA %
Average annual gift: $ NA **Average per student:** $ NA

3-2 Programs (2 degrees in 5 years)

In-house Engineering & Physics

Observation and Opinion of:

Undergraduates and graduates ____________________

____

College counselor ____________________

____

UNIVERSITY OF CHICAGO (Private)

1116 East 59th Street
Chicago, IL 60637

MOST SELECTIVE
(Composite rating of guide books)

Main tel.: 312-702-1234
Admissions tel.: 312-702-8650
Financial aid tel.: 312-702-8850
Scheduled Airline Service: Chicago
Miles to airport: 25

Founded: 1892
Nickname: Maroons
Religious affiliation: None
(Coed since 1892)

Student Body

Undergraduates: 3,400 **Men:** 60 % **Women:** 40 %
Graduate students: 7,400 **Freshman class:** 850

Academics

SAT Averages: 1300 **Verbal:** 640 **Math:** 660 **(Taking SATs:** 80 %)
700-800: V 20 % **M** 38 % **500-600: V** 25 % **M** 13 %
600-700: V 47 % **M** 47 % **400-500: V** 8 % **M** 2 % **300-400: V** NA % **M** NA %
High school class rank: Top fifth 90 % **2nd fifth** NA % **3rd fifth** NA %

Admissions

Applied: 5,500 **Accepted:** 40 % **Matriculated:** %
Deadline: Jan. 15 **Accept common application:** No
Interview recommended: Yes **Off-campus interview available:** Yes
Evaluative: Yes **Informational only:** NA **LD program:** NA
Night in dorm provided: Yes **Non-refundable application fee:** $40
Early decision program: Yes **Applied:** 255 **Accepted:** 77 % **Deadline:** Nov. 15
Freshmen accepted other than Fall term: 0 % **SAT/FAF Code #** 1832

Transfers

Applied: 812 **Accepted:** 22 % **Application deadline for Fall:** Apr. 1 **Spring:** NA
Minimum grades recommended: 3.0 **All new students who were transfers into all classes:** 11 %

Class Experience

Return 2nd year: 93 % **Graduate after 4 years:** 71 % **To graduate school within 5 years:** 80 %

Cost

Tuition deposit: $200 **Total cost (Including school's estimate on fees and books):** $24,600
Tuition: $17,061 **(In state:** $ **)** **Room and board:** $5,940
Annual giving by parents: $126,000 **Average per student:** $12

Financial Aid

Average total package per student: $12,450 **Number receiving aid:** 65 %
Average scholarships and grants: $10,000 **Average loans:** $1,850 **Work-study program:** Yes
Undergraduates working on campus: 80 % **Average earnings:** $2,000
Non-need scholarships 5 % **Athletic scholarships:** NA **FAF deadline:** Feb. 1
Off-campus part-time employment: Excellent **CO-OP program:** No
ROTC: at U of Ill **NROTC:** at U of Ill **AFROTC:** Ill Inst of Tech

Endowment

Total: $1.1 Million **Per student (including graduate students):** $100,000

Location

Acres: 175 **Setting:** Urban **Miles from town center:** 4 (Pop. 3 Mil.)
Miles from (Pop.) **Miles from** (Pop.)

Class Composition

Asian: 15 % **Black:** 4 % **Hispanic:** 3 % **White:** 78 % **Other:** NA %
Total minority : 22% **Foreign countries:** 2 % (80 students)
From public schools: 67 % **Students from in state:** 25 %

Housing (on campus)

Freshmen required to live on campus: Yes **Guaranteed for:** 4 years
Available for all students: 70 % **Fraternity / Sorority housing:** Yes / No
On-campus married student housing: Yes **Women-only dorms available:** NA

Campus Life

Students living on campus: 67 % **Remain weekends:** 90 % **Handicap access:** 50 %
Car regulations: None
Number with cars: 15 % **Adequacy of on-campus parking:** Good
Number of fraternities: 8 **Chapter houses:** 5 **Number of sororities:** 2 **Chapter houses:** 0
Students belonging to fraternities: 8 % **Students belonging to sororities:** 2 %

Libraries and Computers

Books: 5.1 Million **Periodicals:** 50,000 **Microform items:** 1.5 Mil.
Microcomputers available: Yes **Microcomputers networked:** Yes

Classes

Faculty / Student Ratio: 1/6 **Classes taught by teacher assistants:** 15 %
Most popular majors: Economics, English **Classes begin:** Early Oct.
Baccalaureate degrees offered: BA, BS

Sports

Division: III **Except:** **Physical ed requirements:** Three quarters
Students participating in intercollegiate sports: 15 % **In intramural sports:** 75 %
Additional intercollegiate and/or intramural sports: (not found at all colleges)

Crew: Yes	**Ice Hockey:** Yes/M	**Lacrosse:** No	**Wrestling:** Yes/M
Rugby: No	**Sailing:** Yes	**Skiing:** Yes	
Squash: Yes	**Ultimate Frisbee:** Yes	**Water Polo:** No	

Alumni

Number living: 103,000 **Annual giving:** $14.7 million **Participation:** 35 %
Average annual gift: $480 **Average per student:** $1,780

3-2 Programs (2 degrees in 5 years)

In-house for Business, Law, Social Work. Also Public Policy and Library Science

Observation and Opinion of:

Undergraduates and graduates ______________________________

____

College counselor ______________________________

____

CLARK UNIVERSITY (Private)

950 Main Street
Worcester, MA 01610-1477

VERY SELECTIVE
(Composite rating of guide books)

Main tel.: 508-793-7711
Admissions tel.: 508-793-7431
Financial aid tel.: 508-793-7478
Scheduled Airline Service: Boston
Miles to airport: 40

Founded: 1887
Nickname: Cougars
Religious affiliation: None
(Coed since 1909)

Student Body

Undergraduates: 2,200 **Men:** 40 % **Women:** 60 %
Graduate students: 700 **Freshman class:** 460

Academics

SAT Averages: 1090 **Verbal:** 510 **Math:** 580 **(Taking SATs:** NA %**)**
700-800: V NA % **M** NA % **500-600: V** NA % **M** NA %
600-700: V NA % **M** NA % **400-500: V`**NA % **M** NA % **300-400: V** NA % **M** NA %
High school class rank: Top fifth 63 % **2nd fifth** 31 % **3rd fifth** 6 %

Admissions

Applied: 3,050 **Accepted:** 71 % **Matriculated:** 21 %
Deadline: Feb. 15 **Accept common application:** Yes
Interview recommended: NA **Off-campus interview available:** No
Evaluative: No **Informational only:** Yes **LD program:** Yes
Night in dorm provided: No **Non-refundable application fee:** $40
Early decision program: Yes **Applied:** 65 **Accepted:** 66 % **Deadline:** Dec. 1
Freshmen accepted other than Fall term: 1 % **SAT/FAF Code #** 3279

Transfers

Applied: 291 **Accepted:** 70 % **Application deadline for Fall:** Apr. 15 **Spring:** Nov. 15
Minimum grades recommended: 2.8 **All new students who were transfers into all classes:** 19 %

Class Experience

Return 2nd year: 87 % **Graduate after 4 years:** 70 % **To graduate school within 5 years:** 70 %

Cost

Tuition deposit: $100 **Total cost (Including school's estimate on fees and books):** $21,365
Tuition: $15,800 **(In state:** $ **)** **Room and board:** $4,500
Annual giving by parents: $480,000 **Average per student:** $160

Financial Aid

Average total package per student: $ **Number receiving aid:** 43 %
Average scholarships and grants: $13,100 **Average loans:** $ **Work-study program:** Yes
Undergraduates working on campus: 36 % **Average earnings:** $1,000
Non-need scholarships % **Athletic scholarships:** No **FAF deadline:** Feb. 1
Off-campus part-time employment: Excellent **CO-OP program:** No
ROTC: at WPI **NROTC:** at Holy Cross **AFROTC:** at WPI

Endowment

Total: $50 Million **Per student (including graduate students):** $18,000

Location

Acres: 45 **Setting:** City
Miles from town center: 3 **(Pop.** 158,000**)**
38 **Miles from** Boston **(Pop.** 600,000 **)**
Miles from **(Pop.** **)**

Class Composition

Asian: 4 % **Black:** 3 % **Hispanic:** 2 % **White:** 74 % **Other:** 17 %
Total minority : 26 % **Foreign countries:** 9 % (200 students)
From public schools: 69 % **Students from in state:** 30 %

Housing (on campus)

Freshmen required to live on campus: Yes
Available for all students: 70 %
On-campus married student housing:
Guaranteed for: 1 year
Fraternity / Sorority housing: No / No
Women-only dorms available: Yes

Campus Life

Students living on campus: 67 % **Remain weekends:** 60 % **Handicap access:** 80 %
Car regulations: Freshmen prohibited
Number with cars: NA %
Adequacy of on-campus parking: Good
Number of fraternities: 0 **Chapter houses:** 0
Students belonging to fraternities: 0 %
Number of sororities: 0 **Chapter houses:** 0
Students belonging to sororities: 0 %

Libraries and Computers

Books: 500,000 **Periodicals:** 2,100 **Microform items:** 58,000
Microcomputers available: Yes **Microcomputers networked:** Yes

Classes

Faculty / Student Ratio: 1/13 **Classes taught by teacher assistants:** 0 %
Most popular majors: Government, Economics, Psychology **Classes begin:** Late Aug.
Baccalaureate degrees offered: BA, BFA, BS

Sports

Division: III **Except:** **Physical ed requirements:** None
Students participating in intercollegiate sports: 15 % **In intramural sports:** 40 %
Additional intercollegiate and/or intramural sports: (not found at all colleges)

Crew: Yes	**Ice Hockey:** Yes	**Lacrosse:** Yes	**Wrestling:** No
Rugby: No	**Sailing:** No	**Skiing:** No	
Squash: Yes	**Ultimate Frisbee:** Yes	**Water Polo:** Yes	

Alumni

Number living: 18,000 **Annual giving:** $2 Million **Participation:** 42 %
Average annual gift: $NA **Average per student:** $700

3-2 Programs (2 degrees in 5 years)

Engineering with Columbia, 5 year BA/MA Program, 5 year BA/MA in Biology, Environment

Observation and Opinion of:

Undergraduates and graduates ______________________________

____

College counselor ______________________________

____

COLBY COLLEGE (Private)

Waterville, Maine 04901

HIGHLY SELECTIVE
(Composite rating of guide books)

Main tel.: 207-872-3060
Admissions tel.: 207-872-3168
Financial aid tel.: 207-872-3379
Scheduled Airline Service: Washington
Miles to airport: NA

Founded: 1813
Nickname: Mules
Religious affiliation: None
(Coed since 1871)

Student Body

Undergraduates: 1,700 **Men:** 50 % **Women:** 50 %
Graduate students: 0 **Freshman class:** 415

Academics

SAT Averages: 1200 **Verbal:** 580 **Math:** 620 **(Taking SATs:** 95 %**)**
700-800: V 1 % **M** 9 % **500-600: V** 50 % **M** 33 %
600-700: V 37 % **M** 52 % **400-500: V** 12 % **M** 6 % **300-400: V** NA % **M** NA %
High school class rank: Top fifth 60 % **2nd fifth** 78 % **3rd fifth** NA %

Admissions

Applied: 3,170 **Accepted:** 41 % **Matriculated:** 32 %
Deadline: Jan. 15 **Accept common application:** No
Interview recommended: Yes **Off-campus interview available:** Yes
Evaluative: Yes **Informational only:** No **LD program:** NA
Night in dorm provided: Yes **Non-refundable application fee:** $40
Early decision program: Yes **Applied:** 309 **Accepted:** 40 % **Deadline:** Nov. 15
Freshmen accepted other than Fall term: 7 % **SAT/FAF Code #** 3280

Transfers

Applied: 209 **Accepted:** 15 % **Application deadline for Fall:** Mar. 1 **Spring:** Dec. 1
Minimum grades recommended: 3.0 **All new students who were transfers into all classes:** 3 %

Class Experience

Return 2nd year: 95 % **Graduate after 4 years:** 81 % **To graduate school within 5 years:** 65 %

Cost

Tuition deposit: $200 **Total cost (Including school's estimate on fees and books):** $23,100
Tuition: $16,810 **(In state:** $ **)** **Room and board:** $5,500
Annual giving by parents: $300,000 **Average per student:** $170

Financial Aid

Average total package per student: $15,500 **Number receiving aid:** 31 %
Average scholarships and grants: $13,400 **Average loans:** $2,100 **Work-study program:** Yes
Undergraduates working on campus: 65 % **Average earnings:** $1,400
Non-need scholarships 0 % **Athletic scholarships:** No **FAF deadline:** Feb. 1
Off-campus part-time employment: Fair **CO-OP program:** No
ROTC: at U of Maine **NROTC:** No **AFROTC:** at U of Maine

Endowment

Total: $78 Million **Per student (including graduate students):** $45,000

Location

Acres: 80 **Setting:** NW Washington **Miles from town center:** 3 (Pop. 700,000)
Miles from (Pop.) **Miles from** (Pop.)

Class Composition

Asian: 3 % **Black:** 7 % **Hispanic:** 4 % **White:** 78 % **Other:** 8 %
Total minority : 22 % **Foreign countries:** 12 % (1000 students)
From public schools: 80 % **Students from in state:** 10 %

Housing (on campus)

Freshmen required to live on campus: No **Guaranteed for:** 1 year
Available for all students: 60 % **Fraternity / Sorority housing:** No / No
On-campus married student housing: No **Women-only dorms available:** No

Campus Life

Students living on campus: 60 % **Remain weekends:** NA % **Handicap access:** 90 %
Car regulations: No freshmen or sophomores
Number with cars: 30 % **Adequacy of on-campus parking:** Poor
Number of fraternities: 7 **Chapter houses:** 3 **Number of sororities:** 7 **Chapter houses:** 0
Students belonging to fraternities: 11 % **Students belonging to sororities:** 7 %

Libraries and Computers

Books: 500,000 **Periodicals:** 2,700 **Microform items:** 500,000
Microcomputers available: 150 **Microcomputers networked:** NA

Classes

Faculty / Student Ratio: 1/15 **Classes taught by teacher assistants:** 15 %
Most popular majors: Communications, International Studies **Classes begin:** Aug. & Jan.
Baccalaureate degrees offered: BA, BFA, BOS, B Mus, BS, BSBA, BA Tech Mgmt

Sports

Division: I **Except:** **Physical ed requirements:** None
Students participating in intercollegiate sports: 5 % **In intramural sports:** 58 %
Additional intercollegiate and/or intramural sports: (not found at all colleges)

Crew:	**Ice Hockey:**	**Lacrosse:**	**Wrestling:** No
Rugby: Yes/M	**Sailing:**	**Skiing:**	
Squash: Yes	**Ultimate Frisbee:**	**Water Polo:**	

Alumni

Number living: 50,000 **Annual giving:** $2.9 million **Participation:** 13 %
Average annual gift: $470 **Average per student:** $320

3-2 Programs (2 degrees in 5 years)

Engineering U of Maryland & Washington U

Observation and Opinion of:

Undergraduates and graduates ____________________

____

College counselor ____________________

____

COLGATE UNIVERSITY (Private)

13 Oak Drive
Hamilton, NY 13346

HIGHLY SELECTIVE
(Composite rating of guide books)

Main tel.: 315-824-1000
Admissions tel.: 315-824-7401
Financial aid tel.: 315-824-7431
Scheduled Airline Service: Syracuse
Miles to airport: 40

Founded: 1817
Nickname: Red Raiders
Religious affiliation: None
(Coed since 1970)

Student Body

Undergraduates: 2,700 **Men:** 55 % **Women:** 45 %
Graduate students: 0 **Freshman class:** 685

Academics

SAT Averages: 1250 **Verbal:** 595 **Math:** 655 **(Taking SATs:** 98 %)
700-800: V 2 % M 5 % **500-600:** V 48 % M 47 %
600-700: V 24 % M 40 % **400-500:** V 23 % M 7 % **300-400:** V NA % M NA %
High school class rank: Top fifth 83 % **2nd fifth** 14 % **3rd fifth** NA %

Admissions

Applied: 5,200 **Accepted:** 43 % **Matriculated:** 30 %
Deadline: Jan. 15 **Accept common application:** Yes
Interview recommended: No **Off-campus interview available:** Yes
Evaluative: No **Informational only:** Yes **LD program:** No
Night in dorm provided: Yes **Non-refundable application fee:** $50
Early decision program: Yes **Applied:** 311 **Accepted:** 49 % **Deadline:** Jan. 15
Freshmen accepted other than Fall term: 10 % **SAT/FAF Code #** 2086

Transfers

Applied: 207 **Accepted:** 30 % **Application deadline for Fall:** Mar. 15 **Spring:** Nov. 15
Minimum grades recommended: 3.0 **All new students who were transfers into all classes:** 5 %

Class Experience

Return 2nd year: 96 % **Graduate after 4 years:** 85 % **To graduate school within 5 years:** 30 %

Cost

Tuition deposit: $300 **Total cost (Including school's estimate on fees and books):** $22,690
Tuition: $17,275 **(In state:** $) **Room and board:** $5,275
Annual giving by parents: $400,000 **Average per student:** $150

Financial Aid

Average total package per student: $14,100 **Number receiving aid:** 40 %
Average scholarships and grants: $12,100 **Average loans:** $2,000 **Work-study program:** Yes
Undergraduates working on campus: 60 % **Average earnings:** $1,000
Non-need scholarships 0 % **Athletic scholarships:** NA **FAF deadline:** Feb. 1
Off-campus part-time employment: Poor **CO-OP program:** No
ROTC: No **NROTC:** No **AFROTC:** No

Endowment

Total: $147 Million **Per student (including graduate students):** $55,000

Location

Acres: 1400 **Setting:** Rural
Miles from town center: 0 **(Pop.** 3,000**)**
38 **Miles from** Syracuse **(Pop.** 170,000 **)**
30 **Miles from** Utica **(Pop.** 75,000 **)**

Class Composition

Asian: 5 % **Black:** 5 % **Hispanic:** 2 % **White:** 84 % **Other:** 4 %
Total minority : 16 % **Foreign countries:** 4 % (110 students)
From public schools: % **Students from in state:** 35 %

Housing (on campus)

Freshmen required to live on campus: Yes
Guaranteed for: 1 year
Available for all students: 65 %
Fraternity / Sorority housing: Yes / Yes
On-campus married student housing: Yes
Women-only dorms available: Yes

Campus Life

Students living on campus: 65 % **Remain weekends:** 90 % **Handicap access:** 50 %
Car regulations: All classes
Number with cars: 42 %
Adequacy of on-campus parking: Fair
Number of fraternities: 9 **Chapter houses:** 9
Number of sororities: 5 **Chapter houses:** 3
Students belonging to fraternities: 37 %
Students belonging to sororities: 32%

Libraries and Computers

Books: 473,000 **Periodicals:** 2,550 **Microform items:** 318,000
Microcomputers available: Yes **Microcomputers networked:** NA

Classes

Faculty / Student Ratio: 1/11 **Classes taught by teacher assistants:** 0 %
Most popular majors: Poly Science, English, History **Classes begin:** Late Aug.
Baccalaureate degrees offered: BA

Sports

Division: I **Except:** **Physical ed requirements:** 4 semesters
Students participating in intercollegiate sports: 34 % **In intramural sports:** 47 %
Additional intercollegiate and/or intramural sports: (not found at all colleges)

Crew: Yes	**Ice Hockey:** Yes	**Lacrosse:** Yes	**Wrestling:** No
Rugby: Yes	**Sailing:** Yes	**Skiing:** Yes	
Squash: Yes	**Ultimate Frisbee:** Yes	**Water Polo:** Yes	

Alumni

Number living: 24,000 **Annual giving:** $5.8 Million **Participation:** 51 %
Average annual gift: $500 **Average per student:** $500

3-2 Programs (2 degrees in 5 years)

Engineering: with Columbia, Cornell, Dartmouth and RPI
Architecture with Washington U

Observation and Opinion of:

Undergraduates and graduates ________________________________

____

College counselor ________________________________

____

COLORADO COLLEGE (Private)

Colorado, Springs, CO 80903

HIGHLY SELECTIVE
(Composite rating of guide books)

Main tel.: 719-389-6000
Admissions tel.: 719-389-6344
Financial aid tel.: 719-389-6651
Scheduled Airline Service: Colorado Springs
Miles to airport: 8

Founded: 1874
Nickname: Tigers
Religious affiliation: None
(Coed since 1874)

Student Body

Undergraduates: 1,900 **Men:** 45 % **Women:** 55 %
Graduate students: 22 **Freshman class:** 494

Academics

SAT Averages: 1160 **Verbal:** 560 **Math:** 600 **(Taking SATs: 87 %)**
700-800: V 4 % **M** 11 % **500-600: V** 40 % **M** 36 %
600-700: V 24 % **M** 40 % **400-500: V** 21 % **M** 9 % **300-400: V** 4 % **M** 2 %
High school class rank: Top fifth 75 % **2nd fifth** 19 % **3rd fifth** 3 %

Admissions

Applied: 2,770 **Accepted:** 50 % **Matriculated:** 36 %
Deadline: Feb. 1 **Accept common application:** Yes
Interview recommended: No **Off-campus interview available:** Yes
Evaluative: No **Informational only:** Yes **LD program:** Yes
Night in dorm provided: **Non-refundable application fee:** $30
Early decision program: Yes **Applied:** NA **Accepted:** NA % **Deadline:** NA
Freshmen accepted other than Fall term: 0 % **SAT/FAF Code #** 4072

Transfers

Applied: 453 **Accepted:** 37 % **Application deadline for Fall:** Apr. 1 **Spring:** Nov. 1
Minimum grades recommended: C **All new students who were transfers into all classes:** 11 %

Class Experience

Return 2nd year: 90 % **Graduate after 4 years:** 75 % **To graduate school within 5 years:** 55 %

Cost

Tuition deposit: $100 **Total cost (Including school's estimate on fees and books):** $18,700
Tuition: $14,760 **(In state:** $ **)** **Room and board:** $3,800
Annual giving by parents: $370,000 **Average per student:** $360

Financial Aid

Average total package per student: $12,700 **Number receiving aid:** 40 %
Average scholarships and grants: $10,900 **Average loans:** $1,800 **Work-study program:** Yes
Undergraduates working on campus: 38 % **Average earnings:** $800
Non-need scholarships 12 % **Athletic scholarships:** Yes **FAF deadline:** Feb. 15
Off-campus part-time employment: Good **CO-OP program:** No
ROTC: at U of Colorado **NROTC:** No **AFROTC:** No

Endowment

Total: $144 Million **Per student (including graduate students):** $65,000

Location

Acres: 90 **Setting:** Urban
70 Miles from Denver (Pop. 490,000)
Miles from town center: 0 (Pop. 273,000)
Miles from (Pop.)

Class Composition

Asian: 2 % **Black:** 1 % **Hispanic:** 4 % **White:** 82 % **Other:** 10 %
Total minority : 18 % **Foreign countries:** 4 % (40 students)
From public schools: 75 % **Students from in state:** 30 %

Housing (on campus)

Freshmen required to live on campus: Yes
Available for all students: 70 %
On-campus married student housing: Yes
Guaranteed for: 4 years
Fraternity / Sorority housing: Yes / Yes
Women-only dorms available: Yes

Campus Life

Students living on campus: 67 % **Remain weekends:** NA % **Handicap access:** 85 %
Car regulations: All 4 years
Number with cars: 38 %
Adequacy of on-campus parking: Good
Number of fraternities: 4 **Chapter houses:** 4
Number of sororities: 4 **Chapter houses:** 4
Students belonging to fraternities: 33 %
Students belonging to sororities: 33 %

Libraries and Computers

Books: 475,000 **Periodicals:** 1,300 **Microform items:** 20,000
Microcomputers available: Yes **Microcomputers networked:** NA

Classes

Faculty / Student Ratio: 1/13 **Classes taught by teacher assistants:** 0 %
Most popular majors: English, Biology, Economics **Classes begin:** Early Sept.
Baccalaureate degrees offered: BA

Sports

Division: III **Except:** **Physical ed requirements:** None
Students participating in intercollegiate sports: 16 % **In intramural sports:** 70 %
Additional intercollegiate and/or intramural sports: (not found at all colleges)

Crew: No	**Ice Hockey:** Yes	**Lacrosse:** Yes	**Wrestling:** No
Rugby: Yes	**Sailing:** No	**Skiing:** Yes	
Squash: Yes	**Ultimate Frisbee:** Yes	**Water Polo:** No	

Alumni

Number living: 18,000 **Annual giving:** $1.5 Million **Participation:** 40 %
Average annual gift: $250 **Average per student:** $800

3-2 Programs (2 degrees in 5 years)

Engineering with Columbia, RPI, So Cal, Wash U
Computer Science with Wash U, Forestry and Environmental Studies with Duke U
6 Year BA/JD Program with Columbia

Observation and Opinion of:

Undergraduates and graduates ____________________

____

College counselor ____________________

____

UNIVERSITY OF COLORADO (Public)

Regent Drive
Colorado Springs, CO 80309

SELECTIVE
(Composite rating of guide books)

Main tel.: 303-492-1411
Admissions tel.: 303-492-6301
Financial aid tel.: 303-492-5091
Scheduled Airline Service: Denver
Miles to airport: 30

Founded: 1876
Nickname: Buffalos
Religious affiliation: None
(Coed since 1876)

Student Body

Undergraduates: 20,000 **Men:** 55 % **Women:** 45 %
Graduate students: 4,700 **Freshman class:** 3,777

Academics

SAT Averages: 1085 **Verbal:** 500 **Math:** 585 (Taking SATs: 82 %)
700-800: V 1 % **M** 9 % **500-600: V** 45 % **M** 40 %
600-700: V 13 % **M** 35 % **400-500: V** 40 % **M** 15 % **300-400: V** NA % **M** NA %
High school class rank: Top fifth 59 % **2nd fifth** 30 % **3rd fifth** 8 %

Admissions

Applied: 13,200 **Accepted:** 74 % **Matriculated:** 39 %
Deadline: Feb. 15 **Accept common application:** Yes
Interview recommended: Yes **Off-campus interview available:** No
Evaluative: No **Informational only:** Yes **LD program:** No
Night in dorm provided: No **Non-refundable application fee:** $30
Early decision program: No **Applied:** NA **Accepted:** NA % **Deadline:** NA
Freshmen accepted other than Fall term: 10 % **SAT/FAF Code #** 4841

Transfers

Applied: 4,570 **Accepted:** 65 % **Application deadline for Fall:** Apr. 1 **Spring:** Nov. 1
Minimum grades recommended: 2.5 **All new students who were transfers into all classes:** 9 %

Class Experience

Return 2nd year: 82 % **Graduate after 4 years:** 55 % **To graduate school within 5 years:** NA %

Cost

Tuition deposit: $200 **Total cost (Including school's estimate on fees and books):** $14,500
Tuition: $10,900 **(In state:** $ 2,200**)** **Room and board:** $3,550
Annual giving by parents: $110,000 **Average per student:** $5

Financial Aid

Average total package per student: $3,050 **Number receiving aid:** 30 %
Average scholarships and grants: $1,750 **Average loans:** $1,300 **Work-study program:** Yes
Undergraduates working on campus: 70 % **Average earnings:** $1,500
Non-need scholarships 10 % **Athletic scholarships:** Yes **FAF deadline:** Apr. 1
Off-campus part-time employment: Excellent **CO-OP program:** Yes
ROTC: Yes **NROTC:** Yes **AFROTC:** Yes

Endowment

Total: $68 Million **Per student (including graduate students):** $2,600

Location

Acres: 600 **Setting:** Urban
Miles from town center: 1 **(Pop.** 80,000**)**
27 **Miles from** Denver **(Pop.** 490,000 **)**
Miles from **(Pop.** **)**

Class Composition

Asian: 5 **%** **Black:** 2 **%** **Hispanic:** 5 **%** **White:** 87 **%** **Other:** 1 **%**
Total minority : 13 **%** **Foreign countries:** 1 **%** (200 students)
From public schools: NA **% Students from in state:** 65 **%**

Housing (on campus)

Freshmen required to live on campus: No
Guaranteed for: 1 year
Available for all students: 30 **%**
Fraternity / Sorority housing: Yes / Yes
On-campus married student housing: Yes
Women-only dorms available: Yes

Campus Life

Students living on campus: 25 **%** **Remain weekends:** NA **%** **Handicap access:** 85 **%**
Car regulations: $80 for permit
Number with cars: N/A **%**
Adequacy of on-campus parking: OK
Number of fraternities: 22 **Chapter houses:** 18
Number of sororities: 14 **Chapter houses:** 11
Students belonging to fraternities: 15 **%**
Students belonging to sororities: 15 **%**

Libraries and Computers

Books: 2.3 Million **Periodicals:** 25,700 **Microform items:** 4 Million
Microcomputers available: Yes **Microcomputers networked:** Yes

Classes

Faculty / Student Ratio: 1/15 **Classes taught by teacher assistants:** 15 **%**
Most popular majors: Communications, International Studies **Classes begin:** Aug. & Jan.
Baccalaureate degrees offered: BA, BFA, BOS, B Mus, BS, BSBA, BA Tech Mgmt

Sports

Division: I **Except:** **Physical ed requirements:** None
Students participating in intercollegiate sports: 2 **%** **In intramural sports:** 33 **%**
Additional intercollegiate and/or intramural sports: (not found at all colleges)

Crew: No	**Ice Hockey:** Yes/M	**Lacrosse:** Yes	**Wrestling:** Yes
Rugby: Yes	**Sailing:** No	**Skiing:** Yes	
Squash: Yes	**Ultimate Frisbee:** Yes	**Water Polo:** Yes	

Alumni

Number living: N/A **Annual giving:** $5.2 Million **Participation:** NA **%**
Average annual gift: $ NA **Average per student:** $320

3-2 Programs (2 degrees in 5 years)

In-house in Engineering and Business

Observation and Opinion of:

Undergraduates and graduates ______________________________

____

College counselor ______________________________

____

COLUMBIA UNIVERSITY (Private)

New York, NY 10027

MOST SELECTIVE
(Composite rating of guide books)

Main tel.: 212-854-1754
Admissions tel.: 212-854-2521
Financial aid tel.: 212-854-3711
Scheduled Airline Service: NYC
Miles to airport: 12

Founded: 1754
Nickname: Lions
Religious affiliation: None
(Coed since 1983)

Student Body

Undergraduates: 3,200 **Men:** 55 % **Women:** 45 %
Graduate students: 0 **Freshman class:** 780

Academics

SAT Averages: 1270 **Verbal:** 610 **Math:** 660 **(Taking SATs:** 100 %**)**
700-800: V 15 % M 35 % **500-600:** V 25 % M 20 %
600-700: V 50 % M 40 % **400-500:** V 10 % M 5 % **300-400:** V NA % M NA %
High school class rank: Top fifth 95 % **2nd fifth** 5 % **3rd fifth** NA %

Admissions

Applied: 6,500 **Accepted:** 28 % **Matriculated:** 43 %
Deadline: Jan. 15 **Accept common application:** No
Interview recommended: Yes **Off-campus interview available:** Yes
Evaluative: Yes **Informational only:** No **LD program:** No
Night in dorm provided: No **Non-refundable application fee:** $50
Early decision program: Yes **Applied:** NA **Accepted:** NA % **Deadline:** Nov. 1
Freshmen accepted other than Fall term: 0 % **SAT/FAF Code #** 2116

Transfers

Applied: 721 **Accepted:** 16 % **Application deadline for Fall:** Apr. 1 **Spring:** Nov. 1
Minimum grades recommended: 3.0 **All new students who were transfers into all classes:** NA %

Class Experience

Return 2nd year: 98 % **Graduate after 4 years:** 92 % **To graduate school within 5 years:** 90 %

Cost

Tuition deposit: $250 **Total cost (Including school's estimate on fees and books):** $24,000
Tuition: $16,500 **(In state:** $ **)** **Room and board:** $6,500
Annual giving by parents: $180,000 **Average per student:** $70

Financial Aid

Average total package per student: $10,500 **Number receiving aid:** 60 %
Average scholarships and grants: $8,000 **Average loans:** $2,500 **Work-study program:** Yes
Undergraduates working on campus: 60 % **Average earnings:** $1,500
Non-need scholarships 0 % **Athletic scholarships:** 0 **FAF deadline:** Feb. 1
Off-campus part-time employment: Good **CO-OP program:** No
ROTC: at Fordham **NROTC:** No **AFROTC:** at Manhattan

Endowment

Total: $1.5 Million **Per student (including graduate students):** $90,000

Location

Acres: 27 **Setting:** City **Miles from town center:** 6 (Pop. 8 Million)
Miles from (Pop.) **Miles from** (Pop.)

Class Composition

Asian: 12 % **Black:** 7 % **Hispanic:** 7 % **White:** 71 % **Other:** 3 %
Total minority : 29 % **Foreign countries:** 3 % (95 students)
From public schools: 88 % **Students from in state:** 20 %

Housing (on campus)

Freshmen required to live on campus: No **Guaranteed for:** 1 year
Available for all students: 95 % **Fraternity / Sorority housing:** Yes / No
On-campus married student housing: No **Women-only dorms available:** No

Campus Life

Students living on campus: 92 % **Remain weekends:** 85 % **Handicap access:** NA %
Car regulations: Students advised against
Number with cars: 1 % **Adequacy of on-campus parking:** No Parking
Number of fraternities: 17 **Chapter houses:** 15 **Number of sororities:** 5 **Chapter houses:** 0
Students belonging to fraternities: 13 % **Students belonging to sororities:** 13 %

Libraries and Computers

Books: 6 Million **Periodicals:** 60,000 **Microform items:** 9 Million
Microcomputers available: Yes **Microcomputers networked:** Yes

Classes

Faculty / Student Ratio: 1/8 **Classes taught by teacher assistants:** 10 %
Most popular majors: English, History, Poly Science **Classes begin:** Early Sept.
Baccalaureate degrees offered: BA

Sports

Division: I **Except:** **Physical ed requirements:** 2 semesters
Students participating in intercollegiate sports: 15 % **In intramural sports:** 50 %
Additional intercollegiate and/or intramural sports: (not found at all colleges)

Crew: Yes	**Ice Hockey:** Yes/M	**Lacrosse:** Yes	**Wrestling:** Yes/M
Rugby: Yes/M	**Sailing:** Yes	**Skiing:** Yes	
Squash: Yes	**Ultimate Frisbee:** Yes	**Water Polo:** Yes/M	

Alumni

Number living: 196,000 **Annual giving:** $32 Million **Participation:** 20 %
Average annual gift: $850 **Average per student:** $10,000

3-2 Programs (2 degrees in 5 years)

In-house Engineering
BA/MA Music with Julliard School

Observation and Opinion of:

Undergraduates and graduates ______________________________

____

College counselor ______________________________

____

CONNECTICUT COLLEGE (Private)

270 Muhegan Avenue
New London, CT 06320-4196

HIGHLY SELECTIVE
(Composite rating of guide books)

Main tel.: 203-447-1911
Admissions tel.: 203-439-2200
Financial aid tel.: 203-439-2059
Scheduled Airline Service: Hartford
Miles to airport: 58

Founded: 1911
Nickname: Camels
Religious affiliation: None
(Coed since 1969)

Student Body

Undergraduates: 1,600 **Men:** 45 % **Women:** 55 %
Graduate students: 75 **Freshman class:** 450

Academics

SAT Averages: 1225 **Verbal:** 600 **Math:** 625 **(Taking SATs:** 92 %**)**
700-800: V 6 % M 15 % **500-600:** V 35 % M 30 %
600-700: V 50 % M 50 % **400-500:** V 8 % M 5 % **300-400:** V NA % M NA %
High school class rank: Top fifth 67 % **2nd fifth** 27 % **3rd fifth** 6 %

Admissions

Applied: 3,300 **Accepted:** 45 % **Matriculated:** 30 %
Deadline: Jan. 15 **Accept common application:** Yes
Interview recommended: Yes **Off-campus interview available:** Yes
Evaluative: Yes **Informational only:** No **LD program:** NA
Night in dorm provided: Yes **Non-refundable application fee:** $35
Early decision program: Yes **Applied:** NA **Accepted:** NA % **Deadline:** Nov. 15
Freshmen accepted other than Fall term: 0 % **SAT/FAF Code #** 3284

Transfers

Applied: 180 **Accepted:** 45 % **Application deadline for Fall:** Apr. 1 **Spring:** Dec.1
Minimum grades recommended: 3.0 **All new students who were transfers into all classes:** 2 %

Class Experience

Return 2nd year: 98 % **Graduate after 4 years:** 85 % **To graduate school within 5 years:** 21 %

Cost

Tuition deposit: $250 **Total cost (Including school's estimate on fees and books):** $23,500
Tuition: $17,000 **(In state:** $ **)** **Room and board:** $5,700
Annual giving by parents: $277,000 **Average per student:** $170

Financial Aid

Average total package per student: $12,800 **Number receiving aid:** 42 %
Average scholarships and grants: $10,400 **Average loans:** $2,400 **Work-study program:** Yes
Undergraduates working on campus: NA % **Average earnings:** $950
Non-need scholarships 0 % **Athletic scholarships:** 0 **FAF deadline:** Feb. 15
Off-campus part-time employment: Good **CO-OP program:** No
ROTC: No **NROTC:** No **AFROTC:** No

Endowment

Total: $43 Million **Per student (including graduate students):** $27,000

Location

Acres: 700 **Setting:** Urban
47 **Miles from** Hartford **(Pop.** 135,000 **)**
Miles from town center: 2 **(Pop.** 35,000 **)**
Miles from **(Pop.** **)**

Class Composition

Asian: 4 % **Black:** 5 % **Hispanic:** 4 % **White:** 87 % **Other:** NA %
Total minority : 13 % **Foreign countries:** 5 % (80 students)
From public schools: 50 % **Students from in state:** 20 %

Housing (on campus)

Freshmen required to live on campus: Yes
Available for all students: NA %
On-campus married student housing: NA
Guaranteed for: 4 years
Fraternity / Sorority housing: No / No
Women Only Dorms Available No

Campus Life

Students living on campus: 98 % **Remain weekends:** 95 % **Handicap access:** 50 %
Car regulations: All may have
Number with cars: 50 %
Adequacy of on-campus parking: Fair
Number of fraternities: 0 **Chapter houses:** 0
Number of sororities: 0 **Chapter houses:** 0
Students belonging to fraternities: 0 %
Students belonging to sororities: 0 %

Libraries and Computers

Books: 500,000 **Periodicals:** 2,700 **Microform items:** 500,000
Microcomputers available: 150 **Microcomputers networked:** NA

Classes

Faculty / Student Ratio: 1/12 **Classes taught by teacher assistants:** 0 %
Most popular majors: Government, History, Psychology **Classes begin:** Late Aug.
Baccalaureate degrees offered: BA

Sports

Division: III **Except:** **Physical ed requirements:** None
Students participating in intercollegiate sports: 70 % **In intramural sports:** 80 %
Additional intercollegiate and/or intramural sports: (not found at all colleges)

Crew: Yes	**Ice Hockey:** Yes	**Lacrosse:** Yes	**Wrestling:** No
Rugby: Yes	**Sailing:** Yes	**Skiing:** Yes	
Squash: Yes	**Ultimate Frisbee:** Yes	**Water Polo:** Yes	

Alumni

Number living: 16,000 **Annual giving:** $4.5 Million **Participation:** 40 %
Average annual gift: $700 **Average per student:** $2,600

3-2 Programs (2 degrees in 5 years)

Engineering with Washington U
Cross-registration with Trinity, Wesleyan and Coast Guard
Member of 12 College Exchange Programs

Observation and Opinion of:

Undergraduates and graduates ______________________

____

College counselor ______________________

____

CORNELL UNIVERSITY (Private)

Ithaca, NY 14853

MOST SELECTIVE
(Composite rating of guide books)

Main tel.: 607-255-2000
Admissions tel.: 607-255-5241
Financial aid tel.: 607-255-5145
Scheduled Airline Service: Ithaca
Miles to airport: 10

Founded: 1865
Nickname: Big Red
Religious affiliation: None
(Coed since 1891)

Student Body

Undergraduates: 12,400 **Men:** 57 % **Women:** 43 %
Graduate students: 5,500 **Freshman class:** 2,900

Academics

SAT Averages: 1290 **Verbal:** 500 **Math:** 690 **(Taking SATs:** 99 %**)**
700-800: V 10 % **M** 43 % **500-600: V** 34 % **M** 13 %
600-700: V 49 % **M** 43 % **400-500: V** 10 % **M** 1 % **300-400: V** 2 % **M** 1 %
High school class rank: Top fifth 96 % **2nd fifth** 4 % **3rd fifth** NA %

Admissions

Applied: 20,200 **Accepted:** 30 % **Matriculated:** 49 %
Deadline: Jan. 1 **Accept common application:** No
Interview recommended: Yes **Off-campus interview available:** Yes
Evaluative: No **Informational only:** Yes **LD program:** Yes
Night in dorm provided: Yes **Non-refundable application fee:** $50
Early decision program: Yes **Applied:** 2,300 **Accepted:** 37 % **Deadline:** Nov. 1
Freshmen accepted other than Fall term: 3 % **SAT/FAF Code #** 2098

Transfers

Applied: 2,500 **Accepted:** 38 % **Application deadline for Fall:** Mar. 1 **Spring:** Oct. 15
Minimum grades recommended: NA **All new students who were transfers into all classes:** 15 %

Class Experience

Return 2nd year: 95 % **Graduate after 4 years:** 80 % **To graduate school within 5 years:** 26 %

Cost

Tuition deposit: $200 **Total cost (Including school's estimate on fees and books):** $20,000
Tuition: $13,250 **(In state:** $7,000**)** **Room and board:** $5,765
Annual giving by parents: $0 **Average per student:** $NA

Financial Aid

Average total package per student: $10,850 **Number receiving aid:** 46 %
Average scholarships and grants: $7,100 **Average loans:** $3,750 **Work-study program:** Yes
Undergraduates working on campus: 41 % **Average earnings:** $1,250
Non-need scholarships 1 % **Athletic scholarships:** NA **FAF deadline:** Feb. 15
Off-campus part-time employment: Fair **CO-OP program:** Yes
ROTC: Yes **NROTC:** Yes **AFROTC:** Yes

Endowment

Total: $954 Million **Per student (including graduate students):** $50,000

Location

Acres: 740 **Setting:** Urban **Miles from town center:** 2 **(Pop.** 29,500)
60 **Miles from** Syracuse **(Pop.** 120,000) **Miles from** **(Pop.**)

Class Composition

Asian: 13 % **Black:** 5 % **Hispanic:** 5 % **White:** 73 % **Other:** 1 %
Total minority : 17 % **Foreign countries:** 4 % (500 students)
From public schools: 75 % **Students from in state:** 47 %

Housing (on campus)

Freshmen required to live on campus: No **Guaranteed for:** 0 year
Available for all students: 45 % **Fraternity / Sorority housing:** Yes / Yes
On-campus married student housing: Yes **Women-only dorms available:** Yes

Campus Life

Students living on campus: 43 % **Remain weekends:** % **Handicap access:** 80%
Car regulations: All may have, expensive
Number with cars: 50 % **Adequacy of on-campus parking:** Fair
Number of fraternities: 47 **Chapter houses:** 47 **Number of sororities:** 16 **Chapter houses:** 15
Students belonging to fraternities: 37 % **Students belonging to sororities:** 32 %

Libraries and Computers

Books: 5.4 Million **Periodicals:** 62,000 **Microform items:** 5 Million
Microcomputers available: Yes **Microcomputers networked:** Yes

Classes

Faculty / Student Ratio: 1/11 **Classes taught by teacher assistants:** 10 %
Most popular majors: Economics, Engineering, Bio Sciences **Classes begin:** Late Aug.
Baccalaureate degrees offered: BA, BARCH, BFA, BS

Sport

Division: I **Except:** **Physical ed requirements:** 2 semesters
Students participating in intercollegiate sports: 10 % **In intramural sports:** 85 %
Additional intercollegiate and/or intramural sports: (not found at all colleges)

Crew: Yes **Ice Hockey:** Yes **Lacrosse:** Yes **Wrestling:** Yes/M
Rugby: Yes **Sailing:** Yes **Skiing:** Yes
Squash: Yes **Ultimate Frisbee:** Yes **Water Polo:** Yes

Alumni

Number living: 137,000 **Annual giving:** $57 million **Participation:** 37 %
Average annual gift: $1,200 **Average per student:** $3,200

3-2 Programs (2 degrees in 5 years)

BA/MA Program in Business Administration
6 Year BS/MBA/ME Program
Cornell-in-Washington Program

Observation and Opinion of:

Undergraduates and graduates ________________

____

College counselor ________________

____

DARTMOUTH COLLEGE (Private)

Hanover, NH 03755

MOST SELECTIVE
(Composite rating of guide books)

Founded: 1769
Nickname: Big Green
Religious affiliation: None
(Coed since 1972)

Main tel.: 603-646-1110
Admissions tel.: 603-646-2875
Financial aid tel.: 603-646-2451
Scheduled Airline Service: Lebanon
Miles to airport: 5

Student Body

Undergraduates: 4,400 **Men:** 56 % **Women:** 44 %
Graduate students: 1,000 **Freshman class:** 1,054

Academics

SAT Averages: 1300 **Verbal:** 618 **Math:** 682 **(Taking SATs:** NA **%)**
700-800: V 15 % **M** 50 % **500-600: V** 26 % **M** 10 %
600-700: V 52 % **M** 38 % **400-500: V** 7 % **M** 2 % **300-400: V** NA % **M** NA %
High school class rank: Top fifth 95 % **2nd fifth** 4 % **3rd fifth** NA %

Admissions

Applied: 8,000 **Accepted:** 25 % **Matriculated:** 52 %
Deadline: Jan. 1 **Accept common application:** No
Interview recommended: Yes **Off-campus interview available:** Yes
Evaluative: Yes **Informational only:** NA **LD program:** Yes
Night in dorm provided: Yes **Non-refundable application fee:** $50
Early decision program: Yes **Applied:** 1100 **Accepted:** 34 % **Deadline:** Nov. 10
Freshmen accepted other than Fall term: 0 % **SAT/FAF Code #** 3351

Transfers

Applied: 298 **Accepted:** 12 % **Application deadline for Fall:** Apr. 15 **Spring:** Nov. 10
Minimum grades recommended: NA **All new students who were transfers into all classes:** 3 %

Class Experience

Return 2nd year: 95 % **Graduate after 4 years:** 94 % **To graduate school within 5 years:** 75 %

Cost

Tuition deposit: $NA **Total cost (Including school's estimate on fees and books):** $24,315
Tuition: $17,229 **(In state:** $ **)** **Room and board:** $3,025
Annual giving by parents: $1.5 Million **Average per student:** $300

Financial Aid

Average total package per student: $NA **Number receiving aid:** 41 %
Average scholarships and grants: $8,800 **Average loans:** $NA **Work-study program:** Yes
Undergraduates working on campus: 50 % **Average earnings:** $1,500
Non-need scholarships 0 % **Athletic scholarships:** No **FAF deadline:** Feb. 10
Off-campus part-time employment: Good **CO-OP program:** No
ROTC: No **NROTC:** No **AFROTC:** No

Endowment

Total: $595 Million **Per student (including graduate students):** $120,000

Location

Acres: 265 **Setting:** Hanover **Miles from town center:** 0 (**Pop.** 10,000)
68 **Miles from** Manchester (**Pop.**) 130 **Miles from** Boston (**Pop.** 600,000)

Class Composition

Asian: 6 % **Black:** 6 % **Hispanic:** 3 % **White:** 80 % **Other:** 5 %
Total minority : 20 % **Foreign countries:** 5 % (220 students)
From public schools: 60 % **Students from in state:** 5 %

Housing (on campus)

Freshmen required to live on campus: Yes **Guaranteed for:** 1 year
Available for all students: 95 % **Fraternity / Sorority housing:** Yes / Yes
On-campus married student housing: Yes **Women-only dorms available:** No

Campus Life

Students living on campus: 88 % **Remain weekends:** NA % **Handicap access:** 50%
Car regulations: Freshmen not allowed
Number with cars: 20 % **Adequacy of on-campus parking:** Limited
Number of fraternities: 22 **Chapter houses:** 22 **Number of sororities:** 9 **Chapter houses:** 5
Students belonging to fraternities: 60 % **Students belonging to sororities:** 60 %

Libraries and Computers

Books: 1.7 Million **Periodicals:** 20,500 **Microform items:** 1.9 Million
Microcomputers available: Yes **Microcomputers networked:** Yes

Classes

Faculty / Student Ratio: 1/12 **Classes taught by teacher assistants:** 0 %
Most popular majors: History, English, Government **Classes begin:** Sept.
Baccalaureate degrees offered: AB, BE

Sports

Division: I **Except:** **Physical ed requirements:** None
Students participating in intercollegiate sports: 42 % **In intramural sports:** 60 %
Additional intercollegiate and/or intramural sports: (not found at all colleges)

Crew: Yes **Ice Hockey:** Yes **Lacrosse:** Yes **Wrestling:** Yes
Rugby: Yes/M **Sailing:** Yes **Skiing:** Yes
Squash: Yes **Ultimate Frisbee:** Yes **Water Polo:** Yes

Alumni

Number living: 45,000 **Annual giving:** $24.4 Million **Participation:** 60 %
Average annual gift: $1,050 **Average per student:** $5,000

3-2 Programs (2 degrees in 5 years)

In-house Engineering, Business and Medicine
Business Administration with Tuck School of Business

Observation and Opinion of:

Undergraduates and graduates ______________________________

____

College counselor ______________________________

____

DAVIDSON COLLEGE (Private)

P.O. Box 1737
Davidson, NC 28036

HIGHLY SELECTIVE
(Composite rating of guide books)

Main tel.: 704-892-2000
Admissions tel.: 704-892-2230
Financial aid tel.: 704-892-2232
Scheduled Airline Service: Charlotte
Miles to airport: 22

Founded: 1837
Nickname: Wildcats
Religious affiliation: Presbyterian
(Coed since 1972)

Student Body

Undergraduates: 1,400 **Men:** 60 % **Women:** 40 %
Graduate students: 0 **Freshman class:** 425

Academics

SAT Averages: 1240 **Verbal:** 600 **Math:** 640 **(Taking SATs:** 80 %**)**
700-800: V 15 % **M** 25 % **500-600: V** 33 % **M** 33 %
600-700: V 50 % **M** 52 % **400-500: V** 2 % **M** 2 % **300-400: V** NA % **M** NA %
High school class rank: Top fifth 90 % **2nd fifth** 92 % **3rd fifth** NA %

Admissions

Applied: 2,000 **Accepted:** 34 % **Matriculated:** 50 %
Deadline: Feb. 1 **Accept common application:** No
Interview recommended: No **Off-campus interview available:** Yes
Evaluative: No **Informational only:** Yes **LD program:** No
Night in dorm provided: Yes **Non-refundable application fee:** $35
Early decision program: Yes **Applied:** 240 **Accepted:** 48 % **Deadline:** Nov. 20
Freshmen accepted other than Fall term: 0 % **SAT/FAF Code #** 5150

Transfers

Applied: 80 **Accepted:** 15 % **Application deadline for Fall:** Apr. 15 **Spring:** Nov. 15
Minimum grades recommended: B **All new students who were transfers into all classes:** NA %

Class Experience

Return 2nd year: 98 % **Graduate after 4 years:** 90 % **To graduate school within 5 years:** 50 %

Cost

Tuition deposit: $300 **Total cost (Including school's estimate on fees and books):** $19,420
Tuition: $14,400 **(In state:** $ **)** **Room and board:** $4,500
Annual giving by parents: $465,000 **Average per student:** $340

Financial Aid

Average total package per student: $9,000 **Number receiving aid:** 30 %
Average scholarships and grants: $7,000 **Average loans:** $2,000 **Work-study program:** Yes
Undergraduates working on campus: 22 % **Average earnings:** $1,200
Non-need scholarships 10 % **Athletic scholarships:** Yes **FAF deadline:** Feb. 15
Off-campus part-time employment: Poor **CO-OP program:** No
ROTC: Yes **NROTC:** No **AFROTC:** at UNC

Endowment

Total: $93 Million **Per student (including graduate students):** $65,000

Location

Acres: 450 **Setting:** Rural
20 **Miles from** Charlotte **(Pop.** 315,000 **)**
Miles from town center: 0 **(Pop.** 3,000**)**
Miles from **(Pop.** **)**

Class Composition

Asian: 3 % **Black:** 4 % **Hispanic:** 1 % **White:** 92 % **Other:** NA %
Total minority : 8 % **Foreign countries:** 5 % (70 students)
From public schools: % **Students from in state:** 30 %

Housing (on campus)

Freshmen required to live on campus: Yes
Available for all students: 90 %
On-campus married student housing: NA
Guaranteed for: 1 year
Fraternity / Sorority housing: Yes / No
Women-only dorms available: Yes

Campus Life

Students living on campus: 89 % **Remain weekends:** 90 % **Handicap access:** 20 %
Car regulations: No freshmen
Number with cars: 60 %
Number of fraternities: 7 **Chapter houses:** 6
Students belonging to fraternities: 50 %
Adequacy of on-campus parking: Good
Number of sororities: 0 **Chapter houses:** 0
Students belonging to sororities: 0 %

Libraries and Computers

Books: 330,000 **Periodicals:** 1,700 **Microform items:** NA
Microcomputers available: Yes **Microcomputers networked:** NA

Classes

Faculty / Student Ratio: 1/12 **Classes taught by teacher assistants:** 0 %
Most popular majors: English, History, Economics **Classes begin:** Late Aug.
Baccalaureate degrees offered: AB, BS

Sports

Division: III **Except:** **Physical ed requirements:** 3 sports by sophomore yr.
Students participating in intercollegiate sports: 25 % **In intramural sports:** 75 %
Additional intercollegiate and/or intramural sports: (not found at all colleges)

Crew: Yes **Ice Hockey:** No **Lacrosse:** Yes **Wrestling:** Yes/M
Rugby: Yes **Sailing:** Yes **Skiing:** Yes
Squash: Yes **Ultimate Frisbee:** Yes **Water Polo:** No

Alumni

Number living: 13,400 **Annual giving:** $6 Million **Participation:** 51 %
Average annual gift: $900 **Average per student:** $4,400

3-2 Programs (2 degrees in 5 years)

Engineering with Columbia, Duke, N Carolina State, Georgia Tech and Washington U

Observation and Opinion of:

Undergraduates and graduates ____________________

____

College counselor ____________________

____

UNIVERSITY OF DELAWARE (Public)

Newark, Delaware 19716

SELECTIVE
(Composite rating of guide books)

Main tel.: 302-831-2000
Admissions tel.: 302-831-1557
Financial aid tel.: 302-831-8761
Scheduled Airline Service: Philadelphia
Miles to airport: 29

Founded: 1833
Nickname: Blue Hens
Religious affiliation: None
(Coed since 1914)

Student Body

Undergraduates: 13,000 **Men:** 37 % **Women:** 63 %
Graduate students: 2,500 **Freshman class:** 2,950

Academics

SAT Averages: 1085 **Verbal:** 510 **Math:** 575 (Taking SATs: 99 %)
700-800: V 1 % **M** 4 % **500-600: V** 33 % **M** 45 %
600-700: V 8 % **M** 26 % **400-500: V** 47 % **M** 21 % **300-400: V** 11 % **M** 4 %
High school class rank: Top fifth 65 % **2nd fifth** 85 % **3rd fifth** NA %

Admissions

Applied: 12,800 **Accepted:** 70 % **Matriculated:** 33 %
Deadline: Mar. 1 **Accept common application:** No
Interview recommended: No **Off-campus interview available:** No
Evaluative: No **Informational only:** Yes **LD program:** Yes
Night in dorm provided: Yes **Non-refundable application fee:** $35
Early decision program: No **Applied:** NA **Accepted:** NA % **Deadline:** NA
Freshmen accepted other than Fall term: 2 % **SAT/FAF Code #** 5811

Transfers

Applied: 2,120 **Accepted:** 67 % **Application deadline for Fall:** Mar. 1 **Spring:** Nov. 15
Minimum grades recommended: C **All new students who were transfers into all classes:** 21 %

Class Experience

Return 2nd year: 87 % **Graduate after 4 years:** 50 % **To graduate school within 1 year:** 17 %

Cost

Tuition deposit: $200 **Total cost (Including school's estimate on fees and books):** $14,800
Tuition: $8,000 (In state: $3,400) **Room and board:** $3,800
Annual giving by parents: $NA **Average per student:** $NA

Financial Aid

Average total package per student: $3,300 **Number receiving aid:** 30 %
Average scholarships and grants: $2,100 **Average loans:** $1,200 **Work-study program:** Yes
Undergraduates working on campus: 12 % **Average earnings:** $1,000
Non-need scholarships 3 % **Athletic scholarships:** Yes **FAF deadline:** May 1
Off-campus part-time employment: Fair **CO-OP program:** No
ROTC: Yes **NROTC:** No **AFROTC:** Yes

Endowment

Total: $390 Million **Per student (including graduate students):** $22,000

Location

Acres: 1,100 **Setting:** Urban
12 Miles from Wilmington **(Pop.** 70,000)
Miles from town center: 0 **(Pop.** 24,000**)**
30 Miles from Philadelphia **(Pop.**1.7 Million)

Class Composition

Asian: 2 % **Black:** 4 % **Hispanic:** 1 % **White:** 93 % **Other:** NA%
Total minority : 7 % **Foreign countries:** 1 % (135 students)
From public schools: 80 % **Students from in state:** 43 %

Housing (on campus)

Freshman required to live on campus: Yes
Available for all students: 55 %
On-campus married student housing: Yes
Guaranteed for: 1 year
Fraternity / Sorority housing: Yes / Yes
Women-only dorms available: Yes

Campus Life

Students living on campus: 55 % **Remain weekends:** NA % **Handicap access:** 90 %
Car regulations: No, unless need shown
Number with cars: NA %
Adequacy of on-campus parking: NA
Number of fraternities: 17 **Chapter houses:** 11
Number of sororities: 13 **Chapter houses:** 4
Students belonging to fraternities: 17 %
Students belonging to sororities: 17 %

Libraries and Computers

Books: 1.9 Million **Periodicals:** 24,000 **Microform items:** 1.8 Million
Microcomputers available: Yes **Microcomputers networked:** NA

Classes

Faculty / Student Ratio: 1/17 **Classes taught by teacher assistants:** 10 %
Most popular majors: Teacher ED, Business ED **Classes begin:** Aug. & Jan.
Baccalaureate degrees offered: BA, BAED, BS, BCE, BSN, B MUS

Sports

Division: I **Except:** **Physical ed requirements:** None
Students participating in intercollegiate sports: 6 % **In intramural sports:** 60 %
Additional intercollegiate and/or intramural sports: (not found at all colleges)

Crew: No	**Ice Hockey:** Yes	**Lacrosse:** Yes	**Wrestling:** Yes/M
Rugby: Yes	**Sailing:** Yes	**Skiing:** No	
Squash: Yes	**Ultimate Frisbee:** Yes	**Water Polo:** Yes	

Alumni

Number living: NA **Annual giving:** $ NA **Participation:** NA %
Average annual gift: $ NA **Average per student:** $ NA

3-2 Programs (2 degrees in 5 years)

In-house Engineering and MBA Program

Observation and Opinion of:

Undergraduates and graduates ______________________________

____

College counselor ______________________________

____

DENISON UNIVERSITY (Private)

Box H
Granville, Ohio 48023

SELECTIVE
(Composite rating of guide books)

Main tel.: 614-587-0810
Admissions tel.: 614-587-6276
Financial aid tel.: 614-587-6279
Scheduled Airline Service: Columbus
Miles to airport: 26

Founded: 1831
Nickname: Big Red
Religious affiliation: None
(Coed since 1900)

Student Body

Undergraduates: 2,000 **Men:** 48 % **Women:** 52 %
Graduate students: 0 **Freshman class:** 555

Academics

SAT Averages: 1085 **Verbal:** 520 **Math:** 565 **(Taking SATs:** 75 %)
700-800: V 1 % **M** 5 % **500-600: V** 40 % **M** 46 %
600-700: V 8 % **M** 26 % **400-500: V** 46 % **M** 80 % **300-400: V** 5 % **M** 3 %
High school class rank: Top fifth 48 % **2nd fifth** 31 % **3rd fifth** 16 %

Admissions

Applied: 3,270 **Accepted:** 70 % **Matriculated:** 24 %
Deadline: Feb. 1 **Accept common application:** Yes
Interview recommended: Yes **Off-campus interview available:** Yes
Evaluative: Yes **Informational only:** No **LD program:** Yes
Night in dorm provided: Yes **Non-refundable application fee:** $35
Early decision program: Yes **Applied:** 158 **Accepted:** 33 % **Deadline:** Jan. 1
Freshmen accepted other than Fall term: 1 % **SAT/FAF Code #** 1164

Transfers

Applied: 102 **Accepted:** 45 % **Application deadline for Fall:** June **Spring:** Dec.
Minimum grades recommended: 2.5 **All new students who were transfers into all classes:** 2 %

Class Experience

Return 2nd year: 90 % **Graduate after 4 years:** 77 % **To graduate school within 5 years:** 40 %

Cost

Tuition deposit: $250 **Total cost (Including school's estimate on fees and books):** $20,200
Tuition: $14,900 (In state: $) **Room and board:** $4,250
Annual giving by parents: $594,000 **Average per student:** $295

Financial Aid

Average total package per student: $10,300 **Number receiving aid:** 38 %
Average scholarships and grants: $8,300 **Average loans:** $2,000 **Work-study program:** Yes
Undergraduates working on campus: 45 % **Average earnings:** $1,000
Non-need scholarships 12 % **Athletic scholarships:** NA **FAF deadline:** March 1
Off-campus part-time employment: Fair **CO-OP program:** NA
ROTC: No **NROTC:** No **AFROTC:** No

Endowment

Total: $86 Million **Per student (including graduate students):** $40,000

Location

Acres: 1200 **Setting:** in small town
28 Miles from Columbus (Pop. 565,000)
Miles from town center: 1/2 (Pop. 5,000)
Miles from (Pop.)

Class Composition

Asian: 2 % **Black:** 5 % **Hispanic:** 1 % **White:** 91 % **Other:** 1 %
Total minority : 9 % **Foreign countries:** 2 % (40 students)
From public schools: 67 % **Students from in state:** 25 %

Housing (on campus)

Freshmen required to live on campus: Yes
Available for all students: 100 %
On-campus married student housing: No
Guaranteed for: 4 years
Fraternity / Sorority housing: Yes / Yes
Women-only dorms available: Yes

Campus Life

Students living on campus: 97 % **Remain weekends:** 85 % **Handicap access:** 85 %
Car regulations: No freshmen
Number with cars: 34 %
Adequacy of on-campus parking: Limited
Number of fraternities: 9 **Chapter houses:** 9
Students belonging to fraternities: 58 %
Number of sororities: 7 **Chapter houses:** 6
Students belonging to sororities: 62 %

Libraries and Computers

Books: 290,000 **Periodicals:** 1,035 **Microform items:** 29,500
Microcomputers available: Yes **Microcomputers networked:** Yes

Classes

Faculty / Student Ratio: 1/13 **Classes taught by teacher assistants:** 0 %
Most popular majors: Economics, History, English **Classes begin:** Late Aug.
Baccalaureate degrees offered: BA, BFA, B. MUS, BS

Sports

Division: III **Except:** **Physical ed requirements:** None
Students participating in intercollegiate sports: 40 % **In intramural sports:** 35 %
Additional intercollegiate and/or intramural sports: (not found at all colleges)

Crew: No **Ice Hockey:** Yes **Lacrosse:** Yes **Wrestling:** Yes
Rugby: Yes **Sailing:** Yes **Skiing:** Yes
Squash: Yes **Ultimate Frisbee:** Yes **Water Polo:** Yes/M

Alumni

Number living: 20,400 **Annual giving:** $5.6 Million **Participation:** 42 %
Average annual gift: $600 **Average per student:** $2,800

3-2 Programs (2 degrees in 5 years)

Engineering with Case Western, RPI, U of Rochester, Columbia, Washington U
Forestry & Natural Resources with Duke, U of Michigan
4-3 in Dentistry with Case Western

Observation and Opinion of:

Undergraduates and graduates ________________________________

____

College counselor ________________________________

____

DEPAUW UNIVERSITY (Private)

313 South Locust Street
Greencastle, IN 46135

VERY SELECTIVE
(Composite rating of guide books)

Main tel.: 317-658-4800
Admissions tel.: 800-447-2495
Financial aid tel.: 800-446-5299
Scheduled Airline Service: Indianapolis
Miles to airport: 40

Founded: 1837
Nickname: Tigers
Religious affiliation: Methodist
(Coed since 1867)

Student Body

Undergraduates: 2,300 **Men:** 40 % **Women:** 60 %
Graduate students: 2,350 **Freshman class:** 611

Academics

SAT Averages: 1140 **Verbal:** 540 **Math:** 600 (Taking SATs: 92 %)
700-800: V 3% **M** 13 % **500-600: V** 50 % **M** 35 %
600-700: V 22% **M** 42% **400-500: V** 25 % **M** 10% **300-400: V** NA % **M** NA %
High school class rank: Top fifth 65 % **2nd fifth** 26 % **3rd fifth** 8 %

Admissions

Applied: 1,925 **Accepted:** 84 % **Matriculated:** 38 %
Deadline: Feb. 15 **Accept common application:** Yes
Interview recommended: Optional **Off-campus interview available:** Yes
Evaluative: No **Informational only:** Yes **LD program:**
Night in dorm provided: Yes **Non-refundable application fee:** $25
Early decision program: Yes **Applied:** 293 **Accepted:** 85 % **Deadline:** Dec. 15
Freshmen accepted other than Fall term: 5 % **SAT/FAF Code #** 1166

Transfers

Applied: 56 **Accepted:** 75 % **Application deadline for Fall:** Apr. 1 **Spring:** Dec. 1
Minimum grades recommended: 3.0 **All new students who were transfers into all classes:** 5 %

Class Experience

Return 2nd year: 87 % **Graduate after 4 years:** 78 % **To graduate school within 3 years:** 50 %

Cost

Tuition deposit: $200 **Total cost (Including school's estimate on fees and books):** $18,200
Tuition: $13,000 (In state: $) **Room and board:** $4,640
Annual giving by parents: $592,000 **Average per student:** $240

Financial Aid

Average total package per student: $10,800 **Number receiving aid:** 55 %
Average scholarships and grants: $7,900 **Average loans:** $2,900 **Work-study program:** Yes
Undergraduates working on campus: 25 % **Average earnings:** $875
Non-need scholarships 35 % **Athletic scholarships:** Yes **FAF deadline:** Feb. 1
Off-campus part-time employment: Good **CO-OP program:** No
ROTC: at Rose-Hulman **NROTC:** No **AFROTC:** at Indiana U

Endowment

Total: $99 Million **Per student (including graduate students):** $40,000

Location

Acres: 125 **Setting:** Suburban
Miles from town center: 0 **(Pop.** 10,000**)**
40 **Miles from** Indianapolis **(Pop.** 70,000**)**
Miles from **(Pop.** **)**

Class Composition

Asian: 2% **Black:** 6 % **Hispanic:** 1 % **White:** 91 % **Other:** NA %
Total minority : 9 % **Foreign countries:** 2 % (45 students)
From public schools: 86 % **Students from in state:** 40 %

Housing (on campus)

Freshmen required to live on campus: Yes
Guaranteed for: 2 years
Available for all students: 96%
Fraternity / Sorority housing: Yes / Yes
On-campus married student housing: Yes
Women-only dorms available: Yes

Campus Life

Students living on campus: 96 % **Remain weekends:** 95 % **Handicap access:** 50 %
Car regulations: No restrictions but discouraged
Number with cars: 42 %
Adequacy of on-campus parking: OK
Number of fraternities: 14 **Chapter houses:** 13
Number of sororities: 11 **Chapter houses:** 10
Students belonging to fraternities: 80 %
Students belonging to sororities: 80 %

Libraries and Computers

Books: 264,000 **Periodicals:** 1,380 **Microform items:** 9,475
Microcomputers available: Yes **Microcomputers networked:** Yes

Classes

Faculty / Student Ratio: 1/12 **Classes taught by teacher assistants:** NA %
Most popular majors: Communications, Economics **Classes begin:** Late Aug.
Baccalaureate degrees offered: BA, B. MUS, BS, BSN

Sports

Division: III **Except:** **Physical ed requirements:** None
Students participating in intercollegiate sports: 13 % **In intramural sports:** 65 %
Additional intercollegiate and/or intramural sports: (not found at all colleges)

Crew: Yes	**Ice Hockey:** No	**Lacrosse:** Yes	**Wrestling:** Yes/M
Rugby: No	**Sailing:** Yes	**Skiing:** No	
Squash: No	**Ultimate Frisbee:** Yes	**Water Polo:** No	

Alumni

Number living: 29,000 **Annual giving:** $5.4 Million **Participation:** 38 %
Average annual gift: $700 **Average per student:** $2,300

3-2 Programs (2 degrees in 5 years)

Engineering with Case Western, Columbia, Georgia Tech, Washington U

Observation and Opinion of:

Undergraduates and graduates ____________________

____

College counselor ____________________

____

DICKINSON COLLEGE (Private)

P. O. Box 1773
Carlisle, PA 17013-2896

HIGHLY SELECTIVE
(Composite rating of guide books)

Founded: 1773
Nickname:
Religious affiliation: Methodist
(Coed since 1884)

Main tel.: 717-245-5121
Admissions tel.: 717-245-1231
Financial aid tel.: 717-245-1308
Scheduled Airline Service: Harrisburg
Miles to airport: 18

Student Body

Undergraduates: 2,050 **Men:** 42 % **Women:** 58 %
Graduate students: 0 **Freshman class:** 555

Academics

SAT Averages: 1130 **Verbal:** 560 **Math:** 570 **(Taking SATs:** 92 %**)**
700-800: V 2 % **M** 5 % **500-600: V** 55 % **M** 45 %
600-700: V 20 % **M** 40 % **400-500: V** 20 % **M** 10 % **300-400: V** NA % **M** NA %
High school class rank: Top fifth 76 % **2nd fifth** 23 % **3rd fifth** 1 %

Admissions

Applied: 3,640 **Accepted:** 66 % **Matriculated:** 23 %
Deadline: Mar. 1 **Accept common application:** No
Interview recommended: Yes **Off-campus interview available:** Yes
Evaluative: No **Informational only:** Yes **LD program:** Yes
Night in dorm provided: Yes **Non-refundable application fee:** $25
Early decision program: Yes **Applied:** 252 **Accepted:** 75 % **Deadline:** Dec. 15
Freshmen accepted other than Fall term: 0 % **SAT/FAF Code #** 2186

Transfers

Applied: 160 **Accepted:** 54 % **Application deadline for Fall:** Jun. 1 **Spring:** Dec. 1
Minimum grades recommended: 2.0 **All new students who were transfers into all classes:** 5 %

Class Experience

Return 2nd year: 95 % **Graduate after 4 years:** 82 % **To graduate school within 5 years:** 50 %

Cost

Tuition deposit: $200 **Total cost (Including school's estimate on fees and books):** $21,360
Tuition: $16,645 **(In state:** $ **)** **Room and board:** $4,715
Annual giving by parents: $344,000 **Average per student:** $175

Financial Aid

Average total package per student: $16,100 **Number receiving aid:** 46 %
Average scholarships and grants: $13,400 **Average loans:** $2,750 **Work-study program:** Yes
Undergraduates working on campus: 49 % **Average earnings:** $950
Non-need scholarships 15 % **Athletic scholarships:** NA **FAF deadline:** Feb. 1
Off-campus part-time employment: Good **CO-OP program:** No
ROTC: Yes **NROTC:** No **AFROTC:** No

Endowment

Total: $61 Million **Per student (including graduate students):** $30,000

Location

Acres: 87 **Setting:** Urban **Miles from town center:** 0 **(Pop.** 23,000)
18 **Miles from** Harrisburg **(Pop.** 53,000) 130 **Miles from** Philadelphia **(Pop.** 1.8 Mil)

Class Composition

Asian: 3 % **Black:** 1 % **Hispanic:** 2 % **White:** 94 % **Other:** NA %
Total minority : 6 % **Foreign countries:**1 % (20 students)
From public schools: 70 % **Students from in state:** 40 %

Housing (on campus)

Freshmen required to live on campus: Yes
Available for all students: 92 %
On-campus married student housing: No
Guaranteed for: 1 year
Fraternity / Sorority housing: No / No
Women-only dorms available: Yes

Campus Life

Students living on campus: 92 % **Remain weekends:** 85 % **Handicap access:** NA %
Car regulations: No freshmen
Number with cars: 30 % **Adequacy of on-campus parking:** NA
Number of fraternities: 8 **Chapter houses:** 0 **Number of sororities:** 5 **Chapter houses:** 0
Students belonging to fraternities: 34 % **Students belonging to sororities:** 42 %

Libraries and Computers

Books: 485,000 **Periodicals:** 1,670 **Microform items:** 140,000
Microcomputers available: Yes **Microcomputers networked:** NA

Classes

Faculty / Student Ratio: 1/13 **Classes taught by teacher assistants:** 0 %
Most popular majors: Poly Science, Economics **Classes begin:** Late Aug.
Baccalaureate degrees offered: BA, BS

Sports

Division: III **Except:** **Physical ed requirements:** 6 Terms
Students participating in intercollegiate sports: 40 % **In intramural sports:** 55 %
Additional intercollegiate and/or intramural sports: (not found at all colleges)

Crew: No	**Ice Hockey:** Yes	**Lacrosse:** Yes	**Wrestling:** Yes
Rugby: Yes	**Sailing:** No	**Skiing:** Yes	
Squash: Yes	**Ultimate Frisbee:** No	**Water Polo:** No	

Alumni

Number living: 16,200 **Annual giving:** $1.9 Million **Participation:** 34 %
Average annual gift: $ NA **Average per student:** $950

3-2 Programs (2 degrees in 5 years)

Engineering with Case Western, RPI, and U of Pennsylvania

Observation and Opinion of:

Undergraduates and graduates ____________________

____

College counselor ____________________

____

DUKE UNIVERSITY (Private)

2138 Campus Drive
Durham, NC 27706

MOST SELECTIVE
(Composite rating of guide books)

Main tel.: 919-684-2323
Admissions tel.: 919-684-3214
Financial aid tel.: 919-684-6225
Scheduled Airline Service: Raleigh-Durham
Miles to airport: 20

Founded: 1839
Nickname: Blue Devils
Religious affiliation: Methodist
(Coed since 1896)

Student Body

Undergraduates: 5,950 **Men:** 58 % **Women:** 42 %
Graduate students: 4,400 **Freshman class:** 1,475

Academics

SAT Averages: 1320 **Verbal:** 630 **Math:** 690 **(Taking SATs: NA %)**
700-800: V 12 % **M** 49 % **500-600: V** 26 % **M** 10 %
600-700: V 58 % **M** 39 % **400-500: V** 4 % **M** 2 % **300-400: V** NA % **M** NA %
High school class rank: Top fifth 97 % **2nd fifth** 3 % **3rd fifth** NA %

Admissions

Applied: 13,400 **Accepted:** 25 % **Matriculated:** 44 %
Deadline: Jan. 1 **Accept common application:** No
Interview recommended: Yes **Off-campus interview available:** Yes
Evaluative: Yes **Informational only:** No **LD program:** Yes
Night in dorm provided: Yes **Non-refundable application fee:** $50
Early decision program: Yes **Applied:** 885 **Accepted:** 40 % **Deadline:** Nov. 1
Freshmen accepted other than Fall term: 1 % **SAT/FAF Code #** 5156

Transfers

Applied: 563 **Accepted:** 7 % **Application deadline for Fall:** Apr. 1 **Spring:** Oct. 15
Minimum grades recommended: 3.5 **All new students who were transfers into all classes:** 1 %

Class Experience

Return 2nd year: 99 % **Graduate after 4 years:** 93 % **To graduate school within 5 years:** NA %

Cost

Tuition deposit: $400 **Total cost (Including school's estimate on fees and books):** $21,600
Tuition: $15,430 **(In state:** $ **)** **Room and board:** $5,300
Annual giving by parents: $2.5 Million **Average per student:** $404

Financial Aid

Average total package per student: $NA **Number receiving aid:** 40 %
Average scholarships and grants: $10,000 **Average loans:** $NA **Work-study program:** Yes
Undergraduates working on campus: 26 % **Average earnings:** $1,500
Non-need scholarships 10 % **Athletic scholarships:** Yes **FAF deadline:** Feb. 15
Off-campus part-time employment: Excellent **CO-OP program:** No
ROTC: Yes **NROTC:** Yes **AFROTC:** Yes

Endowment

Total: $527 Million **Per student (including graduate students):** $50,000

Location

Acres: 8500 **Setting:** Surburban
30 **Miles from** Raleigh **(Pop.** 150,000)
Miles from town center: 2 **(Pop.** 115,000)
Miles from **(Pop.**)

Class Composition

Asian: 6 % **Black:** 6 % **Hispanic:** 3 % **White:** 85 % **Other:** NA %
Total minority : 15 % **Foreign countries:** 2 % (100 students)
From public schools: 68 % **Students from in state:** 15 %

Housing (on campus)

Freshmen required to live on campus: Yes
Available for all students: 91 %
On-campus married student housing: Yes
Guaranteed for: 1 year
Fraternity / Sorority housing: Yes /Yes
Women-only dorms available: Yes

Campus Life

Students living on campus: 91 % **Remain weekends:** 95 % **Handicap access:** 50 %
Car regulations: Allowed all 4 years
Number with cars: 40 % **Adequacy of on-campus parking:** Poor
Number of fraternities: 21 **Chapter houses:** 21 **Number of sororities:** 14 **Chapter houses:** 14
Students belonging to fraternities: 40 % **Students belonging to sororities:** 35 %

Libraries and Computers

Books: 3.8 Million **Periodicals:** 30,000 **Microform items:** 1.4 Million
Microcomputers available: Yes **Microcomputers networked:** Yes

Classes

Faculty / Student Ratio: 1/13 **Classes taught by teacher assistants:** 10 %
Most popular majors: Poly Science, Economics **Classes begin:** Late Aug.
Baccalaureate degrees offered: BA, BHS, BS, BSE

Sports

Division: I **Except:** **Physical ed requirements:** None
Students participating in intercollegiate sports: 16 % **In intramural sports:** 60 %
Additional intercollegiate and/or intramural sports: (not found at all colleges)

Crew: Yes **Ice Hockey:** Yes **Lacrosse:** Yes **Wrestling:** Yes/M
Rugby: Yes **Sailing:** Yes **Skiing:** Yes
Squash: Yes **Ultimate Frisbee:** No **Water Polo:** Yes/M

Alumni

Number living: 79,000 **Annual giving:** $21.5 million **Participation:** 53 %
Average annual gift: $500 **Average per student:** $2,000

3-2 Programs (2 degrees in 5 years)

In-house, Forestry and Environmental Studies, Business Program, and 3-2 Law Program

Observation and Opinion of:

Undergraduates and graduates ______________________________

____

College counselor ______________________________

____

EARLHAM COLLEGE (Private)

National Road West
Richmond, IN 47374

VERY SELECTIVE
(Composite rating of guide books)

Main tel.: 317-983-1200
Admissions tel.: 800-327-5426
Financial aid tel.: 317-983-1217
Scheduled Airline Service: Dayton, OH
Miles to airport: 40

Founded: 1847
Nickname: Hustling Quakers
Religious affiliation: Quaker
(Coed since 1847)

Student Body

Undergraduates: 1,150 **Men:** 40 % **Women:** 60 %
Graduate students: 0 **Freshman class:** 330

Academics

SAT Averages: 1120 **Verbal:** 560 **Math:** 560 **(Taking SATs:** 90 %**)**
700-800: V 8 % **M** 9 % **500-600: V** 41 % **M** 39 %
600-700: V 27 % **M** 31 % **400-500: V** 20 % **M** 19 % **300-400: V** 4 % **M** 2 %
High school class rank: Top fifth 42 % **2nd fifth** 22 % **3rd fifth** 11 %

Admissions

Applied: 1,240 **Accepted:** 74 % **Matriculated:** 36 %
Deadline: Feb. 15 **Accept common application:** Yes
Interview recommended: Yes **Off-campus interview available:** Yes
Evaluative: Yes **Informational only:** No **LD program:** Yes
Night in dorm provided: Yes **Non-refundable application fee:** $25
Early decision program: Yes **Applied:** 45 **Accepted:** 99 % **Deadline:** Dec. 1
Freshmen accepted other than Fall term: 1 % **SAT/FAF Code #** 1195

Transfers

Applied: 79 **Accepted:** 52 % **Application deadline for Fall:** Apr. 1 **Spring:** Feb. 15
Minimum grades recommended: 2.8 **All new students who were transfers into all classes:** 7 %

Class Experience

Return 2nd year: 72 % **Graduate after 4 years:** 75 % **To graduate school within 5 years:** NA %

Cost

Tuition deposit: $200 **Total cost (Including school's estimate on fees and books):** $19,000
Tuition: $14,130 **(In state:** $ **)** **Room and board:** $4,100
Annual giving by parents: $514,000 **Average per student:** $450

Financial Aid

Average total package per student: $9,230 **Number receiving aid:** 60 %
Average scholarships and grants: $6,530 **Average loans:** $2,700 **Work-study program:** Yes
Undergraduates working on campus: 40 % **Average earnings:** $1,200
Non-need scholarships NA % **Athletic scholarships:** NA **FAF deadline:** March 1
Off-campus part-time employment: Fair **CO-OP program:** No
ROTC: No **NROTC:** No **AFROTC:** No

Endowment

Total: $130 Million **Per student (including graduate students):** $110,000

Location

Acres: 800 **Setting:** Small city
40 Miles from Dayton **(Pop.** 235,000)
Miles from town center: 2 **(Pop.** 40,000)
70 **Miles from Indianapolis (Pop.** 700,000)

Class Composition

Asian: 3 % **Black:** 8 % **Hispanic:** 1 % **White:** 82 % **Other:** 3 %
Total minority : 18 % **Foreign countries:** 3 % (33 students)
From public schools: 74 % **Students from in state:** 15 %

Housing (on campus)

Freshmen required to live on campus: Yes
Available for all students: 85 %
On-campus married student housing: No
Guaranteed for: 4 years
Fraternity / Sorority housing: 0 / 0
Women-only dorms available: No

Campus Life

Students living on campus: 80 % **Remain weekends:** 95 % **Handicap access:** NA %
Car regulations: No restrictions
Number with cars: 5 %
Number of fraternities: 0 **Chapter houses:**
Students belonging to fraternities: 0 %
Adequacy of on-campus parking: Good
Number of sororities: 0 **Chapter houses:**
Students belonging to sororities: 0 %

Libraries and Computers

Books: 341,000 **Periodicals:** 1,365 **Microform items:** 147,000
Microcomputers available: Yes **Microcomputers networked:**

Classes

Faculty / Student Ratio: 1/12 **Classes taught by teacher assistants:** 0 %
Most popular majors: Biology, Social Relations **Classes begin:** Early Sept.
Baccalaureate degrees offered: BA

Sports

Division: III **Except:** **Physical ed requirements:** None
Students participating in intercollegiate sports: 35 % **In intramural sports:** 50 %
Additional intercollegiate and/or intramural sports: (not found at all colleges)

Crew: No	**Ice Hockey:** No	**Lacrosse:** Yes	**Wrestling:** No
Rugby: No	**Sailing:** Yes	**Skiing:** Yes	
Squash: Yes	**Ultimate Frisbee:** Yes	**Water Polo:** Yes/W	

Alumni

Number living: 14,000 **Annual giving:** $1.5 million **Participation:** 32 %
Average annual gift: $360 **Average per student:** $1300

3-2 Programs (2 degrees in 5 years)

Engineering with Case Western, RPI, Michigan, Rochester, and Washington U
Architecture with Washington U
Forestry with Duke

Observation and Opinion of:

Undergraduates and graduates ______________________________

____

College counselor ______________________________

____

EMORY UNIVERSITY (Private)

1380 Oxford Road
Atlanta, GA 30322

HIGHLY SELECTIVE
(Composite rating of guide books)

Main tel.: 404-727-6123
Admissions tel.: 404-727-6036
Financial aid tel.: 404-727-6039
Scheduled Airline Service: Atlanta
Miles to airport: 14

Founded: 1836
Nickname: Eagles
Religious affiliation: Methodist
(Coed since 1953)

Student Body

Undergraduates: 4,600 **Men:** 45 % **Women:** 55 %
Graduate students: 4,100 **Freshman class:** 1,112

Academics

SAT Averages: 1210 **Verbal:** 570 **Math:** 640 **(Taking SATs:** 97 **%)**
700-800: V 4 % **M** 16 % **500-600: V** 55 % **M** %
600-700: V 25% **M** 52 % **400-500: V** 16 % **M** 0 % **300-400: V** NA % **M** NA %
High school class rank: Top fifth 75 % **2nd fifth** 16 % **3rd fifth** 4 %

Admissions

Applied: 5,900 **Accepted:** 66 % **Matriculated:** 29 %
Deadline: Feb. 1 **Accept common application:** Yes
Interview recommended: No **Off-campus interview available:** No
Evaluative: No **Informational only:** Yes **LD program:** Yes
Night in dorm provided: Yes **Non-refundable application fee:** $35
Early decision program: Yes **Applied:** 290 **Accepted:** 80 % **Deadline:** Nov. 15
Freshmen accepted other than Fall term: Yes % **SAT/FAF Code #** 5187

Transfers

Applied: 325 **Accepted:** 64 % **Application deadline for Fall:** July 1 **Spring:** Nov. 1
Minimum grades recommended: 3.0 **All new students who were transfers into all classes:** 8 %

Class Experience

Return 2nd year: 90 % **Graduate after 4 years:** 75 % **To graduate school within 5 years:** 65 %

Cost

Tuition deposit: $150 **Total cost (Including school's estimate on fees and books):** $21,900
Tuition: $15,820 **(In state:** $ **)** **Room and board:** $4,800
Annual giving by parents: $53,000 **Average per student:** $43

Financial Aid

Average total package per student: $12,400 **Number receiving aid:** 43 %
Average scholarships and grants: $9,750 **Average loans:** $2,625 **Work-study program:** Yes
Undergraduates working on campus: 40 % **Average earnings:** $1,300
Non-need scholarships 23 % **Athletic scholarships:** NA **FAF deadline:** Apr. 1
Off-campus part-time employment: Good **CO-OP program:** No
ROTC: No **NROTC:** No **AFROTC:** No

Endowment

Total: $1.3 Billion **Per student (including graduate students):** $145,000

Location

Acres: 630 **Setting:** Surburban **Miles from town center:** 6 (Pop. 450,000)
Miles from (Pop.) **Miles from** (Pop.)

Class Composition

Asian: 5 % **Black:** 7 % **Hispanic:** 2 % **White:** 82 % **Other:** 4 %
Total minority : 18 % **Foreign countries:** 4 % (170 students)
From public schools: 70 % **Students from in state:** 20 %

Housing (on campus)

Freshmen required to live on campus: Yes **Guaranteed for:** 1 year
Available for all students: 75 % **Fraternity / Sorority housing:** Yes / Yes
On-campus married student housing: Yes **Women-only dorms available:** Yes

Campus Life

Students living on campus: 75 % **Remain weekends:** 95 % **Handicap access:** 95 %
Car regulations: No freshmen 7am - 5pm
Number with cars: 75 % **Adequacy of on-campus parking:** Poor
Number of fraternities: 15 **Chapter houses:** 14 **Number of sororities:** 10 **Chapter houses:** 10
Students belonging to fraternities: 40 % **Students belonging to sororities:** 45 %

Libraries and Computers

Books: 2.2 Million **Periodicals:** 17,000 **Microform items:** 1.8 Million
Microcomputers available: Yes **Microcomputers networked:** NA

Classes

Faculty / Student Ratio: 1/9 **Classes taught by teacher assistants:** 16 %
Most popular majors: Poly Science, Business **Classes begin:** Late Aug.
Baccalaureate degrees offered: BA, BBA, BS, BSN

Sports

Division: III **Except:** **Physical ed requirements:** 4 semesters
Students participating in intercollegiate sports: 16 % **In intramural sports:** 80 %
Additional intercollegiate and/or intramural sports: (not found at all colleges)

Crew: Yes	**Ice Hockey:** Yes	**Lacrosse:** Yes	**Wrestling:** Yes/M
Rugby: Yes/M	**Sailing:** No	**Skiing:** No	
Squash: No	**Ultimate Frisbee:** Yes	**Water Polo:** Yes	

Alumni

Number living: 57,000 **Annual giving:** $ 4.5 Million **Participation:** 28 %
Average annual gift: $ 290 **Average per student:** $500

3-2 Programs (2 degrees in 5 years)

Engineering with Georgia Tech, In-house BA/MA in Psychology, 4-year BA/MA or BS/MS in Chemistry, English, History, Math/Computer Science, Philosophy, Poly Science

Observation and Opinion of:

Undergraduates and graduates ______________________________

____

College counselor ______________________________

____

FAIRFIELD UNIVERSITY (Private)

North Benson Road
Fairfield, CT 06430-7524

HIGHLY SELECTIVE
(Composite rating of guide books)

Main tel.: 203-254-4000
Admissions tel.: 203-254-4100
Financial aid tel.: 203-254-4000, Ext. 2485
Scheduled Airline Service: New York City
Miles to airport: 60

Founded: 1942
Nickname: The Stags
Religious affiliation: Catholic
(Coed since 1970)

Student Body

Undergraduates: 2,900 **Men:** 46 % **Women:** 54 %
Graduate students: 770 **Freshman class:** 750

Academics

SAT Averages: 1115 **Verbal:** 525 **Math:** 590 **(Taking SATs:** 100 %**)**
700-800: V 1 % M 6 % **500-600:** V 49 % M 43 %
600-700: V 15 % M 40 % **400-500:** V 32 % M 10 % **300-400:** V 3 % M 1 %
High school class rank: Top fifth 57 % **2nd fifth** 27 % **3rd fifth** 5 %

Admissions

Applied: 4,980 **Accepted:** 54 % **Matriculated:** 28 %
Deadline: Mar. 1 **Accept common application:** Yes
Interview recommended: Yes **Off-campus interview available:** Yes
Evaluative: No **Informational only:** Yes **LD program:** NA
Night in dorm provided: No **Non-refundable application fee:** $35
Early decision program: Yes **Applied:** 180 **Accepted:** 63 % **Deadline:** Dec. 1
Freshmen accepted other than Fall term: NA % **SAT/FAF Code #** 3390

Transfers

Applied: 312 **Accepted:** 27 % **Application deadline for Fall:** June 1 **Spring:** Dec. 1
Minimum grades recommended: 2.5 **All new students who were transfers into all classes:** 2 %

Class Experience

Return 2nd year: 91 % **Graduate after 4 years:** 84 % **To graduate school within 5 years:** 15 %

Cost

Tuition deposit: $200 **Total cost (Including school's estimate on fees and books):** $20,000
Tuition: $13,450 **(In state:** $ **)** **Room and board:** $5,650
Annual giving by parents: $3.1 Million **Average per student:** $3,000

Financial Aid

Average total package per student: $NA **Number receiving aid:** 51 %
Average scholarships and grants: $5,265 **Average loans:** $NA **Work-study program:** Yes
Undergraduates working on campus: 15 % **Average earnings:** $1,200
Non-need scholarships 26 % **Athletic scholarships:** Yes **FAF deadline:** Feb. 1
Off-campus part-time employment: Good **CO-OP program:** No
ROTC: No **NROTC:** No **AFROTC:** No

Endowment

Total: $25 Million **Per student (including graduate students):** $7,000

Location

Acres: 225 **Setting:** Surburban **Miles from town center:** 2 (Pop. 60,000)
5 **Miles from** Bridgeport (**Pop.** 140,000) 60 **Miles from** NYC (**Pop.** 14 Million)

Class Composition

Asian: 3 % **Black:** 1 % **Hispanic:** 3 % **White:** 92 % **Other:** 1 %
Total minority : 8 % **Foreign countries:** 1 % (30 students)
From public schools: 50 % **Students from in state:** 35 %

Housing (on campus)

Freshmean required to live on campus: Yes **Guaranteed for:** 4 years
Available for all students: 80 % **Fraternity / Sorority housing:** No / No
On-campus married student housing: Yes **Women-only dorms available:** No

Campus Life

Students living on campus: 80 % **Remain weekends:** 70 % **Handicap access:** 85 %
Car regulations: No freshmen
Number with cars: 40 % **Adequacy of on-campus parking:** Good
Number of fraternities: 0 **Chapter houses:** **Number of sororities:** 0 **Chapter houses:**
Students belonging to fraternities: 0 % **Students belonging to sororities:** 0 %

Libraries and Computers

Books: 249,000 **Periodicals:** 1,800 **Microform items:** 355,000
Microcomputers available: Yes **Microcomputers networked:** NA

Classes

Faculty / Student Ratio: **Classes taught by teacher assistants:** 0 %
Most popular majors: English, Poly Science, Marketing **Classes begin:** Early Sept.
Baccalaureate degrees offered: BA, BS, BS Business

Sports

Division: I **Except:** **Physical ed requirements:** None
Students participating in intercollegiate sports: 20 % **In intramural sports:** 65 %
Additional intercollegiate and/or intramural sports: (not found at all colleges)

Crew: No	**Ice Hockey:** Yes/M	**Lacrosse:** Yes	**Wrestling:** No
Rugby: Yes/M	**Sailing:** Yes	**Skiing:** Yes	
Squash: No	**Ultimate Frisbee:** No	**Water Polo:** Yes	

Alumni

Number living: 22,000 **Annual giving:** $1.7 million **Participation:** 31 %
Average annual gift: $300 **Average per student:** $400

3-2 Programs (2 degrees in 5 years)

Engineering with U of Connecticut
Dental Program with NYU

Observation and Opinion of:

Undergraduates and graduates ____________________

____

College counselor ____________________

____

UNIVERSITY OF FLORIDA (Public)

Gainesville, FL 32611

VERY SELECTIVE
(Composite rating of guide books)

Main tel.: 904-392-3261
Admissions tel.: 904-392-1365
Financial aid tel.: 904-392-1275
Scheduled Airline Service: Jacksonville
Miles to airport: 73

Founded: 1853
Nickname: Gators
Religious affiliation: None
(Coed since 1946)

Student Body

Undergraduates: 23,000 **Men:** 58 % **Women:** 42 %
Graduate students: 8,700 **Freshman class:** 2,900

Academics

SAT Averages: 1155 **Verbal:** 530 **Math:** 625 **(Taking SATs:** 65 %**)**
700-800: V 3 % **M** 13 % **500-600: V** 46 % **M** 37 %
600-700: V 18 % **M** 44 % **400-500: V** 30 % **M** 6 % **300-400: V** 3 % **M** 0 %
High school class rank: Top fifth NA % **2nd fifth** NA % **3rd fifth** NA %

Admissions

Applied: 10,900 **Accepted:** 66 % **Matriculated:** 40 %
Deadline: Feb. 1 **Accept common application:** No
Interview recommended: No **Off-campus interview available:** No
Evaluative: No **Informational only:** Yes **LD program:** Yes
Night in dorm provided: No **Non-refundable application fee:** $15
Early decision program: Yes **Applied:** NA **Accepted:** NA % **Deadline:** Oct. 1
Freshmen accepted other than Fall term: NA % **SAT/FAF Code #** 5812

Transfers

Applied: 9,400 **Accepted:** 48 % **Application deadline for Fall:** June 15 **Spring:** Nov. 1
Minimum grades recommended: 2.0 **All new students who were transfers into all classes:** 42 %

Class Experience

Return 2nd year: 88 % **Graduate after 4 years:** 40 % **To graduate school within 5 years:** NA %

Cost

Tuition deposit: $175 **Total cost (Including school's estimate on fees and books):** $10,000
Tuition: $6,030 **(In state:** $ 1,580 **)** **Room and board:** $3,800
Annual giving by parents: $100,000 **Average per student:** $42

Financial Aid

Average total package per student: $4,615 **Number receiving aid:** 32 %
Average scholarships and grants: $2,500 **Average loans:** $2,115 **Work-study program:** Yes
Undergraduates working on campus: 22 % **Average earnings:** $1,800
Non-need scholarships 5 % **Athletic scholarships:** Yes **FAF deadline:** April 1
Off-campus part-time employment: Fair **CO-OP program:** Yes
ROTC: Yes **NROTC:** Yes **AFROTC:** Yes

Endowment

Total: $225 Million **Per student (including graduate students):** $7,000

Location

Acres: 2,000 **Setting:** Surburban
90 **Miles from** Orlando **(Pop.** 130,000 **)**
Miles from town center: 2 **(Pop.** 81,000**)**
Miles from **(Pop.** **)**

Class Composition

Asian: 4 % **Black:** 6 % **Hispanic:** 5 % **White:** 79 % **Other:** 6 %
Total minority : 21 % **Foreign countries:** 5 % (1100 students)
From public schools: 80 % **Students from in state:** 92 %

Housing (on campus)

Freshmen required to live on campus: No
Available for all students: 25 %
On-campus married student housing: Yes
Guaranteed for: 0 years
Fraternity / Sorority housing: Yes / Yes
Women-only dorms available: Yes

Campus Life

Students living on campus: 25 % **Remain weekends:** NA % **Handicap access:** NA %
Car regulations: All 4 years
Number with cars: 55 %
Adequacy of on-campus parking: Fair
Number of fraternities: 32 **Chapter houses:** 28
Number of sororities: 18 **Chapter houses:** 15
Students belonging to fraternities: 18 %
Students belonging to sororities: 14 %

Libraries and Computers

Books: 2.8 Million **Periodicals:** 28,000 **Microform items:** 2.7 Million
Microcomputers available: Yes **Microcomputers networked:** NA

Classes

Faculty / Student Ratio: 1/25 **Classes taught by teacher assistants:** 10 %
Most popular majors: Business, Communications, Engineering **Classes begin:** Late Aug.
Baccalaureate degrees offered: BA, BAED, Bldg. Construction, Bldg. Design, BFA, BLA, BMUS, BS

Sports

Division: I **Except:** **Physical ed requirements:** None
Students participating in intercollegiate sports: 5 % **In intramural sports:** 10 %
Additional intercollegiate and/or intramural sports: (not found at all colleges)

Crew: No **Ice Hockey:** No **Lacrosse:** No **Wrestling:** No
Rugby: No **Sailing:** No **Skiing:** No
Squash: No **Ultimate Frisbee:** Yes **Water Polo:** No

Alumni

Number living: 190,000 **Annual giving:** $10.1 Million **Participation:** 20 %
Average annual gift: $330 **Average per student:** $350

3-2 Programs (2 degrees in 5 years)

In-house Engineering/MBA

Observation and Opinion of:

Undergraduates and graduates ______________________________

____

College counselor ______________________________

____

FORDHAM UNIVERSITY (Private)

East Fordham Road
Bronx, New York 10458

VERY SELECTIVE
(Composite rating of guide books)

Main tel.: 212-579-2000
Admissions tel.: 212-579-2133
Financial aid tel.:
Scheduled Airline Service: NYC
Miles to airport: 10

Founded: 1841
Nickname: Rams
Religious affiliation: Catholic
(Coed since 1974)

Student Body

Undergraduates: 5,050 **Men:** 50 % **Women:** 50 %
Graduate students: 6,500 **Freshman class:** 1,290

Academics

SAT Averages: 1085 **Verbal:** 535 **Math:** 550 **(Taking SATs:** 70 %**)**
700-800: V 2 % **M** 3 % **500-600: V** 45 % **M** 55 %
600-700: V 12 % **M** 17 % **400-500: V** 40 % **M** 25 % **300-400: V** NA % **M** NA %
High school class rank: Top fifth 60 % **2nd fifth** NA % **3rd fifth** NA %

Admissions

Applied: 4,250 **Accepted:** 67 % **Matriculated:** 40 %
Deadline: Apr. 1 **Accept common application:** Yes
Interview recommended: Yes **Off-campus interview available:** Yes
Evaluative: Yes **Informational only:** NA **LD program:** NA
Night in dorm provided: Yes **Non-refundable application fee:** $25
Early decision program: Yes **Applied:** NA **Accepted:** NA% **Deadline:** Nov. 1
Freshmen accepted other than Fall term: Yes **SAT/FAF Code #** 2259

Transfers

Applied: NA **Accepted:** NA % **Application deadline for Fall:** NA **Spring:** NA
Minimum grades recommended: NA **All new students who were transfers into all classes:** 10 %

Class Experience

Return 2nd year: 78 % **Graduate after 4 years:** 78 % **To graduate school within 5 years:** 60 %

Cost

Tuition deposit: $100 **Total cost (Including school's estimate on fees and books):** $18,800
Tuition: $10,950 **(In state:** $ **)** **Room and board:** $6,700
Annual giving by parents: $100,000 **Average per student:** $NA

Financial Aid

Average total package per student: $ **Number receiving aid:** 75 %
Average scholarships and grants: $3,500 **Average loans:** $NA **Work-study program:** Yes
Undergraduates working on campus: 40 % **Average earnings:** $1,200
Non-need scholarships 10 % **Athletic scholarships:** NA **FAF deadline:** NA
Off-campus part-time employment: Excellent **CO-OP program:** No
ROTC: Yes **NROTC:** No **AFROTC:** No

Endowment

Total: $73 Million **Per student (including graduate students):** $6,500

Location

Acres: 86 **Setting:** City **Miles from town center:** 6 (**Pop.** 7 Million)
55 **Miles from** Harrisburg (**Pop.** 53,000) **Miles from** (**Pop.** 1.6 Million)

Class Composition

Asian: 3 % **Black:** 10 % **Hispanic:** 11 % **White:** 66 % **Other:** 10 %
Total minority : 34 % **Foreign countries:** 2 % (100 students)
From public schools: 40 % **Students from in state:** 75 %

Housing (on campus)

Freshmen required to live on campus: Yes **Guaranteed for:** 1 year
Available for all students: 50 % **Fraternity / Sorority housing:** No / No
On-campus married student housing: No **Women-only dorms available:** Yes

Campus Life

Students living on campus: 50 % **Remain weekends:** NA % **Handicap access:** NA %
Car regulations: No freshmen or sophomores
Number with cars: NA % **Adequacy of on-campus parking:** NA
Number of fraternities: 0 **Chapter houses:** 0 **Number of sororities:** 0 **Chapter houses:** 0
Students belonging to fraternities: 0 % **Students belonging to sororities:** 0 %

Libraries and Computers

Books: 1.4 Million **Periodicals:** 4,700 **Microform items:** 1.2 Million
Microcomputers available: **Microcomputers networked:** NA

Classes

Faculty / Student Ratio: 1/17 **Classes taught by teacher assistants:** 20 %
Most popular majors: Business, Communications **Classes begin:** Early Sept.
Baccalaureate degrees offered: BA, BS, BSBA

Sports

Division: I **Except:** **Physical ed requirements:** None
Students participating in intercollegiate sports: 17 % **In intramural sports:** 8 %
Additional intercollegiate and/or intramural sports: (not found at all colleges)

Crew: Yes **Ice Hockey:** Yes/M **Lacrosse:** Yes **Wrestling:** Yes
Rugby: Yes/M **Sailing:** No **Skiing:** Yes
Squash: Yes **Ultimate Frisbee:** No **Water Polo:** Yes/M

Alumni

Number living: NA **Annual giving:** $ NA **Participation:** NA %
Average annual gift: $ NA **Average per student:** $NA

3-2 Programs (2 degrees in 5 years)

Engineering with Columbia, Pharmacy with Long Island U, 3-3 In-house Law Program
5-year MA Program

Observation and Opinion of:

Undergraduates and graduates ______________________________

____

College counselor ______________________________

____

FRANKLIN & MARSHALL COLLEGE (Private)

Lancaster, PA 17604

HIGHLY SELECTIVE
(Composite rating of guide books)

Main tel.: 717-291-7911
Admissions tel.: 717-291-3951
Financial aid tel.: 717-291-3991
Scheduled Airline Service: Harrisburg
Miles to airport: 25

Founded: 1787
Nickname: Diplomats
Religious affiliation: None
(Coed since 1969)

Student Body

Undergraduates: 5,050 **Men:** 50 % **Women:** 50 %
Graduate students: 6,500 **Freshman class:** 1,290

Academics

SAT Averages 1800 **Verbal:** 560 **Math:** 620 **(Taking SATs:** NA %)
700-800: V 3 % M 12 % **500-600:** V 52 % M 34 %
600-700: V 25 % M 51 % **400-500:** V 20 % M 3 % **300-400:** V NA % M NA %
High school class rank: Top fifth 43% **2nd fifth** 19 % **3rd fifth** 5 %

Admissions

Applied: 3,160 **Accepted:** 59 % **Matriculated:** 27 %
Deadline: **Accept common application:** Yes
Interview recommended: NA **Off-campus interview available:** NA
Evaluative: NA **Informational only:** NA **LD program:** NA
Night in dorm provided: Yes **Non-refundable application fee:** $35
Early decision program: Yes **Applied:** 199 **Accepted:** 60 % **Deadline:** NA
Freshmen accepted other than Fall term: 1 % **SAT/FAF Code #** 2261

Transfers

Applied: NA **Accepted:** NA % **Application deadline for Fall:** May 15 **Spring:** Dec. 1
Minimum grades recommended: 3.0 **All new students who were transfers into all classes:** 5 %

Class Experience

Return 2nd year: 92 % **Graduate after 4 years:** 79 % **To graduate school within 5 years:** 36 %

Cost

Tuition deposit: $200 **Total cost (Including school's estimate on fees and books):** $22,900
Tuition: $22,330 **(In state:** $) **Room and board:** Included
Annual giving by parents: $120,000 **Average per student:** $70

Financial Aid

Average total package per student: $14,500 **Number receiving aid:** 47 %
Average scholarships and grants: $11,900 **Average loans:** $2,600 **Work-study program:** Yes
Undergraduates working on campus: 49 % **Average earnings:** $1,350
Non-need scholarships 0 % **Athletic scholarships:** 0 **FAF deadline:** Feb. 10
Off-campus part-time employment: Good **CO-OP program:** No
ROTC: No **NROTC:** No **AFROTC:** No

Endowment

Total: $105 Million **Per student (including graduate students):** $60,000

Location

Acres: 125 **Setting:** Surburban **Miles from town center:** 2 **(Pop.** 60,000)
60 **Miles from** Philadelphia **(Pop.** 1.7 Mil.) 30 **Miles from** Harrisburg **(Pop.** 53,000)

Class Composition

Asian: 6 % **Black:** 3 % **Hispanic:** 2 % **White:** 89 % **Other:** NA %
Total minority : 11 % **Foreign countries:** 5 % (80 students)
From public schools: 60 % **Students from in state:** 38 %

Housing (on campus)

Freshmen required to live on campus: Yes **Guaranteed for:** 4 years
Available for all students: 75 % **Fraternity / Sorority housing:** Yes / Yes
On-campus married student housing: No **Women-only dorms available:** No

Campus Life

Students living on campus: 71 % **Remain weekends:** 90 % **Handicap access:** 80 %
Car regulations: All classes can have
Number with cars: NA % **Adequacy of on-campus parking:** Fair
Number of fraternities: 9 **Chapter houses:** 9 **Number of sororities:** 3 **Chapter houses:** 3
Students belonging to fraternities: 40 % **Students belonging to sororities:** 30 %

Libraries and Computers

Books: 338,000 **Periodicals:** 2,000 **Microform items:** 228,000
Microcomputers available: Yes **Microcomputers networked:** NA

Classes

Faculty / Student Ratio: 11/1 **Classes taught by teacher assistants:** 0 %
Most popular majors: Gov't., Biology, Bus. Administration **Classes begin:** Late Aug.
Baccalaureate degrees offered: BA

Sports

Division: III **Except:** **Physical ed requirements:** None
Students participating in intercollegiate sports: 35 % **In intramural sports:** 28 %
Additional intercollegiate and/or intramural sports: (not found at all colleges)

Crew: Yes **Ice Hockey:** Yes/M **Lacrosse:** Yes/M **Wrestling:** Yes/M
Rugby: Yes **Sailing:** Yes **Skiing:** No
Squash: Yes **Ultimate Frisbee:** No **Water Polo:** Yes

Alumni

Number living: 18,500 **Annual giving:** $2 Million **Participation:** 29 %
Average annual gift: $ 400 **Average per student:** $1,050

3-2 Programs (2 degrees in 5 years)

Engineering with Case Western, Columbia, Georgia Tech, RPI, U of Pennsylvania, Washington U, Forestry with Duke

Observation and Opinion of:

Undergraduates and graduates ________________________________

____

College counselor ________________________________

____

FURMAN UNIVERSITY (Private)

Greenville, SC 29613

VERY SELECTIVE
(Composite rating of guide books)

Main tel.: 803-294-2000
Admissions tel.: 803-294-2034
Financial aid tel.: 803-294-2204
Scheduled Airline Service: Greenville
Miles to airport: 16

Founded: 1826
Nickname: NA
Religious affiliation: Baptist
(Coed since 1933)

Student Body

Undergraduates: 2,450 **Men:** 50 % **Women:** 50 %
Graduate students: 400 **Freshman class:** 600

Academics

SAT Averages: 1190 **Verbal:** 570 **Math:** 620 **(Taking SATs:** NA %)
700-800: V 3 % M 12 % **500-600:** V 50 % M 45 %
600-700: V 22 % M 38 % **400-500:** V 25 % M 5 % **300-400:** V NA % M NA %
High school class rank: Top fifth 80 % 2nd fifth 16 % 3rd fifth 4 %

Admissions

Applied: 2,973 **Accepted:** 43 % **Matriculated:** 47 %
Deadline: Feb. 1 **Accept common application:** No
Interview recommended: No **Off-campus interview available:** Yes
Evaluative: No **Informational only:** Yes **LD program:** No
Night in dorm provided: Yes **Non-refundable application fee:** $25
Early decision program: Yes **Applied:** 749 **Accepted:** 50 % **Deadline:** Dec. 1
Freshmen accepted other than Fall term: 0 % **SAT/FAF Code #** 5222

Transfers

Applied: 155 **Accepted:** 16 % **Application deadline for Fall:** Feb. 1 **Spring:**
Minimum grades recommended: 3.0 **All new students who were transfers into all classes:** 5 %

Class Experience

Return 2nd year: 95 % **Graduate after 4 years:** 75 % **To graduate school within 5 years:** 70 %

Cost

Tuition deposit: $100 **Total cost (Including school's estimate on fees and books):** $16,300
Tuition: $11,584 **(In state:** $) **Room and board:** $4,000
Annual giving by parents: $185,000 **Average per student:** $70

Financial Aid

Average total package per student: $3,100 **Number receiving aid:** 60 %
Average scholarships and grants: $1,600 **Average loans:** $1,500 **Work-study program:** Yes
Undergraduates working on campus: 20 % **Average earnings:** $1,000
Non-need scholarships 32 % **Athletic scholarships:** Yes **FAF deadline:** Feb. 1
Off-campus part-time employment: Good **CO-OP program:** No
ROTC: Yes **NROTC:** No **AFROTC:** No

Endowment

Total: $85 Million **Per student (including graduate students):** $31,000

Location

Acres: 750 **Setting:** Rural
Miles from town center: 5 (**Pop.** 300,000)
145 **Miles from** Atlanta (**Pop.** 500,000)
Miles from (**Pop.**)

Class Composition

Asian: 1 % **Black:** 4 % **Hispanic:** 1 % **White:** 94 % **Other:** NA %
Total minority : 6 % **Foreign countries:** 5 % (125 students)
From public schools: 72 % **Students from in state:** 35 %

Housing (on campus)

Freshmen required to live on campus: Yes
Available for all students: 65 %
On-campus married student housing: No
Guaranteed for: 2 years
Fraternity / Sorority housing: No / No
Women-only dorms available: Yes

Campus Life

Students living on campus: 60 % **Remain weekends:** 85 % **Handicap access:** 100 %
Car regulations: OK all 4 years
Number with cars: 50 %
Adequacy of on-campus parking: Good
Number of fraternities: 8 **Chapter houses:** 0
Number of sororities: 6 **Chapter houses:** 0
Students belonging to fraternities: 35 %
Students belonging to sororities: 30 %

Libraries and Computers

Books: 500,000 **Periodicals:** 2,500 **Microform items:** 455,000
Microcomputers available: Yes **Microcomputers networked:** NA

Classes

Faculty / Student Ratio: 1/13 **Classes taught by teacher assistants:** 0 %
Most popular majors: Business, Poly Science **Classes begin:** Sept.
Baccalaureate degrees offered: BA, BGS, BMUS, BS

Sports

Division: I **Except:** **Physical ed requirements:** 1 course
Students participating in intercollegiate sports: 25 % **In intramural sports:** 50 %
Additional intercollegiate and/or intramural sports: (not found at all colleges)

Crew: Yes **Ice Hockey:** No **Lacrosse:** Yes **Wrestling:** Yes/M
Rugby: Yes **Sailing:** Yes **Skiing:** Yes
Squash: No **Ultimate Frisbee:** Yes **Water Polo:** Yes

Alumni

Number living: 24,500 **Annual giving:** $3.5 Million **Participation:** 35 %
Average annual gift: $550 **Average per student:** $1,200

3-2 Programs (2 degrees in 5 years)

Engineering with Georgia Tech, Clemson, N. Carolina State and Auburn
Forestry with Duke

Observation and Opinion of:

Undergraduates and graduates ______________________________

____

College counselor ______________________________

____

GEORGETOWN UNIVERSITY (Private)

37 and O Streets, N.W.
Washington, DC 20057

MOST SELECTIVE
(Composite rating of guide books)

Main tel.: 202-687-5055
Admissions tel.: 202-687-3600
Financial aid tel.: 202-687-4547
Scheduled Airline Service: Washington
Miles to airport: 4

Founded: 1789
Nickname: Hoyas
Religious affiliation: Catholic
(Coed since 1969)

Student Body

Undergraduates: 5,600 **Men:** 50 % **Women:** 50 %
Graduate students: 5,600 **Freshman class:** 1,360

Academics

SAT Averages:1230 **Verbal:** 591 **Math:** 639 **(Taking SATs:** 97 %**)**
700-800: V 10 % M 24% **500-600:** V 33 % M 20 %
600-700: V 44 % M 52 % **400-500:** V 11 % M 4 % **300-400:** V 2 % M 0 %
High school class rank: Top fifth 85 % **2nd fifth** 10 % **3rd fifth** 5 %

Admissions

Applied: 9,400 **Accepted:** 29 % **Matriculated:** 50 %
Deadline: Jan. 10 **Accept common application:** NA
Interview recommended: Yes **Off-campus interview available:** Yes
Evaluative: Yes **Informational only:** NA **LD program:** Yes
Night in dorm provided: No **Non-refundable application fee:** $45
Early decision program: NA **Applied:** 2,041 **Accepted:** 26 % **Deadline:** Nov. 1
Freshmen accepted other than Fall term: 0 % **SAT/FAF Code #** 5244

Transfers

Applied: 1,254 **Accepted:** 33 % **Application deadline for Fall:** Mar. 1 **Spring:** Dec. 1
Minimum grades recommended: 3.0 **All new students who were transfers into all classes:** 4 %

Class Experience

Return 2nd year: 95 % **Graduate after 4 years:** 78 % **To graduate school within 5 years:** 26 %

Cost

Tuition deposit: $650 **Total cost (Including school's estimate on fees and books):** $24,500
Tuition: $16,500 **(In state:** $ **)** **Room and board:** $7,000
Annual giving by parents: $1.4 Million **Average per student:** $NA

Financial Aid

Average total package per student: $10,400 **Number receiving aid:** 45 %
Average scholarships and grants: $8,000 **Average loans:** $2,400 **Work-study program:** Yes
Undergraduates working on campus: 47% **Average earnings:** $1,900
Non-need scholarships 10 % **Athletic scholarships:** Yes **FAF deadline:** Jan. 10
Off-campus part-time employment: Excellent **CO-OP program:** No
ROTC: Yes **NROTC:** at Geo Wash **AFROTC:** at Howard

Endowment

Total: $242 Million **Per student (including graduate students):** $22,000

Location

Acres: 110 **Setting:** City **Miles from town center:** 2 **(Pop.** 700,000**)**
Miles from **(Pop.** **)** **Miles from** **(Pop.** **)**

Class Composition

Asian: 5 % **Black:** 8 % **Hispanic:** 5 % **White:** 73 % **Other:** 9 %
Total minority : 27 % **Foreign countries:** 10 % (560 students)
From public schools: 40 % **Students from in state:** 2 %

Housing (on campus)

Freshmen required to live on campus: Yes **Guaranteed for:** 2 years
Available for all students: 80 % **Fraternity / Sorority housing:** No / No
On-campus married student housing: No **Women-only dorms available:** No

Campus Life

Students living on campus: 80 % **Remain weekends:** NA % **Handicap access:** 85 %
Car regulations: No freshmen
Number with cars: 8 % **Adequacy of on-campus parking:** Poor
Number of fraternities: 0 **Chapter houses:** **Number of sororities:** 0 **Chapter houses:**
Students belonging to fraternities: 0 % **Students belonging to sororities:** 0 %

Libraries and Computers

Books: 1.3 Million **Periodicals:** 12,000 **Microform items:** 715,000
Microcomputers available: Yes **Microcomputers networked:** NA

Classes

Faculty / Student Ratio: 1/14 **Classes taught by teacher assistants:** 0 %
Most popular majors: Government, International Politics **Classes begin:** Late Aug.
Baccalaureate degrees offered: BA, BS, BSBA, BSN

Sports

Division: I **Except:** Football III **Physical ed requirements:** NA
Students participating in intercollegiate sports: 15 % **In intramural sports:** 50 %
Additional intercollegiate and/or intramural sports: (not found at all colleges)
Crew: Yes **Ice Hockey:** Yes **Lacrosse:** Yes **Wrestling:** No
Rugby: Yes **Sailing:** Yes **Skiing:** No
Squash: Yes **Ultimate Frisbee:** No **Water Polo:** No

Alumni

Number living: 70,000 **Annual giving:** $10 Million **Participation:** 29 %
Average annual gift: $550 **Average per student:** $800

3-2 Programs (2 degrees in 5 years)

Engineering with Catholic U

Observation and Opinion of:

Undergraduates and graduates ____________________

____

College counselor ____________________

____

GEORGE WASHINGTON UNIVERSITY (Private)

Washington, DC 20052

VERY SELECTIVE
(Composite rating of guide books)

Main tel.: 202-994-1000
Admissions tel.: 202-994-6040
Financial aid tel.: 202-994-6620
Scheduled Airline Service: Washington
Miles to airport: 4

Founded: 1821
Nickname: Colonials
Religious affiliation: None
(Coed since 1888)

Student Body

Undergraduates: 5,900 **Men:** 49 % **Women:** 51 %
Graduate students: 8,600 **Freshman class:** 1,160

Academics

SAT Averages: 1130 **Verbal:** 540 **Math:** 590 **(Taking SATs: 92 %)**
700-800: V 4 % **M** 9 % **500-600: V** 44 % **M** 43 %
600-700: V 22 % **M** 36 % **400-500: V** 21 % **M** 11% **300-400: V** 3 % **M** 1 %
High school class rank: Top fifth 65 % **2nd fifth** 20 % **3rd fifth** 15 %

Admissions

Applied: 6,100 **Accepted:** 51 % **Matriculated:** 24 %
Deadline: Feb. 1 **Accept common application:** NA
Interview recommended: No **Off-campus interview available:** Yes
Evaluative: No **Informational only:** Yes **LD program:** Yes
Night in dorm provided: No **Non-refundable application fee:** $45
Early decision program: Yes **Applied:** 127 **Accepted:** 65 % **Deadline:** Nov. 15
Freshmen accepted other than Fall term: NA % **SAT/FAF Code #** 5246

Transfers

Applied: 1,394 **Accepted:** 73 % **Application deadline for Fall:** June 1 **Spring:** Nov. 1
Minimum grades recommended: 2.5 **All new students who were transfers into all classes:** 27 %

Class Experience

Return 2nd year: 85 % **Graduate after 4 years:** 63 % **To graduate school within 5 years:** NA %

Cost

Tuition deposit: $300 **Total cost (Including school's estimate on fees and books):** $22,400
Tuition: $15,200 **(In state: $)** **Room and board:** $6,000
Annual giving by parents: $273,000 **Average per student:** $50

Financial Aid

Average total package per student: $13,450 **Number receiving aid:** 52 %
Average scholarships and grants: $9,000 **Average loans:** $4,450 **Work-study program:** Yes
Undergraduates working on campus: NA % **Average earnings:** $1,350
Non-need scholarships 28 % **Athletic scholarships:** **FAF deadline:** Feb. 1
Off-campus part-time employment: Excellent **CO-OP program:** Yes
ROTC: at Georgetown **NROTC:** Yes **AFROTC:** at Howard

Endowment

Total: $297 Million **Per student (including graduate students):** $16,000

Location

Acres: 36 **Setting:** City **Miles from town center:** 0 (Pop. 700,000)
Miles from (Pop.) **Miles from** (Pop.)

Class Composition

Asian: 8 % **Black:** 6 % **Hispanic:** 3 % **White:** 52 % **Other:** 1%
Total minority : 18% **Foreign countries:** 14 % (800 students)
From public schools: 80 % **Students from in state:** 6 %

Housing (on campus)

Freshmen required to live on campus: No **Guaranteed for:** 1 year
Available for all students: 50 % **Fraternity / Sorority housing:** Yes / No
On-campus married student housing: No **Women-only dorms available:** Yes

Campus Life

Students living on campus: 50 % **Remain weekends:** NA % **Handicap access:** 90 %
Car regulations: No restrictions (expensive)
Number with cars: 10 % **Adequacy of on-campus parking:** Poor
Number of fraternities: 16 **Chapter houses:** 9 **Number of sororities:** 11 **Chapter houses:** 0
Students belonging to fraternities: 26 % **Students belonging to sororities:** 18 %

Libraries and Computers

Books: 1.6 Million **Periodicals:** 13,000 **Microform items:** 1.6 Million
Microcomputers available: Yes **Microcomputers networked:** NA

Classes

Faculty / Student Ratio: 1/14 **Classes taught by teacher assistants:** 0 %
Most popular majors: International Affairs, Finance **Classes begin:** Early Sept.
Baccalaureate degrees offered: BA, BBA, BMUS, BS, BSACC, BSHS

Sports

Division: I **Except:** **Physical ed requirements:** None
Students participating in intercollegiate sports: 4 % **In intramural sports:** 75 %
Additional intercollegiate and/or intramural sports: (not found at all colleges)

Crew: Yes **Ice Hockey:** No **Lacrosse:** Yes **Wrestling:** No
Rugby: Yes **Sailing:** Yes **Skiing:** No
Squash: Yes **Ultimate Frisbee:** No **Water Polo:** Yes

Alumni

Number living: 107,000 **Annual giving:** $3.1 Million **Participation:** 37 %
Average annual gift: $190 **Average per student:** $210

3-2 Programs (2 degrees in 5 years)

Engineering with Bowie State, Gallaudet U, etc.

Observation and Opinion of:

Undergraduates and graduates ____

____

College counselor ____

____

GEORGIA INSTITUTE OF TECHNOLOGY (Public)

225 North Avenue, NW
Atlanta, GA 30332

HIGHLY SELECTIVE
(Composite rating of guide books)

Main tel.: 404-894-2000
Admissions tel.: 404-894-4154
Financial aid tel.: 404-894-4160
Scheduled Airline Service: Atlanta
Miles to airport: 9

Founded: 1885
Nickname: Yellow Jackets
Religious affiliation: None
(Coed since 1952)

Student Body

Undergraduates: 8,600 **Men:** 76 % **Women:** 24 %
Graduate students: 2,750 **Freshman class:** 1,605

Academics

SAT Averages: 1190 **Verbal:** 540 **Math:** 650 **(Taking SATs: 98 %)**
700-800: V 4 % **M** 26 % **500-600: V** 44 % **M** 23 %
600-700: V 19 % **M** 47 % **400-500: V** 28 % **M** 4 % **300-400: V** NA % **M** NA %
High school class rank: Top fifth 88 % **2nd fifth** 11 % **3rd fifth** 1 %

Admissions

Applied: 5,840 **Accepted:** 69 % **Matriculated:** 40 %
Deadline: Feb. 1 **Accept common application:** NA
Interview recommended: No **Off-campus interview available:** Yes
Evaluative: No **Informational only:** Yes **LD program:** Yes
Night in dorm provided: No **Non-refundable application fee:** $15
Early decision program: Yes **Applied:** NA **Accepted:** NA % **Deadline:** NA
Freshmen accepted other than Fall term: 15 % **SAT/FAF Code #** 5248

Transfers

Applied: 1023 **Accepted:** 43 % **Application deadline for Fall:** NA **Spring:** NA
Minimum grades recommended: 3.0 **All new students who were transfers into all classes:** 12 %

Class Experience

Return 2nd year: 86 % **Graduate after 4 years:** 66 % **To graduate school within 5 years:** 20 %

Cost

Tuition deposit: $100 **Total cost (Including school's estimate on fees and books):** $11,000
Tuition: $6,600 (In state: $ 2,200) **Room and board:** $4,000
Annual giving by parents: $22,000 **Average per student:** $NA

Financial Aid

Average total package per student: $3,250 **Number receiving aid:** 36 %
Average scholarships and grants: $750 **Average loans:** $2,500 **Work-study program:** Yes
Undergraduates working on campus: 25 % **Average earnings:** $1,000
Non-need scholarships 10 % **Athletic scholarships:** Yes **FAF deadline:** Feb. 15
Off-campus part-time employment: Excellent **CO-OP program:** Yes
ROTC: Yes **NROTC:** Yes **AFROTC:** Yes

Endowment

Total: $223 Million **Per student (including graduate students):** $19,000

Location

Acres: 330 **Setting:** City **Miles from town center:** 1 (Pop. 500,000)
Miles from (Pop.) **Miles from** (Pop.)

Class Composition

Asian: 11% **Black:** 7 % **Hispanic:** 4 % **White:** 78 % **Other:** NA %
Total minority : 22 % **Foreign countries:** 2 % (190 students)
From public schools: 87 % **Students from in state:** 34 %

Housing (on campus)

Freshmen required to live on campus: No **Guaranteed for:** 1 year
Available for all students: 36 % **Fraternity / Sorority housing:** Yes / Yes
On-campus married student housing: Yes **Women-only dorms available:** Yes

Campus Life

Students living on campus: 36 % **Remain weekends:** NA % **Handicap access:** 30 %
Car regulations: All four years
Number with cars: 60 % **Adequacy of on-campus parking:** NA
Number of fraternities: 33 **Chapter houses:** 31 **Number of sororities:** 8 **Chapter houses:** 7
Students belonging to fraternities: 26 % **Students belonging to sororities:** 23 %

Libraries and Computers

Books: 2.5 Million **Periodicals:** 23,400 **Microform items:** 3 Million
Microcomputers available: Yes **Microcomputers networked:** NA

Classes

Faculty / Student Ratio: 1/20 **Classes taught by teacher assistants:** 20 %
Most popular majors: Engineering, Management **Classes begin:** Mid Sept.
Baccalaureate degrees offered: B. Eng, BS

Sports

Division: I **Except:** **Physical ed requirements:** 2 Terms
Students participating in intercollegiate sports: 16 % **In intramural sports:** 60 %
Additional intercollegiate and/or intramural sports: (not found at all colleges)

Crew: No	**Ice Hockey:** Yes	**Lacrosse:** Yes	**Wrestling:** Yes/M
Rugby: Yes	**Sailing:** Yes	**Skiing:** No	
Squash: Yes	**Ultimate Frisbee:** No	**Water Polo:** Yes	

Alumni

Number living: 64,000 **Annual giving:** $ 11.6 Million **Participation:** 34 %
Average annual gift: $ 600 **Average per student:** $1,000

3-2 Programs (2 degrees in 5 years)

Engineering with 80 other colleges, In-house 6-year Master's Program in Architecture

Observation and Opinion of:

Undergraduates and graduates ______________________________

____

College counselor ______________________________

____

GETTYSBURG COLLEGE (Private)

Gettysburg, PA

HIGHLY SELECTIVE
(Composite rating of guide books)

Main tel.: 717-337-6000
Admissions tel.: 800-431-0803
Financial aid tel.: 717-337-6611
Scheduled Airline Service: Harrisburg
Miles to airport: 36

Founded: 1832
Nickname: NA
Religious affiliation: Lutheran
(Coed since 1888)

Student Body

Undergraduates: 1,900 **Men:** 50 % **Women:** 50 %
Graduate students: 0 **Freshman class:** 550

Academics

SAT Averages: 1120 **Verbal:** 535 **Math:** 585 **(Taking SATs:** NA %**)**
700-800: V 3 % **M** 5 % **500-600: V** 55 % **M** 50 %
600-700: V 15 % **M** 35 % **400-500: V** 25 % **M** 10 % **300-400: V** 2 % **M** NA %
High school class rank: Top fifth 75 % **2nd fifth** NA % **3rd fifth** NA %

Admissions

Applied: 3,500 **Accepted:** 49 % **Matriculated:** 29 %
Deadline: Feb. 15 **Accept common application:** Yes
Interview recommended: No **Off-campus interview available:** No
Evaluative: Yes **Informational only:** NA **LD program:** No
Night in dorm provided: Yes **Non-refundable application fee:** $35
Early decision program: Yes **Applied:** NA **Accepted:** NA % **Deadline:** NA
Freshmen accepted other than Fall term: 1 % **SAT/FAF Code #** 2275

Transfers

Applied: NA **Accepted:** NA % **Application deadline for Fall:** Feb. 15 **Spring:** NA
Minimum grades recommended: 3.0 **All new students who were transfers into all classes:** NA %

Class Experience

Return 2nd year: 90 % **Graduate after 4 years:** 76 % **To graduate school within 5 years:** 40 %

Cost

Tuition deposit: $200 **Total cost (Including school's estimate on fees and books):** $22,300
Tuition: $17,650 **(In state:** $ **)** **Room and board:** $3,900
Annual giving by parents: $166,000 **Average per student:** $80

Financial Aid

Average total package per student: $ **Number receiving aid:** 40 %
Average scholarships and grants: $NA **Average loans:** $NA **Work-study program:** Yes
Undergraduates working on campus: 35 % **Average earnings:** $900
Non-need scholarships 10 % **Athletic scholarships:** No **FAF deadline:** Feb. 2
Off-campus part-time employment: Good **CO-OP program:** No
ROTC: Yes **NROTC:** No **AFROTC:** No

Endowment

Total: $45 Million **Per student (including graduate students):** $24,000

Location

Acres: 200 **Setting:** Rural **Miles from town center:** 1 **(Pop.** 8,500**)**
36 **Miles from** Harrisburg **(Pop.** 53,000 **)** **Miles from** Baltimore **(Pop.** 655,000 **)**

Class Composition

Asian: 3 % **Black:** 2 % **Hispanic:** 3 % **White:** 92 % **Other:** 1 %
Total minority : 8 % **Foreign countries:** 2 % (40 students)
From public schools: NA % **Students from in state:** 25 %

Housing (on campus)

Freshmen required to live on campus: Yes **Guaranteed for:** 4 years
Available for all students: 90 % **Fraternity / Sorority housing:** Yes / No
On-campus married student housing: No **Women-only dorms available:** Yes

Campus Life

Students living on campus: 88 % **Remain weekends:** 85 % **Handicap access:** 75 %
Car regulations: All may have
Number with cars: 35 % **Adequacy of on-campus parking:** NA
Number of fraternities: 12 **Chapter houses:** 12 **Number of sororities:** 7 **Chapter houses:** 0
Students belonging to fraternities: 0 % **Students belonging to sororities:** 45 %

Libraries and Computers

Books: 308,000 **Periodicals:** 1,350 **Microform items:** 35,000
Microcomputers available: Yes **Microcomputers networked:** NA

Classes

Faculty / Student Ratio: 1/13 **Classes taught by teacher assistants:** 0 %
Most popular majors: NA **Classes begin:** August
Baccalaureate degrees offered: BA, BS

Sports

Division: **Except:** **Physical ed requirements:** 1-1/2
Students participating in intercollegiate sports: 25 % **In intramural sports:** 70 %
Additional intercollegiate and/or intramural sports: (not found at all colleges)

Crew: No	**Ice Hockey:** Yes/M	**Lacrosse:** Yes	**Wrestling:** Yes/M
Rugby: Yes/M	**Sailing:** No	**Skiing:** Yes	
Squash: No	**Ultimate Frisbee:** No	**Water Polo:** No	

Alumni

Number living: 22 **Annual giving:** $ 2.9 Million **Participation:** 34 %
Average annual gift: $ 400 **Average per student:** $1,500

3-2 Programs (2 degrees in 5 years)

Engineering with Penn State, RPI, Washington U, Forestry with Duke

Observation and Opinion of:

Undergraduates and graduates

College counselor ______________________________

GMI ENGINEERING & MANAGEMENT INSTITUTE (Private)

1700 West Third Avenue
Flint, MI 48504-4898

HIGHLY SELECTIVE
(Composite rating of guide books)

Main tel.: 313-762-9500
Admissions tel.: 313-762-7865
Financial aid tel.: 313-762-7859
Scheduled Airline Service: Detroit
Miles to airport: 66

Founded: 1919
Nickname: NA
Religious affiliation: None
(Coed since 1966)

Student Body

Undergraduates: 2,500 **Men:** 79 % **Women:** 21 %
Graduate students: 700 **Freshman class:** 640

Academics

SAT Averages: 1150 **Verbal:** 510 **Math:** 640 **(Taking SATs:** 74 %)
700-800: V 1 % M 20 % **500-600:** V 55 % M 22 %
600-700: V 17 % M 57 % **400-500:** V 23 % M 1% **300-400:** V NA % M NA %
High school class rank: Top fifth 87 % 2nd fifth 12 % 3rd fifth 1 %

Admissions

Applied: 2,215 **Accepted:** 67 % **Matriculated:** 43 %
Deadline: NA **Accept common application:** NA
Interview recommended: Yes **Off-campus interview available:** Yes
Evaluative: No **Informational only:** Yes **LD program:** No
Night in dorm provided: No **Non-refundable application fee:** $25
Early decision program: NA **Applied:** NA **Accepted:** NA % **Deadline:** NA
Freshmen accepted other than Fall term: 1 % **SAT/FAF Code #** 1246

Transfers

Applied: 247 **Accepted:** 53 % **Application deadline for Fall:** NA **Spring:** NA
Minimum grades recommended: 3.0 **All new students who were transfers into all classes:** 10 %

Class Experience

Return 2nd year: 91 % **Graduate after 4 years:** 72 % **To graduate school within 5 years:** 55 %

Cost

Tuition deposit: $100 **Total cost (Including school's estimate on fees and books):** $13,800
Tuition: $10,150 (In state: $) **Room and board:** $3,000 (Room Only)
Annual giving by parents: $1,500 **Average per student:** $NA

Financial Aid

Average total package per student: $NA **Number receiving aid:** 48 %
Average scholarships and grants: $2,500 **Average loans:** $3,700 **Work-study program:** Yes
Undergraduates working on campus: 17 % **Average earnings:** $800
Non-need scholarships NA % **Athletic scholarships:** NA **FAF deadline:** May 1
Off-campus part-time employment: Excellent **CO-OP program:** Yes
ROTC: No **NROTC:** No **AFROTC:** No

Endowment

Total: $10 Million **Per student (including graduate students):** $3,300

Location

Acres: 45 **Setting:** Surburban **Miles from town center:** 2 **(Pop.** 150,000**)**
61 **Miles from** Detroit **(Pop.** 1.2 Mi.) **Miles from (Pop.)**

Class Composition

Asian: 7 % **Black:** 6 % **Hispanic:** 2 % **White:** 77 % **Other:** 8 %
Total minority : 23 % **Foreign countries:**7 % (180 students)
From public schools: 85 % **Students from in state:** 48 %

Housing (on campus)

Freshmen required to live on campus: Yes **Guaranteed for:** 1 year
Available for all students: 35 % **Fraternity / Sorority housing:** Yes / Yes
On-campus married student housing: NA **Women-only dorms available:** No

Campus Life

Students living on campus: 32 % **Remain weekends:** NA % **Handicap access:** 100 %
Car regulations: All may have
Number with cars: 80 % **Adequacy of on-campus parking:** NA
Number of fraternities: 14 **Chapter houses:** 11 **Number of sororities:** 6 **Chapter houses:** 2
Students belonging to fraternities: 60 % **Students belonging to sororities:** 60 %

Libraries and Computers

Books: 61,000 **Periodicals:** 740 **Microform items:** 23
Microcomputers available: Yes **Microcomputers networked:** Yes

Classes

Faculty / Student Ratio: 1/14 **Classes taught by teacher assistants:** 0 %
Most popular majors: Engineering & Management **Classes begin:** July, Jan. Oct., March
Baccalaureate degrees offered: BS

Sports

Division: Except: Physical ed requirements: None
Students participating in intercollegiate sports: 1 % **In intramural sports:** 40 %
Additional intercollegiate and/or intramural sports: (not found at all colleges)
Crew: No **Ice Hockey:** Yes/M **Lacrosse:** No **Wrestling:** Yes
Rugby: No **Sailing:** Yes **Skiing:** Yes
Squash: No **Ultimate Frisbee:** No **Water Polo:** No

Alumni

Number living: 22,600 **Annual giving:** $500,000 **Participation:** 23 %
Average annual gift: $ 130 **Average per student:** $176

3-2 Programs (2 degrees in 5 years)

Double Majors - Dual Degrees

Observation and Opinion of:

Undergraduates and graduates ____________________

____

College counselor ____________________

____

GRINNELL COLLEGE (Private)

Grinnell, Iowa 50112

HIGHLY SELECTIVE
(Composite rating of guide books)

Main tel.: 515-269-4000
Admissions tel.: 515-269-3600
Financial aid tel.: 515-289-3250
Scheduled Airline Service: Des Moines
Miles to airport: 60

Founded: 1846
Nickname: Pioneers
Religious affiliation: None
(Coed since 1846)

Student Body

Undergraduates: 1,250 **Men:** 52% **Women:** 48 %
Graduate students: 0 **Freshman class:** 343

Academics

SAT Averages: 1235 **Verbal:** 602 **Math:** 634 **(Taking SATs:** 89 %)
700-800: V 11 % **M** 24 % **500-600: V** 39 % **M** 24 %
600-700: V 40 % **M** 50 % **400-500: V** 10 % **M** 6 % **300-400: V** NA % **M** NA %
High school class rank: Top fifth 78 % **2nd fifth** 16 % **3rd fifth** 4 %

Admissions

Applied: 1,600 **Accepted:** 69 % **Matriculated:** 31 %
Deadline: Feb. 1 **Accept common application:** Yes
Interview recommended: Yes **Off-campus interview available:** Yes
Evaluative: Yes **Informational only:** No **LD program:** No
Night in dorm provided: Yes **Non-refundable application fee:** $25
Early decision program: Yes **Applied:** 172 **Accepted:** 75% **Deadline:** Dec. 1
Freshmen accepted other than Fall term: 0 % **SAT/FAF Code #** 6252

Transfers

Applied: 153 **Accepted:** 50 % **Application deadline for Fall:** May 1 **Spring:** Dec. 15
Minimum grades recommended: 3.0 **All new students who were transfers into all classes:** 11 %

Class Experience

Return 2nd year: 95 % **Graduate after 4 years:** 78 % **To graduate school within 5 years:** N/A %

Cost

Tuition deposit: $100 **Total cost (Including school's estimate on fees and books):** $19,470
Tuition: $14,195 **(In state:** $ **)** **Room and board:** $4,138
Annual giving by parents: $235,000 **Average per student:** $200

Financial Aid

Average total package per student: $9,100 **Number receiving aid:** 69 %
Average scholarships and grants: $6,700 **Average loans:** $2,400 **Work-study program:** Yes
Undergraduates working on campus: NA % **Average earnings:** $1,000
Non-need scholarships 11 % **Athletic scholarships:** NA **FAF deadline:** Mar. 1
Off-campus part-time employment: Fair **CO-OP program:** Yes
ROTC: No **NROTC:** No **AFROTC:** No

Endowment

Total: $292 Million **Per student (including graduate students):** $230,000

Location

Acres: 90 **Setting:** Rural **Miles from town center:** 0 **(Pop.** 8,900**)**
55 **Miles from** Des Moines **(Pop.** 191,000 **)** **Miles from** **(Pop.** **)**

Class Composition

Asian: 4 **%** **Black:** 5 **%** **Hispanic:** 1 **%** **White:** 82 **%** **Other:** 8 **%**
Total minority : 18 **%** **Foreign countries:** 8 **%** (90 students)
From public schools: 72 **%** **Students from in state:** 25 **%**

Housing (on campus)

Freshmen required to live on campus: Yes **Guaranteed for:** 4 years
Available for all students: 86 **%** **Fraternity / Sorority housing:** No / No
On-campus married student housing: Yes **Women-only dorms available:** Yes

Campus Life

Students living on campus: 86 **%** **Remain weekends:** NA **%** **Handicap access:** 35 **%**
Car regulations: Restricted if on financial aid
Number with cars: 10**%** **Adequacy of on-campus parking:** Good
Number of fraternities: 0 **Chapter houses:** 0 **Number of sororities:** 0 **Chapter houses:** 0
Students belonging to fraternities: 0 **%** **Students belonging to sororities:** 0 **%**

Libraries and Computers

Books: 304,000 **Periodicals:** 1,650 **Microform items:** 5,230
Microcomputers available: Yes **Microcomputers networked:** NA

Classes

Faculty / Student Ratio: 1/10 **Classes taught by teacher assistants:** 0 **%**
Most popular majors: Biology, History, Psychology **Classes begin:** Late Aug.
Baccalaureate degrees offered: BA

Sports

Division: III **Except:** **Physical ed requirements:** None
Students participating in intercollegiate sports: 50 **%** **In intramural sports:** 25 **%**
Additional intercollegiate and/or intramural sports: (not found at all colleges)

Crew: No	**Ice Hockey:** No	**Lacrosse:** No	**Wrestling:** No
Rugby: No	**Sailing:** No	**Skiing:** No	
Squash: Yes	**Ultimate Frisbee:** Yes	**Water Polo:** No	

Alumni

Number living: 16,600 **Annual giving:** $ 4.1 Million **Participation:** 48 **%**
Average annual gift: $ 550 **Average per student:** $3,300

3-2 Programs (2 degrees in 5 years)

Engineering with Cal Tech, Columbia, RPI and Wash U, 3-3 Law with Columbia, 3-4 Architecture with Wash U

Observation and Opinion of:

Undergraduates and graduates ______________________________

____

College counselor ______________________________

____

HAMILTON COLLEGE (Private)

Clinton, NY 13323

HIGHLY SELECTIVE
(Composite rating of guide books)

Main tel.: 315-859-4011
Admissions tel.: 315-859-4421
Financial aid tel.: 315-859-4434
Scheduled Airline Service: Utica
Miles to airport: 15

Founded: 1812
Nickname: Continentals
Religious affiliation: None
(Coed since 1978)

Student Body

Undergraduates: 1,650 **Men:** 55 % **Women:** 45 %
Graduate students: 0 **Freshman class:** 448

Academics

SAT Averages: 1170 **Verbal:** 555 **Math:** 615 **(Taking SATs:** 99 %**)**
700-800: V 3 % **M** 12 % **500-600: V** 51 % **M** 35 %
600-700: V 26 % **M** 46 % **400-500: V** 19 % **M** 6 % **300-400: V** 1 % **M** 1 %
High school class rank: Top fifth 78 % **2nd fifth** 17 % **3rd fifth** 5 %

Admissions

Applied: 3,780 **Accepted:** 43 % **Matriculated:** 27 %
Deadline: Jan. 15 **Accept common application:** NA
Interview recommended: Yes **Off-campus interview available:** Yes
Evaluative: Yes **Informational only:** No **LD program:** No
Night in dorm provided: Yes **Non-refundable application fee:** $40
Early decision program: Yes **Applied:** 303 **Accepted:** 47 % **Deadline:** Nov. 15
Freshman accepted other than Fall term: 0 % **SAT/FAF Code #** 2286

Transfers

Applied: 97 **Accepted:** 33 % **Application deadline for Fall:** Mar. 15 **Spring:** Dec. 15
Minimum grades recommended: 3.0 **All new students who were transfers into all classes:** 4 %

Class Experience

Return 2nd year: 94% **Graduate after 4 years:** 85 % **To graduate school within 5 years:** 50 %

Cost

Tuition deposit: $200 **Total cost (Including school's estimate on fees and books):** $22,900
Tuition: $17,150 **(In state: $** **)** **Room and board:** $4,750
Annual giving by parents: $517,000 **Average per student:** $460

Financial Aid

Average total package per student: $12,000 **Number receiving aid:** 42 %
Average scholarships and grants: $10,140 **Average loans:** $1,900 **Work-study program:** Yes
Undergraduates working on campus: 30 % **Average earnings:** $1,200
Non-need scholarships 0 % **Athletic scholarships:** NA **FAF deadline:** Feb. 1
Off-campus part-time employment: Fair **CO-OP program:** No
ROTC: At Utica College **NROTC:** No **AFROTC:** No

Endowment

Total: $115 Million **Per student (including graduate students):** $80,000

Location

Acres: 1,200 **Setting:** Rural
Miles from town center: 1 **(Pop.** 3,000**)**
50 **Miles from** Syracuse **(Pop.** 170,000 **)**
9 **Miles from** Utica **(Pop.** 75,000 **)**

Class Composition

Asian: 3 % **Black:** 3 % **Hispanic:** 3 % **White:** 86 % **Other:** 5 %
Total minority : 14 % **Foreign countries:** 5 % (80 students)
From public schools: 58 % **Students from in state:** 48 %

Housing (on campus)

Freshmen required to live on campus: Yes
Guaranteed for: 4 years
Available for all students: 100 %
Fraternity / Sorority housing: No / No
On-campus married student housing: Yes
Women-only dorms available: No

Campus Life

Students living on campus: 99 % **Remain weekends:** 95 % **Handicap access:** NA %
Car regulations: No freshmen
Number with cars: 30 %
Adequacy of on-campus parking: Poor
Number of fraternities: 8 **Chapter houses:** 0
Number of sororities: 2 **Chapter houses:** 0
Students belonging to fraternities: 45 %
Students belonging to sororities: 10 %

Libraries and Computers

Books: 453,000 **Periodicals:** 2,200 **Microform items:** 318,000
Microcomputers available: Yes **Microcomputers networked:**

Classes

Faculty / Student Ratio: 1/11 **Classes taught by teacher assistants:** 0 %
Most popular majors: Government, Economics, English **Classes begin:** Late Aug.
Baccalaureate degrees offered: BA

Sports

Division: III **Except:** **Physical ed requirements:** 2 sports
Students participating in intercollegiate sports: 35 % **In intramural sports:** 67 %
Additional intercollegiate and/or intramural sports: (not found at all colleges)

Crew: Yes	**Ice Hockey:** Yes	**Lacrosse:** Yes	**Wrestling:** No
Rugby: Yes	**Sailing:** Yes	**Skiing:** Yes	
Squash: Yes	**Ultimate Frisbee:** Yes	**Water Polo:** Yes/M	

Alumni

Number living: 10,800 **Annual giving:** $4 Million **Participation:** 63 %
Average annual gift: $ 600 **Average per student:** $2,400

3-2 Programs (2 degrees in 5 years)

Engineering with Columbia, RPI, Washington U, 3-3 Law Program with Columbia U

Observation and Opinion of:

Undergraduates and graduates ______________________________

____

College counselor ______________________________

____

HAMPSHIRE COLLEGE (Private)

Amherst, MA 01002

SELECTIVE
(Composite rating of guide books)

Main tel.: 413-549-4600
Admissions tel.: 413-549-4600, Ext. 471
Financial aid tel.: 413-549-4600, Ext. 484
Scheduled Airline Service: Hartford
Miles to airport: 30

Founded: 1965
Nickname: NA
Religious affiliation: None
(Coed since 1965)

Student Body

Undergraduates: 1,250 **Men:** 40 % **Women:** 60 %
Graduate students: 0 **Freshman class:** 310

Academics

SAT Averages: 1105 **Verbal:** NA **Math:** NA (**Taking SATs:** NA %)
700-800: V NA % **M** NA % **500-600: V** NA % **M** NA %
600-700: V NA% **M** NA % **400-500: V** NA % **M** NA % **300-400: V** NA % **M** NA %
High school class rank: Top fifth 27 % **2nd fifth** 17 % **3rd fifth** 5 %

Admissions

Applied: 1,450 **Accepted:** 61 % **Matriculated:** 35 %
Deadline: NA **Accept common application:** Yes
Interview recommended: No **Off-campus interview available:**
Evaluative: NA **Informational only:** Yes **LD program:** No
Night in dorm provided: Yes **Non-refundable application fee:** No
Early decision program: Yes **Applied:** 92 **Accepted:** 50 % **Deadline:** Dec. 1
Freshmen accepted other than Fall term: 3 % **SAT/FAF Code #** 3447

Transfers

Applied: 176 **Accepted:** 60 % **Application deadline for Fall:** Feb. 1 **Spring:** Dec. 1
Minimum grades recommended: 1.3 **All new students who were transfers into all classes:** 16 %

Class Experience

Return 2nd year: 84 % **Graduate after 4 years:** 60 % **To graduate school within 5 years:** 50 %

Cost

Tuition deposit: $200 **Total cost (Including school's estimate on fees and books):** $24,000
Tuition: $18,385 **(In state:** $ **)** **Room and board:** $4,800
Annual giving by parents: $185,000 **Average per student:** $150

Financial Aid

Average total package per student: $17,000 **Number receiving aid:** 60 %
Average scholarships and grants: $14,325 **Average loans:** $2,625 **Work-study program:** Yes
Undergraduates working on campus: 85 % **Average earnings:** $1,450
Non-need scholarships NA % **Athletic scholarships:** NA **FAF deadline:** Feb. 15
Off-campus part-time employment: Good **CO-OP program:** No
ROTC: Yes **NROTC:** No **AFROTC:** at U of Mass

Endowment

Total: $10 Million **Per student (including graduate students):** $8,000

Location

Acres: 800 **Setting:** City
20 Miles from (Pop. 150,000)
Miles from town center: 2 (Pop. 28,000)
Miles from Hartford (Pop. 800,000)

Class Composition

Asian: 4 % **Black:** 3 % **Hispanic:** 3 % **White:** 88% **Other:** 2 %
Total minority : 12 % **Foreign countries:** 3 % (40 students)
From public schools: 67 % **Students from in state:** 14 %

Housing (on campus)

Freshmen required to live on campus: Yes
Available for all students: 87 %
On-campus married student housing: Yes
Guaranteed for: 4 years
Fraternity / Sorority housing: No / No
Women-only dorms available: Yes

Campus Life

Students living on campus: 87 % **Remain weekends:** 75 % **Handicap access:** 90 %
Car regulations: All 4 years
Number with cars: 60%
Number of fraternities: 0 **Chapter houses:** 0
Students belonging to fraternities: 0 %
Adequacy of on-campus parking: NA
Number of sororities: 0 **Chapter houses:** 0
Students belonging to sororities: 0 %

Libraries and Computers

Books: 100,000 **Periodicals:** 750 **Microform items:** 280
Microcomputers available: Yes **Microcomputers networked:** NA

Classes

Faculty / Student Ratio: 1/13 **Classes taught by teacher assistants:** 0 %
Most popular majors: NA **Classes begin:** Early Sept.
Baccalaureate degrees offered: BA

Sports

Division: None **Except:** **Physical ed requirements:** None
Students participating in intercollegiate sports: 65 % **In intramural sports:** 35 %
Additional intercollegiate and/or intramural sports: (not found at all colleges)

Crew: No	**Ice Hockey:** No	**Lacrosse:** No	**Wrestling:** No
Rugby: No	**Sailing:** No	**Skiing:** Yes	
Squash: No	**Ultimate Frisbee:** Yes	**Water Polo:** Yes	

Alumni

Number living: 5,500 **Annual giving:** $157,000 **Participation:** 31 %
Average annual gift: $ 76 **Average per student:** $120

3-2 Programs (2 degrees in 5 years)

Member of 5-college consortium (Amherst, Mt. Holyoke, Smith, U of Mass.)

Observation and Opinion of:

Undergraduates and graduates ____________________

____

College counselor ____________________

____

HARVARD UNIVERSITY (Private)

Beverly Hall, 18 Garden Street
Cambridge, MA 02138

MOST SELECTIVE
(Composite rating of guide books)

Main tel.: 617-495-1000
Admissions tel.: 617-495-1551
Financial aid tel.: 617-495-1581
Scheduled Airline Service: Boston
Miles to airport: 4

Founded: 1636
Nickname: Crimson
Religious affiliation: None
(Coed since 1943)

Student Body

Undergraduates: 6,600 **Men:** 60 % **Women:** 40 %
Graduate students: 11,200 **Freshman class:** 1,600

Academics

SAT Averages: 1365 **Verbal:** 665 **Math:** 700 **(Taking SATs:** NA %**)**
700-800: V NA % **M** NA % **500-600:** V NA % **M** NA %
600-700: V NA % **M** NA % **400-500:** V NA % **M** NA % **300-400:** V NA % **M** NA %
High school class rank: Top fifth 98 % **2nd fifth** 2 % **3rd fifth** NA%

Admissions

Applied: 12,190 **Accepted:** 18 % **Matriculated:** 73 %
Deadline: Jan. 1 **Accept common application:** No
Interview recommended: No **Off-campus interview available:** Yes
Evaluative: Yes **Informational only:** Yes **LD program:** Yes
Night in dorm provided: Yes **Non-refundable application fee:** $50
Early decision program: Yes **Applied:** 1,777 **Accepted:** 39 % **Deadline:** Nov. 1
Freshmen accepted other than Fall term: 0 % **SAT/FAF Code #** 5222

Transfers

Applied: 1,020 **Accepted:** 13 % **Application deadline for Fall:** Apr. 15 **Spring:** Nov. 15
Minimum grades recommended: C **All new students who were transfers into all classes:** 5 %

Class Experience

Return 2nd year: 97 % **Graduate after 4 years:** 95 % **To graduate school within 5 years:** 33 %

Cost

Tuition deposit: $ **Total cost (Including school's estimate on fees and books):** $23,500
Tuition: $15,870 **(In state:** $ **)** **Room and board:** $5,835
Annual giving by parents: $NA **Average per student:** $NA

Financial Aid

Average total package per student: $11,000 **Number receiving aid:** 40 %
Average scholarships and grants: $8,500 **Average loans:** $2,400 **Work-study program:** Yes
Undergraduates working on campus: 67 % **Average earnings:** $1,000
Non-need scholarships 0 % **Athletic scholarships:** No **FAF deadline:** Feb. 15
Off-campus part-time employment: Good **CO-OP program:** No
ROTC: No **NROTC:** No **AFROTC:** No

Endowment

Total: $4.7 Billion **Per student (including graduate students):** $300,000

Location

Acres: 300 **Setting:** Urban **Miles from town center:** 0 **(Pop.** 95,000**)**
2 **Miles from** Boston **(Pop.** 700,000 **)** **Miles from (Pop.)**

Class Composition

Asian: 14 % **Black:** 5 % **Hispanic:** 8 % **White:** 73 % **Other:** NA %
Total minority : 27 % **Foreign countries:** 6 % (400 students)
From public schools: 66 % **Students from in state:** 22 %

Housing (on campus)

Freshmen required to live on campus: Yes **Guaranteed for:** 1 year
Available for all students: 100 % **Fraternity / Sorority housing:** No / No
On-campus married student housing: Yes **Women-only dorms available:** No

Campus Life

Students living on campus: 99 % **Remain weekends:** NA % **Handicap access:** 50 %
Car regulations: All 4 years
Number with cars: 3 % **Adequacy of on-campus parking:** Poor
Number of fraternities: 0 **Chapter houses:** 0 **Number of sororities:** 0 **Chapter houses:** 0
Students belonging to fraternities: 0 % **Students belonging to sororities:** 0 %

Libraries and Computers

Books: 11 Million **Periodicals:** 100,000 **Microform items:** 3 Million
Microcomputers available: Yes **Microcomputers networked:** NA

Classes

Faculty / Student Ratio: 1/8 **Classes taught by teacher assistants:** 20 %
Most popular majors: Economics, Biology, Government **Classes begin:** Late Sept.
Baccalaureate degrees offered: AB, BS

Sports

Division: I **Except:** **Physical ed requirements:** None
Students participating in intercollegiate sports: 20 % **In intramural sports:** 70 %
Additional intercollegiate and/or intramural sports: (not found at all colleges)

Crew: Yes	**Ice Hockey:** Yes	**Lacrosse:** Yes	**Wrestling:** Yes/M
Rugby: Yes	**Sailing:** Yes	**Skiing:** Yes	
Squash: Yes	**Ultimate Frisbee:** Yes	**Water Polo:** Yes	

Alumni

Number living: 244,000 **Annual giving:** $71 Million **Participation:** 27 %
Average annual gift: $ 1,100 **Average per student:** $4,060

3-2 Programs (2 degrees in 5 years)

A number of dual degrees

Observation and Opinion of:

Undergraduates and graduates ____________________

College counselor ____________________

HAVERFORD COLLEGE (Private)

370 Lancaster Avenue
Haverford, PA 19041-1392

MOST SELECTIVE
(Composite rating of guide books)

Founded: 1833
Nickname: Fords
Religious affiliation: Quaker
(Coed since 1980)

Main tel.: 215-896-1000
Admissions tel.: 215-896-1350
Financial aid tel.: 215-896-1350
Scheduled Airline Service: Philadelphia
Miles to airport: 10

Student Body

Undergraduates: 1,150 **Men:** 58 % **Women:** 42 %
Graduate students: 0 **Freshman class:** 287

Academics

SAT Averages: 1290 **Verbal:** 640 **Math:** 650 **(Taking SATs: 100 %)**
700-800: V 13 % **M** 30 % **500-600: V** 24 % **M** 15 %
600-700: V 55 % **M** 51 % **400-500: V** 6 % **M** 4 % **300-400: V** 2 % **M** 0 %
High school class rank: Top fifth 94 % **2nd fifth** 6 % **3rd fifth** 0 %

Admissions

Applied: 2,148 **Accepted:** 40 % **Matriculated:** 34 %
Deadline: Apr. 15 **Accept common application:** Yes
Interview recommended: Yes **Off-campus interview available:** Yes
Evaluative: No **Informational only:** Yes **LD program:** Yes
Night in dorm provided: Yes **Non-refundable application fee:** $40
Early decision program: Yes **Applied:** 159 **Accepted:** 46 % **Deadline:** Apr. 15
Freshmen accepted other than Fall term: 0 % **SAT/FAF Code #** 2289

Transfers

Applied: 125 **Accepted:** 3 % **Application deadline for Fall:** Mar. 1 **Spring:** NA
Minimum grades recommended: 3.0 **All new students who were transfers into all classes:** 1 %

Class Experience

Return 2nd year: 97 % **Graduate after 4 years:** 89 % **To graduate school within 5 years:** 80 %

Cost

Tuition deposit: $100 **Total cost (Including school's estimate on fees and books):** $23,500
Tuition: $16,960 **(In state:** $ **)** **Room and board:** $5,700
Annual giving by parents: $200,000 **Average per student:** $180

Financial Aid

Average total package per student: $12,400 **Number receiving aid:** 55 %
Average scholarships and grants: $9,600 **Average loans:** $2,700 **Work-study program:** Yes
Undergraduates working on campus: NA % **Average earnings:** $NA
Non-need scholarships 0 % **Athletic scholarships:** No **FAF deadline:** Jan. 15
Off-campus part-time employment: Good **CO-OP program:** No
ROTC: No **NROTC:** No **AFROTC:** No

Endowment

Total: $84 Million **Per student (including graduate students):** $75,000

Location

Acres: 216 **Setting:** Surburban **Miles from town center:** 0 **(Pop.** 8,000**)**
10 **Miles from** Phila. **(Pop.** 1.3 Mil**)** **Miles from (Pop.)**

Class Composition

Asian: 9 % **Black:** 5 % **Hispanic:** 4 % **White:** 82 % **Other:** NA %
Total minority : 18 % **Foreign countries:** 5 % (52 students)
From public schools: 61 % **Students from in state:** 14 %

Housing (on campus)

Freshmen required to live on campus: Yes **Guaranteed for:** 4 years
Available for all students: 99 % **Fraternity / Sorority housing:** No / No
On-campus married student housing: Yes **Women-only dorms available:** No

Campus Life

Students living on campus: 99 % **Remain weekends:** 90 % **Handicap access:** 50%
Car regulations: No freshmen
Number with cars: NA % **Adequacy of on-campus parking:** Fair
Number of fraternities: 0 **Chapter houses:** 0 **Number of sororities:** 0 **Chapter houses:** 0
Students belonging to fraternities: 0 % **Students belonging to sororities:** 0 %

Libraries and Computers

Books: 470,000 **Periodicals:** 1,040 **Microform items:** N/A
Microcomputers available: Yes **Microcomputers networked:** NA

Classes

Faculty / Student Ratio: 1/11 **Classes taught by teacher assistants:** 0 %
Most popular majors: English, History, Biology **Classes begin:** Early Sept.
Baccalaureate degrees offered: BA, BS

Sports

Division: III **Except:** **Physical ed requirements:** 3 semesters
Students participating in intercollegiate sports: 50 % **In intramural sports:** 60 %
Additional intercollegiate and/or intramural sports: (not found at all colleges)

Crew: No	**Ice Hockey:** Yes	**Lacrosse:** Yes	**Wrestling:** Yes/M
Rugby: Yes	**Sailing:** Yes	**Skiing:** No	
Squash: Yes	**Ultimate Frisbee:** Yes	**Water Polo:** Yes	

Alumni

Number living: 8,300 **Annual giving:** $1.8 Million **Participation:** 58 %
Average annual gift: $ 210 **Average per student:** $1,500

3-2 Programs (2 degrees in 5 years)

Engineering with U of Pennsylvania
Cross registration with Bryn Mawr, Swarthmore and U of Pennsylvania

Observation and Opinion of:

Undergraduates and graduates ______________________________

____

College counselor ______________________________

____

HOBART AND WILLIAM SMITH COLLEGES (Private)

639 South Main Street
Geneva, NY 14456

HIGHLY SELECTIVE
(Composite rating of guide books)

Main tel.: 315-789-5501
Admissions tel.: 800-852-2256
Financial aid tel.: 315-781-3315
Scheduled Airline Service: Rochester
Miles to airport: 50

Founded: 1822
Nickname: NA
Religious affiliation: Episcopal
(Coed since 1908)

Student Body

Undergraduates: 1,850 **Men:** 60 % **Women:** 40 %
Graduate students: 0 **Freshman class:** 518

Academics

SAT Averages: 1110 **Verbal:** NA **Math:** NA (Taking SATs: 94 %)
700-800: V 1% M 4 % **500-600:** V 61 % M 48 %
600-700: V 14 % M 36 % **400-500:** V 24 % M 12 % **300-400:** V NA % M NA %
High school class rank: Top fifth 55 % 2nd fifth 36 % 3rd fifth 9 %

Admissions

Applied: 3,150 **Accepted:** 62 % **Matriculated:** 27 %
Deadline: Feb. 15 **Accept common application:** No
Interview recommended: Yes **Off-campus interview available:** Yes
Evaluative: Yes **Informational only:** NA **LD program:** No
Night in dorm provided: Yes **Non-refundable application fee:** $40
Early decision program: Yes **Applied:** 150 **Accepted:** 65 % **Deadline:** Jan. 1
Freshmen accepted other than Fall term: 0 % **SAT/FAF Code #** 2294(H) 2978(WS)

Transfers

Applied: 54 **Accepted:** 55 % **Application deadline for Fall:** Jun. 1 **Spring:** Jan. 1
Minimum grades recommended: 3.0 **All new students who were transfers into all classes:** 1%

Class Experience

Return 2nd year: 93 % **Graduate after 4 years:** 77 % **To graduate school within 5 years:** 60 %

Cost

Tuition deposit: $250 **Total cost (Including school's estimate on fees and books):** $22,650
Tuition: $16,992 (In state: $) **Room and board:** $5,350
Annual giving by parents: $185,000 **Average per student:** $195

Financial Aid

Average total package per student: $15,800 **Number receiving aid:** 40 %
Average scholarships and grants: $13,500 **Average loans:** $2,300 **Work-study program:** Yes
Undergraduates working on campus: 23 % **Average earnings:** $850
Non-need scholarships NA% **Athletic scholarships:** NA **FAF deadline:** Feb. 15
Off-campus part-time employment: Fair **CO-OP program:** No
ROTC: No **NROTC:** No **AFROTC:** No

Endowment

Total: $37.5 Million **Per student (including graduate students):** $19,000

Location

Acres: 270 **Setting:** Rural **Miles from town center:** 2 **(Pop.** 15,000**)**
50 **Miles from** Syracuse **(Pop.** 170,000**)** 40 **Miles from** Utica **(Pop.** 29,000 **)**

Class Composition

Asian: 2 % **Black:** 4 % **Hispanic:** 2 % **White:** 89 % **Other:** 3 %
Total minority : 11 % **Foreign countries:** 2 % (40 students)
From public schools: 55 % **Students from in state:** 45 %

Housing (on campus)

Freshmen required to live on campus: Yes **Guaranteed for:** 4 years
Available for all students: 85 % **Fraternity / Sorority housing:** Yes / No
On-campus married student housing: **Women-only dorms available:** Yes

Campus Life

Students living on campus: 85 % **Remain weekends:** 80% **Handicap access:** 50 %
Car regulations: All 4 years
Number with cars: 20% **Adequacy of on-campus parking:** Fair
Number of fraternities: 8 **Chapter houses:** 8 **Number of sororities:** 0 **Chapter houses:** 0
Students belonging to fraternities: 35 % **Students belonging to sororities:** 0 %

Libraries and Computers

Books: 280,000 **Periodicals:** 1,800 **Microform items:** 42,000
Microcomputers available: Yes **Microcomputers networked:** NA

Classes

Faculty / Student Ratio: 1/14 **Classes taught by teacher assistants:** 0 %
Most popular majors: English, Psychology, Poly Science **Classes begin:** Sept.
Baccalaureate degrees offered: BA, BS

Sports

Division: III **Except:** **Physical ed requirements:** None
Students participating in intercollegiate sports: 50 % **In intramural sports:** 70 %
Additional intercollegiate and/or intramural sports: (not found at all colleges)

Crew: Yes **Ice Hockey:** Yes **Lacrosse:** Yes **Wrestling:** No
Rugby: Yes **Sailing:** Yes **Skiing:** Yes
Squash: Yes **Ultimate Frisbee:** Yes **Water Polo:** No

Alumni

Number living: 14,000 **Annual giving:** $1.9 Million **Participation:** 44 %
Average annual gift: $ 300 **Average per student:** $1,000

3-2 Programs (2 degrees in 5 years)

Engineering with RPI, U of Rochester and Columbia
4-3 Architecture with Washington U

Observation and Opinion of:

Undergraduates and graduates ______________________________

____

College counselor ______________________________

____

COLLEGE OF THE HOLY CROSS (Private)

College Street
Worcester, MA 01610

HIGHLY SELECTIVE
(Composite rating of guide books)

Main tel.: 508-793-2041
Admissions tel.: 508-793-2443
Financial aid tel.: 508-793-2265
Scheduled Airline Service: Boston
Miles to airport: 43

Founded: 1843
Nickname: Crusaders
Religious affiliation: Catholic
(Coed since 1972)

Student Body

Undergraduates: 2,650 **Men:** 50 % **Women:** 50 %
Graduate students: 0 **Freshman class:** 627

Academics

SAT Averages: 1210 **Verbal:** 580 **Math:** 630 **(Taking SATs:** 99 %)
700-800: V 1 % M 9 % **500-600:** V 50 % M 45 %
600-700: V 28 % M 51 % **400-500:** V 25 % M 5 % **300-400:** V NA % M NA %
High school class rank: Top fifth 88 % **2nd fifth** 10 % **3rd fifth** 1 %

Admissions

Applied: 3,900 **Accepted:** 43 % **Matriculated:** 38 %
Deadline: Feb. 1 **Accept common application:** No
Interview recommended: Yes **Off-campus interview available:** Yes
Evaluative: Yes **Informational only:** Yes **LD program:** No
Night in dorm provided: Yes **Non-refundable application fee:** $50
Early decision program: Yes **Applied:** 363 **Accepted:** 50 % **Deadline:** Dec. 1
Freshmen accepted other than Fall term: 1 % **SAT/FAF Code #** 3282

Transfers

Applied: NA **Accepted:** NA % **Application deadline for Fall:** May 1 **Spring:** Dec. 1
Minimum grades recommended: 2.0 **All new students who were transfers into all classes:** 1 %

Class Experience

Return 2nd year: 99% **Graduate after 4 years:** 87 % **To graduate school within 5 years:** 30 %

Cost

Tuition deposit: $200 **Total cost (Including school's estimate on fees and books):** $23,000
Tuition: $16,300 **(In state:** $) **Room and board:** $6,000
Annual giving by parents: $130,000 **Average per student:** $50

Financial Aid

Average total package per student: $15,100 **Number receiving aid:** 40 %
Average scholarships and grants: $12,500 **Average loans:** $2,600 **Work-study program:** Yes
Undergraduates working on campus: 34 % **Average earnings:** $1,100
Non-need scholarships 1 % **Athletic scholarships:** No **FAF deadline:** Feb. 1
Off-campus part-time employment: Fair **CO-OP program:** No
ROTC: at WPI **NROTC:** Yes **AFROTC:** at WPI

Endowment

Total: $88 Million **Per student (including graduate students):** $35,000

Location

Acres: 175 **Setting:** Surburban **Miles from town center:** 2 **(Pop.** 160,000**)**
35 **Miles from** Boston **(Pop.** 700,000 **)** **Miles from** **(Pop.** **)**

Class Composition

Asian: 2 % **Black:** 4 % **Hispanic:** 2 % **White:** 92 % **Other:** NA %
Total minority : 8 % **Foreign countries:** 1 % (25 students)
From public schools: 49 % **Students from in state:** 35 %

Housing (on campus)

Freshmen required to live on campus: No **Guaranteed for:** 1 year
Available for all students: 80 % **Fraternity / Sorority housing:** No / No
On-campus married student housing: No **Women-only dorms available:** No

Campus Life

Students living on campus: 80 % **Remain weekends:** 87 % **Handicap access:** NA %
Car regulations: No freshmen or sophomores
Number with cars: 26 % **Adequacy of on-campus parking:** Fair
Number of fraternities: 0 **Chapter houses:** 0 **Number of sororities:** 0 **Chapter houses:** 0
Students belonging to fraternities: 0 % **Students belonging to sororities:** 0 %

Libraries and Computers

Books: 440,000 **Periodicals:** 2,500 **Microform items:** 18,000
Microcomputers available: Yes **Microcomputers networked:** Yes

Classes

Faculty / Student Ratio: 1/14 **Classes taught by teacher assistants:** 0 %
Most popular majors: English, Economics, History **Classes begin:** Early Sept.
Baccalaureate degrees offered: BA

Sports

Division: I **Except:** **Physical ed requirements:** None
Students participating in intercollegiate sports: 25 % **In intramural sports:** 45 %
Additional intercollegiate and/or intramural sports: (not found at all colleges)

Crew: Yes	**Ice Hockey:** Yes	**Lacrosse:** Yes	**Wrestling:** No
Rugby: Yes	**Sailing:** Yes	**Skiing:** No	
Squash: Yes	**Ultimate Frisbee:** No	**Water Polo:** No	

Alumni

Number living: 23,000 **Annual giving:** $ 5.3 Million **Participation:** 55 %
Average annual gift: $ 400 **Average per student:** $2,000

3-2 Programs (2 degrees in 5 years)

Engineering with Columbia, Dartmouth, and Washington U

Observation and Opinion of:

Undergraduates and graduates ____________________

____

College counselor ____________________

____

UNIVERSITY OF ILLINOIS, URBANA (Public)

506 South Wright Street
Urbana, IL 61801

HIGHLY SELECTIVE
(Composite rating of guide books)

Main tel.: 217-333-1000
Admissions tel.: 217-333-0302
Financial aid tel.: 217-333-0100
Scheduled Airline Service: Chicago
Miles to airport: 13

Founded: 1867
Nickname: Fighting Illini
Religious affiliation: None
(Coed since 1869)

Student Body

Undergraduates: 25,000 **Men:** 61 % **Women:** 39 %
Graduate students: 6,200 **Freshman class:** 5,900

Academics

SAT Averages: 1145 **Verbal:** 520 **Math:** 625 **(Taking SATs:** NA %)
700-800: V 2 % **M** 19 % **500-600: V** 41 % **M** 29 %
600-700: V 17 % **M** 40 % **400-500: V** 33 % **M** 10 % **300-400: V** 7 % **M** 2 %
High school class rank: Top fifth 82 % **2nd fifth** 15 % **3rd fifth** 3 %

Admissions

Applied: 14,470 **Accepted:** 77 % **Matriculated:** 53 %
Deadline: Jan. 1 **Accept common application:** No
Interview recommended: Yes **Off-campus interview available:** No
Evaluative: Yes **Informational only:** NA **LD program:** Yes
Night in dorm provided: No **Non-refundable application fee:** $25
Early decision program: Yes **Applied:** NA **Accepted:** NA% **Deadline:** NA
Freshmen accepted other than Fall term: 2 % **SAT/FAF Code #** 1836

Transfers

Applied: 3,300 **Accepted:** 30 % **Application deadline for Fall:** Mar. 1 **Spring:** Nov. 1
Minimum grades recommended: 3.25 **All new students who were transfers into all classes:** 5 %

Class Experience

Return 2nd year: 95 % **Graduate after 4 years:** 72% **To graduate school within 5 years:** NA %

Cost

Tuition deposit: $100 **Total cost (Including school's estimate on fees and books):** $11,800
Tuition: $6,300 **(In state:** $ 3,200) **Room and board:** $3,900
Annual giving by parents: $NA **Average per student:** $NA

Financial Aid

Average total package per student: $NA **Number receiving aid:** NA %
Average scholarships and grants: $NA **Average loans:** $NA **Work-study program:** NA
Undergraduates working on campus: 40 % **Average earnings:** $650
Non-need scholarships 5 % **Athletic scholarships:** Yes **FAF deadline:** Mar. 15
Off-campus part-time employment: Good **CO-OP program:** Yes
ROTC: Yes **NROTC:** No **AFROTC:** No

Endowment

Total: $NA **Per student (including graduate students):** $NA

Location

Acres: 705 **Setting:** Urban **Miles from town center:** 2 **(Pop.** 100,000)
130 **Miles from** Chicago **(Pop.** 3 Mil.) 160 **Miles from** Indianapolis **(Pop.** 700,000)

Class Composition

Asian: 10 % **Black:** 7 % **Hispanic:** 4 % **White:** 77 % **Other:** 2 %
Total minority : 13 % **Foreign countries:** 1 % (250 students)
From public schools: NA % **Students from in state:** 94 %

Housing (on campus)

Freshmen required to live on campus: Yes **Guaranteed for:** 1 year
Available for all students: 33 % **Fraternity / Sorority housing:** Yes / Yes
On-campus married student housing: Yes **Women-only dorms available:** Yes

Campus Life

Students living on campus: 33 % **Remain weekends:** NA % **Handicap access:** 100 %
Car regulations: All 4 years
Number with cars: NA % **Adequacy of on-campus parking:** Poor
Number of fraternities: 61 **Chapter houses:** 54 **Number of sororities:** 31 **Chapter houses:** 25
Students belonging to fraternities: 0 % **Students belonging to sororities:** 29 %

Libraries and Computers

Books: 7.5 Million **Periodicals:** 92,000 **Microform items:** 3.2 Million
Microcomputers available: Yes **Microcomputers networked:** Yes

Classes

Faculty / Student Ratio: 1/10 **Classes taught by teacher assistants:** 30 %
Most popular majors: Electrical Engineering, Accounting **Classes begin:** Late Aug.
Baccalaureate degrees offered: AB, BFA, BLA, B MUS, BS, BSAG, BSED, BS Journalism, BSW, BVM

Sports

Division: I **Except:** **Physical ed requirements:** NA
Students participating in intercollegiate sports: 1 % **In intramural sports:** 15 %
Additional intercollegiate and/or intramural sports: (not found at all colleges)

Crew: No	**Ice Hockey:** Yes	**Lacrosse:** No	**Wrestling:** Yes/M
Rugby: Yes	**Sailing:** Yes	**Skiing:** Yes	
Squash: Yes	**Ultimate Frisbee:** Yes	**Water Polo:** Yes	

Alumni

Number living: NA **Annual giving:** $ 6 Million **Participation:** NA %
Average annual gift: $ NA **Average per student:** $NA

3-2 Programs (2 degrees in 5 years)

In-house Commerce and Accounting, Host university of 3-2 Engineering Program

Observation and Opinion of:

Undergraduates and graduates ______________________

____

College counselor ______________________

____

JAMES MADISON UNIVERSITY (Public)

Harrisburg, VA 22807

VERY SELECTIVE
(Composite rating of guide books)

Main tel.: 703-568-6211
Admissions tel.: 703-568-6147
Financial aid tel.: 703-568-6644
Scheduled Airline Service: Charlottesville
Miles to airport: 45

Founded: 1908
Nickname: Dukes
Religious affiliation: None
(Coed since 1966)

Student Body

Undergraduates: 9,300 **Men:** 42 % **Women:** 58 %
Graduate students: 400 **Freshman class:** 1,900

Academics

SAT Averages: 1090 **Verbal:** 510 **Math:** 580 **(Taking SATs:** 100 %)
700-800: V 1 % **M** 4 % **500-600: V** 45 % **M** 44 %
600-700: V 10 % **M** 36 % **400-500: V** 36 % **M** 14 % **300-400: V** 8 % **M** 2 %
High school class rank: Top fifth 64 % **2nd fifth** 24 % **3rd fifth** 10 %

Admissions

Applied: 11,200 **Accepted:** 43 % **Matriculated:** 39 %
Deadline: Feb. 1 **Accept common application:** NA
Interview recommended: No **Off-campus interview available:** No
Evaluative: NA **Informational only:** **LD program:** Yes
Night in dorm provided: No **Non-refundable application fee:** $20
Early decision program: Yes **Applied:** NA **Accepted:** NA % **Deadline:** NA
Freshmen accepted other than Fall term: 0 % **SAT/FAF Code #** 5392

Transfers

Applied: 1,585 **Accepted:** 53 % **Application deadline for Fall:** Feb. 1 **Spring:** Nov. 15
Minimum grades recommended: 2.0 **All new students who were transfers into all classes:** 21 %

Class Experience

Return 2nd year: 92 % **Graduate after 4 years:** 60 % **To graduate school within 5 years:** NA %

Cost

Tuition deposit: $100 **Total cost (Including school's estimate on fees and books):** $12,800
Tuition: $7,300 **(In state:** $ 3,500) **Room and board:** $4,300
Annual giving by parents: $188,000 **Average per student:** $NA

Financial Aid

Average total package per student: $3,200 **Number receiving aid:** 50 %
Average scholarships and grants: $1,000 **Average loans:** $2,200 **Work-study program:** Yes
Undergraduates working on campus: 26 % **Average earnings:** $1,050
Non-need scholarships 10 % **Athletic scholarships:** Yes **FAF deadline:** Feb. 15
Off-campus part-time employment: Good **CO-OP program:** No
ROTC: Yes **NROTC:** No **AFROTC:** No

Endowment

Total: $9 Million **Per student (including graduate students):** $900

Location

Acres: 470 **Setting:** City **Miles from town center:** 1 **(Pop.** 30,000)
120 **Miles from** Wash. **(Pop.** 700,000) **Miles from (Pop.**)

Class Composition

Asian: 2 % **Black:** 9 % **Hispanic:** 1 % **White:** 87 % **Other:** 1 %
Total minority : 13 % **Foreign countries:** 1 % (90 students)
From public schools: 95 % **Students from in state:** 77 %

Housing (on campus)

Freshmen required to live on campus: Yes **Guaranteed for:** 1 year
Available for all students: 25 % **Fraternity / Sorority housing:** Yes / Yes
On-campus married student housing: No **Women-only dorms available:** Yes

Campus Life

Students living on campus: 51 % **Remain weekends:** N/A % **Handicap access:** NA %
Car regulations: No freshmen or sophomores
Number with cars: NA % **Adequacy of on-campus parking:** Good
Number of fraternities: 14 **Chapter houses:** 10 **Number of sororities:** 11 **Chapter houses:** 7
Students belonging to fraternities: 19 % **Students belonging to sororities:** 16 %

Libraries and Computers

Books: 377,000 **Periodicals:** 2,600 **Microform items:** 1.2 Million
Microcomputers available: Yes **Microcomputers networked:** Yes

Classes

Faculty / Student Ratio: 1/19 **Classes taught by teacher assistants:** 20 %
Most popular majors: Communications, Marketing **Classes begin:** Late Aug.
Baccalaureate degrees offered: BA, BBA, BEA, BGS, B MUS, BS, BSN, BSW

Sports

Division: I **Except:** **Physical ed requirements:** 2 credit hours
Students participating in intercollegiate sports: 11 % **In intramural sports:** 65 %
Additional intercollegiate and/or intramural sports: (not found at all colleges)

Crew: No **Ice Hockey:** No **Lacrosse:** Yes **Wrestling:** Yes/M
Rugby: Yes **Sailing:** No **Skiing:** Yes
Squash: No **Ultimate Frisbee:** No **Water Polo:** Yes

Alumni

Number living: 36,000 **Annual giving:** $450,000 **Participation:** 30 %
Average annual gift: $ 45 **Average per student:** $45

3-2 Programs (2 degrees in 5 years)

2-year transfer programs in Engineering

Observation and Opinion of:

Undergraduates and graduates ______________________________

____

College counselor ______________________________

____

THE JOHNS HOPKINS UNIVERSITY (Private)

34th and Charles Street
Baltimore, MD 21218

MOST SELECTIVE
(Composite rating of guide books)

Main tel.: 301-516-8000
Admissions tel.: 301-516-8171
Financial aid tel.: 301-516-8028
Scheduled Airline Service: Baltimore
Miles to airport: 15

Founded: 1876
Nickname: Blue Jays
Religious affiliation: None
(Coed since 1971)

Student Body

Undergraduates: 3,000 **Men:** 62 % **Women:** 38 %
Graduate students: 1,300 **Freshman class:** 840

Academics

SAT Averages: 1290 **Verbal:** 610 **Math:** 680 **(Taking SATs 75 %)**
700-800: V 9 % **M** 48 % **500-600: V** 31 % **M** 9 %
600-700: V 50 % **M** 42 % **400-500: V** 8 % **M** 1 % **300-400: V** 1 % **M** 0 %
High school class rank: Top fifth 85 % **2nd fifth** NA % **3rd fifth** NA %

Admissions

Applied: 5,240 **Accepted:** 55 % **Matriculated:** 29 %
Deadline: Jan. 1 **Accept common application:** No
Interview recommended: NA **Off-campus interview available:** Yes
Evaluative: No **Informational only:** Yes **LD program:** Yes
Night in dorm provided: Yes **Non-refundable application fee:** $45
Early decision program: Yes **Applied:** 376 **Accepted:** 64 % **Deadline:** Nov. 15
Freshmen accepted other than Fall term: 0 % **SAT/FAF Code #** 5332

Transfers

Applied: 273 **Accepted:** 50 % **Application deadline for Fall:** May 1 **Spring:** Nov. 1
Minimum grades recommended: 3.0 **All new students who were transfers into all classes:** 8%

Class Experience

Return 2nd year: 93% **Graduate after 4 years:** 80 % **To graduate school within 5 years:** NA %

Cost

Tuition deposit: $100 **Total cost (Including school's estimate on fees and books):** $24,200
Tuition: $17,000 (In state: $) **Room and board:** $6,300
Annual giving by parents: $1.1 Million **Average per student:** $370

Financial Aid

Average total package per student: $11,600 **Number receiving aid:** 25 %
Average scholarships and grants: $9,100 **Average loans:** $2,500 **Work-study program:** Yes
Undergraduates working on campus: 50 % **Average earnings:** $1,700
Non-need scholarships 4 % **Athletic scholarships:** NA **FAF deadline:** Jan. 15
Off-campus part-time employment: Good **CO-OP program:** No
ROTC: Yes **NROTC:** No **AFROTC:** at U of MD

Endowment

Total: $561 Million **Per student (including graduate students):** $145,000

Location

Acres: 140 **Setting:** Urban **Miles from town center:** 2 **(Pop.** 900,000**)**
Miles from **(Pop.** **)** **Miles from** **(Pop.** **)**

Class Composition

Asian: 17 % **Black:** 6 % **Hispanic:** 3 % **White:** 73 % **Other:** 1 %
Total minority : 27 % **Foreign countries:** 5 % (150 students)
From public schools: 70 % **Students from in state:** 20 %

Housing (on campus)

Freshmen required to live on campus: Yes **Guaranteed for:** 1 year
Available for all students: 50 % **Fraternity / Sorority housing:** Yes / No
On-campus married student housing: No **Women-only dorms available:** Yes

Campus Life

Students living on campus: 50 % **Remain weekends:** 98 % **Handicap access:** 90 %
Car regulations: No parking on campus
Number with cars: NA % **Adequacy of on-campus parking:** Poor
Number of fraternities: 12 **Chapter houses:** 8 **Number of sororities:** 5 **Chapter houses:** 0
Students belonging to fraternities: 25 % **Students belonging to sororities:** 30 %

Libraries and Computers

Books: 2 Million **Periodicals:** 18,000 **Microform items:** 2,000
Microcomputers available: Yes **Microcomputers networked:** Yes

Classes

Faculty / Student Ratio: 1/10 **Classes taught by teacher assistants:** 10 %
Most popular majors: Biology, Political Science **Classes begin:** Sept.
Baccalaureate degrees offered: BA, BS

Sports

Division: III **Except:** Lacrosse I **Physical ed requirements:** None
Students participating in intercollegiate sports: 25 % **In intramural sports:** 20 %
Additional intercollegiate and/or intramural sports: (not found at all colleges)

Crew: Yes	**Ice Hockey:** Yes/M	**Lacrosse:** Yes	**Wrestling:** Yes/M
Rugby: No	**Sailing:** No	**Skiing:** No	
Squash: Yes	**Ultimate Frisbee:** Yes	**Water Polo:** Yes	

Alumni

Number living: 71,000 **Annual giving:** $ 31.6 Million **Participation:** 41 %
Average annual gift: $ 1,400 **Average per student:** $10,000

3-2 Programs (2 degrees in 5 years)

In-house BA/PhD in Psychology and BA/MA with School of Advanced International Studies

Observation and Opinion of:

Undergraduates and graduates ____________________

College counselor ____________________

KENYON COLLEGE (Private)

Gambier, OH 43022-9623

HIGHLY SELECTIVE
(Composite rating of guide books)

Main tel.: 614-427-5000
Admissions tel.: 800-848-2468
Financial aid tel.: 614-427-5782
Scheduled Airline Service: Columbus
Miles to airport: 50

Founded: 1824
Nickname: Lords & Ladies
Religious affiliation: Episcopal
(Coed since 1969)

Student Body

Undergraduates: 1,550 **Men:** 52 % **Women:** 48 %
Graduate students: 0 **Freshman class:** 400

Academics

SAT Averages: 1170 **Verbal:** 570 **Math:** 600 **(Taking SATs:** NA %**)**
700-800: V 5 % **M** 15 % **500-600: V** 50 % **M** 42 %
600-700: V 27 % **M** 38 % **400-500: V** 18 % **M** 5 % **300-400: V** NA % **M** NA %
High school class rank: Top fifth 70 % **2nd fifth** 20 % **3rd fifth** %

Admissions

Applied: 2,500 **Accepted:** 55 % **Matriculated:** 33%
Deadline: Feb. 15 **Accept common application:** Yes
Interview recommended: Yes **Off-campus interview available:** Yes
Evaluative: No **Informational only:** No **LD program:** No
Night in dorm provided: Yes **Non-refundable application fee:** $35
Early decision program: Yes **Applied:** NA **Accepted:** NA % **Deadline:** Dec. 1
Freshmen accepted other than Fall term: 0 % **SAT/FAF Code #** 1370

Transfers

Applied: **Accepted:** % **Application deadline for Fall:** May 1 **Spring:** NA
Minimum grades recommended: 3.0 **All new students who were transfers into all classes:** 4 %

Class Experience

Return 2nd year: 90 % **Graduate after 4 years:** 80 % **To graduate school within 5 years:** 60 %

Cost

Tuition deposit: $250 **Total cost (Including school's estimate on fees and books):** $21,180
Tuition: $17,060 **(In state:** $ **)** **Room and board:** $3,500
Annual giving by parents: $775,000 **Average per student:** $500

Financial Aid

Average total package per student: $7,400 **Number receiving aid:** 30 %
Average scholarships and grants: $NA **Average loans:** $NA **Work-study program:** Yes
Undergraduates working on campus: NA % **Average earnings:** $700
Non-need scholarships NA % **Athletic scholarships:** Yes **FAF deadline:** Feb. 15
Off-campus part-time employment: Poor **CO-OP program:** No
ROTC: No **NROTC:** No **AFROTC:** No

Endowment

Total: $35 Million **Per student (including graduate students):** $23,000

Location

Acres: 600 **Setting:** Rural
Miles from town center: 0 (**Pop.** 2,000)
50 **Miles from** Columbus (**Pop.** 550,000)
Miles from (**Pop.**)

Class Composition

Asian: 5 % **Black:** 4 % **Hispanic:** 1 % **White:** 90 % **Other:** NA %
Total minority : 10 % **Foreign countries:** 2 % (28 students)
From public schools: 60 % **Students from in state:** 23 %

Housing (on campus)

Freshmen required to live on campus: Yes
Guaranteed for: 4 years
Available for all students: 10 %
Fraternity / Sorority housing: No / No
On-campus married student housing: Yes
Women-only dorms available: Yes

Campus Life

Students living on campus: 100 % **Remain weekends:** 95 % **Handicap access:** 50 %
Car regulations: All 4 years
Number with cars: 22 %
Adequacy of on-campus parking: Poor
Number of fraternities: 9 **Chapter houses:** No
Number of sororities: 1 **Chapter houses:** No
Students belonging to fraternities: 55 %
Students belonging to sororities: %

Libraries and Computers

Books: 350,000 **Periodicals:** 1,000 **Microform items:** 200,000
Microcomputers available: Yes **Microcomputers networked:** NA

Classes

Faculty / Student Ratio: 1/13 **Classes taught by teacher assistants:** 0 %
Most popular majors: NA **Classes begin:** Early Sept.
Baccalaureate degrees offered: AB

Sports

Division: III **Except:** **Physical ed requirements:** None
Students participating in intercollegiate sports: 50 % **In intramural sports:** 75 %
Additional intercollegiate and/or intramural sports: (not found at all colleges)

Crew: Yes/M **Ice Hockey:** Yes/M **Lacrosse:** Yes **Wrestling:** Yes
Rugby: Yes **Sailing:** Yes **Skiing:** Yes
Squash: Yes **Ultimate Frisbee:** Yes **Water Polo:** Yes

Alumni

Number living: 10,000 **Annual giving:** $1.8 Million **Participation:** 45 %
Average annual gift: $ 800 **Average per student:** $1,200

3-2 Programs (2 degrees in 5 years)

Engineering with Case Western, RPI, Washington U
4-1 program in Education with Columbia U Teachers College

Observation and Opinion of:

Undergraduates and graduates ____________________

College counselor ____________________

LAFAYETTE COLLEGE (Private)

118 Markle Hall
Easton, PA 18042

HIGHLY SELECTIVE
(Composite rating of guide books)

Main tel.: 215-250-5000
Admissions tel.: 215-250-5100
Financial aid tel.: 215-250-5055
Scheduled Airline Service: Bethlehem
Miles to airport: 13

Founded: 1826
Nickname: Leopards
Religious affiliation: Presbyterian
(Coed since 1970)

Student Body

Undergraduates: 2,300 **Men:** 59 % **Women:** 41 %
Graduate students: 0 **Freshman class:** 520

Academics

SAT Averages: 1200 **Verbal:** 570 **Math:** 630 **(Taking SATs:** 99 %**)**
700-800: V 2 % **M** 17 % **500-600: V** 50 % **M** 30 %
600-700: V 25 % **M** 50 % **400-500: V** 20 % **M** 3 % **300-400: V** NA % **M** NA %
High school class rank: Top fifth 80 % **2nd fifth** 18 % **3rd fifth** %

Admissions

Applied: 4,140 **Accepted:** 44 % **Matriculated:** 28 %
Deadline: Feb. 1 **Accept common application:** Yes
Interview recommended: Yes **Off-campus interview available:** Yes
Evaluative: Yes **Informational only:** No **LD program:** No
Night in dorm provided: Yes **Non-refundable application fee:** $35
Early decision program: Yes **Applied:** 228 **Accepted:** 40 % **Deadline:** Nov. 1
Freshmen accepted other than Fall term: 3 % **SAT/FAF Code #** 2361

Transfers

Applied: 194 **Accepted:** 50 % **Application deadline for Fall:** Jun. 1 **Spring:** Dec. 1
Minimum grades recommended: 2.0 **All new students who were transfers into all classes:** 7 %

Class Experience

Return 2nd year: 95 % **Graduate after 4 years:** 75 % **To graduate school within 5 years:** 70 %

Cost

Tuition deposit: $NA **Total cost (Including school's estimate on fees and books):** $22,500
Tuition: $16,725 **(In state:** $ **)** **Room and board:** $5,150
Annual giving by parents: $160,000 **Average per student:** $70

Financial Aid

Average total package per student: $13,850 **Number receiving aid:** NA %
Average scholarships and grants: $10,850 **Average loans:** $3,000 **Work-study program:** Yes
Undergraduates working on campus: NA % **Average earnings:** $1,075
Non-need scholarships 0 % **Athletic scholarships:** **FAF deadline:** Feb. 15
Off-campus part-time employment: Good **CO-OP program:** No
ROTC: Yes **NROTC:** No **AFROTC:** at LeHigh

Endowment

Total: $206 Million **Per student (including graduate students):** $110,000

Location

Acres: 100 **Setting:** Surburban **Miles from town center:** 2 **(Pop.** 20,000)
60 **Miles from** Phila. (Pop. 1.7 Mil.) 80 **Miles from** NYC **(Pop.** 7 **Mil.)**

Class Composition

Asian: NA % **Black:** 5 % **Hispanic:** 2 % **White:** 83 % **Other:** 10 %
Total minority : 17 % **Foreign countries:** 10 % (200 students)
From public schools: 70 % **Students from in state:** 20 %

Housing (on campus)

Freshmen required to live on campus: Yes **Guaranteed for:** 1 year
Available for all students: 90 % **Fraternity / Sorority housing:** Yes / Yes
On-campus married student housing: Yes **Women-only dorms available:** Yes

Campus Life

Students living on campus: 90 % **Remain weekends:** 95 % **Handicap access:** 50%
Car regulations: Not 1st 2 years
Number with cars: 35 % **Adequacy of on-campus parking:** Good
Number of fraternities: 11 **Chapter houses:** 11 **Number of sororities:** 5 **Chapter houses:** 3
Students belonging to fraternities: 53 % **Students belonging to sororities:** 46 %

Libraries and Computers

Books: 226,000 **Periodicals:** 1,750 **Microform items:** 75,000
Microcomputers available: Yes **Microcomputers networked:** NA

Classes

Faculty / Student Ratio: 1/12 **Classes taught by teacher assistants:** 0 %
Most popular majors: Engineering, Government, Law **Classes begin:** Late Aug.
Baccalaureate degrees offered: AB, BS

Sports

Division: I **Except:** **Physical ed requirements:** None
Students participating in intercollegiate sports: 25 % **In intramural sports:** 20 %
Additional intercollegiate and/or intramural sports: (not found at all colleges)

Crew: Yes **Ice Hockey:** Yes/M **Lacrosse:** Yes **Wrestling:** Yes
Rugby: Yes/M **Sailing:** No **Skiing:** Yes
Squash: Yes **Ultimate Frisbee:** Yes **Water Polo:** Yes

Alumni

Number living: 20,000 **Annual giving:** $ 11 Million **Participation:** 37 %
Average annual gift: $ NA **Average per student:** $5,500

3-2 Programs (2 degrees in 5 years)

Member LeHigh Valley Association of Colleges/ Cross registration possible

Observation and Opinion of:

Undergraduates and graduates ______________________________

____

College counselor ______________________________

____

LEHIGH UNIVERSITY (Private)

Provost's Office
Bethlehem, PA 18015-3035

HIGHLY SELECTIVE
(Composite rating of guide books)

Main tel.: 215-758-3000
Admissions tel.: 215-758-3100
Financial aid tel.: 215-758-3181
Scheduled Airline Service: Bethlehem
Miles to airport: 10

Founded: 1865
Nickname: NA
Religious affiliation: None
(Coed since 1971)

Student Body

Undergraduates: 4,500 **Men:** 62 % **Women:** 38 %
Graduate students: 4,500 **Freshman class:** 1,135

Academics

SAT Averages: 1180 **Verbal:** NA **Math:** NA **(Taking SATs:** 100 %**)**
700-800: V 2 % **M** 20 % **500-600: V** 52 % **M** 24 %
600-700: V 15 % **M** 53 % **400-500: V** 30 % **M** 3 % **300-400: V** 1 % **M** 0 %
High school class rank: Top fifth 71 % **2nd fifth** 20 % **3rd fifth** 5 %

Admissions

Applied: 5,185 **Accepted:** 72 % **Matriculated:** 31 %
Deadline: Feb. 15 **Accept common application:** Yes
Interview recommended: Yes **Off-campus interview available:** Yes
Evaluative: Yes **Informational only:** NA **LD program:** No
Night in dorm provided: Yes **Non-refundable application fee:** $40
Early decision program: Yes **Applied:** 285 **Accepted:** 61 % **Deadline:** Dec. 1
Freshmen accepted other than Fall term: 1 % **SAT/FAF Code #** 2365

Transfers

Applied: 277 **Accepted:** 54 % **Application deadline for Fall:** Apr. 1 **Spring:** Nov. 1
Minimum grades recommended: 3.0 **All new students who were transfers into all classes:** 5 %

Class Experience

Return 2nd year: 95% **Graduate after 4 years:** 85 % **To graduate school within 1 years:** 15 %

Cost

Tuition deposit: $100 **Total cost (Including school's estimate on fees and books):** $21,940
Tuition: $16,700 **(In state:** $ **)** **Room and board:** $5,240
Annual giving by parents: $0 **Average per student:** $18

Financial Aid

Average total package per student: $11,250 **Number receiving aid:** 40 %
Average scholarships and grants: $8,500 **Average loans:** $2,650 **Work-study program:** Yes
Undergraduates working on campus: NA % **Average earnings:** $1,135
Non-need scholarships 1 % **Athletic scholarships:** NA **FAF deadline:** Feb. 8
Off-campus part-time employment: Good **CO-OP program:** No
ROTC: Yes **NROTC:** No **AFROTC:** Yes

Endowment

Total: $262 Million **Per student (including graduate students):** $30,000

Location

Acres: 1,600 **Setting:** City
Miles from town center: 2 **(Pop.** 75,500**)**
60 **Miles from** Phila. **(Pop.** 1.7 Mil. **)**
Miles from (Pop.)

Class Composition

Asian: 4 **%** **Black:** 2 **%** **Hispanic:** 2 **%** **White:** 92 **%** **Other:** NA **%**
Total minority : 8 **%** **Foreign countries:** 3 **%** (130 **Students)**
From public schools: 70 **%** **Students from in state:** 29 **%**

Housing (on campus)

Freshmen required to live on campus: Yes
Guaranteed for: 1 year
Available for all students: 75 **%**
Fraternity / Sorority housing: Yes / Yes
On-campus married student housing: Yes
Women-only dorms available: Yes

Campus Life

Students living on campus: 75 **%** **Remain weekends:** 75 **%** **Handicap access:** 80 **%**
Car regulations: No freshmen
Number with cars: 80 **%**
Adequacy of on-campus parking: NA
Number of fraternities: 30 **Chapter houses:** 30
Number of sororities: 8 **Chapter houses:** 8
Students belonging to fraternities: 51 **%**
Students belonging to sororities: 45 **%**

Libraries and Computers

Books: 969,000 **Periodicals:** 9,700 **Microform items:** 1.5 Million
Microcomputers available: Yes **Microcomputers networked:** NA

Classes

Faculty / Student Ratio: 1/11 **Classes taught by teacher assistants:** 10 **%**
Most popular majors: Mechanical Engineering & Finance **Classes begin:** Late Aug.
Baccalaureate degrees offered: BA, BS

Sports

Division: I **Except:** **Physical ed requirements:** None
Students participating in intercollegiate sports: 25 **%** **In intramural sports:** 80 **%**
Additional intercollegiate and/or intramural sports: (not found at all colleges)

Crew: Yes	**Ice Hockey:** Yes	**Lacrosse:** Yes	**Wrestling:** Yes/M
Rugby: Yes	**Sailing:** Yes	**Skiing:** Yes	
Squash: Yes	**Ultimate Frisbee:** Yes/M	**Water Polo:** Yes/M	

Alumni

Number living: 48,000 **Annual giving:** $ 14 Million **Participation:** 45 **%**
Average annual gift: $ 210 **Average per student:** $2,100

3-2 Programs (2 degrees in 5 years)

In-house Engineering
6-year BA/MD with Medical College of Pennsylvania

Observation and Opinion of:

Undergraduates and graduates ______________________________

____

College counselor ______________________________

____

LEWIS AND CLARK COLLEGE (Private)

Portland, OR 97219

SELECTIVE
(Composite rating of guide books)

Main tel.: 503-244-6161
Admissions tel.: 503-768-7040
Financial aid tel.: 503-768-7090
Scheduled Airline Service: Portland
Miles to airport: 10

Founded: 1867
Nickname: Pioneers
Religious affiliation: Presbyterian
(Coed since 1867)

Student Body

Undergraduates: 2,000 **Men:** 45 % **Women:** 55 %
Graduate students: 700 **Freshman class:** 474

Academics

SAT Averages: 1105 **Verbal:** NA **Math:** NA **(Taking SATs: 88 %)**
700-800: V 1 % **M** 4 % **500-600: V** 39 % **M** 44 %
600-700: V 13% **M** 22 % **400-500: V** 38 % **M** 27 % **300-400: V** 8 % **M** 3 %
High school class rank: Top fifth 53 % **2nd fifth** 30 % **3rd fifth** 14 %

Admissions

Applied: 2,370 **Accepted:** 79 % **Matriculated:** 25 %
Deadline: Feb. 15 **Accept common application:** Yes
Interview recommended: Yes **Off-campus interview available:** Yes
Evaluative: Yes **Informational only:** NA **LD program:** Yes
Night in dorm provided: Yes **Non-refundable application fee:** $35
Early decision program: Yes **Applied:** NA **Accepted:** NA % **Deadline:** NA
Freshmen accepted other than Fall term: 1 % **SAT/FAF Code #** 4384

Transfers

Applied: 294 **Accepted:** 67 % **Application deadline for Fall:** May 1 **Spring:** Feb. 1
Minimum grades recommended: 3.0 **All new students who were transfers into all classes:** 22 %

Class Experience

Return 2nd year: 85 % **Graduate after 4 years:** 65 % **To graduate school within 5 years:** NA %

Cost

Tuition deposit: $200 **Total cost (Including school's estimate on fees and books):** $20,000
Tuition: $14,265 **(In state:** $ **)** **Room and board:** $4,839
Annual giving by parents: $33,000 **Average per Student** $ 16

Financial Aid

Average total package per student: $10,700 **Number receiving aid:** 53 %
Average scholarships and grants: $7,500 **Average loans:** $3,200 **Work-study program:** Yes
Undergraduates working on campus: 60 % **Average earnings:** $1,100
Non-need scholarships 5 % **Athletic scholarships:** **FAF deadline:** Feb. 15
Off-campus part-time employment: Excellent **CO-OP program:** No
ROTC: No **NROTC:** No **AFROTC:** at U of Portland

Endowment

Total: $35 Million **Per student (including graduate students):** $17,000

Location

Acres: 130 **Setting:** Surburban **Miles from town center:** 6 **(Pop.** 388,000)
Miles from (Pop. 53,000) **Miles from** **(Pop.**)

Class Composition

Asian: 7 % **Black:** 2 % **Hispanic:** 2 % **White:** 88 % **Other:** 1 %
Total minority : 12 % **Foreign countries:** 5 % (100 students)
From public schools: 70 % **Students from in state:** 25 %

Housing (on campus)

Freshmen required to live on campus: Yes **Guaranteed for:** 4 years
Available for all students: 55 % **Fraternity / Sorority housing:** No / No
On-campus married student housing: No **Women-only dorms available:** Yes

Campus Life

Students living on campus: 55 % **Remain weekends:** 85 % **Handicap access:** 50 %
Car regulations: No freshmen
Number with cars: 25 % **Adequacy of on-campus parking:** Good
Number of fraternities: 2 **Chapter houses:** 0 **Number of sororities:** 0 **Chapter houses:** 0
Students belonging to fraternities: 1 % **Students belonging to sororities:** 0 %

Libraries and Computers

Books: 343,000 **Periodicals:** 1,100 **Microform items:** 48,000
Microcomputers available: Yes **Microcomputers networked:** NA

Classes

Faculty / Student Ratio: 13/1 **Classes taught by teacher assistants:** 0 %
Most popular majors: Business, English **Classes begin:** Early Sept.
Baccalaureate degrees offered: BA, BS

Sports

Division: **Except:** **Physical ed requirements:** NA
Students participating in intercollegiate sports: 25 % **In intramural sports:** 60 %
Additional intercollegiate and/or intramural sports: (not found at all colleges)

Crew: Yes **Ice Hockey:** No **Lacrosse:** Yes **Wrestling:** No
Rugby: Yes **Sailing:** Yes **Skiing:** Yes
Squash: Yes **Ultimate Frisbee:** Yes **Water Polo:** Yes

Alumni

Number living: 14,000 **Annual giving:** $ 270,000 **Participation:** 28 %
Average annual gift: $ 70 **Average per student:** $100

3-2 Programs (2 degrees in 5 years)

Engineering with Columbia, Wash U, Southern California
4-2 Engineering Programs with Columbia and Washington U

Observation and Opinion of:

Undergraduates and graduates ____________________

____

College counselor ____________________

____

LOYOLA COLLEGE (Private)

4501 North Charles Street
Baltimore, MD 21210

SELECTIVE
(Composite rating of guide books)

Main tel.: 800-221-9107
Admissions tel.: 800-221-9107
Financial aid tel.: 800-221-9107
Scheduled Airline Service: Baltimore
Miles to airport: 10

Founded: 1852
Nickname: Greyhounds
Religious affiliation: Catholic
(Coed since 1971)

Student Body

Undergraduates: 3,100 **Men:** 45 % **Women:** 55 %
Graduate students: 2,800 **Freshman class:** 840

Academics

SAT Averages: 1100 **Verbal:** 520 **Math:** 580 **(Taking SATs:** 100 %**)**
700-800: V 1 % M 4 % **500-600:** V 44 % M 54 %
600-700: V 12 % M 27 % **400-500:** V 46 % M 14 % **300-400:** V 3 % M 1 %
High school class rank: Top fifth 45 % **2nd fifth** 30 % **3rd fifth** 18 %

Admissions

Applied: 3,600 **Accepted:** 72 % **Matriculated:** 32 %
Deadline: Feb. 1 **Accept common application:** NA
Interview recommended: No **Off-campus interview available:** No
Evaluative: No **Informational only:** NA **LD program:** No
Night in dorm provided: No **Non-refundable application fee:** $25
Early decision program: Yes **Applied:** NA **Accepted:** NA % **Deadline:** NA
Freshmen accepted other than Fall term: 2 % **SAT/FAF Code #** 6374

Transfers

Applied: 65 **Accepted:** % **Application deadline for Fall:** Aug. 1 **Spring:** Dec. 15
Minimum grades recommended: 2.5 **All new students who were transfers into all classes:** 21 %

Class Experience

Return 2nd year: 90 % **Graduate after 4 years:** 65 % **To graduate school within 5 years:** 30 %

Cost

Tuition deposit: $100 **Total cost (Including school's estimate on fees and books):** $17,900
Tuition: $11,100 **(In state:** $ **)** **Room and board:** $5,900
Annual giving by parents: $NA **Average per student:** $NA

Financial Aid

Average total package per student: $NA **Number receiving aid:** 60 %
Average scholarships and grants: $5,700 **Average loans:** $
Undergraduates working on campus: 15 %
Non-need scholarships NA % **Athletic scholarships:** NA
Off-campus part-time employment: Excellent
ROTC: Yes **NROTC:** No

Work-study program:
Average earnings: $1,100
FAF deadline: Mar. 1
CO-OP program: No
AFROTC: U of Maryland

Endowment

Total: $42 Million **Per student (including graduate students):** $13,000

Location

Acres: 63 **Setting:** City **Miles from town center:** 0 **(Pop.** 1 Million**)**
Miles from (Pop.) **Miles from (Pop.)**

Class Composition

Asian: 4 % **Black:** 3 % **Hispanic:** 2 % **White:** 90 % **Other:** 1 %
Total minority : 10 % **Foreign countries:** 2 % (80 students)
From public schools: 51 % **Students from in state:** 41 %

Housing (on campus)

Freshmen required to live on campus: Yes **Guaranteed for:** 1 year
Available for all students: 40 % **Fraternity / Sorority housing:** No / No
On-campus married student housing: Yes **Women-only dorms available:** Yes

Campus Life

Students living on campus: 40 % **Remain weekends:** 80 % **Handicap access:** 90 %
Car regulations: No freshmen
Number with cars: 40 % **Adequacy of on-campus parking:** Fair
Number of fraternities: 0 **Chapter houses:** 0 **Number of sororities:** 0 **Chapter houses:** 0
Students belonging to fraternities: 0 % **Students belonging to sororities:** 0 %

Libraries and Computers

Books: 230,000 **Periodicals:** 1,850 **Microform items:** 280,000
Microcomputers available: Yes **Microcomputers networked:** NA

Classes

Faculty / Student Ratio: 1/15 **Classes taught by teacher assistants:** 0 %
Most popular majors: Business, Communications **Classes begin:** Early Sept.
Baccalaureate degrees offered: BA, BBA, BS, BSEE

Sports

Division: I **Except:** **Physical ed requirements:** None
Students participating in intercollegiate sports: 13 % **In intramural sports:** 25 %
Additional intercollegiate and/or intramural sports: (not found at all colleges)

Crew: Yes	**Ice Hockey:** No	**Lacrosse:** Yes	**Wrestling:** No
Rugby: Yes	**Sailing:** Yes	**Skiing:** No	
Squash: Yes	**Ultimate Frisbee:** No	**Water Polo:** Yes	

Alumni

Number living: **Annual giving:** $850,000 **Participation:** 28 %
Average annual gift: $ 120 **Average per student:** $140

3-2 Programs (2 degrees in 5 years)

Speech, Pathology with Goucher, Johns Hopkins
3-4 Dentistry with Georgetown

Observation and Opinion of:

Undergraduates and graduates ______________________________

____

College counselor ______________________________

____

MACALESTER COLLEGE (Private)

1600 Grand Avenue
St. Paul, MN 55105

HIGHLY SELECTIVE
(Composite rating of guide books)

Main tel.: 612-696-6000
Admissions tel.: 612-696-6357
Financial aid tel.: 612-696-6214
Scheduled Airline Service: Minneapolis-St.Paul
Miles to airport: 10

Founded: 1874
Nickname: Fighting Scotts
Religious affiliation: Presbyterian
(Coed since 1893)

Student Body

Undergraduates: 1,750 **Men:** 45 % **Women:** 55 %
Graduate students: 0 **Freshman class:** 430

Academics

SAT Averages: 1220 **Verbal:** 600 **Math:** 620 **(Taking SATs: 70 %)**
700-800: V 10 % M 17 % **500-600:** V 38 % M 28 %
600-700: V 40 % M 48 % **400-500:** V 12 % M 6 % **300-400:** V 0 % M 1 %
High school class rank: Top fifth 78 % **2nd fifth** 17 % **3rd fifth** NA %

Admissions

Applied: 2,300 **Accepted:** 56 % **Matriculated:** 33 %
Deadline: Feb. 1 **Accept common application:** No
Interview recommended: Yes **Off-campus interview available:** Yes
Evaluative: Yes **Informational only:** No **LD program:** No
Night in dorm provided: Yes **Non-refundable application fee:** $30
Early decision program: Yes **Applied:** 749 **Accepted:** 65 % **Deadline:** Dec. 1
Freshmen accepted other than Fall term: 1 % **SAT/FAF Code** #6390

Transfers

Applied: 202 **Accepted:** 40 % **Application deadline for Fall:** Apr. 1 **Spring:** Dec. 1
Minimum grades recommended: 3.0 **All new students who were transfers into all classes:** 10 %

Class Experience

Return 2nd year: 90 % **Graduate after 4 years:** 61 % **To graduate school within 5 years:** N/A %

Cost

Tuition deposit: $150 **Total cost (Including school's estimate on fees and books):** $18,800
Tuition: $14,024 **(In state:** $ **)** **Room and board:** $4,200
Annual giving by parents: $240,000 **Average per student:** $150

Financial Aid

Average total package per student: $ **Number receiving aid:** 60 %
Average scholarships and grants: $7,400 **Average loans:** $NA **Work-study program:** Yes
Undergraduates working on campus: 20 % **Average earnings:** $1,350
Non-need scholarships 4 % **Athletic scholarships:** NA **FAF deadline:** Feb. 1
Off-campus part-time employment: Excellent **CO-OP program:** No
ROTC: No **NROTC:** No **AFROTC:** Col. St. Thomas

Endowment

Total: $390 Million **Per student (including graduate students):** $180,000

Location

Acres: 50 **Setting:** Surburban **Miles from town center:**2 **(Pop.** 620,000)
Miles from **(Pop.**) **Miles from** **(Pop.**)

Class Composition

Asian: 3 % **Black:** 4 % **Hispanic:** 2 % **White:** 75 % **Other:** 12 %
Total minority : 21 % **Foreign countries:** 11 % (190 students)
From public schools: 68 % **Students from in state:** 25 %

Housing (on campus)

Freshmen required to live on campus: Yes **Guaranteed for:** 1 year
Available for all students: 70 % **Fraternity / Sorority housing:** No / No
On-campus married student housing: No **Women-only dorms available:** Yes

Campus Life

Students living on campus: 70 % **Remain weekends:** 95 % **Handicap access:** 80 %
Car regulations: All 4 years
Number with cars: NA % **Adequacy of on-campus parking:** Fair
Number of fraternities: 0 **Chapter houses:** 0 **Number of sororities:** 0 **Chapter houses:** 0
Students belonging to fraternities: 0 % **Students belonging to sororities:** 0 %

Libraries and Computers

Books: 317,000 **Periodicals:** 1,300 **Microform items:** 50,000
Microcomputers available: Yes **Microcomputers networked:** NA

Classes

Faculty / Student Ratio: 1/12 **Classes taught by teacher assistants:** 0 %
Most popular majors: Business, Communications **Classes begin:** Early Sept.
Baccalaureate degrees offered: BA

Sports

Division: III **Except:** **Physical ed requirements:** None
Students participating in intercollegiate sports: 20 % **In intramural sports:** 50 %
Additional intercollegiate and/or intramural sports: (not found at all colleges)

Crew: Yes **Ice Hockey:** No **Lacrosse:** Yes **Wrestling:** No
Rugby: Yes **Sailing:** No **Skiing:** No
Squash: Yes **Ultimate Frisbee:** No **Water Polo:** Yes

Alumni

Number living: 16,500 **Annual giving:** $2.2 Million **Participation:** 31 %
Average annual gift: $ 400 **Average per student:** $1,250

3-2 Programs (2 degrees in 5 years)

Engineering with U of Minnesota and Washington U, Occupational Therapy with Washington U, 3-3 Architecture program with Washington U

Observation and Opinion of:

Undergraduates and graduates ______________________________

____

College counselor ______________________________

____

MARQUETTE UNIVERSITY (Private)

1217 West Wisconsin Avenue
Milwaukee, WI 53233

SELECTIVE
(Composite rating of guide books)

Main tel.: 414-288-7700
Admissions tel.: 414-288-7302
Financial aid tel.: 414-288-7390
Scheduled Airline Service: Milwaukee
Miles to airport: 10

Founded: 1881
Nickname: Warriors
Religious affiliation: Catholic
(Coed since 1912)

Student Body

Undergraduates: 7,850 **Men:** 50 % **Women:** 50 %
Graduate students: 3,000 **Freshman class:** 1,650

Academics

SAT Averages: 1085 **Verbal:** 500 **Math:** 585 **(Taking SATs: 64 %)**
700-800: V 1 % **M** 4 % **500-600: V** 34 % **M** 38 %
600-700: V 7 % **M** 25 % **400-500: V** 45 % **M** 27 % **300-400: V** 13 % **M** 6%
High school class rank: Top fifth 54 % **2nd fifth** 28 % **3rd fifth** 14 %

Admissions

Applied: 6,400 **Accepted:** 80 % **Matriculated:** 32 %
Deadline: Rolling **Accept common application:** No
Interview recommended: No **Off-campus interview available:** Yes
Evaluative: No **Informational only:** Yes **LD program:** No
Night in dorm provided: No **Non-refundable application fee:** $25
Early decision program: NA **Applied:** NA **Accepted:** NA % **Deadline:** NA
Freshmen accepted other than Fall term: 2 % **SAT/FAF Code #** 1448

Transfers

Applied: 892 **Accepted:** 58 % **Application deadline for Fall:** NA **Spring:** NA
Minimum grades recommended: 2.0 **All new students who were transfers into all classes:** 13 %

Class Experience

Return 2nd year: 89 % **Graduate after 4 years:** 72 % **To graduate school within 5 years:** 75 %

Cost

Tuition deposit: $200 **Total cost (Including school's estimate on fees and books):** $14,800
Tuition: $9,900 (In state: $) **Room and board:** $4,200
Annual giving by parents: $295,000

Financial Aid

Average total package per student: $7,900 **Number receiving aid:** 60 %
Average scholarships and grants: $4,100 **Average loans:** $3,800 **Work-study program:** Yes
Undergraduates working on campus: 33 % **Average earnings:** $930
Non-need scholarships 10 % **Athletic scholarships:** NA **FAF deadline:** Feb. 1
Off-campus part-time employment: Excellent **CO-OP program:** Yes
ROTC: Yes **NROTC:** No **AFROTC:** Milwaukee Eng.

Endowment

Total: $95 Million **Per student (including graduate students):** $8,000

Location

Acres: 80 **Setting:** City **Miles from town center:** 0 **(Pop.** 680,000**)**
Miles from **(Pop.** **)** **Miles from** **(Pop.** **)**

Class Composition

Asian: 4 % **Black:** 4 % **Hispanic:** 3 % **White:** 89 % **Other:** NA %
Total minority : 11 % **Foreign countries:** NA % ( )
From public schools: 55 % **Students from in state:** 53 %

Housing (on campus)

Freshmen required to live on campus: Yes **Guaranteed for:** 4 years
Available for all students: 65 % **Fraternity / Sorority housing:** No / No
On-campus married student housing: Yes **Women-only dorms available:** Yes

Campus Life

Students living on campus: 65 % **Remain weekends:** 95 % **Handicap access:** 80 %
Car regulations: All 4 years
Number with cars: NA % **Adequacy of on-campus parking:** NA
Number of fraternities: 8 **Chapter houses:** 0 **Number of sororities:** 4 **Chapter houses:** 0
Students belonging to fraternities: 0 % **Students belonging to sororities:** 1%

Libraries and Computers

Books: 743,000 **Periodicals:** 5,700 **Microform items:** 256,000
Microcomputers available: Yes **Microcomputers networked:** NA

Classes

Faculty / Student Ratio: 1/12 **Classes taught by teacher assistants:** 10 %
Most popular majors: Marketing, Electrical Engineering **Classes begin:** Late Aug.
Baccalaureate degrees offered: BA, BS, BSCE, BS Dental, HVG., BSEE, BSME, BSMT, BSN, BSPT

Sports

Division: I **Except:** **Physical ed requirements:** None
Students participating in intercollegiate sports: 2 % **In intramural sports:** 50 %
Additional intercollegiate and/or intramural sports: (not found at all colleges)

Crew: No	**Ice Hockey:** Yes	**Lacrosse:** Yes	**Wrestling:** Yes/M
Rugby: Yes	**Sailing:** Yes	**Skiing:** Yes	
Squash: Yes	**Ultimate Frisbee:** No	**Water Polo:** Yes	

Alumni

Number living: 73,000 **Annual giving:** $ 6 Million **Participation:** 23 %
Average annual gift: $ 380 **Average per student:** $550

3-2 Programs (2 degrees in 5 years)

Exchange program with U of Madrid

Observation and Opinion of:

Undergraduates and graduates ____________________

____

College counselor ____________________

____

MASSACHUSETTS INSTITUTE OF TECHNOLOGY (Private)

77 Massachusetts Avenue
Cambridge, MA

MOST SELECTIVE
(Composite rating of guide books)

Main tel.: 617-253-1000
Admissions tel.: 617-253-4791
Financial aid tel.: 617-253-4971
Scheduled Airline Service: Boston
Miles to airport: 5

Founded: 1861
Nickname: Engineers
Religious affiliation: None
(Coed since 1861)

Student Body

Undergraduates: 4,400 **Men:** 67 % **Women:** 33 %
Graduate students: 5,000 **Freshman class:** 1,100

Academics

SAT Averages: 1355 **Verbal:** 620 **Math:** 735 **(Taking SATs: 99 %)**
700-800: V 21 % **M** 84% **500-600: V** 23 % **M** 1 %
600-700: V 48 % **M** 15 % **400-500: V** 7 % **M** 0 % **300-400: V** 1 % **M** 0 %
High school class rank: Top fifth 99 % **2nd fifth** 1 % **3rd fifth** NA %

Admissions

Applied: 6,425 **Accepted:** 32 % **Matriculated:** 54 %
Deadline: Jan. 1 **Accept common application:** No
Interview recommended: Yes **Off-campus interview available:** Yes
Evaluative: Yes **Informational only:** No **LD program:** No
Night in dorm provided: Yes **Non-refundable application fee:** $45
Early decision program: Yes **Applied:** 1,214 **Accepted:** 33 % **Deadline:** Nov. 1
Freshmen accepted other than Fall term: 0 % **SAT/FAF Code #** 3514

Transfers

Applied: NA **Accepted:** NA % **Application deadline for Fall:** Apr. 1 **Spring:** Nov. 15
Minimum grades recommended: B **All new students who were transfers into all classes:** 2 %

Class Experience

Return 2nd year: 97 % **Graduate after 4 years:** 87 % **To graduate school within 1 years:** 52 %

Cost

Tuition deposit: $0 **Total cost (Including school's estimate on fees and books):** $24,200
Tuition: $18,000 **(In state:** $ **)** **Room and board:** $5,560
Annual giving by parents: $0 **Average per student:** $NA

Financial Aid

Average total package per student: $15,400 **Number receiving aid:** 60 %
Average scholarships and grants: $10,700 **Average loans:** $4,700 **Work-study program:** Yes
Undergraduates working on campus: 55 % **Average earnings:** $1,000
Non-need scholarships 0 % **Athletic scholarships:** NA **FAF deadline:** NA
Off-campus part-time employment: Good **CO-OP program:** No
ROTC: Yes **NROTC:** Yes **AFROTC:** Yes

Endowment

Total: $1.4 Billion **Per student (including graduate students):** $150,000

Location

Acres: 142 **Setting:** Urban **Miles from town center:** 0 **(Pop.** 107,000**)**
5 **Miles from** Boston **(Pop.** 700,000 **)** **Miles from** **(Pop.** **)**

Class Composition

Asian: 21 % **Black:** 7 % **Hispanic:** 8 % **White:** 63 % **Other:** 1 %
Total minority : 37 % **Foreign countries:** NA% ( )
From public schools: 77 % **Students from in state:** 10 %

Housing (on campus)

Freshmen required to live on campus: Yes **Guaranteed for:** 4 years
Available for all students: 95 % **Fraternity / Sorority housing:** Yes / No
On-campus married student housing: Yes **Women-only dorms available:** NA

Campus Life

Students living on campus: 95 % **Remain weekends:** 80 % **Handicap access:** 75 %
Car regulations: All 4 years
Number with cars: 30% **Adequacy of on-campus parking:** Poor
Number of fraternities: 33 **Chapter houses:** 33 **Number of sororities:** 4 **Chapter houses:** 0
Students belonging to fraternities: 55 % **Students belonging to sororities:** 18 %

Libraries and Computers

Books: 2.1 Million **Periodicals:** 21,400 **Microform items:** 1.6 Million
Microcomputers available: Yes **Microcomputers networked:** Yes

Classes

Faculty / Student Ratio: 1/4 **Classes taught by teacher assistants:** 10 %
Most popular majors: Electrical Engineering, Computer Science **Classes begin:** Mid Sept.
Baccalaureate degrees offered: SB

Sports

Division: III **Except:** **Physical ed requirements:** NA
Students participating in intercollegiate sports: 40 % **In intramural sports:** 70 %
Additional intercollegiate and/or intramural sports: (not found at all colleges)
Crew: Yes **Ice Hockey:** Yes **Lacrosse:** Yes **Wrestling:** Yes/M
Rugby: Yes **Sailing:** Yes **Skiing:** Yes
Squash: Yes **Ultimate Frisbee:** Yes **Water Polo:** Yes

Alumni

Number living: 78,000 **Annual giving:** $ 34 Million **Participation:** 38 %
Average annual gift: $ 1,200 **Average per student:** $8,000

3-2 Programs (2 degrees in 5 years)

S.B./M.C.P. Program
Cross registration with Harvard and Wellesley

Observation and Opinion of:

Undergraduates and graduates ____________________

____

College counselor ____________________

____

UNIVERSITY OF MIAMI (Private)

Box 248025
Coral Gables, FL 33124

SELECTIVE
(Composite rating of guide books)

Main tel.: 305-284-2211
Admissions tel.: 305-284-4329
Financial aid tel.: 305-284-5212
Scheduled Airline Service: Miami
Miles to airport: 24

Founded: 1925
Nickname: Hurricanes
Religious affiliation: None
(Coed since 1925)

Student Body

Undergraduates: 7,750 **Men:** 55 % **Women:** 45 %
Graduate students: 5,100 **Freshman class:** 1,960

Academics

SAT Averages: 1100 **Verbal:** 520 **Math:** 580 **(Taking SATs:** NA %)
700-800: V 2 % **M** 15 % **500-600: V** 45 % **M** 35 %
600-700: V 18% **M** 35 % **400-500: V** 35 % **M** 15 % **300-400: V** NA % **M** NA %
High school class rank: Top fifth 59 % **2nd fifth** 23 % **3rd fifth** 12 %

Admissions

Applied: 8,370 **Accepted:** 74 % **Matriculated:** 32 %
Deadline: Mar. 1 **Accept common application:** No
Interview recommended: Yes **Off-campus interview available:** Yes
Evaluative: No **Informational only:** Yes **LD program:** No
Night in dorm provided: No **Non-refundable application fee:** $35
Early decision program: Yes **Applied:** NA **Accepted:** NA % **Deadline:** Nov. 1
Freshmen accepted other than Fall term: 4 % **SAT/FAF Code #** 5815

Transfers

Applied: 1,940 **Accepted:** 60 % **Application deadline for Fall:** Jul. 1 **Spring:** Nov. 1
Minimum grades recommended: 2.5 **All new students who were transfers into all classes:** 7 %

Class Experience

Return 2nd year: 93% **Graduate after 4 years:** 68 % **To graduate school within 5 years:** NA %

Cost

Tuition deposit: $200 **Total cost (Including school's estimate on fees and books):** $21,500
Tuition: $15,050 **(In state:** $ **)** **Room and board:** $5,900
Annual giving by parents: $175,000 **Average per student:** $13

Financial Aid

Average total package per student: $NA **Number receiving aid:** 32 %
Average scholarships and grants: $NA **Average loans:** $NA **Work-study program:** Yes
Undergraduates working on campus: 38 % **Average earnings:** $2,000
Non-need scholarships 5 % **Athletic scholarships:** Yes **FAF deadline:** Mar. 1
Off-campus part-time employment: Good **CO-OP program:** Yes
ROTC: Yes **NROTC:** No **AFROTC:** Yes

Endowment

Total: $196 Million **Per student (including graduate students):** $13,000

Location

Acres: 260 **Setting:** Surburban
6 **Miles from** Miami **(Pop.** 346,000)
16 **Miles from town center:** 6 **(Pop.** 38,000)
Miles from (Pop.)

Class Composition

Asian: 3 % **Black:** 7 % **Hispanic:** 19 % **White:** 61 % **Other:** 10 %
Total minority : 39 % **Foreign countries:** 10 % (750 students)
From public schools: NA % **Students from in state:** 45 %

Housing (on campus)

Freshmen required to live on campus: Yes
Available for all students: 50 %
On-campus married student housing: Yes
Guaranteed for: 4 years
Fraternity / Sorority housing: Yes / No
Women-only dorms available: Yes

Campus Life

Students living on campus: 80 % **Remain weekends:** 70 % **Handicap access:** 99 %
Car regulations: All 4 years
Number with cars: NA %
Adequacy of on-campus parking: Poor
Number of fraternities: 16 **Chapter houses:** 7
Number of sororities: 8 **Chapter houses:** 0
Students belonging to fraternities: 18 %
Students belonging to sororities: 11 %

Libraries and Computers

Books: 1.7 Million **Periodicals:** 16,700 **Microform items:** 1 Million
Microcomputers available: **Microcomputers networked:** NA

Classes

Faculty / Student Ratio: 1/13 **Classes taught by teacher assistants:** 20 %
Most popular majors: Finance, Accounting **Classes begin:** Late Aug.
Baccalaureate degrees offered: BA, B ARCH, BSSA, BBA, BFA, BSS, B MUS, BA, BS ARCHE, BSCE, BS COMM, BSED, BSN

Sports

Division: I **Except:** **Physical ed requirements:** None
Students participating in intercollegiate sports: 35 % **In intramural sports:** 50 %
Additional intercollegiate and/or intramural sports: (not found at all colleges)

Crew: Yes	**Ice Hockey:** No	**Lacrosse:** Yes	**Wrestling:** Yes
Rugby: Yes	**Sailing:** Yes	**Skiing:** No	
Squash: No	**Ultimate Frisbee:** No	**Water Polo:** Yes	

Alumni

Number living: 75,000 **Annual giving:** $ 5.2 Mil **Participation:** 17 %
Average annual gift: $ 420 **Average per student:** $400

3-2 Programs (2 degrees in 5 years)

In-house BA/JD Program and BS/PAO Program and Marine Science and Business Administration

Observation and Opinion of:

Undergraduates and graduates ______________________

____

College counselor ______________________

____

MIAMI UNIVERSITY (Private)

Oxford, OH 45056

VERY SELECTIVE
(Composite rating of guide books)

Main tel.: 513-529-1809
Admissions tel.: 513-529-2531
Financial aid tel.: 513-529-4734
Scheduled Airline Service: Cincinnati
Miles to airport: 35

Founded: 1809
Nickname: Redskins
Religious affiliation: None
(Coed since 1888)

Student Body

Undergraduates: 13,600 **Men:** 45 % **Women:** 55 %
Graduate students: 1,600 **Freshman class:** 3,460

Academics

SAT Averages: 1140 **Verbal:** 535 **Math:** 605 **(Taking SATs:** 65 %**)**
700-800: V 2 % **M** 13 % **500-600: V** 25 % **M** 8 %
600-700: V 16 % **M** 26 % **400-500: V** 4 % **M** 0 % **300-400: V** NA % **M** NA %
High school class rank: Top fifth 69 % **2nd fifth** 18 % **3rd fifth** 3 %

Admissions

Applied: 9,300 **Accepted:** 78 % **Matriculated:** 48 %
Deadline: Jan. 31 **Accept common application:** Yes
Interview recommended: Yes **Off-campus interview available:** Yes
Evaluative: No **Informational only:** Yes **LD program:** Yes
Night in dorm provided: Yes **Non-refundable application fee:** $30
Early decision program: Yes **Applied:** 971 **Accepted:** 67 % **Deadline:** Nov. 1
Freshmen accepted other than Fall term: 2 % **SAT/FAF Code #** 1463

Transfers

Applied: 850 **Accepted:** 38 % **Application deadline for Fall:** May 1 **Spring:** Dec. 10
Minimum grades recommended: 3.0 **All new students who were transfers into all classes:** 6 %

Class Experience

Return 2nd year: 93 % **Graduate after 4 years:** 68 % **To graduate school within 5 years:** N/A %

Cost

Tuition deposit: $70 **Total cost (Including school's estimate on fees and books):** $13,000
Tuition: $8,600 **(In state:** $ 4,000 **)** **Room and board:** $3,620
Annual giving by parents: $94,000 **Average per student:** $NA

Financial Aid

Average total package per student: $6,200 **Number receiving aid:** 32 %
Average scholarships and grants: $3,100 **Average loans:** $3,087 **Work-study program:** NA
Undergraduates working on campus: 34 % **Average earnings:** $1,120
Non-need scholarships 38 % **Athletic scholarships:** Yes **FAF deadline:** Feb. 15
Off-campus part-time employment: Good **CO-OP program:** No
ROTC: Yes **NROTC:** No **AFROTC:** Yes

Endowment

Total: $31 Million **Per student (including graduate students):** $2,400

Location

Acres: 1,200 **Setting:** Rural
Miles from town center: 1 **(Pop.** 9,500**)**
35 **Miles from** Cincinnati **(Pop.)**
Miles from (Pop.)

Class Composition

Asian: 1 % **Black:** 2 % **Hispanic:** 1 % **White:** 95 % **Other:** 1%
Total minority : 5 % **Foreign countries:** NA% ( )
From public schools: NA % **Students from in state:** 77 %

Housing (on campus)

Freshmen required to live on campus: Yes
Guaranteed for: 1 year
Available for all students: 60 %
Fraternity / Sorority housing: Yes / No
On-campus married student housing: Yes
Women-only dorms available: Yes

Campus Life

Students living on campus: 60 % **Remain weekends:** 80 % **Handicap access:** 80 %
Car regulations: Special permission required
Number with cars: NA %
Adequacy of on-campus parking: Limited
Number of fraternities: 29 **Chapter houses:** 26
Number of sororities: 23 **Chapter houses:** 0
Students belonging to fraternities: 38 %
Students belonging to sororities: 42 %

Libraries and Computers

Books: 1.3 Million **Periodicals:** 6,500 **Microform items:** 2 Million
Microcomputers available: Yes **Microcomputers networked:** Yes

Classes

Faculty / Student Ratio: 1/21 **Classes taught by teacher assistants:** 10 %
Most popular majors: Marketing, Finance **Classes begin:** Late Aug.
Baccalaureate degrees offered: AB, BA INT'L ST, BEA, B MUS,B PHIL, BS, BS APPL SCI, BS BUSINESS, BSED, BSHE

Sports

Division: I **Except:** **Physical ed requirements:** NA
Students participating in intercollegiate sports: 3 % **In intramural sports:** 90 %
Additional intercollegiate and/or intramural sports: (not found at all colleges)

Crew: No **Ice Hockey:** Yes **Lacrosse:** Yes **Wrestling:** Yes
Rugby: Yes **Sailing:** Yes **Skiing:** Yes
Squash: Yes **Ultimate Frisbee:** No **Water Polo:** Yes

Alumni

Number living: 93,000 **Annual giving:** $ 5.6 Mil. **Participation:** 30 %
Average annual gift: $ 220 **Average per student:** $250

3-2 Programs (2 degrees in 5 years)

Engineering and Forestry with Case Western, Columbia and Duke

Observation and Opinion of:

Undergraduates and graduates ______________________________

____

College counselor ______________________________

____

UNIVERSITY OF MICHIGAN (Public)

Ann Arbor, MI 48109-1316

HIGHLY SELECTIVE
(Composite rating of guide books)

Main tel.: 313-764-1817
Admissions tel.: 313-764-7433
Financial aid tel.: 313-763-6600
Scheduled Airline Service: Detroit
Miles to airport: 50

Founded: 1817
Nickname: Wolverines
Religious affiliation: None
(Coed since 1879)

Student Body

Undergraduates: 21,800 **Men:** 53 % **Women:** 47 %
Graduate students: 13,200 **Freshman class:** 4,630

Academics

SAT Averages: 1190 **Verbal:** 554 **Math:** 635 **(Taking SATs:** 71 %**)**
700-800: V 4 % **M** 25 % **500-600: V** 43 % **M** 23 %
600-700: V 25 % **M** 44 % **400-500: V** 24 % **M** 7 % **300-400: V** 4 % **M** 1 %
High school class rank: Top fifth 90 % **2nd fifth** 9 % **3rd fifth** 1 %

Admissions

Applied: 17,500 **Accepted:** 60 % **Matriculated:** 44 %
Deadline: Feb. 1 **Accept common application:** No
Interview recommended: No **Off-campus interview available:** No
Evaluative: No **Informational only:** Yes **LD program:** Yes
Night in dorm provided: Yes **Non-refundable application fee:** $30
Early decision program: No **Applied:** NA **Accepted:** NA% **Deadline:** NA
Freshmen accepted other than Fall term: Yes **SAT/FAF Code #** 1839

Transfers

Applied: 3,290 **Accepted:** 50 % **Application deadline for Fall:** Feb. 1 **Spring:** NA
Minimum grades recommended: C **All new students who were transfers into all classes:** 9 %

Class Experience

Return 2nd year: 90 % **Graduate after 4 years:** 75 % **To graduate school within 5 years:** %

Cost

Tuition deposit: $200 **Total cost (Including school's estimate on fees and books):** $20,800
Tuition: $14,000 **(In state:** $ 4,000 **)** **Room and board:** $4,200
Annual giving by parents: $347,000 **Average per student:** $14

Financial Aid

Average total package per student: $ **Number receiving aid:** 40 %
Average scholarships and grants: $3,000 **Average loans:** $5,000 **Work-study program:** Yes
Undergraduates working on campus: 56 % **Average earnings:** $1,200
Non-need scholarships 3 % **Athletic scholarships:** Yes **FAF deadline:** Feb. 15
Off-campus part-time employment: Excellent **CO-OP program:** Yes
ROTC: Yes **NROTC:** Yes **AFROTC:** Yes

Endowment

Total: $500 Million **Per student (including graduate students):** $14,000

Location

Acres: 2,600 **Setting:** City
Miles from town center: 0 **(Pop.** 100,000**)**
50 **Miles from** Detroit **(Pop.** **)**
Miles from **(Pop.** **)**

Class Composition

Asian: 6 **%** **Black:** 6 **%** **Hispanic:** 3 **%** **White:** 84 **%** **Other:** NA **%**
Total minority : 16 **%** **Foreign countries:** 2 **%** (220 students)
From public schools: 75 **%** **Students from in state:** 70 **%**

Housing (on Campus)

Freshmen required to live on campus: No
Guaranteed for: 1 year
Available for all students: 52 **%**
Fraternity / Sorority housing: No / No
On-campus married student housing: Yes
Women-only dorms available: Yes

Campus Life

Students living on campus: 52 **%** **Remain weekends:** 90 **%** **Handicap access:** 80 **%**
Car regulations: OK for all students
Number with cars: NA **%**
Adequacy of on-campus parking: Poor
Number of fraternities: 38 **Chapter houses:** 0
Number of sororities: 22 **Chapter houses:** 0
Students belonging to fraternities: 0 **%**
Students belonging to sororities: 25 **%**

Libraries and Computers

Books: 6 Million **Periodicals:** 30,000 **Microform items:**
Microcomputers available: Yes **Microcomputers networked:** Yes

Classes

Faculty / Student Ratio: 1/13 **Classes taught by teacher assistants:** 35 **%**
Most popular majors: English, Poly Science **Classes begin:** Early Sept.
Baccalaureate degrees offered: AB, BA ED, BBA, BFA, BGS, B MUS, BS, BSE, BS ED, BS MED CHEM, BSN

Sports

Division: I **Except:** **Physical ed requirements:** None
Students participating in intercollegiate sports: 3 **%** **In intramural sports:** 90 **%**
Additional intercollegiate and/or intramural sports: (not found at all colleges)

Crew: Yes	**Ice Hockey:** Yes/M	**Lacrosse:** Yes	**Wrestling:** Yes
Rugby: Yes	**Sailing:** Yes	**Skiing:** Yes	
Squash: Yes	**Ultimate Frisbee:** No	**Water Polo:** Yes	

Alumni

Number living: 294,000 **Annual giving:** $ 33 Mil. **Participation:** 22 **%**
Average annual gift: $ 500 **Average per student:** $950

3-2 Programs (2 degrees in 5 years)

Internal Engineering
2-2 with School of Business Administration

Observation and Opinion of:

Undergraduates and graduates ____________________

College counselor ____________________

MIDDLEBURY COLLEGE (Private)

Middlebury, VT 05753

HIGHLY SELECTIVE
(Composite rating of guide books)

Main tel.: 802-388-3711
Admissions tel.: 802-388-3711, Ext. 5153
Financial aid tel.: 802-388-3711, Ext. 5158
Scheduled Airline Service: Burlington
Miles to airport: 35

Founded: 1800
Nickname: Panthers
Religious affiliation: None
(Coed since 1883)

Student Body

Undergraduates: 1,950 **Men:** 50 % **Women:** 50 %
Graduate students: 0 **Freshman class:** 530

Academics

SAT Averages: 1250 **Verbal:** NA **Math:** NA **(Taking SATs:** NA %
700-800: V NA % **M** NA % **500-600: V** NA % **M** NA %
600-700: V NA % **M** NA % **400-500: V** NA % **M** NA % **300-400: V** NA % **M** NA %
High school class rank: Top fifth 86 % **2nd fifth** 10 % **3rd fifth** NA %

Admissions

Applied: 3,700 **Accepted:** 40 % **Matriculated:** 36 %
Deadline: Jan. 15 **Accept common application:** No
Interview recommended: Yes **Off-campus interview available:** Yes
Evaluative: No **Informational only:** Yes **LD program:** No
Night in dorm provided: No **Non-refundable application fee:** $50
Early decision program: Yes **Applied:** 343 **Accepted:** 28 % **Deadline:** Nov. 15
Freshmen accepted other than Fall term: NA % **SAT/FAF Code #** 3526

Transfers

Applied: 225 **Accepted:** 36 % **Application deadline for Fall:** NA **Spring:** No
Minimum grades recommended: B **All new students who were transfers into all classes:** 2 %

Class Experience

Return 2nd year: 85% **Graduate after 4 years:** 91 % **To graduate school within 5 years:** 40 %

Cost

Tuition deposit: $200 **Total cost (Including school's estimate on fees and books):** $22,900
Tuition: $NA **(In state:** $ **)** **Room and board:** $NA
Annual giving by parents: $476,000 **Average per student:** $260

Financial Aid

Average total package per student: $NA **Number receiving aid:** 35 %
Average scholarships and grants: $11,400 **Average loans:** $NA **Work-study program:** Yes
Undergraduates working on campus: 60 % **Average earnings:** $700
Non-need scholarships NA% **Athletic scholarships:** NA **FAF deadline:** Feb. 1
Off-campus part-time employment: Good **CO-OP program:** NA
ROTC: No **NROTC:** No **AFROTC:** No

Endowment

Total: $209 Million **Per student (including graduate students):** $105,000

Location

Acres: 350 **Setting:** Small Town **Miles from town center:** 1/2 **(Pop.** 7 Million)
35 **Miles from** Burlington **(Pop.**) **Miles from** **(Pop.**)

Class Composition

Asian: 4 % **Black:** 3 % **Hispanic:** 3 % **White:** 90 % **Other:** NA %
Total minority : 10 % **Foreign countries:** 9 % (175 students)
From public schools: NA% **Students from in state:** NA %

Housing (on campus)

Freshmen required to live on campus: Yes **Guaranteed for:** 4 years
Available for all students: 100 % **Fraternity / Sorority housing:** No / No
On-campus married student housing: No **Women-only dorms available:** Yes

Campus Life

Students living on campus: 98 % **Remain weekends:** 85 % **Handicap access:** NA %
Car regulations: Restricted if on financial aid
Number with cars: 33 % **Adequacy of on-campus parking:** Good
Number of fraternities: 6 **Chapter houses:** 0 **Number of sororities:** 0 **Chapter houses:** 0
Students belonging to fraternities: 10 % **Students belonging to sororities:** 0 %

Libraries and Computers

Books: 630,000 **Periodicals:** 1,950 **Microform items:** 63,400
Microcomputers available: Yes **Microcomputers networked:** NA

Classes

Faculty / Student Ratio: 1/11 **Classes taught by teacher assistants:** 0 %
Most popular majors: Poly Science, Economics **Classes begin:** Sept.
Baccalaureate degrees offered: AB

Sports

Division: III **Except:** **Physical ed requirements:** 3 semesters
Students participating in intercollegiate sports: 35 % **In intramural sports:** 62 %
Additional intercollegiate and/or intramural sports: (not found at all colleges)
Crew: No **Ice Hockey:** Yes **Lacrosse:** Yes **Wrestling:** No
Rugby: Yes **Sailing:** No **Skiing:** Yes
Squash: Yes **Ultimate Frisbee:** Yes **Water Polo:** Yes

Alumni

Number living: 18,600 **Annual giving:** $ 6.3 Million **Participation:** 51 %
Average annual gift: $ 650 **Average per student:** $3,100

3-2 Programs (2 degrees in 5 years)

Observation and Opinion of:

Undergraduates and graduates ______________________________

____

College counselor ______________________________

____

MOUNT HOLYOKE COLLEGE (Private)

College Street
South Hadley, MA 01075-1497

HIGHLY SELECTIVE
(Composite rating of guide books)

Main tel.: 413-538-2000
Admissions tel.: 413-538-2023
Financial aid tel.: 413-538-2291
Scheduled Airline Service: Hartford
Miles to airport: 39

Founded: 1837
Nickname: NA
Religious affiliation: None
(Coed since 1837)

Student Body

Undergraduates: 1,950 **Men:** 0 % **Women:** 100 %
Graduate students: 0 **Freshman class:** NA

Academics

SAT Averages: 1160 **Verbal:** 570 **Math:** 590 (Taking SATs: NA %)
700-800: V 5 % M 9 % **500-600:** V 45 % M 45 %
600-700: V 30 % M 31 % **400-500:** V 20 % M 15 % **300-400:** V NA % M NA %
High school class rank: Top fifth NA % **2nd fifth** NA % **3rd fifth** NA %

Admissions

Applied: 2,000 **Accepted:** 60 % **Matriculated:** 45 %
Deadline: Feb. 1 **Accept common application:** Yes
Interview recommended: Yes **Off-campus interview available:** Yes
Evaluative: No **Informational only:** Yes **LD program:** Yes
Night in dorm provided: Yes **Non-refundable application fee:** $40
Early decision program: Yes **Applied:** NA **Accepted:** 50 % **Deadline:** Nov. 15
Freshmen accepted other than Fall term: 11 % **SAT/FAF Code #** 3529

Transfers

Applied: NA **Accepted:** NA% **Application deadline for Fall:** NA **Spring:** NA
Minimum grades recommended: 3.0 **All new students who were transfers into all classes:** 4 %

Class Experience

Return 2nd year: 95 % **Graduate after 4 years:** 80 % **To graduate school within 5 years:** 70 %

Cost

Tuition deposit: $300 **Total cost (Including school's estimate on fees and books):** $22,800
Tuition: $16,870 **(In state:** $ **)** **Room and board:** $5,180
Annual giving by parents: $383,000 **Average per student:** $200

Financial Aid

Average total package per student: $11,500 **Number receiving aid:** 50 %
Average scholarships and grants: $9,000 **Average loans:** $2,500 **Work-study program:** Yes
Undergraduates working on campus: 85 % **Average earnings:** $1,100
Non-need scholarships NA % **Athletic scholarships:** NA **FAF deadline:** Feb. 1
Off-campus part-time employment: Fair **CO-OP program:** No
ROTC: at U of Mass **NROTC:** No **AFROTC:** at U of Mass

Endowment

Total: $180 Million **Per student (including graduate students):** $90,000

Location

Acres: 800 **Setting:** Small town **Miles from town center:** 0 **(Pop.** 16,000**)**
50 **Miles from** Hartford **(Pop.** 800,000**)** **Miles from (Pop.)**

Class Composition

Asian: NA % **Black:** NA % **Hispanic:** NA % **White:** NA % **Other:** NA %
Total minority : NA% **Foreign countries:** 8 % (160 students)
From public schools: NA % **Students from in state:** 20 %

Housing (on campus)

Freshmen required to live on campus: Yes **Guaranteed for:** 4 years
Available for all students: 97 % **Fraternity / Sorority housing:** No / No
On-campus married student housing: No **Women-only dorms available:** Yes

Campus Life

Students living on campus: 97 % **Remain weekends:** 75 % **Handicap access:** 50 %
Car regulations: All may have
Number with cars: 32 % **Adequacy of on-campus parking:** Fair
Number of fraternities: 0 **Chapter houses:** 0 **Number of sororities:** 0 **Chapter houses:** 0
Students belonging to fraternities: 0% **Students belonging to sororities:** 0 %

Libraries and Computers

Books: 556,000 **Periodicals:** 1,800 **Microform items:** 14,100
Microcomputers available: Yes **Microcomputers networked:** Yes

Classes

Faculty / Student Ratio: 1/10 **Classes taught by teacher assistants:** 0 %
Most popular majors: NA **Classes begin:** Early Sept.
Baccalaureate degrees offered: AB

Sports

Division: III **Except:** **Physical ed requirements:** 3 semesters
Students participating in intercollegiate sports: 10 % **In intramural sports:** 20 %
Additional intercollegiate and/or intramural sports: (not found at all colleges)

Crew: Yes **Ice Hockey:** No **Lacrosse:** Yes **Wrestling:** No
Rugby: Yes **Sailing:** No **Skiing:** Yes
Squash: Yes **Ultimate Frisbee:** No **Water Polo:** Yes

Alumni

Number living: 27,000 **Annual giving:** $ 10.7 Mil. **Participation:** 60 %
Average annual gift: $ 800 **Average per student:** $5,400

3-2 Programs (2 degrees in 5 years)

Member of 12-College Exchange Program

Observation and Opinion of:

Undergraduates and graduates ______________________________

____

College counselor ______________________________

____

MUHLENBERG COLLEGE (Private)

2400 Chew Street
Allentown, PA 18104-5586

VERY SELECTIVE
(Composite rating of guide books)

Main tel.: 215-821-3100
Admissions tel.: 215-821-3200
Financial aid tel.: 215-821-3175
Scheduled Airline Service: Philadelphia
Miles to airport: 57

Founded: 1848
Nickname: Mules
Religious affiliation: Lutheran
(Coed since 1957)

Student Body

Undergraduates: 1,600 **Men:** 45 % **Women:** 54 %
Graduate students: 0 **Freshman class:** 415

Academics

SAT Averages: 1100 **Verbal:** 520 **Math:** 580 **(Taking SATs: 96 %)**
700-800: V 1 % M 5 % **500-600:** V 43 % M 47 %
600-700: V 13 % M 35 % **400-500:** V 40 % M 12 % **300-400:** V 3 % M 1 %
High school class rank: Top fifth 63 % 2nd fifth 28 % 3rd fifth 4 %

Admissions

Applied: 2,400 **Accepted:** 60 % **Matriculated:** 29 %
Deadline: Feb. 15 **Accept common application:** Yes
Interview recommended: Yes **Off-campus interview available:** Yes
Evaluative: Yes **Informational only:** NA **LD program:** Yes
Night in dorm provided: Yes **Non-refundable application fee:** $30
Early decision program: Yes **Applied:** 141 **Accepted:** 70 % **Deadline:** Jan. 15
Freshmen accepted other than Fall term: 1 % **SAT/FAF Code #** 2424

Transfers

Applied: 141 **Accepted:** 70 % **Application deadline for Fall:** Feb. 1 **Spring:** NA
Minimum grades recommended: 2.5 **All new students who were transfers into all classes:** 8 %

Class Experience

Return 2nd year: 90 % **Graduate after 4 years:** 85 % **To graduate school within 5 years:** NA %

Cost

Tuition deposit: $400 **Total cost (Including school's estimate on fees and books):** $21,000
Tuition: $15,740 **(In state:** $ **)** **Room and board:** $4,260
Annual giving by parents: $64,000 **Average per student:** $40

Financial Aid

Average total package per student: $14,700 **Number receiving aid:** 50 %
Average scholarships and grants: $7,500 **Average loans:** $7,200 **Work-study program:** Yes
Undergraduates working on campus: 32 % **Average earnings:** $1,300
Non-need scholarships 1 % **Athletic scholarships:** NA **FAF deadline:** Feb. 15
Off-campus part-time employment: Fair **CO-OP program:** No
ROTC: at LeHigh U **NROTC:** No **AFROTC:** at LeHigh U

Endowment

Total: $29 Million **Per student (including graduate students):** $18,000

Location

Acres: 75 **Setting:** Surburban **Miles from town center:** 2 **(Pop.** 104,000)
55 Miles from Phila. **(Pop.** 53,000) 90 Miles from NYC **(Pop.** 7 Million)

Class Composition

Asian: 6 % **Black:** 2 % **Hispanic:** 1 % **White:** 81 % **Other:** NA%
Total minority : 9 % **Foreign countries:** 2 % (30 students)
From public schools: 78 % **Students from in state:** 34 %

Housing (on campus)

Freshmen required to live on campus: No **Guaranteed for:** 4 years
Available for all students: 90 % **Fraternity / Sorority housing:** Yes / Yes
On-campus married student housing: Yes **Women-only dorms available:** Yes

Campus Life

Students living on campus: 88 % **Remain weekends:** 85 % **Handicap access:** 50 %
Car regulations: No freshmen
Number with cars: NA % **Adequacy of on-campus parking:** Poor
Number of fraternities: 6 **Chapter houses:** 6 **Number of sororities:** 3 **Chapter houses:** 3
Students belonging to fraternities: 50 % **Students belonging to sororities:** 40 %

Libraries and Computers

Books: 300,000 **Periodicals:** 1,600 **Microform items:** 20,000
Microcomputers available: Yes **Microcomputers networked:** NA

Classes

Faculty / Student Ratio: 1/12 **Classes taught by teacher assistants:** 0 %
Most popular majors: Biology, Business Administration **Classes begin:** August
Baccalaureate degrees offered: BA, BS

Sports

Division: III **Except:** **Physical ed requirements:** 2 semesters
Students participating in intercollegiate sports: 25 % **In intramural sports:** 60 %
Additional intercollegiate and/or intramural sports: (not found at all colleges)
Crew: No **Ice Hockey:** Yes **Lacrosse:** Yes **Wrestling:** Yes/M
Rugby: Yes **Sailing:** No **Skiing:** No
Squash: No **Ultimate Frisbee:** No **Water Polo:** Yes

Alumni

Number living: 13,000 **Annual giving:** $ 1 Mil. **Participation:** 35 %
Average annual gift: $ 220 **Average per student:** $700

3-2 Programs (2 degrees in 5 years)

Engineering with Columbia and Washington U, Forestry with Duke, Nursing with Columbia
3-4 Dentistry with U of Pennsylvania

Observation and Opinion of:

Undergraduates and graduates ______________________________

____

College counselor ______________________________

____

NEW YORK UNIVERSITY (Private)

22 Washington Square North
New York, NY 10011

HIGHLY SELECTIVE
(Composite rating of guide books)

Main tel.: 212-998-1212
Admissions tel.: 212-998-4500
Financial aid tel.: 212-998-4444
Scheduled Airline Service: NYC
Miles to airport: 12

Founded: 1831
Nickname: Violets
Religious affiliation: None
(Coed since 1873)

Student Body

Undergraduates: 14,500 **Men:** 43 % **Women:** 57 %
Graduate students: 14,000 **Freshman class:** 2,530

Academics

SAT Averages: 1140 **Verbal:** 550 **Math:** 590 **(Taking SATs: 93 %)**
700-800: V 5 % **M** 12 % **500-600: V** 48 % **M** 37 %
600-700: V 34 % **M** 43 % **400-500: V** 11 % **M** 8 % **300-400: V** 2 % **M** 0 %
High school class rank: Top fifth 45 % **2nd fifth** 8 % **3rd fifth** 4 %

Admissions

Applied: 10,600 **Accepted:** 54 % **Matriculated:** 44 %
Deadline: Feb. 1 **Accept common application:** Yes
Interview recommended: Yes **Off-campus interview available:** No
Evaluative: No **Informational only:** Yes **LD program:** Yes
Night in dorm provided: No **Non-refundable application fee:** $45
Early decision program: Yes **Applied:** 877 **Accepted:** 65 % **Deadline:** Dec. 15
Freshmen accepted other than Fall term: 8 % **SAT/FAF Code #** 2562

Transfers

Applied: 3,225 **Accepted:** 64 % **Application deadline for Fall:** Apr. 1 **Spring:** Dec. 1
Minimum grades recommended: C **All new students who were transfers into all classes:** 39 %

Class Experience

Return 2nd year: 87 % **Graduate after 4 years:** 70 % **To graduate school within 5 years:** 65 %

Cost

Tuition deposit: $200 **Total cost (Including school's estimate on fees and books):** $24,000
Tuition: $16,750 (In state: $) **Room and board:** $6,780
Annual giving by parents: $120,000 **Average per student:** $8

Financial Aid

Average total package per student: $10,000 **Number receiving aid:** 60 %
Average scholarships and grants: $7,500 **Average loans:** $2,500 **Work-study program:** Yes
Undergraduates working on campus: 27 % **Average earnings:** $1,900
Non-need scholarships 2 % **Athletic scholarships:** NA **FAF deadline:** Feb. 1
Off-campus part-time employment: Excellent **CO-OP program:** No
ROTC: at PolyTech **NROTC:** No **AFROTC:** at Manhat Coll

Endowment

Total: $582 Million **Per student (including graduate students):** $21,000

Location

Acres: 29 **Setting:** City **Miles from town center:** 0 **(Pop.** 7 Million**)**
Miles from **(Pop.** **)** **Miles from** **(Pop.** **)**

Class Composition

Asian: 16 % **Black:** 7 % **Hispanic:** 7 % **White:** 52 % **Other:** 18 %
Total minority : 48 % **Foreign countries:** 7 % (1,000 students)
From public schools: % **Students from in state:** 50 %

Housing (on campus)

Freshmen required to live on campus: No **Guaranteed for:** 4 years
Available for all students: 48 % **Fraternity / Sorority housing:** Yes / Yes
On-campus married student housing: No **Women-only dorms available:** No

Campus Life

Students living on campus: 48 % **Remain weekends:** % **Handicap access:** 90 %
Car regulations: All may have
Number with cars: 2 % **Adequacy of on-campus parking:** Very poor
Number of fraternities: 12 **Chapter houses:** 10 **Number of sororities:** 9 **Chapter houses:** 6
Students belonging to fraternities: 8 % **Students belonging to sororities:** 8 %

Libraries and Computers

Books: 3 Million **Periodicals:** 29,500 **Microform items:** 2,745,000
Microcomputers available: Yes **Microcomputers networked:** NA

Classes

Faculty / Student Ratio: 1/13 **Classes taught by teacher assistants:** 30 %
Most popular majors: NA **Classes begin:** Early Sept.
Baccalaureate degrees offered: BA, BFA, B MUS, BS

Sports

Division: III **Except:** **Physical ed requirements:** None
Students participating in intercollegiate sports: 5 % **In intramural sports:** 3 %
Additional intercollegiate and/or intramural sports: (not found at all colleges)

Crew: Yes	**Ice Hockey:** Yes	**Lacrosse:** Yes	**Wrestling:** Yes
Rugby: No	**Sailing:** No	**Skiing:** No	
Squash: Yes	**Ultimate Frisbee:** No	**Water Polo:** Yes	

Alumni

Number living: 225,000 **Annual giving:** $ 14.6 Mil. **Participation:** 18 %
Average annual gift: $ 360 **Average per student:** $600

3-2 Programs (2 degrees in 5 years)

Engineering with Stevens Institute

Observation and Opinion of:

Undergraduates and graduates ______________________________

____

College counselor ______________________________

____

NORTHWESTERN UNIVERSITY (Private)

P.O. Box 3060, 1801 Hinman Avenue
Evanston, IL 60204-3060

MOST SELECTIVE
(Composite rating of guide books)

Main tel.: 708-491-3741
Admissions tel.: 708-491-7271
Financial aid tel.: 708-491-7271
Scheduled Airline Service: Chicago
Miles to airport: 8

Founded: 1851
Nickname: Wildcats
Religious affiliation: None
(Coed since 1851)

Student Body

Undergraduates: 7,250 **Men:** 51 % **Women:** 49 %
Graduate students: 4,000 **Freshman class:** 1,775

Academics

SAT Averages: 1260 **Verbal:** 590 **Math:** 670 **(Taking SATs:** NA %**)**
700-800: V 5 % **M** 31 % **500-600: V** 43 % **M** 18 %
600-700: V 39 % **M** 46 % **400-500: V** 12 % **M** 4 % **300-400: V** 1 % **M** 0 %
High school class rank: Top fifth 89 % **2nd fifth** 4 % **3rd fifth** 1 %

Admissions

Applied: 10,850 **Accepted:** 47 % **Matriculated:** 35 %
Deadline: Jan. 1 **Accept common application:** No
Interview recommended: Yes **Off-campus interview available:** Yes
Evaluative: Yes **Informational only:** NA **LD program:** No
Night in dorm provided: Yes **Non-refundable application fee:** $40
Early decision program: Yes **Applied:** 943 **Accepted:** 55 % **Deadline:** Nov. 1
Freshmen accepted other than Fall term: 1 % **SAT/FAF Code #** 1565

Transfers

Applied: 634 **Accepted:** 40 % **Application deadline for Fall:** NA **Spring:** NA
Minimum grades recommended: 3.0 **All new students who were transfers into all classes:** 6 %

Class Experience

Return 2nd year: 95 % **Graduate after 4 years:** 84 % **To graduate school within 5 years:** 50 %

Cost

Tuition deposit: $200 **Total cost (Including school's estimate on fees and books):** $21,000
Tuition: $15,075 **(In state:** $ **)** **Room and board:** $5,080
Annual giving by parents: $1.5 Million **Average per student:** $200

Financial Aid

Average total package per student: $11,600 **Number receiving aid:** 50 %
Average scholarships and grants: $8,900 **Average loans:** $2,700 **Work-study program:** Yes
Undergraduates working on campus: 70 % **Average earnings:** $1,500
Non-need scholarships 0 % **Athletic scholarships:** Yes **FAF deadline:** Feb. 15
Off-campus part-time employment: Excellent **CO-OP program:** Yes
ROTC: at Loyola **NROTC:** Yes **AFROTC:** at IL Institute

Endowment

Total: $1.2 Billion **Per student (including graduate students):** $90,000

Location

Acres: 250 **Setting:** Surburban **Miles from town center:** 35 **(Pop.** 75,000**)**
12 **Miles from** Chicago **(Pop.** 3 Mil. **)** **Miles from (Pop.)**

Class Composition

Asian: 14 % **Black:** 8 % **Hispanic:** 1 % **White:** 76 % **Other:** 1 %
Total minority : 14 % **Foreign countries:** 2 % (150 students)
From public schools: 72 % **Students from in state:** 25 %

Housing (on campus)

Freshmen required to live on campus: Yes **Guaranteed for:** 1 year
Available for all students: 50 % **Fraternity / Sorority housing:** Yes / Yes
On-campus married student housing: Yes **Women-only dorms available:** Yes

Campus Life

Students living on campus: 80 % **Remain weekends:** 60 % **Handicap access:** 90 %
Car regulations: No freshmen or sophomores
Number with cars: NA % **Adequacy of on-campus parking:** NA
Number of fraternities: 28 **Chapter houses:** 24 **Number of sororities:** 16 **Chapter houses:** 13
Students belonging to fraternities: 36 % **Students belonging to sororities:** 39 %

Libraries and Computers

Books: 3 Million **Periodicals:** 25,000 **Microform items:** 1.5 Million
Microcomputers available: Yes **Microcomputers networked:** NA

Classes

Faculty / Student Ratio: 1/10 **Classes taught by teacher assistants:** 10 %
Most popular majors: Poly Science, Communications **Classes begin:** NA
Baccalaureate degrees offered: BA, BME, B MUS ED, BS, BS ED, BS Journalism, BS Speech

Sports

Division: I **Except:** **Physical ed requirements:** None
Students participating in intercollegiate sports: 65 % **In intramural sports:** 80 %
Additional intercollegiate and/or intramural sports: (not found at all colleges)

Crew: Yes	**Ice Hockey:** Yes	**Lacrosse:** Yes	**Wrestling:** Yes/M
Rugby: No	**Sailing:** Yes	**Skiing:** Yes	
Squash: No	**Ultimate Frisbee:** Yes	**Water Polo:** Yes	

Alumni

Number living: 138,000 **Annual giving:** $16.3 Mil. **Participation:** 26 %
Average annual gift: $ 500 **Average per student:** $1,300

3-2 Programs (2 degrees in 5 years)

3-4 Honors Program with Northwestern Medical

Observation and Opinion of:

Undergraduates and graduates ______________________________

____

College counselor ______________________________

____

UNIVERSITY OF NOTRE DAME (Private)

113 Administration Building
Notre Dame, IN 46556

MOST SELECTIVE
(Composite rating of guide books)

Main tel.: 219-239-5000
Admissions tel.: 219-239-7505
Financial aid tel.: 219-239-6436
Scheduled Airline Service: Chicago
Miles to airport: 90

Founded: 1842
Nickname: Fighting Irish
Religious affiliation: Catholic
(Coed since 1973)

Student Body

Undergraduates: 7,500 **Men:** 64 % **Women:** 36 %
Graduate students: 2,200 **Freshman class:** 1,800

Academics

SAT Averages: 1250 **Verbal:** 590 **Math:** 660 **(Taking SATs:** 99 %)
700-800: V 5 % **M** 30 % **500-600: V** 42 % **M** 19 %
600-700: V 38 % **M** 48 % **400-500: V** 14 % **M** 3 % **300-400: V** 1 % **M** 0 %
High school class rank: Top fifth 95 % **2nd fifth** 4 % **3rd fifth** 1 %

Admissions

Applied: 9,100 **Accepted:** 37 % **Matriculated:** 53 %
Deadline: Jan. 10 **Accept common application:** NA
Interview recommended: No **Off-campus interview available:** No
Evaluative: No **Informational only:** Yes **LD program:** NA
Night in dorm provided: Yes **Non-refundable application fee:** $35
Early decision program: Yes **Applied:** 900 **Accepted:** 33 % **Deadline:** NA
Freshmen accepted other than Fall term: 0 % **SAT/FAF Code #** 1841

Transfers

Applied: 750 **Accepted:** 33 % **Application deadline for Fall:** NA **Spring:** NA
Minimum grades recommended: 3.5 **All new students who were transfers into all classes:** 5 %

Class Experience

Return 2nd year: 96 % **Graduate after 4 years:** 92 % **To graduate school within 1 year:** 45 %

Cost

Tuition deposit: $200 **Total cost (Including school's estimate on fees and books):** $18,800
Tuition: $14,200 **(In state:** $) **Room and board:** $4,000
Annual giving by parents: $3.1 Million **Average per student:** $400

Financial Aid

Average total package per student: $9,000 **Number receiving aid:** 25 %
Average scholarships and grants: $6,000 **Average loans:** $3,000 **Work-study program:** Yes
Undergraduates working on campus: 40 % **Average earnings:** $1,200
Non-need scholarships 25 % **Athletic scholarships:** Yes **FAF deadline:** Feb. 28
Off-campus part-time employment: Good **CO-OP program:** No
ROTC: Yes **NROTC:** No **AFROTC:** No

Endowment

Total: $637 Million **Per student (including graduate students):** $65,000

Location

Acres: 1,250 **Setting:** Surburban **Miles from town center:** 2 **(Pop.** 100,000**)**
90 **Miles from** Chicago **(Pop.** 3 Mil.**)** **Miles from** **(Pop.** **)**

Class Composition

Asian: 3 **%** **Black:** 4 **%** **Hispanic:** 5 **%** **White:** 85 **%** **Other:** 2 **%**
Total minority : 15 **%** **Foreign countries:** 2 **%** (150 students)
From public schools: 40 **%** **Students from in state:** 10 **%**

Housing (on campus)

Freshmen required to live on campus: Yes **Guaranteed for:** 1 year only
Available for all students: 85 **%** **Fraternity / Sorority housing:** No / No
On-campus married student housing: Yes **Women-only dorms available:** Yes

Campus Life

Students living on campus: 85 **%** **Remain weekends:** 75 **%** **Handicap access:** 90 **%**
Car regulations: No freshmen
Number with cars: 50**%** **Adequacy of on-campus parking:** None
Number of fraternities: 0 **Chapter houses:** 0 **Number of sororities:** 0 **Chapter houses:** 0
Students belonging to fraternities: 0 **%** **Students belonging to sororities:** 0 **%**

Libraries and Computers

Books: 1.9 Million **Periodicals:** 16,300 **Microform items:** 1.2 Million
Microcomputers available: Yes **Microcomputers networked:** NA

Classes

Faculty / Student Ratio: 1/11 **Classes taught by teacher assistants** 10 **%**
Most popular majors: Government, Accounting **Classes begin:** Late Aug.
Baccalaureate degrees offered: BA, B ARCH, BBA, BFA, B MUS, BS

Sports

Division: I **Except:** **Physical ed requirements:** 2 semesters
Students participating in intercollegiate sports: 10 **%** **In intramural sports:** 90 **%**
Additional intercollegiate and/or intramural sports: (not found at all colleges)

Crew: Yes **Ice Hockey:** Yes/M **Lacrosse:** Yes/M **Wrestling:** Yes/M
Rugby: Yes/M **Sailing:** Yes **Skiing:** Yes
Squash: No **Ultimate Frisbee:** No **Water Polo:** Yes/M

Alumni

Number living: 79,000 **Annual giving:** $ 24 Mil. **Participation:** 50 **%**
Average annual gift: $ 670 **Average per student:** $2,200

3-2 Programs (2 degrees in 5 years)

Engineering with Bethel, St. Anselm and St. Mary's

Observation and Opinion of:

Undergraduates and graduates ______________________

____

College counselor ______________________

____

OBERLIN COLLEGE (Private)

Oberlin, OH 44074-1075

MOST SELECTIVE
(Composite rating of guide books)

Main tel.: 216-775-8121
Admissions tel.: 216-775-8411
Financial aid tel.: 216-775-8142
Scheduled Airline Service: Cleveland
Miles to airport: 35

Founded: 1833
Nickname: Yeoman
Religious affiliation: None
(Coed since 1837)

Student Body

Undergraduates: 2,700 **Men:** 46 % **Women:** 54 %
Graduate students: 0 **Freshman class:** 570

Academics

SAT Averages: 1250 **Verbal:** 610 **Math:** 640 **(Taking SATs:** 96 %**)**
700-800: V 10 % **M** 21 % **500-600: V** 33 % **M** 21 %
600-700: V 47 % **M** 51 % **400-500: V** 7 % **M** 5 % **300-400: V** 2 % **M** 2 %
High school class rank: Top fifth NA % **2nd fifth** NA % **3rd fifth** NA %

Admissions

Applied: 3,480 **Accepted:** 54 % **Matriculated:** 30 %
Deadline: Jan. 15 **Accept common application:** Yes
Interview recommended: Yes **Off-campus interview available:** Yes
Evaluative: Yes **Informational only:** No **LD program:** Yes
Night in dorm provided: Yes **Non-refundable application fee:** $45
Early decision program: Yes **Applied:** 265 **Accepted:** 75 % **Deadline:** Nov. 15
Freshmen accepted other than Fall term: 0 % **SAT/FAF Code #** 1587

Transfers

Applied: 270 **Accepted:** 45 % **Application deadline for Fall:** Mar. 16 **Spring:** Nov. 15
Minimum grades recommended: 3.0 **All new students who were transfers into all classes:** NA %

Class Experience

Return 2nd year: 90 % **Graduate after 4 years:** 77 % **To graduate school within 2 years:** 75 %

Cost

Tuition deposit: $200 **Total cost (Including school's estimate on fees and books):** $23,100
Tuition: $17,600 **(In state: $)** **Room and board:** $5,300
Annual giving by parents: $421,000 **Average per student:** $170

Financial Aid

Average total package per student: $12,800 **Number receiving aid:** 45 %
Average scholarships and grants: $9,200 **Average loans:** $3,600 **Work-study program:** Yes
Undergraduates working on campus: 55 % **Average earnings:** $1,140
Non-need scholarships 30 % **Athletic scholarships:** NA **FAF deadline:** Feb. 1
Off-campus part-time employment: Good **CO-OP program:** No
ROTC: No **NROTC:** No **AFROTC:** No

Endowment

Total: $245 Million **Per student (including graduate students):** $85,000

Location

Acres: 440 **Setting:** Surburban
Miles from town center: 0 **(Pop.** 8,500**)**
34 **Miles from** Cleveland **(Pop.** 580,000**)**
Miles from (Pop.)

Class Composition

Asian: 8 % **Black:** 8 % **Hispanic:** 3 % **White:** 80 % **Other:** 1 %
Total minority : 20 % **Foreign countries:** 4 % (110 students)
From public schools: 67 % **Students from in state:** 11 %

Housing (on campus)

Freshmen required to live on campus: Yes
Guaranteed for: 4 years
Available for all students: 75 %
Fraternity / Sorority housing: No / No
On-campus married student housing: No
Women-only dorms available: Yes

Campus Life

Students living on campus: 71 % **Remain weekends:** 95 % **Handicap access:** 90 %
Car regulations: No freshmen
Number with cars: 15 %
Adequacy of on-campus parking: Good
Number of fraternities: 0 **Chapter houses:** 0
Number of sororities: 0 **Chapter houses:** 0
Students belonging to fraternities: 0 %
Students belonging to sororities: 0 %

Libraries and Computers

Books: 1 Million **Periodicals:** 4,500 **Microform items:** 275,000
Microcomputers available: Yes **Microcomputers networked:** NA

Classes

Faculty / Student Ratio: 1/13 **Classes taught by teacher assistants:** 0 %
Most popular majors: Biology, Government/History **Classes begin:** Sept.
Baccalaureate degrees offered: AB, BFA, MUS, BMus

Sports

Division: I **Except:** **Physical ed requirements:** NA
Students participating in intercollegiate sports: NA % **In intramural sports:** NA %
Additional intercollegiate and/or intramural sports: (not found at all colleges)

Crew: No	**Ice Hockey:** Yes/M	**Lacrosse:** Yes	**Wrestling:** No
Rugby: Yes	**Sailing:** No	**Skiing:** No	
Squash: Yes	**Ultimate Frisbee:** Yes	**Water Polo:** Yes/M	

Alumni

Number living: 26,000 **Annual giving:** $ 6.2 Mil. **Participation:** 52 %
Average annual gift: $ 440 **Average per student:** $NA

3-2 Programs (2 degrees in 5 years)

Engineering with Case Western, U of Pennsylvania and Washington U

Observation and Opinion of:

Undergraduates and graduates ______________________________

____

College counselor ______________________________

____

OCCIDENTAL COLLEGE (Private)

1600 Campus Road
Los Angeles, CA 90041

HIGHLY SELECTIVE
(Composite rating of guide books)

Main tel.: 213-259-2500
Admissions tel.: 213-259-2700
Financial aid tel.: 213-259-2548
Scheduled Airline Service: Burbank
Miles to airport: 10

Founded: 1887
Nickname: Tigers
Religious affiliation: None
(Coed since 1887)

Student Body

Undergraduates: 1,650 **Men:** 47 % **Women:** 53 %
Graduate students: 20 **Freshman class:** 412

Academics

SAT Averages: 1650 **Verbal:** 560 **Math:** 610 **(Taking SATs:** 99 %**)**
700-800: V 3 % **M** 12 % **500-600: V** 41 % **M** 32 %
600-700: V 30 % **M** 41 % **400-500: V** 24 % **M** 14 % **300-400: V** 2 % **M** 1 %
High school class rank: Top fifth 76 % **2nd fifth** 18 % **3rd fifth** 4 %

Admissions

Applied: 2,525 **Accepted:** 49 % **Matriculated:** 33 %
Deadline: Jan. 15 **Accept common application:** Yes
Interview recommended: Yes **Off-campus interview available:** Yes
Evaluative: No **Informational only:** Yes **LD program:** NA
Night in dorm provided: Yes **Non-refundable application fee:** $30
Early decision program: Yes **Applied:** NA **Accepted:** NA % **Deadline:** Nov. 15
Freshmen accepted other than Fall term: 0 % **SAT/FAF Code #** 4581

Transfers

Applied: NA **Accepted:** NA % **Application deadline for Fall:** Apr. 15 **Spring:** No
Minimum grades recommended: 3.0 **All new students who were transfers into all classes:** 14 %

Class Experience

Return 2nd year: 92 % **Graduate after 4 years:** 75 % **To graduate school within 5 years:** 46 %

Cost

Tuition deposit: $200 **Total cost (Including school's estimate on fees and books):** $21,500
Tuition: $15,500 **(In state:** $ **)** **Room and board:** $5,200
Annual giving by parents: $87,000 **Average per student:** $54

Financial Aid

Average total package per student: $NA **Number receiving aid:** 60 %
Average scholarships and grants: $NA **Average loans:** $NA **Work-study program:** Yes
Undergraduates working on campus: NA % **Average earnings:** $NA
Non-need scholarships NA % **Athletic scholarships:** NA **FAF deadline:** Feb. 1
Off-campus part-time employment: Good **CO-OP program:** No
ROTC: at USC **NROTC:** No **AFROTC:** at UCLA

Endowment

Total: $147 Million **Per student (including graduate students):** $85,000

Location

Acres: 120 **Setting:** Surburban **Miles from town center:** 6 **(Pop.** 3 Million**)**
Miles from **(Pop.** **)** **Miles from** **(Pop.** **)**

Class Composition

Asian: 12 % **Black:** 4 % **Hispanic:** 8 % **White:** 71 % **Other:** 5 %
Total minority : 29 % **Foreign countries:** 4 % (65 students)
From public schools: 62 % **Students from in state:** 54 %

Housing (on campus)

Freshmen required to live on campus: Yes **Guaranteed for:** 1 year only
Available for all students: 75 % **Fraternity / Sorority housing:** Yes / Yes
On-campus married student housing: No **Women-only dorms available:** Yes

Campus Life

Students living on campus: 75 % **Remain weekends:** 75 % **Handicap access:** NA %
Car regulations: All may have
Number with cars: 50 % **Adequacy of on-campus parking:** Good
Number of fraternities: 4 **Chapter houses:** 4 **Number of sororities:** 3 **Chapter houses:** 3
Students belonging to fraternities: 18 % **Students belonging to sororities:** 18 %

Libraries and Computers

Books: 486,000 **Periodicals:** 1,930 **Microform items:** 175,000
Microcomputers available: Yes **Microcomputers networked:** NA

Classes

Faculty / Student Ratio: 1/12 **Classes taught by teacher assistants:** 0 %
Most popular majors: NA **Classes begin:** Late Sept.
Baccalaureate degrees offered: BA

Sports

Division: III **Except:** **Physical ed requirements:** None
Students participating in intercollegiate sports: 25 % **In intramural sports:** 30 %
Additional intercollegiate and/or intramural sports: (not found at all colleges)

Crew: No **Ice Hockey:** No **Lacrosse:** Yes **Wrestling:** No
Rugby: Yes/M **Sailing:** No **Skiing:** No
Squash: No **Ultimate Frisbee:** No **Water Polo:** Yes

Alumni

Number living: 19,000 **Annual giving:** $ 900,000 **Participation:** 27 %
Average annual gift: $ 190 **Average per student:** $550

3-2 Programs (2 degrees in 5 years)

Engineering with Cal Tech and Columbia
3-3 Law Program with Columbia

Observation and Opinion of:

Undergraduates and graduates ____________________

____

College counselor ____________________

____

OHIO WESLEYAN UNIVERSITY (Private)

168 Sandusky Street
Delaware, OH 43015

SELECTIVE
(Composite rating of guide books)

Main tel.: 614-369-4431
Admissions tel.: 614-368-3020
Financial aid tel.: 614-368-3050
Scheduled Airline Service: Columbus
Miles to airport: 24

Founded: 1842
Nickname: Battling Bishops
Religious affiliation: Methodist
(Coed since 1842)

Student Body

Undergraduates: 2,000 **Men:** 51 % **Women:** 49 %
Graduate students: 0 **Freshman class:** 563

Academics

SAT Averages: NA **Verbal:** NA **Math:** NA **(Taking SATs:** NA **%)**
700-800: V 1 % **M** 11 % **500-600: V** 40 % **M** 34 %
600-700: V 18 % **M** 31 % **400-500: V** 35 % **M** 20 % **300-400: V** 6 % **M** 4 %
High school class rank: Top fifth 50 % **2nd fifth** 22 % **3rd fifth** 16 %

Admissions

Applied: 2,560 **Accepted:** 74 % **Matriculated:** 30 %
Deadline: Feb. 1 **Accept common application:** Yes
Interview recommended: Yes **Off-campus interview available:** Yes
Evaluative: No **Informational only:** Yes **LD program:** Yes
Night in dorm provided: NA **Non-refundable application fee:** $30
Early decision program: Yes **Applied:** 215 **Accepted:** 85 % **Deadline:** Dec. 31
Freshmen accepted other than Fall term: 0 % **SAT/FAF Code #** 1594

Transfers

Applied: 118 **Accepted:** 70 % **Application deadline for Fall:** NA **Spring:** NA
Minimum grades recommended: 3.0 **All new students who were transfers into all classes:** 7 %

Class Experience

Return 2nd year: 85 % **Graduate after 4 years:** 71 % **To graduate school within 5 years:** 55 %

Cost

Tuition deposit: $300 **Total cost (Including school's estimate on fees and books):** $20,500
Tuition: $14,650 **(In state:** $ **)** **Room and board:** $5,100
Annual giving by parents: $266,000 **Average per student:** $130

Financial Aid

Average total package per student: $14,200 **Number receiving aid:** 60 %
Average scholarships and grants: $12,000 **Average loans:** $2,200 **Work-study program:** Yes
Undergraduates working on campus: 38 % **Average earnings:** $1,100
Non-need scholarships 16 % **Athletic scholarships:** NA **FAF deadline:** Mar. 15
Off-campus part-time employment: Excellent **CO-OP program:** No
ROTC: No **NROTC:** No **AFROTC:** at Ohio State

Endowment

Total: $41 Million **Per student (including graduate students):** $22,000

Location

Acres: 200 **Setting:** Rural
Miles from town center: 1 **(Pop.** 20,000**)**
25 **Miles from** Columbus **(Pop.)**
Miles from (Pop.)

Class Composition

Asian: NA % **Black:** NA % **Hispanic:** NA % **White:** NA % **Other:** NA %
Total minority : NA % **Foreign countries:** NA% ( )
From public schools: 72 % **Students from in state:** 47 %

Housing (on campus)

Freshmen required to live on campus: Yes
Guaranteed for: 4 years
Available for all students: 100 %
Fraternity / Sorority housing: Yes / Yes
On-campus married student housing: NA
Women-only dorms available: NA

Campus Life

Students living on campus: NA % **Remain weekends:** NA % **Handicap access:** NA%
Car regulations: Freshmen discouraged
Number with cars: 27 %
Adequacy of on-campus parking: Poor
Number of fraternities: 10 **Chapter houses:** 10
Number of sororities: 5 **Chapter houses:** 5
Students belonging to fraternities: NA %
Students belonging to sororities: NA %

Libraries and Computers

Books: 435,000 **Periodicals:** 1,300 **Microform items:**
Microcomputers available: Yes **Microcomputers networked:** NA

Classes

Faculty / Student Ratio: 1/14 **Classes taught by teacher assistants:** 0 %
Most popular majors: Politics/Government **Classes begin:** Aug.
Baccalaureate degrees offered: AB, BFA, B MUS, BSN

Sports

Division: III **Except:** **Physical ed requirements:** None
Students participating in intercollegiate sports: 40 % **In intramural sports:** 63 %
Additional intercollegiate and/or intramural sports: (not found at all colleges)

Crew: No **Ice Hockey:** Yes/M **Lacrosse:** Yes **Wrestling:** No
Rugby: Yes/M **Sailing:** Yes **Skiing:** No
Squash: Yes **Ultimate Frisbee:** No **Water Polo:** No

Alumni

Number living: 30,000 **Annual giving:** $ 6 Mil. **Participation:** 39 %
Average annual gift: $ 700 **Average per student:** $3,100

3-2 Programs (2 degrees in 5 years)

Engineering with Ga Tech, Cal Tech, RPI and Case Western

Observation and Opinion of:

Undergraduates and graduates ____________________

College counselor ____________________

PENNSYLVANIA STATE UNIVERSITY (Public)

308 Old Main
University Park, PA 16802

SELECTIVE
(Composite rating of guide books)

Main tel.: 814-865-4700
Admissions tel.: 814-865-5471
Financial aid tel.: 814-865-6301
Scheduled Airline Service: Harrisburg
Miles to airport: 90

Founded: 1855
Nickname: Nittany Lions
Religious affiliation: None
(Coed since 1871)

Student Body

Undergraduates: 30,000 **Men:** 55 % **Women:** 45 %
Graduate students: 6,500 **Freshman class:** 4,490

Academics

SAT Averages: 1095 **Verbal:** 505 **Math:** 590 **(Taking SATs: 96 %)**
700-800: V 2 % **M** 11 % **500-600: V** 39 % **M** 35 %
600-700: V 13 % **M** 37 % **400-500: V** 38 % **M** 14 % **300-400: V** 7 % **M** 2 %
High school class rank: Top fifth 73 % **2nd fifth** 18 % **3rd fifth** 4 %

Admissions

Applied: 22,578 **Accepted:** 50 % **Matriculated:** 40 %
Deadline: Rolling **Accept common application:** NA
Interview recommended: No **Off-campus interview available:** Yes
Evaluative: No **Informational only:** Yes **LD program:** No
Night in dorm provided: Yes **Non-refundable application fee:** $35
Early decision program: No **Applied:** NA **Accepted:** NA % **Deadline:** NA
Freshmen accepted other than Fall term: 24 % **SAT/FAF Code #** 2660

Transfers

Applied: 2,300 **Accepted:** 33 % **Application deadline for Fall:** Nov. 30 **Spring:** NA
Minimum grades recommended: 2.0 **All new students who were transfers into all classes:** 9 %

Class Experience

Return 2nd year: 84 % **Graduate after 4 years:** 35 % **To graduate school within 5 years:** NA %

Cost

Tuition deposit: $75 **Total cost (Including school's estimate on fees and books):** $14,000
Tuition: $9,000 **(In state:** $ 4,400**)** **Room and board:** $3,500
Annual giving by parents: $255,000 **Average per student:** $NA

Financial Aid

Average total package per student: $5,350 **Number receiving aid:** 57 %
Average scholarships and grants: $2,350 **Average loans:** $3,000 **Work-study program:** NA
Undergraduates working on campus: 27 % **Average earnings:** $1,085
Non-need scholarships NA % **Athletic scholarships:** Yes **FAF deadline:** Feb. 15
Off-campus part-time employment: Good **CO-OP program:** Yes
ROTC: Yes **NROTC:** Yes **AFROTC:** Yes

Endowment

Total: $208 Million **Per student (including graduate students):** $5,500

Location

Acres: 5,000 **Setting:** Small city
Miles from town center: 0 **(Pop.** 35,000)
90 **Miles from** Harrisburg **(Pop.**)
35 **Miles from** Lewiston **(Pop.**)

Class Composition

Asian: 3 % **Black:** 3 % **Hispanic:** 1 % **White:** 91 % **Other:** 2 %
Total minority : 9 % **Foreign countries:** 1 % (300 students)
From public schools: % **Students from in state:** 83 %

Housing (on campus)

Freshmen required to live on campus: Yes
Available for all students: 40 %
On-campus married student housing: Yes
Guaranteed for: 1 year
Fraternity / Sorority housing: Yes / Yes
Women-only dorms available: Yes

Campus Life

Students living on campus: 40 % **Remain weekends:** 40 % **Handicap access:** 90 %
Car regulations: No freshmen
Number with cars: %
Adequacy of on-campus parking: Poor
Number of fraternities: 56 **Chapter houses:** 50
Number of sororities: 23 **Chapter houses:** 0
Students belonging to fraternities: 14 %
Students belonging to sororities: 14 %

Libraries and Computers

Books: 2.2 Million **Periodicals:** 25,500 **Microform items:** 2 Million
Microcomputers available: Yes **Microcomputers networked:** NA

Classes

Faculty / Student Ratio: 1/19 **Classes taught by teacher assistants:** 10 %
Most popular majors: Education, Electrical Engineering **Classes begin:** Mid-Aug.
Baccalaureate degrees offered: BA, B ARCH, B ARCH ENG, BFA, B MUS, B PHIL, BS

Sports

Division: I **Except:** **Physical ed requirements:** 3 credits
Students participating in intercollegiate sports: 18 % **In intramural sports:** 35 %
Additional intercollegiate and/or intramural sports: (not found at all colleges)

Crew: No **Ice Hockey:** Yes **Lacrosse:** Yes **Wrestling:** Yes/M
Rugby: Yes/M **Sailing:** Yes **Skiing:** Yes
Squash: Yes **Ultimate Frisbee:** No **Water Polo:** Yes

Alumni

Number living: 297,000 **Annual giving:** $ 12.2 Mil. **Participation:** 22 %
Average annual gift: $ 250 **Average per student:** $350

3-2 Programs (2 degrees in 5 years)

6-year combined medical program with Thomas Jefferson U

Observation and Opinion of:

Undergraduates and graduates ______________________________

____

College counselor ______________________________

____

UNIVERSITY OF PENNSYLVANIA (Private)

Philadelphia, PA 19104

MOST SELECTIVE
(Composite rating of guide books)

Main tel.: 215-898-5000
Admissions tel.: 215-898-7507
Financial aid tel.: 215-898-1988
Scheduled Airline Service: Philadelphia
Miles to airport: 10

Founded: 1740
Nickname: Quakers
Religious affiliation: None
(Coed since 1933)

Student Body

Undergraduates: 9,200 **Men:** 60 % **Women:** 40 %
Graduate students: 10,300 **Freshman class:** 2,230

Academics

SAT Averages: 1270 **Verbal:** 590 **Math:** 680 **(Taking SATs:** 100 %)
700-800: V 8 % M 45 % **500-600:** V 37 % M 12 %
600-700: V 45 % M 42 % **400-500:** V 10 % M 1 % **300-400:** V 1 % M 0 %
High school class rank: Top fifth 93 % 2nd fifth 6 % 3rd fifth 1 %

Admissions

Applied: 10,665 **Accepted:** 42 % **Matriculated:** 49 %
Deadline: Jan. 1 **Accept common application:** No
Interview recommended: Yes **Off-campus interview available:** Yes
Evaluative: No **Informational only:** Yes **LD program:** Yes
Night in dorm provided: Yes **Non-refundable application fee:** $60
Early decision program: Yes **Applied:** 1,229 **Accepted:** 52 % **Deadline:** Nov. 1
Freshmen accepted other than Fall term: 0 % **SAT/FAF Code #** 2926

Transfers

Applied: 1,228 **Accepted:** 34 % **Application deadline for Fall:** Apr. 1 **Spring:** Oct.
Minimum grades recommended: 3.2 **All new students who were transfers into all classes:** 14 %

Class Experience

Return 2nd year: 96 % **Graduate after 4 years:** 90 % **To graduate school within 1 years:** 23 %

Cost

Tuition deposit: $50 **Total cost (Including school's estimate on fees and books):** $23,000
Tuition: $14,350 **(In state:** $) **Room and board:** $6,200
Annual giving by parents: $2 Million **Average per student:** $100

Financial Aid

Average total package per student: $13,500 **Number receiving aid:** 40 %
Average scholarships and grants: $10,600 **Average loans:** $2,900 **Work-study program:** Yes
Undergraduates working on campus: 27 % **Average earnings:** $1,600
Non-need scholarships NA % **Athletic scholarships:** NA **FAF deadline:** Feb. 15
Off-campus part-time employment: Good **CO-OP program:** No
ROTC: Yes **NROTC:** Yes **AFROTC:** No

Endowment

Total: $826 Million **Per student (including graduate students):** $40,000

Location

Acres: 260 **Setting:** City **Miles from town center:** 4 **(Pop.** 1.7 Million**)**
Miles from **(Pop.)** **Miles from** **(Pop.)**

Class Composition

Asian: 14 % **Black:** 7 % **Hispanic:** 4 % **White:** 75 % **Other:** %
Total minority : 25 % **Foreign countries:** 6 % (540 students)
From public schools: 62 % **Students from in state:** 20 %

Housing (on campus)

Freshmen required to live on campus: No **Guaranteed for:** NA
Available for all students: 63 % **Fraternity / Sorority housing:** Yes / Yes
On-campus married student housing: Yes **Women-only dorms available:** No

Campus Life

Students living on campus: 63 % **Remain weekends:** 80 % **Handicap access:** 90 %
Car regulations: All may have
Number with cars: NA % **Adequacy of on-campus parking:** Poor
Number of fraternities: 32 **Chapter houses:** 22 **Number of sororities:** 12 **Chapter houses:** 1
Students belonging to fraternities: 35 % **Students belonging to sororities:** 35 %

Libraries and Computers

Books: 3.7 Million **Periodicals:** 31,900 **Microform items:** 1.4 Million
Microcomputers available: NA **Microcomputers networked:** NA

Classes

Faculty / Student Ratio: 1/7 **Classes taught by teacher assistants:** 0 %
Most popular majors: Banking/Finance, Economics **Classes begin:**
Baccalaureate degrees offered: BA, BAS, BS, BSE, BS ECON, BSN

Sports

Division: I **Except:** **Physical ed requirements:** None
Students participating in intercollegiate sports: 25 % **In intramural sports:** 80 %
Additional intercollegiate and/or intramural sports: (not found at all colleges)

Crew: Yes	**Ice Hockey:** Yes	**Lacrosse:** Yes	**Wrestling:** Yes/M
Rugby: Yes/M	**Sailing:** Yes	**Skiing:** Yes	
Squash: Yes	**Ultimate Frisbee:** Yes	**Water Polo:** Yes/M	

Alumni

Number living: 207,000 **Annual giving:** $ 52 Mil. **Participation:** 45 %
Average annual gift: $ 700 **Average per student:** $2,700

3-2 Programs (2 degrees in 5 years)

3-4 Program in Veterinary Medicine

Observation and Opinion of:

Undergraduates and graduates ____________________

College counselor ____________________

PEPPERDINE UNIVERSITY (Private)

Malibu, CA 90263

SELECTIVE
(Composite rating of guide books)

Main tel.: 213-456-4000
Admissions tel.: 213-456-4392
Financial aid tel.: 213-456-4301
Scheduled Airline Service: Los Angeles
Miles to airport: 30

Founded: 1937
Nickname: Waves
Religious affiliation: Church of Christ
(Coed since 1937)

Student Body

Undergraduates: 2,600 **Men:** 50 % **Women:** 50 %
Graduate students: 85 **Freshman class:** 680

Academics

SAT Averages: 1085 **Verbal:** NA **Math:** NA **(Taking SATs:** 77 %)
700-800: V 5 % **M** 1 % **500-600: V** 47 % **M** 38 %
600-700: V 24 % **M** 8 % **400-500: V** 20 % **M** 44 % **300-400: V** 4 % **M** 9 %
High school class rank: Top fifth 90 % **2nd fifth** 9 % **3rd fifth** NA %

Admissions

Applied: 2,640 **Accepted:** 74 % **Matriculated:** 35 %
Deadline: Feb. 15 **Accept common application:** NA
Interview recommended: Yes **Off-campus interview available:** Yes
Evaluative: No **Informational only:** Yes **LD program:** NA
Night in dorm provided: No **Non-refundable application fee:** $35
Early decision program: Yes **Applied:** 360 **Accepted:** 63 % **Deadline:** Nov. 15
Freshmen accepted other than Fall term: NA % **SAT/FAF Code #** 4630

Transfers

Applied: 405 **Accepted:** 60 % **Application deadline for Fall:** Mar. 1 **Spring:** Oct. 15
Minimum grades recommended: 2.7 **All new students who were transfers into all classes:** 19 %

Class Experience

Return 2nd year: 81 % **Graduate after 4 years:** 80 % **To graduate school within 5 years:** NA %

Cost

Tuition deposit: $150 **Total cost (Including school's estimate on fees and books):** $23,000
Tuition: $16,200 **(In state:** $) **Room and board:** $6,250
Annual giving by parents: $276,000 **Average per student:** $NA

Financial Aid

Average total package per student: $NA **Number receiving aid:** 65 %
Average scholarships and grants: $2,500 **Average loans:** $1,800 **Work-study program:** Yes
Undergraduates working on campus: 65 % **Average earnings:** $1,200
Non-need scholarships NA % **Athletic scholarships:** NA **FAF deadline:** Mar. 1
Off-campus part-time employment: Excellent **CO-OP program:** No
ROTC: at UCLA **NROTC:** No **AFROTC:** at USC

Endowment

Total: $80 Million **Per student (including graduate students):** $30,000

Location

Acres: 830 **Setting:** Rural **Miles from town center:** 0 **(Pop.** 10,000**)**
12 **Miles from** Santa Monica **(Pop.** 53,000 **)** 30 **Miles from** Los Angeles **(Pop.** 7.5 Million**)**

Class Composition

Asian: 6 % **Black:** 2 % **Hispanic:** 5 % **White:** 73 % **Other:** 14 %
Total minority : 17 % **Foreign countries:** 10 % (260 students)
From public schools: 60 % **Students from in state:** 52 %

Housing (on campus)

Freshmen required to live on campus: Yes **Guaranteed for:** 2 years
Available for all students: 62 % **Fraternity / Sorority housing:** No / No
On-campus married student housing: No **Women-only dorms available:** Yes

Campus Life

Students living on campus: 62 % **Remain weekends:** 35 % **Handicap access:** NA %
Car regulations: All may have
Number with cars: 45 % **Adequacy of on-campus parking:** Fair
Number of fraternities: 7 **Chapter houses:** 0 **Number of sororities:** 4 **Chapter houses:** 0
Students belonging to fraternities: 15 % **Students belonging to sororities:** 10 %

Libraries and Computers

Books: 421,000 **Periodicals:** 5,000 **Microform items:** 8,950
Microcomputers available: Yes **Microcomputers networked:** NA

Classes

Faculty / Student Ratio: 1/13 **Classes taught by teacher assistants:** 0 %
Most popular majors: Communications, Advertising **Classes begin:** Late Aug.
Baccalaureate degrees offered: BA, BS

Sports

Division: I **Except:** **Physical ed requirements:** 4 terms
Students participating in intercollegiate sports: NA % **In intramural sports:** 75 %
Additional intercollegiate and/or intramural sports: (not found at all colleges)
Crew: No **Ice Hockey:** Yes **Lacrosse:** Yes/M **Wrestling:** No
Rugby: Yes **Sailing:** Yes **Skiing:** Yes
Squash: No **Ultimate Frisbee:** No **Water Polo:** Yes

Alumni

Number living: 38,000 **Annual giving:** $ 500,000 **Participation:** 6 %
Average annual gift: $ 210 **Average per student:** $200

3-2 Programs (2 degrees in 5 years)

Observation and Opinion of:

Undergraduates and graduates ______________________________

____

College counselor ______________________________

____

POMONA COLLEGE (Private)

(Member of Six-Institution Claremont Colleges)
Claremont, CA 91711-6312

MOST SELECTIVE
(Composite rating of guide books)

Main tel.: 714-621-8000
Admissions tel.: 714-621-8134
Financial aid tel.: 714-621-8205
Scheduled Airline Service: Los Angeles
Miles to airport: 35

Founded: 1887
Nickname: NA
Religious affiliation: None
(Coed since 1887)

Student Body

Undergraduates: 1,400 **Men:** 53 % **Women:** 47 %
Graduate students: 0 **Freshman class:** 370

Academics

SAT Averages: 1320 **Verbal:** 630 **Math:** 690 **(Taking SATs: 94 %)**
700-800: V 15 % **M** 43 % **500-600: V** 23 % **M** 11 %
600-700: V 59 % **M** 44 % **400-500: V** 3 % **M** 2 % **300-400: V** NA % **M** NA %
High school class rank: Top fifth 93 % **2nd fifth** 7 % **3rd fifth** 0%

Admissions

Applied: 2,870 **Accepted:** 37 % **Matriculated:** 35 %
Deadline: Feb. 1 **Accept common application:** Yes
Interview recommended: Yes **Off-campus interview available:** Yes
Evaluative: Yes **Informational only:** No **LD program:** NA
Night in dorm provided: NA **Non-refundable application fee:** $45
Early decision program: Yes **Applied:** 138 **Accepted:** 49 % **Deadline:** Nov. 15
Freshmen accepted other than Fall term: NA % **SAT/FAF Code #** 4607

Transfers

Applied: 250 **Accepted:** 16 % **Application deadline for Fall:** Apr. 15 **Spring:** NA
Minimum grades recommended: C- **All new students who were transfers into all classes:** 5 %

Class Experience

Return 2nd year: 99 % **Graduate after 4 years:** 85 % **To graduate school within 4 years:** 75 %

Cost

Tuition deposit: $200 **Total cost (Including school's estimate on fees and books):** $23,000
Tuition: $15,700 **(In state:** $ **)** **Room and board:** $6,625
Annual giving by parents: $248,000 **Average per student:** $175

Financial Aid

Average total package per student: $12,900 **Number receiving aid:** 55 %
Average scholarships and grants: $10,400 **Average loans:** $2,500 **Work-study program:** Yes
Undergraduates working on campus: 65 % **Average earnings:** $1,600
Non-need scholarships NA % **Athletic scholarships:** No **FAF deadline:** NA
Off-campus part-time employment: Good **CO-OP program:** No
ROTC: at McKenna College **NROTC:** No **AFROTC:** at Harvey Mudd

Endowment

Total: $316 Million **Per student (including graduate students):** $220,000

Location

Acres: 130 Setting: Surburban
Miles from town center: 0 (Pop. 37,000)
35 Miles from Los Angeles (Pop. 7.5 Mil.)
Miles from (Pop.)

Class Composition

Asian: 15 % Black: 4 % Hispanic: 9 % White: 65 % Other: 7 %
Total minority : 35 % Foreign countries: 3 % (40 students)
From public schools: NA % Students from in state: 40 %

Housing (on campus)

Freshmen required to live on campus: Yes
Available for all students: 97 %
On-campus married student housing: No
Guaranteed for: 4 years
Fraternity / Sorority housing: Yes / No
Women-only dorms available: Yes

Campus Life

Students living on campus: 97 % Remain weekends: NA % Handicap access: 90 %
Car regulations: NA
Number with cars: 30 %
Number of fraternities: 7 Chapter houses: 0
Students belonging to fraternities: 10 %
Adequacy of on-campus parking: NA
Number of sororities: 0 Chapter houses: 0
Students belonging to sororities: 5 %

Libraries and Computers

Books: 1.8 Million Periodicals: 7,000 Microform items: 1.1 Million
Microcomputers available: Yes Microcomputers networked: NA

Classes

Faculty / Student Ratio: 1/9 Classes taught by teacher assistants: 0 %
Most popular majors: History, Economics Classes begin: Early Sept.
Baccalaureate degrees offered: BA

Sports

Division: III Except: Physical ed requirements: 1 semester
Students participating in intercollegiate sports: 45 % In intramural sports: 67 %
Additional intercollegiate and/or intramural sports: (not found at all colleges)

Crew: No Ice Hockey: No Lacrosse: Yes Wrestling: Yes/M
Rugby: Yes Sailing: Yes Skiing: Yes
Squash: Yes Ultimate Frisbee: Yes Water Polo: Yes

Alumni

Number living: 17,100 Annual giving: $ 11.4 Mil. Participation: 42 %
Average annual gift: $ 1,450 Average per student: $8,200

3-2 Programs (2 degrees in 5 years)

Engineering with Cal Tech and Washington U

Observation and Opinion of:

Undergraduates and graduates ______________________________

____

College counselor ______________________________

____

PRINCETON UNIVERSITY (Private)

Princeton, NJ 08544

MOST SELECTIVE
(Composite rating of guide books)

Main tel.: 609-258-3000
Admissions tel.: 609-258-3060
Financial aid tel.: 609-258-3330
Scheduled Airline Service: Newark
Miles to airport: 45

Founded: 1746
Nickname: Tigers
Religious affiliation: None
(Coed since 1969)

Student Body

Undergraduates: 4,500 **Men:** 60 % **Women:** 40 %
Graduate students: 1,800 **Freshman class:** 1,175

Academics

SAT Averages: 1350 **Verbal:** 650 **Math:** 700 **(Taking SATs:** NA %)
700-800: V 28 % **M** 59 % **500-600: V** 21 % **M** 8 %
600-700: V 46 % **M** 33 % **400-500: V** 5 % **M** 0 % **300-400: V** NA % **M** NA %
High school class rank: Top fifth 97 % **2nd fifth** 3 % **3rd fifth** NA %

Admissions

Applied: 12,650 **Accepted:** 17 % **Matriculated:** 55 %
Deadline: Jan. 2 **Accept common application:** No
Interview recommended: NA **Off-campus interview available:** Yes
Evaluative: Yes **Informational only:** No **LD program:** Yes
Night in dorm provided: Yes **Non-refundable application fee:** $45
Early decision program: No **Applied:** NA **Accepted:** NA % **Deadline:** NA
Freshmen accepted other than Fall term: 0 % **SAT/FAF Code #** 2672

Transfers

Applied: 421 **Accepted:** 1 % **Application deadline for Fall:** Apr. 1 **Spring:** NA
Minimum grades recommended: 3.5 **All new students who were transfers into all classes:** 1 %

Class Experience

Return 2nd year: 97 % **Graduate after 4 years:** 95 % **To graduate school within 5 years:** NA %

Cost

Tuition deposit: $0 **Total cost (Including school's estimate on fees and books):** $24,000
Tuition: $17,750 **(In state:** $) **Room and board:** $5,500
Annual giving by parents: $4.5 Mil. **Average per student:** $1,000

Financial Aid

Average total package per student: $13,100 **Number receiving aid:** 39 %
Average scholarships and grants: $10,480 **Average loans:** $2,665 **Work-study program:** Yes
Undergraduates working on campus: 60 % **Average earnings:** $860
Non-need scholarships 0 % **Athletic scholarships:** NA **FAF deadline:** Feb. 1
Off-campus part-time employment: Excellent **CO-OP program:** No
ROTC: Yes **NROTC:** No **AFROTC:** at Rutgers

Endowment

Total: $2.5 Million **Per student (including graduate students):** $400,000

Location

Acres: 1,000 **Setting:** Urban
Miles from town center: 0 **(Pop.** 12,000**)**
50 **Miles from** NYC **(Pop.** 14 Mil. **)**
45 **Miles from** Phila. **(Pop.** 1.7 Million **)**

Class Composition

Asian: NA **%** **Black:** NA **%** **Hispanic:** NA **%** **White:** NA **%** **Other:** NA **%**
Total minority : 34 **%** **Foreign countries:** 5 **%** (240 students)
From public schools: 55 **%** **Students from in state:** 14 **%**

Housing (on campus)

Freshmen required to live on campus: Yes
Available for all students: 98 **%**
On-campus married student housing: Yes
Guaranteed for: 2 years
Fraternity / Sorority housing: No / No
Women-only dorms available: Yes

Campus Life

Students living on campus: 98 **%** **Remain weekends:** NA **%** **Handicap access:** NA**%**
Car regulations: All may have
Number with cars: 10 **%** **Adequacy of on-campus parking:** Good
Number of fraternities: 0 **Chapter houses:** 0
Students belonging to fraternities: 0 **%**
Number of sororities: 0 **Chapter houses:** 0
Students belonging to sororities: 0 **%**

Libraries and Computers

Books: 4.3 Million **Periodicals:** 35,100 **Microform items:** 2.4 Million
Microcomputers available: Yes **Microcomputers networked:** Yes

Classes

Faculty / Student Ratio: 1/6 **Classes taught by teacher assistants:** 0 **%**
Most popular majors: History/Politics **Classes begin:** Mid- Sept.
Baccalaureate degrees offered: AB, BSE

Sports

Division: I **Except:** **Physical ed requirements:** None
Students participating in intercollegiate sports: 40 **%** **In intramural sports:** 40 **%**
Additional intercollegiate and/or intramural sports: (not found at all colleges)

Crew: Yes **Ice Hockey:** Yes **Lacrosse:** Yes **Wrestling:** Yes/M
Rugby: Yes **Sailing:** Yes **Skiing:** Yes
Squash: Yes **Ultimate Frisbee:** Yes **Water Polo:** Yes/M

Alumni

Number living: 61,000 **Annual giving:** $ 31.7 **Participation:** 47 **%**
Average annual gift: $ 1,200 **Average per student:** $5,000

3-2 Programs (2 degrees in 5 years)

None

Observation and Opinion of:

Undergraduates and graduates ______________________________

____

College counselor ______________________________

____

PROVIDENCE COLLEGE (Private)

River Avenue and Eaton Street
Providence, RI 02918

SELECTIVE
(Composite rating of guide books)

Main tel.: 401-865-1000
Admissions tel.: 401-865-2535
Financial aid tel.: 401-865-2286
Scheduled Airline Service: Providence
Miles to airport: 5

Founded: 1917
Nickname: Friars
Religious affiliation: Catholic
(Coed since 1971)

Student Body

Undergraduates: 3,800 **Men:** 48 % **Women:** 52 %
Graduate students: 650 **Freshman class:** 925

Academics

SAT Averages: 1085 **Verbal:** 510 **Math:** 575 **(Taking SATs:** 95 %**)**
700-800: V 1 % **M** 3 % **500-600: V** 41 % **M** 48 %
600-700: V 9 % **M** 30 % **400-500: V** 45 % **M** 17 % **300-400: V** 4 % **M** 2 %
High school class rank: Top fifth 70 % **2nd fifth** 12 % **3rd fifth** 6 %

Admissions

Applied: 4,700 **Accepted:** 62 % **Matriculated:** 32 %
Deadline: NA **Accept common application:** NA
Interview recommended: NA **Off-campus interview available:** No
Evaluative: No **Informational only:** NA **LD program:** Yes
Night in dorm provided: NA **Non-refundable application fee:** $30
Early decision program: Yes **Applied:** 415 **Accepted:** 70 % **Deadline:** Dec. 15
Freshmen accepted other than Fall term: 0 % **SAT/FAF Code #** 3693

Transfers

Applied: 321 **Accepted:** 50 % **Application deadline for Fall:** Mar. 1 **Spring:** Dec. 15
Minimum grades recommended: 3.0 **All new students who were transfers into all classes:** 8 %

Class Experience

Return 2nd year: 96 % **Graduate after 4 years:** 87 % **To graduate school within 5 years:** NA %

Cost

Tuition deposit: $300 **Total cost (Including school's estimate on fees and books):** $18,500
Tuition: $12,600 **(In state:** $ **)** **Room and board:** $5,600
Annual giving by parents: $407,000 **Average per student:** $130

Financial Aid

Average total package per student: $10,500 **Number receiving aid:** 55 %
Average scholarships and grants: $8,000 **Average loans:** $2,500 **Work-study program:** Yes
Undergraduates working on campus: 35 % **Average earnings:** $1,600
Non-need scholarships 1 % **Athletic scholarships:** Yes **FAF deadline:** Feb. 15
Off-campus part-time employment: Excellent **CO-OP program:** No
ROTC: Yes **NROTC:** No **AFROTC:** No

Endowment

Total: $18 Million **Per student (including graduate students):** $40,000

Location

Acres: 105 **Setting:** Surburban **Miles from town center:** 2 **(Pop.** 165,000)
35 **Miles from** Newport **(Pop.**) 50 **Miles from** Boston **(Pop.** 600,000)

Class Composition

Asian: 1 % **Black:** 2 % **Hispanic:** 2 % **White:** 94 % **Other:** 1 %
Total minority : 6 % **Foreign countries:** 1 % (38 students)
From public schools: 50 % **Students from in state:** 15 %

Housing (on campus)

Freshmen required to live on campus: No **Guaranteed for:** 1 year
Available for all students: 65 % **Fraternity / Sorority housing:** No / No
On-campus married student housing: Yes **Women-only dorms available:** Yes

Campus Life

Students living on campus: 65 % **Remain weekends:** 90 % **Handicap access:** 90 %
Car regulations: No freshmen
Number with cars: NA % **Adequacy of on-campus parking:** Fair
Number of fraternities: 0 **Chapter houses:** 0 **Number of sororities:** 0 **Chapter houses:** 0
Students belonging to fraternities: 0 % **Students belonging to sororities:** 0 %

Libraries and Computers

Books: 295,000 **Periodicals:** 1,905 **Microform items:** 1,137
Microcomputers available: Yes **Microcomputers networked:** NA

Classes

Faculty / Student Ratio: 1/16 **Classes taught by teacher assistants:** 0 %
Most popular majors: Business **Classes begin:** Early Sept.
Baccalaureate degrees offered: BA, BS

Sports

Division: I **Except:** **Physical ed requirements:** None
Students participating in intercollegiate sports: 12 % **In intramural sports:** 65 %
Additional intercollegiate and/or intramural sports: (not found at all colleges)

Crew: Yes **Ice Hockey:** Yes **Lacrosse:** Yes **Wrestling:** Yes
Rugby: Yes **Sailing:** Yes **Skiing:** Yes
Squash: Yes **Ultimate Frisbee:** Yes **Water Polo:** Yes

Alumni

Number living: 27,700 **Annual giving:** $ 2.8 Mil. **Participation:** 39 %
Average annual gift: $ 280 **Average per student:** $700

3-2 Programs (2 degrees in 5 years)

Engineering with Columbia and Washington U, 5-year MBA Program

Observation and Opinion of:

Undergraduates and graduates ______________________________

____

College counselor ______________________________

____

REED COLLEGE (Private)

3203 S.E. Woodstock Boulevard
Portland, OR

HIGHLY SELECTIVE
(Composite rating of guide books)

Main tel.: 503-771-1112
Admissions tel.: 800-547-4750
Financial aid tel.: 503-771-1112, Ext. 223
Scheduled Airline Service: Portland
Miles to airport: 10

Founded: 1909
Nickname: Griffins
Religious affiliation: None
(Coed since 1909)

Student Body

Undergraduates: 1,250 **Men:** 61 % **Women:** 39 %
Graduate students: 20 **Freshman class:** 288

Academics

SAT Averages: 1250 **Verbal:** 615 **Math:** 635 **(Taking SATs:** NA %**)**
700-800: V 13 % **M** 23 % **500-600: V** 32 % **M** 20 %
600-700: V 48 % **M** 51 % **400-500: V** 7 % **M** 6 % **300-400: V** NA % **M** NA %
High school class rank: Top fifth 93 % **2nd fifth** NA % **3rd fifth** NA %

Admissions

Applied: 1,970 **Accepted:** 62 % **Matriculated:** 24 %
Deadline: Feb. 1 **Accept common application:** Yes
Interview recommended: Yes **Off-campus interview available:** Yes
Evaluative: Yes **Informational only:** No **LD program:** NA
Night in dorm provided: Yes **Non-refundable application fee:** $35
Early decision program: Yes **Applied:** 189 **Accepted:** 40 % **Deadline:** Dec. 1
Freshmen accepted other than Fall term: Yes **SAT/FAF Code #** 4654

Transfers

Applied: 247 **Accepted:** 52 % **Application deadline for Fall:** Apr. 1 **Spring:** Dec. 1
Minimum grades recommended: C **All new students who were transfers into all classes:** NA %

Class Experience

Return 2nd year: 90 % **Graduate after 4 years:** 57 % **To graduate school within 5 years:** NA %

Cost

Tuition deposit: $200 **Total cost (Including school's estimate on fees and books):** $24,000
Tuition: $18,060 **(In state:** $ **)** **Room and board:** $5,000
Annual giving by parents: $688,000 **Average per student:** $500

Financial Aid

Average total package per student: $8,400 **Number receiving aid:** 48 %
Average scholarships and grants: $6,100 **Average loans:** $2,300 **Work-study program:** Yes
Undergraduates working on campus: 55 % **Average earnings:** $1,000
Non-need scholarships 0 % **Athletic scholarships:** No **FAF deadline:** Feb. 15
Off-campus part-time employment: Good **CO-OP program:** No
ROTC: Yes **NROTC:** No **AFROTC:** No

Endowment

Total: $98 Million **Per student (including graduate students):** $70,000

Location

Acres: 100 **Setting:** Surburban **Miles from town center:** 5 **(Pop.** 400,000)
Miles from **(Pop.**) **Miles from** **(Pop.**)

Class Composition

Asian: 5 % **Black:** 1 % **Hispanic:** 2 % **White:** 84 % **Other:** 8 %
Total minority : 16 % **Foreign countries:** 2 % (25 students)
From public schools: 71 % **Students from in state:** 20 %

Housing (on campus)

Freshmen required to live on campus: No **Guaranteed for:** 1 year
Available for all students: 50 % **Fraternity / Sorority housing:** No / No
On-campus married student housing: Yes **Women-only dorms available:** Yes

Campus Life

Students living on campus: 50 % **Remain weekends:** NA % **Handicap access:** NA %
Car regulations: All may have
Number with cars: 40 % **Adequacy of on-campus parking:** Good
Number of fraternities: 0 **Chapter houses:** 0 **Number of sororities:** 0 **Chapter houses:** 0
Students belonging to fraternities: 0 % **Students belonging to sororities:** 0 %

Libraries and Computers

Books: 330,000 **Periodicals:** 1,500 **Microform items:** 37,000
Microcomputers available: Yes **Microcomputers networked:** Yes

Classes

Faculty / Student Ratio: 1/12 **Classes taught by teacher assistants:** 0 %
Most popular majors: English, Psychology **Classes begin:** Early Sept.
Baccalaureate degrees offered: BA

Sports

Division: I **Except:** **Physical ed requirements:** 3 semesters
Students participating in intercollegiate sports: 15 % **In intramural sports:** 25 %
Additional intercollegiate and/or intramural sports: (not found at all colleges)
Crew: Yes **Ice Hockey:** No **Lacrosse:** No **Wrestling:** Yes/M
Rugby: Yes **Sailing:** Yes **Skiing:** Yes
Squash: Yes **Ultimate Frisbee:** No **Water Polo:** Yes

Alumni

Number living: 9,000 **Annual giving:** $ 1.5 Mil. **Participation:** 41 %
Average annual gift: $ NA **Average per student:** $1,200

3-2 Programs (2 degrees in 5 years)

Combined degrees in Computer Technology, Engineering and Environmental Studies

Observation and Opinion of:

Undergraduates and graduates ______________________________

____

College counselor ______________________________

____

RENSSELAER POLYTECHNIC INSTITUTE (Private)

Troy, NY 12180

HIGHLY SELECTIVE
(Composite rating of guide books)

Main tel.: 518-276-6000
Admissions tel.: 518-276-6216
Financial aid tel.: 518-276-6813
Scheduled Airline Service: Albany
Miles to airport: 7

Founded: 1824
Nickname: Engineers
Religious affiliation: None
(Coed since 1824)

Student Body

Undergraduates: 4,400 **Men:** 80 % **Women:** 20 %
Graduate students: 2,050 **Freshman class:** 990

Academics

SAT Averages: 1230 **Verbal:** 560 **Math:** 670 **(Taking SATs:** NA %**)**
700-800: V 1 % **M** 30 % **500-600: V** 47 % **M** 14 %
600-700: V 22 % **M** 53 % **400-500: V** 24 % **M** 2 % **300-400: V** 5 % **M** 1 %
High school class rank: Top fifth 83 % **2nd fifth** 13 % **3rd fifth** 4 %

Admissions

Applied: 4,620 **Accepted:** 77 % **Matriculated:** 28 %
Deadline: Jan. 15 **Accept common application:** Yes
Interview recommended: Yes **Off-campus interview available:** Yes
Evaluative: No **Informational only:** Yes **LD program:** No
Night in dorm provided: Yes **Non-refundable application fee:** $35
Early decision program: Yes **Applied:** 225 **Accepted:** 82 % **Deadline:** Jan. 1
Freshmen accepted other than Fall term: 1 % **SAT/FAF Code #** 2757

Transfers

Applied: 496 **Accepted:** 80 % **Application deadline for Fall:** Aug. 1 **Spring:** Nov. 1
Minimum grades recommended: 3.0 **All new students who were transfers into all classes:** 19 %

Class Experience

Return 2nd year: 85 % **Graduate after 4 years:** 72 % **To graduate school within 5 years:** NA %

Cost

Tuition deposit: $250 **Total cost (Including school's estimate on fees and books):** $22,500
Tuition: $15,900 **(In state:** $ **)** **Room and board:** $5,150
Annual giving by parents: $93,000 **Average per student:** $21

Financial Aid

Average total package per student: $12,000 **Number receiving aid:** 68 %
Average scholarships and grants: $9,200 **Average loans:** $2,800 **Work-study program:** Yes
Undergraduates working on campus: NA % **Average earnings:** $1,300
Non-need scholarships 3 % **Athletic scholarships:** NA **FAF deadline:** Feb. 15
Off-campus part-time employment: Fair **CO-OP program:** No
ROTC: Yes **NROTC:** No **AFROTC:** No

Endowment

Total: $240 Million **Per student (including graduate students):** $35,000

Location

Acres: 260 **Setting:** City **Miles from town center:** 0 **(Pop.** 67,000**)**
15 **Miles from** Albany **(Pop.** 53,000 **)** **Miles from** **(Pop.** **)**

Class Composition

Asian: 12 % **Black:** 3 % **Hispanic:** 4 % **White:** 78 % **Other:** 3 %
Total minority : 22 % **Foreign countries:** 3 % (40 students)
From public schools: % **Students from in state:** 40 %

Housing (on campus)

Freshmen required to live on campus: Yes **Guaranteed for:** 0 years
Available for all students: 70 % **Fraternity / Sorority housing:** Yes / Yes
On-campus married student housing: Yes **Women-only dorms available:** No

Campus Life

Students living on campus: 70 % **Remain weekends:** 70 % **Handicap access:** 90 %
Car regulations: All may have
Number with cars: 35 % **Adequacy of on-campus parking:** Fair
Number of fraternities: 28 **Chapter houses:** 0 **Number of sororities:** 5 **Chapter houses:** 3
Students belonging to fraternities: 35 % **Students belonging to sororities:** 35 %

Libraries and Computers

Books: 487,000 **Periodicals:** 4,835 **Microform items:** 873,000
Microcomputers available: Yes **Microcomputers networked:** NA

Classes

Faculty / Student Ratio: 1/11 **Classes taught by teacher assistants:** 20 %
Most popular majors: Mechanical and Electrical Engineering **Classes begin:** Late Aug.
Baccalaureate degrees offered: B ARCH, BS

Sports

Division: III **Except:** **Physical ed requirements:** 1 1/2 years
Students participating in intercollegiate sports: 15 % **In intramural sports:** 70 %
Additional intercollegiate and/or intramural sports: (not found at all colleges)

Crew: Yes **Ice Hockey:** Yes **Lacrosse:** Yes **Wrestling:** No
Rugby: Yes **Sailing:** Yes **Skiing:** No
Squash: Yes **Ultimate Frisbee:** Yes **Water Polo:** Yes

Alumni

Number living: 49,000 **Annual giving:** $ 7.6 Mil. **Participation:** 25 %
Average annual gift: $ 600 **Average per student:** $1,200

3-2 Programs (2 degrees in 5 years)

Engineering with over 20 colleges

Observation and Opinion of:

Undergraduates and graduates ______________________________

____

College counselor ______________________________

____

RHODES COLLEGE (Private)

2000 North Parkway
Memphis, TN 38112

HIGHLY SELECTIVE
(Composite rating of guide books)

Main tel.: 901-726-3000
Admissions tel.: 800-238-6788
Financial aid tel.: 901-726-3810
Scheduled Airline Service: Memphis
Miles to airport: 10

Founded: 1848
Nickname: Lynx
Religious affiliation: Presbyterian
(Coed since 1916)

Student Body

Undergraduates: 1,350 **Men:** 45 % **Women:** 55 %
Graduate students: 0 **Freshman class:** 388

Academics

SAT Averages: 1200 **Verbal:** 580 **Math:** 620 **(Taking SATs:** NA %)
700-800: V 7 % **M** 13 % **500-600: V** 42 % **M** 33 %
600-700: V 35 % **M** 49 % **400-500: V** 16 % **M** 5 % **300-400: V** NA % **M** NA %
High school class rank: Top fifth 75 % **2nd fifth** 16 % **3rd fifth** 9 %

Admissions

Applied: 1,946 **Accepted:** 72 % **Matriculated:** 28 %
Deadline: Feb. 1 **Accept common application:** Yes
Interview recommended: Yes **Off-campus interview available:** Yes
Evaluative: Yes **Informational only:** No **LD program:** No
Night in dorm provided: Yes **Non-refundable application fee:** $30
Early decision program: Yes **Applied:** 74 **Accepted:** 80 % **Deadline:** Nov. 15
Freshmen accepted other than Fall term: 1 % **SAT/FAF Code #** 1730

Transfers

Applied: 123 **Accepted:** 33 % **Application deadline for Fall:** Feb. 1 **Spring:** Dec. 1
Minimum grades recommended: C **All new students who were transfers into all classes:** 9 %

Class Experience

Return 2nd year: 87% **Graduate after 4 years:** 70 % **To graduate school within 5 years:** 45 %

Cost

Tuition deposit: $100 **Total cost (Including school's estimate on fees and books):** $19,500
Tuition: $13,800 **(In state:** $) **Room and board:** $4,700
Annual giving by parents: $78,000 **Average per student:** $NA

Financial Aid

Average total package per student: $10,000 **Number receiving aid:** 47 %
Average scholarships and grants: $17,800 **Average loans:** $2,120 **Work-study program:** Yes
Undergraduates working on campus: 25 % **Average earnings:** $1,000
Non-need scholarships 32 % **Athletic scholarships:** NA **FAF deadline:** Mar. 1
Off-campus part-time employment: Good **CO-OP program:** No
ROTC: at Memphis State **NROTC:** No **AFROTC:** at Memphis St

Endowment

Total: $84 Million **Per student (including graduate students):** $70,000

Location

Acres: 100 **Setting:** Surburban **Miles from town center:** 4 **(Pop.** 700,000 **)**
Miles from **(Pop.** **)** **Miles from** **(Pop.** **)**

Class Composition

Asian: 3 % **Black:** 4 % **Hispanic:** 1 % **White:** 92 % **Other:** 10 %
Total minority : 8 % **Foreign countries:** 2 % (28 students)
From public schools: 60 % **Students from in state:** 34 %

Housing (on campus)

Freshmen required to live on campus: No **Guaranteed for:** NA
Available for all students: 82 % **Fraternity / Sorority housing:** Yes / Yes
On-campus married student housing: No **Women-only dorms available:** Yes

Campus Life

Students living on campus: 82 % **Remain weekends:** 80 % **Handicap access:** 90 %
Car regulations: NA
Number with cars: 79 % **Adequacy of on-campus parking:** NA
Number of fraternities: 6 **Chapter houses:** 6 **Number of sororities:** 6 **Chapter houses:** 6
Students belonging to fraternities: 56 % **Students belonging to sororities:** 62 %

Libraries and Computers

Books: 215,000 **Periodicals:** 1,135 **Microform items:** 15,250
Microcomputers available: Yes **Microcomputers networked:** Yes

Classes

Faculty / Student Ratio: 1/12 **Classes taught by teacher assistants:** 0 %
Most popular majors: Business Administration, Psychology **Classes begin:** Late Aug.
Baccalaureate degrees offered: BA, BS

Sports

Division: III **Except:** **Physical ed requirements:** 1 1/2 semesters
Students participating in intercollegiate sports: 23 % **In intramural sports:** 45 %
Additional intercollegiate and/or intramural sports: (not found at all colleges)
Crew: No **Ice Hockey:** No **Lacrosse:** Yes **Wrestling:** No
Rugby: Yes **Sailing:** No **Skiing:** No
Squash: No **Ultimate Frisbee:** No **Water Polo:** Yes

Alumni

Number living: 10,700 **Annual giving:** $ 2.5 Mil. **Participation:** 44 %
Average annual gift: $ 550 **Average per student:** $1,900

3-2 Programs (2 degrees in 5 years)

Observation and Opinion of:

Undergraduates and graduates ______________________________

____

College counselor ______________________________

____

RICE UNIVERSITY (Private)

Box 1892
Houston, TX 77251

MOST SELECTIVE
(Composite rating of guide books)

Main tel.: 713-527-8101
Admissions tel.: 713-527-4036
Financial aid tel.: 713-527-4958
Scheduled Airline Service: Houston
Miles to airport: 8

Founded: 1912
Nickname: Owls
Religious affiliation: None
(Coed since 1912)

Student Body

Undergraduates: 2,700 **Men:** 63 % **Women:** 37 %
Graduate students: 1,300 **Freshman class:** 622

Academics

SAT Averages: 1345 **Verbal:** 645 **Math:** 700 **(Taking SATs: 100 %)**
700-800: V 25 % **M** 60 % **500-600: V** 18 % **M** 9 %
600-700: V 51 % **M** 28 % **400-500: V** 6 % **M** 3 % **300-400: V** NA % **M** NA %
High school class rank: Top fifth 74 % **2nd fifth** NA % **3rd fifth** NA %

Admissions

Applied: 5,289 **Accepted:** 25 % **Matriculated:** 47 %
Deadline: Jan. 2 **Accept common application:** Yes
Interview recommended: Yes **Off-campus interview available:** Yes
Evaluative: Yes **Informational only:** No **LD program:** No
Night in dorm provided: Yes **Non-refundable application fee:** $ NA
Early decision program: Yes **Applied:** 193 **Accepted:** 32 % **Deadline:** Nov. 1
Freshmen accepted other than Fall term: 0 % **SAT/FAF Code #** 6609

Transfers

Applied: 500 **Accepted:** 14 % **Application deadline for Fall:** Apr. 1 **Spring:** Nov. 1
Minimum grades recommended: 3.0 **All new students who were transfers into all classes:** 7 %

Class Experience

Return 2nd year: 95 % **Graduate after 4 years:** 88 % **To graduate school within 1 year:** 47 %

Cost

Tuition deposit: $100 **Total cost (Including school's estimate on fees and books):** $14,500
Tuition: $8,500 **(In state: $)** **Room and board:** $5,200
Annual giving by parents: $352,000 **Average per student:** $85

Financial Aid

Average total package per student: $5,350 **Number receiving aid:** 40 %
Average scholarships and grants: $4,500 **Average loans:** $850 **Work-study program:** Yes
Undergraduates working on campus: 20 % **Average earnings:** $1,000
Non-need scholarships 25 % **Athletic scholarships:** NA **FAF deadline:** Mar. 1
Off-campus part-time employment: Good **CO-OP program:** No
ROTC: at U of Houston **NROTC:** Yes **AFROTC:** No

Endowment

Total: $1.14 Billion **Per student (including graduate students):** $290,000

Location

Acres: 300 **Setting:** Urban
Miles from town center: (Pop. 1.7 Million)
Miles from (Pop.)
Miles from (Pop.)

Class Composition

Asian: 8 % **Black:** 6 % **Hispanic:** 6 % **White:** 78 % **Other:** 1 %
Total minority : 22 % **Foreign countries:** 2 % (55 students)
From public schools: 90 % **Students from in state:** 47 %

Housing (on campus)

Freshmen Required to live on campus: No
Available for all students: 70 %
On-campus married student housing: NA
Guaranteed for: 1 year
Fraternity / Sorority housing: No / No
Women-only dorms available: NA

Campus Life

Students living on campus: 70 % **Remain weekends:** 75 % **Handicap access:** 50 %
Car regulations: All may have
Number with cars: 75 %
Number of fraternities: 0 **Chapter houses:** 0
Students belonging to fraternities: 0 %
Adequacy of on-campus parking: Fair
Number of sororities: 0 **Chapter houses:** 0
Students belonging to sororities: 0 %

Libraries and Computers

Books: 1.5 Million **Periodicals:** 12,000 **Microform items:** 1.5 Million
Microcomputers available: Yes **Microcomputers networked:** Yes

Classes

Faculty / Student Ratio: 1/9 **Classes taught by teacher assistants:** 10 %
Most popular majors: English, Electrical Engineering **Classes begin:** Late Aug.
Baccalaureate degrees offered: BA, B ARCH, BFA, B MUS, BS

Sports

Division: I **Except:** **Physical ed requirements:** 2 semesters
Students participating in intercollegiate sports: 10 % **In intramural sports:** 100 %
Additional intercollegiate and/or intramural sports: (not found at all colleges)

Crew: Yes **Ice Hockey:** No **Lacrosse:** Yes **Wrestling:** No
Rugby: Yes **Sailing:** Yes **Skiing:** No
Squash: Yes **Ultimate Frisbee:** Yes **Water Polo:** Yes

Alumni

Number living: 28,000 **Annual giving:** $ 5.2 Mil. **Participation:** 42 %
Average annual gift: $ 420 **Average per student:** $1,200

3-2 Programs (2 degrees in 5 years)

5-year Rice MBA Program, 8-year Medical with Baylor

Observation and Opinion of:

Undergraduates and graduates ____________________

____

College counselor ____________________

____

UNIVERSITY OF RICHMOND (Private)

Richmond, VA 23173

HIGHLY SELECTIVE
(Composite rating of guide books)

Main tel.: 804-289-8000
Admissions tel.: 804-289-8640
Financial aid tel.: 804-289-8438
Scheduled Airline Service: Richmond
Miles to airport: 8

Founded: 1830
Nickname: Spiders
Religious affiliation: Baptist
(Coed since 1914)

Student Body

Undergraduates: 2,825 **Men:** 51 % **Women:** 49 %
Graduate students: 2,000 **Freshman class:** 695

Academics

SAT Averages: 1215 **Verbal:** 575 **Math:** 640 **(Taking SATs:** 65 %**)**
700-800: V 2 % **M** 18 % **500-600: V** 8 % **M** 20 %
600-700: V 33 % **M** 62 % **400-500: V** 7 % **M** 0 % **300-400: V** 2 % **M** 0 %
High school class rank: Top fifth 59 % **2nd fifth** 18 % **3rd fifth** 4 %

Admissions

Applied: 5,550 **Accepted:** 37 % **Matriculated:** 34 %
Deadline: Feb. 1 **Accept common application:** Yes
Interview recommended: Yes **Off-campus interview available:** No
Evaluative: No **Informational only:** Yes **LD program:** No
Night in dorm provided: No **Non-refundable application fee:** $35
Early decision program: Yes **Applied:** 167 **Accepted:** 27 % **Deadline:** Nov. 1
Freshmen accepted other than Fall term: 0 % **SAT/FAF Code #** 5569

Transfers

Applied: 265 **Accepted:** 23 % **Application deadline for Fall:** Feb. 1 **Spring:** Nov. 1
Minimum grades recommended: 2.0 **All new students who were transfers into all classes:** 4 %

Class Experience

Return 2nd year: 93% **Graduate after 4 years:** 76 % **To graduate school within 5 years:** NA %

Cost

Tuition deposit: $300 **Total cost (Including school's estimate on fees and books):** $17,200
Tuition: $12,620 **(In state:** $ **)** **Room and board:** $3,000
Annual giving by parents: $757,000 **Average per student:** $260

Financial Aid

Average total package per student: $NA **Number receiving aid:** 52 %
Average scholarships and grants: $4,600 **Average loans:** $NA **Work-study program:** Yes
Undergraduates working on campus: 25 % **Average earnings:** $900
Non-need scholarships 73 % **Athletic scholarships:** Yes **FAF deadline:** Feb. 25
Off-campus part-time employment: Excellent **CO-OP program:** No
ROTC: Yes **NROTC:** No **AFROTC:** No

Endowment

Total: $297 Million **Per student (including graduate students):** $65,000

Location

Acres: 350 **Setting:** Surburban **Miles from town center:** 6 **(Pop.** 700,000**)**
110 **Miles from** Wash, DC **(Pop.)** **Miles from (Pop.)**

Class Composition

Asian: 1 % **Black:** 3 % **Hispanic:** 1 % **White:** 94 % **Other:** 1 %
Total minority : 94 % **Foreign countries:** 1 % (30 students)
From public schools: 67 % **Students from in state:** 20 %

Housing (on campus)

Freshmen required to live on campus: No **Guaranteed for:** 1 year
Available for all students: 95 % **Fraternity / Sorority housing:** Yes / No
On-campus married student housing: Yes **Women-only dorms available:** Yes

Campus Life

Students living on campus: 95 % **Remain weekends:** 80 % **Handicap access:** 75 %
Car regulations: All may have
Number with cars: 50% **Adequacy of on-campus parking:** Good
Number of fraternities: 11 **Chapter houses:** 11 **Number of sororities:** 6 **Chapter houses:** 0
Students belonging to fraternities: 55 % **Students belonging to sororities:** 60 %

Libraries and Computers

Books: 478,000 **Periodicals:** 5,700 **Microform items:** 33,000
Microcomputers available: Yes **Microcomputers networked:** Yes

Classes

Faculty / Student Ratio: 1/14 **Classes taught by teacher assistants:** 0 %
Most popular majors: Business, Economics **Classes begin:** Late Aug.
Baccalaureate degrees offered: BA, B MUS, BS, BSBA

Sports

Division: I **Except:** **Physical ed requirements:** 4 semesters
Students participating in intercollegiate sports: 15 % **In intramural sports:** 15 %
Additional intercollegiate and/or intramural sports: (not found at all colleges)

Crew: Yes **Ice Hockey:** No **Lacrosse:** Yes **Wrestling:** No
Rugby: Yes **Sailing:** No **Skiing:** Yes
Squash: No **Ultimate Frisbee:** No **Water Polo:** Yes/M

Alumni

Number living: 26,000 **Annual giving:** $ 9.3 Mil. **Participation:** 30 %
Average annual gift: $ 1,200 **Average per student:** $2,600

3-2 Programs (2 degrees in 5 years)

Forestry and Environmental Studies with Duke. Pre-Law and Pre-Medicine with numerous colleges

Observation and Opinion of:

Undergraduates and graduates ______________________________

____

College counselor ______________________________

____

UNIVERSITY OF ROCHESTER (Private)

Wilson Boulevard
Rochester, NY 14627

HIGHLY SELECTIVE
(Composite rating of guide books)

Main tel.: 716-275-2121
Admissions tel.: 716-275-3221
Financial aid tel.: 716-275-3226
Scheduled Airline Service: Rochester
Miles to airport: 10

Founded: 1850
Nickname: Yellow Jackets
Religious affiliation: None
(Coed since 1900)

Student Body

Undergraduates: 4,800 **Men:** 65 % **Women:** 35 %
Graduate students: 2,300 **Freshman class:** 1,190

Academics

SAT Averages: 1150 **Verbal:** 530 **Math:** 620 (Taking SATs: 94 %)
700-800: V 2 % M 16 % **500-600:** V 41 % M 30 %
600-700: V 20 % M 45 % **400-500:** V 30 % M 8 % **300-400:** V 7 % M 1 %
High school class rank: Top fifth 59 % 2nd fifth 16 % 3rd fifth 6 %

Admissions

Applied: 7,100 **Accepted:** 68 % **Matriculated:** 24 %
Deadline: Jan. 15 **Accept common application:** Yes
Interview recommended: Yes **Off-campus interview available:** Yes
Evaluative: Yes **Informational only:** No **LD program:** No
Night in dorm provided: Yes **Non-refundable application fee:** $45
Early decision program: Yes **Applied:** 337 **Accepted:** 62 % **Deadline:** Feb. 1
Freshmen accepted other than Fall term: 1 % **SAT/FAF Code #** 2928

Transfers

Applied: 646 **Accepted:** 54 % **Application deadline for Fall:** NA **Spring:** NA
Minimum grades recommended: C- **All new students who were transfers into all classes:** 16 %

Class Experience

Return 2nd year: 90 % **Graduate after 4 years:** 68 % **To graduate school within 5 years:** 73 %

Cost

Tuition deposit: $400 **Total cost (Including school's estimate on fees and books):** $23,000
Tuition: $16,000 (In state: $) **Room and board:** $6,000
Annual giving by parents: $93,000 **Average per student:** $12

Financial Aid

Average total package per student: $14,300 **Number receiving aid:** 73 %
Average scholarships and grants: $11,425 **Average loans:** $2,850 **Work-study program:** Yes
Undergraduates working on campus: 48 % **Average earnings:** $1,200
Non-need scholarships 11 % **Athletic scholarships:** NA **FAF deadline:** Feb. 1
Off-campus part-time employment: Good **CO-OP program:** No
ROTC: at Rochester Inst **NROTC:** Yes **AFROTC:** at Roch Inst

Endowment

Total: $588 Million **Per student (including graduate students):** $80,000

Location

Acres: 600 **Setting:** Surburban **Miles from town center:** 2 **(Pop.** 1 Million**)**
Miles from **(Pop.)** **Miles from** **(Pop.)**

Class Composition

Asian: 8 % **Black:** 6 % **Hispanic:** 4 % **White:** 78 % **Other:** 4 %
Total minority : 22 % **Foreign countries:** 4 % (200 students)
From public schools: % **Students from in state:** 48 %

Housing (on campus)

Freshmen required to live on campus: Yes **Guaranteed for:** 1 year
Available for all students: 90 % **Fraternity / Sorority housing:** No / No
On-campus married student housing: Yes **Women-only dorms available:** Yes

Campus Life

Students living on campus: 89 % **Remain weekends:** 90 % **Handicap access:** 63 %
Car regulations: All may have
Number with cars: NA % **Adequacy of on-campus parking:** NA
Number of fraternities: 18 **Chapter houses:** 6 **Number of sororities:** 10 **Chapter houses:** 0
Students belonging to fraternities: 26 % **Students belonging to sororities:** 18 %

Libraries and Computers

Books: 2.7 Million **Periodicals:** 16,000 **Microform items:** 3.4 Million
Microcomputers available: Yes **Microcomputers networked:** Yes

Classes

Faculty / Student Ratio: 1/12 **Classes taught by teacher assistants:** 15 %
Most popular majors: Poly Science, Economics **Classes begin:** Early Sept.
Baccalaureate degrees offered: BA, B MUS, BS

Sports

Division: III **Except:** **Physical ed requirements:** NA
Students participating in intercollegiate sports: 15 % **In intramural sports:** 60 %
Additional intercollegiate and/or intramural sports: (not found at all colleges)
Crew: Yes **Ice Hockey:** Yes/M **Lacrosse:** Yes **Wrestling:** No
Rugby: Yes/M **Sailing:** Yes **Skiing:** No
Squash: No **Ultimate Frisbee:** Yes **Water Polo:** Yes

Alumni

Number living: 60,000 **Annual giving:** $ 8.3 Mil. **Participation:** 29 %
Average annual gift: $ 480 **Average per student:** $1,100

3-2 Programs (2 degrees in 5 years)

Engineering with Colby, Hamilton

Observation and Opinion of:

Undergraduates and graduates ______________________________

____

College counselor ______________________________

____

ROLLINS COLLEGE (Private)

1000 Holt Avenue
Winter Park, FL 32789

VERY SELECTIVE
(Composite rating of guide books)

Main tel.: 407-646-2000
Admissions tel.: 407-646-2161
Financial aid tel.: 407-646-2395
Scheduled Airline Service: Orlando
Miles to airport: 7

Founded: 1885
Nickname: Tars
Religious affiliation: None
(Coed since 1885)

Student Body

Undergraduates: 1,500 **Men:** 47 % **Women:** 53 %
Graduate students: 600 **Freshman class:** 410

Academics

SAT Averages: 1085 **Verbal:** 515 **Math:** 570 **(Taking SATs:** 60 %**)**
700-800: V 1 % **M** 4 % **500-600: V** 50 % **M** 52 %
600-700: V 12 % **M** 28 % **400-500: V** 34 % **M** 15 % **300-400: V** 3 % **M** 1 %
High school class rank: Top fifth 53 % **2nd fifth** 29 % **3rd fifth** 13 %

Admissions

Applied: 2,350 **Accepted:** 56 % **Matriculated:** 31 %
Deadline: Feb. 14 **Accept common application:** Yes
Interview recommended: Yes **Off-campus interview available:** No
Evaluative: No **Informational only:** Yes **LD program:** NA
Night in dorm provided: Yes **Non-refundable application fee:** $35
Early decision program: Yes **Applied:** 132 **Accepted:** 60 % **Deadline:** Dec. 15
Freshmen accepted other than Fall term: 1 % **SAT/FAF Code #** 5572

Transfers

Applied: 237 **Accepted:** 50 % **Application deadline for Fall:** Apr. 15 **Spring:** Nov. 15
Minimum grades recommended: 2.7 **All new students who were transfers into all classes:** 14 %

Class Experience

Return 2nd year: 88 % **Graduate after 4 years:** 72 % **To graduate school within 5 years:** 30 %

Cost

Tuition deposit: $500 **Total cost (Including school's estimate on fees and books):** $20,000
Tuition: $14,550 **(In state:** $ **)** **Room and board:** $4,600
Annual giving by parents: $500,000 **Average per student:** $250

Financial Aid

Average total package per student: $9,000 **Number receiving aid:** 30 %
Average scholarships and grants: $6,450 **Average loans:** $2,600 **Work-study program:** Yes
Undergraduates working on campus: 8 % **Average earnings:** $1,000
Non-need scholarships 56 % **Athletic scholarships:** Yes **FAF deadline:** Mar. 1
Off-campus part-time employment: Excellent **CO-OP program:** No
ROTC: No **NROTC:** No **AFROTC:** No

Endowment

Total: $32 Million **Per student (including graduate students):** $16,000

Location

Acres: 65 **Setting:** Surburban **Miles from town center:** 0 **(Pop.** 35,000)
6 **Miles from** Orlando **(Pop.)** **Miles from (Pop.)**

Class Composition

Asian: 2 % **Black:** 4 % **Hispanic:** 5 % **White:** 88 % **Other:** 1 %
Total minority : 12 % **Foreign countries:** 4 % (80 students)
From public schools: 43 % **Students from in state:** 70 %

Housing (on campus)

Freshmen required to live on campus: No **Guaranteed for:** 4 years
Available for all students: 80 % **Fraternity / Sorority housing:** Yes / Yes
On-campus married student housing: No **Women-only dorms available:** No

Campus Life

Students living on campus: 80 % **Remain weekends:** 75 % **Handicap access:** 85 %
Car regulations: No freshmen
Number with cars: NA % **Adequacy of on-campus parking:** Poor
Number of fraternities: 4 **Chapter houses:** 4 **Number of sororities:** 5 **Chapter houses:** 4
Students belonging to fraternities: 24 % **Students belonging to sororities:** 30 %

Libraries and Computers

Books: 233,000 **Periodicals:** 1,400 **Microform items:** 19,100
Microcomputers available: Yes **Microcomputers networked:** NA

Classes

Faculty / Student Ratio: 1/12 **Classes taught by teacher assistants:** 0 %
Most popular majors: Poly Science, Economics **Classes begin:** Early Sept.
Baccalaureate degrees offered: BA

Sports

Division: II **Except:** In Tennis I **Physical ed requirements:** 4 course units
Students participating in intercollegiate sports: NA % **In intramural sports:** NA %
Additional intercollegiate and/or intramural sports: (not found at all colleges)

Crew: Yes **Ice Hockey:** No **Lacrosse:** No **Wrestling:** No
Rugby: No **Sailing:** Yes **Skiing:** No
Squash: No **Ultimate Frisbee:** Yes **Water Polo:** No

Alumni

Number living: 13,000 **Annual giving:** $ 1.8 Mil. **Participation:** 29 %
Average annual gift: $ 450 **Average per student:** $900

3-2 Programs (2 degrees in 5 years)

Engineering with Auburn, Case Western, Columbia, Georgia Tech
Forestry and Environmental Studies with Duke

Observation and Opinion of:

Undergraduates and graduates ______________________________

____

College counselor ______________________________

____

RUTGERS COLLEGE (Public)

New Brunswick, NJ 08903

HIGHLY SELECTIVE
(Composite rating of guide books)

Main tel.: 908-932-1766
Admissions tel.: 908-932-3770
Financial aid tel.: 908-932-8811
Scheduled Airline Service: Newark
Miles to airport: 34

Founded: 1766
Nickname: Scarlet Knights
Religious affiliation: None
(Coed since 1972)

Student Body

Undergraduates: 8,000 **Men:** 52 % **Women:** 48 %
Graduate students: 0 **Freshman class:** 1,650

Academics

SAT Averages: 1140 **Verbal:** 530 **Math:** 610 **(Taking SATs:** 65 %)
700-800: V 2 % **M** 16 % **500-600: V** 48 % **M** 28 %
600-700: V 22 % **M** 50 % **400-500: V** 25 % **M** 6 % **300-400: V** 3 % **M** 0 %
High school class rank: Top fifth 83 % **2nd fifth** 10 % **3rd fifth** 2 %

Admissions

Applied: 14,400 **Accepted:** 44 % **Matriculated:** 26 %
Deadline: Jan. 15 **Accept common application:** No
Interview recommended: NA **Off-campus interview available:** NA
Evaluative: NA **Informational only:** NA **LD program:** Yes
Night in dorm provided: NA **Non-refundable application fee:** $30
Early decision program: Yes **Applied:** NA **Accepted:** 27 % **Deadline:** Jan. 15
Freshmen accepted other than Fall term: 0 % **SAT/FAF Code #** 2765

Transfers

Applied: 3,790 **Accepted:** 30 % **Application deadline for Fall:** Mar. 15 **Spring:** Nov. 1
Minimum grades recommended: C **All new students who were transfers into all classes:** 23 %

Class Experience

Return 2nd year: 91 % **Graduate after 4 years:** 59 % **To graduate school within 5 years:** NA %

Cost

Tuition deposit: $100 **Total cost (Including school's estimate on fees and books):** $12,000
Tuition: $6,900 (In state: $ 3,400) **Room and board:** $4,200
Annual giving by parents: $140,000 **Average per student:** $NA

Financial Aid

Average total package per student: $2,600 **Number receiving aid:** 58 %
Average scholarships and grants: $1,450 **Average loans:** $1,150 **Work-study program:** Yes
Undergraduates working on campus: 31 % **Average earnings:** $990
Non-need scholarships 7 % **Athletic scholarships:** NA **FAF deadline:** Mar. 1
Off-campus part-time employment: Fair **CO-OP program:** No
ROTC: Yes **NROTC:** No **AFROTC:** Yes

Endowment

Total: $126 Million **Per student (including graduate students):** $29,000

Location

Acres: 2,700 **Setting:** Urban
40 Miles from NYC **(Pop.** 7 Mil. **)**
Miles from town center: 1 **(Pop.** 41,000**)**
Miles from (Pop.)

Class Composition

Asian: 10 % **Black:** 8 % **Hispanic:** 10 % **White:** 68 % **Other:** 4 %
Total minority : 32 % **Foreign countries:** 2 % (160 students)
From public schools: NA % **Students from in state:** 88 %

Housing (on campus)

Freshmen required to live on campus: No
Available for all students: 60 %
On-campus married student housing: Yes
Guaranteed for: 1 year
Fraternity / Sorority housing: Yes / No
Women-only dorms available: No

Campus Life

Students living on campus: 59 % **Remain weekends:** NA % **Handicap access:** 90 %
Car regulations: Only juniors and seniors
Number with cars: NA%
Adequacy of on-campus parking: Poor
Number of fraternities: 33 **Chapter houses:** 19
Number of sororities: 14 **Chapter houses:** 0
Students belonging to fraternities: 55 %
Students belonging to sororities: 4 %

Libraries and Computers

Books: 4.1 Million **Periodicals:** 16,000 **Microform items:** 2.2 Million
Microcomputers available: Yes **Microcomputers networked:** NA

Classes

Faculty / Student Ratio: 1/17 **Classes taught by teacher assistants:** 20 %
Most popular majors: Economics, English **Classes begin:** Early Sept.
Baccalaureate degrees offered: BA, BS

Sports

Division: I **Except:** **Physical ed requirements:** None
Students participating in intercollegiate sports: 5 % **In intramural sports:** NA%
Additional intercollegiate and/or intramural sports: (not found at all colleges)
Crew: Yes **Ice Hockey:** No **Lacrosse:** Yes **Wrestling:** Yes/M
Rugby: No **Sailing:** No **Skiing:** No
Squash: No **Ultimate Frisbee:** No **Water Polo:** No

Alumni

Number living: 213,000 **Annual giving:** $ 4.3 Mil. **Participation:** 19 %
Average annual gift: $ 130 **Average per student:** $500

3-2 Programs (2 degrees in 5 years)

2-3 Engineering with Rutgers College of Engineering
BA/MBA Program with Rutgers Graduate School

Observation and Opinion of:

Undergraduates and graduates ______________________________

____

College counselor ______________________________

____

ST. LAWRENCE UNIVERSITY (Private)

Canton, NY 13617

SELECTIVE
(Composite rating of guide books)

Main tel.: 315-379-5011
Admissions tel.: 315-379-5261
Financial aid tel.: 315-379-5265
Scheduled Airline Service: Ottawa
Miles to airport: 70

Founded: 1856
Nickname: Larries
Religious affiliation: None
(Coed since 1856)

Student Body

Undergraduates: 1,925 **Men:** 51 % **Women:** 49 %
Graduate students: 129 **Freshman class:** 534

Academics

SAT Averages: 1085 **Verbal:** 515 **Math:** 570 **(Taking SATs:** NA %**)**
700-800: V 1 % M 4 % **500-600:** V 40 % M 45 %
600-700: V 12 % M 30 % **400-500:** V 41 % M 19 % **300-400:** V 6 % M 2 %
High school class rank: Top fifth 50 % 2nd fifth 29 % 3rd fifth 13 %

Admissions

Applied: 2,550 **Accepted:** 70 % **Matriculated:** 30 %
Deadline: Feb. 1 **Accept common application:** Yes
Interview recommended: NA **Off-campus interview available:** NA
Evaluative: NA **Informational only:** NA **LD program:** Yes
Night in dorm provided: NA **Non-refundable application fee:** $40
Early decision program: Yes **Applied:** 145 **Accepted:** 68 % **Deadline:** Dec. 15
Freshmen accepted other than Fall term: 1 % **SAT/FAF Code #** 2805

Transfers

Applied: 100 **Accepted:** 65 % **Application deadline for Fall:** May 1 **Spring:** Dec. 1
Minimum grades recommended: 3.0 **All new students who were transfers into all classes:** 7 %

Class Experience

Return 2nd year: 89 % **Graduate after 4 years:** 80 % **To graduate school within 1 year:** 33 %

Cost

Tuition deposit: $500 **Total cost (Including school's estimate on fees and books):** $22,700
Tuition: $16,700 **(In state:** $ **)** **Room and board:** $5,300
Annual giving by parents: $16,000 **Average per student:** $NA

Financial Aid

Average total package per student: $12,900 **Number receiving aid:** 40 %
Average scholarships and grants: $10,400 **Average loans:** $2,500 **Work-study program:** Yes
Undergraduates working on campus: 45 % **Average earnings:** $1,000
Non-need scholarships NA % **Athletic scholarships:** NA **FAF deadline:** Feb. 15
Off-campus part-time employment: Fair **CO-OP program:** No
ROTC: Yes **NROTC:** No **AFROTC:** at Clarkson U

Endowment

Total: $86 Million **Per student (including graduate students):** $40,000

Location

Acres: 1,000 **Setting:** Rural
Miles from town center: 0 **(Pop.** 7,500**)**
80 **Miles from** Ottawa **(Pop.** 300,000 **)**
150 **Miles from** Syracuse **(Pop.** 170,000**)**

Class Composition

Asian: 1 % **Black:** 3 % **Hispanic:** 1 % **White:** 94 % **Other:** 1 %
Total minority : 6 % **Foreign countries:** 3 % (60 students)
From public schools: NA % **Students from in state:** 49 %

Housing (on campus)

Freshmen required to live on campus: Yes
Available for all students: 95 %
On-campus married student housing: Yes
Guaranteed for: 4 years
Fraternity / Sorority housing: Yes / Yes
Women-only dorms available: No

Campus Life

Students living on campus: 92 % **Remain weekends:** 90 % **Handicap access:** 50 %
Car regulations: Not if on probation
Number with cars: 50%
Adequacy of on-campus parking: Good
Number of fraternities: 7 **Chapter houses:** 7
Students belonging to fraternities: 45 %
Number of sororities: 5 **Chapter houses:** 5
Students belonging to sororities: 45 %

Libraries and Computers

Books: 395,000 **Periodicals:** 2,400 **Microform items:** 328,000
Microcomputers available: Yes **Microcomputers networked:** Yes

Classes

Faculty / Student Ratio: 1/11 **Classes taught by teacher assistants:** 0 %
Most popular majors: Government, Economics **Classes begin:** Late Aug.
Baccalaureate degrees offered: BA, BS

Sports

Division: III **Except:** **Physical ed requirements:** 1 year
Students participating in intercollegiate sports: 25 % **In intramural sports:** 50 %
Additional intercollegiate and/or intramural sports: (not found at all colleges)

Crew: No	**Ice Hockey:** Yes	**Lacrosse:** Yes	**Wrestling:** Yes/M
Rugby: No	**Sailing:** No	**Skiing:** Yes	
Squash: Yes	**Ultimate Frisbee:** No	**Water Polo:** No	

Alumni

Number living: 16,500 **Annual giving:** $ 2.2 Mil. **Participation:** 45 %
Average annual gift: $ 300 **Average per student:** $1,000

3-2 Programs (2 degrees in 5 years)

Engineering with Columbia, Clarkson, RPI, U of Rochester, USC, Washington U, Worcester Poly
Nursing with Columbia and U of Rochester, 4-1 MBA with Clarkson U

Observation and Opinion of:

Undergraduates and graduates ______________________________

____

College counselor ______________________________

____

ST. OLAF COLLEGE (Private)

North Field, MN 55057

HIGHLY SELECTIVE
(Composite rating of guide books)

Main tel.: 507-663-2222
Admissions tel.: 507-663-3025
Financial aid tel.: 507-663-3019
Scheduled Airline Service: Minneapolis
Miles to airport: 40

Founded: NA
Nickname: Oles
Religious affiliation: Lutheran
(Coed since NA)

Student Body

Undergraduates: 3,000 **Men:** 48 % **Women:** 52 %
Graduate students: 0 **Freshman class:** 755

Academics

SAT Averages: 1110 **Verbal:** 530 **Math:** 620 **(Taking SATs:** 77 %**)**
700-800: V 2 % **M** 11 % **500-600: V** 41 % **M** 39 %
600-700: V 18 % **M** 33 % **400-500: V** 33 % **M** 15 % **300-400: V** 6 % **M** 2 %
High school class rank: Top fifth 68 % **2nd fifth** 22 % **3rd fifth** 7 %

Admissions

Applied: 2,175 **Accepted:** 70 % **Matriculated:** 50 %
Deadline: Feb. 1 **Accept common application:** Yes
Interview recommended: Yes **Off-campus interview available:** No
Evaluative: No **Informational only:** Yes **LD program:** Yes
Night in dorm provided: No **Non-refundable application fee:** $25
Early decision program: Yes **Applied:** 267 **Accepted:** 80 % **Deadline:** Nov. 15
Freshmen accepted other than Fall term: 5 % **SAT/FAF Code #** 6638

Transfers

Applied: 168 **Accepted:** 63 % **Application deadline for Fall:** Mar. 1 **Spring:** Dec. 1
Minimum grades recommended: 3.0 **All new students who were transfers into all classes:** 7 %

Class Experience

Return 2nd year: 95 % **Graduate after 4 years:** 66 % **To graduate school within 1 years:** 23 %

Cost

Tuition deposit: $200 **Total cost (Including school's estimate on fees and books):** $17,200
Tuition: $12,750 **(In state:** $ NA **)** **Room and board:** $3,500
Annual giving by parents: $970,000 **Average per student:** $NA

Financial Aid

Average total package per student: $11,400 **Number receiving aid:** 6 %
Average scholarships and grants: $9,150 **Average loans:** $2,235 **Work-study program:** Yes
Undergraduates working on campus: 65 % **Average earnings:** $900
Non-need scholarships 0 % **Athletic scholarships:** NA **FAF deadline:** Mar. 1
Off-campus part-time employment: Fair **CO-OP program:** No
ROTC: No **NROTC:** No **AFROTC:** No

Endowment

Total: $47 Million **Per student (including graduate students):** $16,000

Location

Acres: 350 **Setting:** Rural
40 **Miles from** St. Paul **(Pop.** 270,000 **)**
Miles from town center: 1 **(Pop.** 13,000**)**
Miles from **(Pop.** **)**

Class Composition

Asian: NA % **Black:** NA % **Hispanic:** NA % **White:** NA % **Other:** NA %
Total minority : NA % **Foreign countries:** NA% (NA students)
From public schools: NA % **Students from in state:** NA %

Housing (on campus)

Freshmen required to live on campus: Yes
Available for all students: 86 %
On-campus married student housing: No
Guaranteed for: 4 years
Fraternity / Sorority housing: No / No
Women-only dorms available: No

Campus Life

Students living on campus: 86 % **Remain weekends:** 80 % **Handicap access:** 60 %
Car regulations: Discouraged
Number with cars: 23 %
Number of fraternities: 0 **Chapter houses:** 0
Students belonging to fraternities: 0 %
Adequacy of on-campus parking: Limited
Number of sororities: 0 **Chapter houses:** 0
Students belonging to sororities: 0 %

Libraries and Computers

Books: 393,000 **Periodicals:** 1,360 **Microform items:** 180,000
Microcomputers available: Yes **Microcomputers networked:** Yes

Classes

Faculty / Student Ratio: 1/12 **Classes taught by teacher assistants:** 0 %
Most popular majors: Economics, Mathematics **Classes begin:** Early Sept.
Baccalaureate degrees offered: BA, BA NURSING, BS NURSING, B MUS

Sports

Division: III **Except:** **Physical ed requirements:** 2 semesters
Students participating in intercollegiate sports: 25 % **In intramural sports:** 50 %
Additional intercollegiate and/or intramural sports: (not found at all colleges)

Crew: No **Ice Hockey:** Yes **Lacrosse:** No **Wrestling:** Yes/M
Rugby: No **Sailing:** No **Skiing:** Yes
Squash: No **Ultimate Frisbee:** Yes **Water Polo:** Yes/M

Alumni

Number living: 24,000 **Annual giving:** $ 4 Mil. **Participation:** 31 %
Average annual gift: $ 570 **Average per student:** $1,300

3-2 Programs (2 degrees in 5 years)

Engineering with Washington U

Observation and Opinion of:

Undergraduates and graduates ____________________

College counselor ____________________

SANTA CLARA UNIVERSITY (Private)

Santa Clara, CA 95053

SELECTIVE
(Composite rating of guide books)

Main tel.: 408-554-4764
Admissions tel.: 408-554-4700
Financial aid tel.: 408-554-4505
Scheduled Airline Service: San Jose
Miles to airport: 2

Founded: 1851
Nickname: Broncos
Religious affiliation: Catholic
(Coed since 1961)

Student Body

Undergraduates: 3,650 **Men:** 52 % **Women:** 48 %
Graduate students: 3,400 **Freshman class:** 927

Academics

SAT Averages: 1085 **Verbal:** 505 **Math:** 580 **(Taking SATs:** 100 %**)**
700-800: V 1 % **M** 8 % **500-600: V** 42 % **M** 43 %
600-700: V 10 % **M** 36 % **400-500: V** 41 % **M** 12 % **300-400: V** 6 % **M** 1 %
High school class rank: Top fifth 60 % **2nd fifth** 26 % **3rd fifth** 7 %

Admissions

Applied: 3,400 **Accepted:** 71 % **Matriculated:** 38 %
Deadline: Feb. 1 **Accept common application:** NA
Interview recommended: Yes **Off-campus interview available:** No
Evaluative: No **Informational only:** Yes **LD program:** No
Night in dorm provided: Yes **Non-refundable application fee:** $300
Early decision program: No **Applied:** NA **Accepted:** NA % **Deadline:** NA
Freshmen accepted other than Fall term: 1 % **SAT/FAF Code #** 4851

Transfers

Applied: 491 **Accepted:** 58 % **Application deadline for Fall:** May 1 **Spring:** Feb. 1
Minimum grades recommended: 3.0 **All new students who were transfers into all classes:** 17 %

Class Experience

Return 2nd year: 90 % **Graduate after 4 years:** 68 % **To graduate school within 5 years:** 68 %

Cost

Tuition deposit: $200 **Total cost (Including school's estimate on fees and books):** $17,100
Tuition: $12,150 **(In state:** $ **)** **Room and board:** $5,555
Annual giving by parents: $2 Million **Average per student:** $250

Financial Aid

Average total package per student: $12,700 **Number receiving aid:** 76 %
Average scholarships and grants: $9,755 **Average loans:** $2,950 **Work-study program:** Yes
Undergraduates working on campus: 18 % **Average earnings:** $900
Non-need scholarships 73 % **Athletic scholarships:** Yes **FAF deadline:** Feb. 1
Off-campus part-time employment: Good **CO-OP program:** Yes
ROTC: Yes **NROTC:** at Berkeley **AFROTC:** at San Jose

Endowment

Total: $115 Million **Per student (including graduate students):** $17,000

Location

Acres: 164 **Setting:** Surburban **Miles from town center:** 0 **(Pop.** 91,000)
3 **Miles from** San Jose **(Pop.** 650,000) 46 **Miles from** San Francisco **(Pop.** 880,000)

Class Composition

Asian: 17 % **Black:** 2 % **Hispanic:** 9 % **White:** 69 % **Other:** 2 %
Total minority : 31 % **Foreign countries:** 8 % (300 students)
From public schools: 52 % **Students from in state:** 68 %

Housing (on campus)

Freshmen required to live on campus: No **Guaranteed for:** 1 year
Available for all students: 50 % **Fraternity / Sorority housing:** Yes / Yes
On-campus married student housing: Yes **Women-only dorms available:** Yes

Campus Life

Students living on campus: 50 % **Remain weekends:** 90 % **Handicap access:** NA%
Car regulations: All may have
Number with cars: 30 % **Adequacy of on-campus parking:** NA
Number of fraternities: 4 **Chapter houses:** 4 **Number of sororities:** 3 **Chapter houses:** 3
Students belonging to fraternities: NA % **Students belonging to sororities:** NA %

Libraries and Computers

Books: 526,000 **Periodicals:** 3,540 **Microform items:** 440,000
Microcomputers available: Yes **Microcomputers networked:** Yes

Classes

Faculty / Student Ratio: 1/14 **Classes taught by teacher assistants:** 0 %
Most popular majors: Finance, Marketing **Classes begin:** Mid Sept.
Baccalaureate degrees offered: BA, B MUS, BS, BS COMMERCE

Sports

Division: II **Except:** **Physical ed requirements:** None
Students participating in intercollegiate sports: 15 % **In intramural sports:** 50 %
Additional intercollegiate and/or intramural sports: (not found at all colleges)

Crew: Yes **Ice Hockey:** No **Lacrosse:** Yes **Wrestling:** No
Rugby: Yes **Sailing:** No **Skiing:** Yes
Squash: No **Ultimate Frisbee:** No **Water Polo:** Yes

Alumni

Number living: 37,000 **Annual giving:** $ 2 Mil. **Participation:** 24 %
Average annual gift: $ 250 **Average per student:** $300

3-2 Programs (2 degrees in 5 years)

Cooperative Program in Engineering

Observation and Opinion of:

Undergraduates and graduates ____________________

____

College counselor ____________________

____

SKIDMORE COLLEGE (Private)

Saratoga Springs, NY 12866

HIGHLY SELECTIVE
(Composite rating of guide books)

Main tel.: 518-587-5000
Admissions tel.: 518-587-2569
Financial aid tel.: 518-587-5000, Ext. 2144
Scheduled Airline Service: Albany
Miles to airport: 30

Founded: 1903
Nickname: Thoroughbreds
Religious affiliation: None
(Coed since 1971)

Student Body

Undergraduates: 2,150 **Men:** 40 % **Women:** 60 %
Graduate students: 0 **Freshman class:** 608

Academics

SAT Averages: 1150 **Verbal:** 550 **Math:** 600 (Taking SATs: 99 %)
700-800: V 2 % M 9 % **500-600:** V 48 % M 39 %
600-700: V 25 % M 42 % **400-500:** V 23 % M 9 % **300-400:** V 2 % M 1 %
High school class rank: Top fifth 38 % **2nd fifth** 17 % **3rd fifth** 5 %

Admissions

Applied: 5,000 **Accepted:** 44 % **Matriculated:** 27 %
Deadline: Feb. 1 **Accept common application:** Yes
Interview recommended: Yes **Off-campus interview available:** Yes
Evaluative: Yes **Informational only:** Yes **LD program:** NA
Night in dorm provided: NA **Non-refundable application fee:** $35
Early decision program: Yes **Applied:** 300 **Accepted:** 47 % **Deadline:** Jan. 15
Freshmen accepted other than Fall term: 0 % **SAT/FAF Code #** 2815

Transfers

Applied: 170 **Accepted:** 37 % **Application deadline for Fall:** Apr. 1 **Spring:** Nov. 15
Minimum grades recommended: 3.0 **All new students who were transfers into all classes:** 4 %

Class Experience

Return 2nd year: 91 % **Graduate after 4 years:** 75 % **To graduate school within 5 years:** 36 %

Cost

Tuition deposit: $300 **Total cost (Including school's estimate on fees and books):** $22,800
Tuition: $16,650 **(In state:** $ **)** **Room and board:** $5,400
Annual giving by parents: $450,000 **Average per student:** $240

Financial Aid

Average total package per student: $10,600 **Number receiving aid:** 25 %
Average scholarships and grants: $8,600 **Average loans:** $2,025 **Work-study program:** Yes
Undergraduates working on campus: 3 % **Average earnings:** $600
Non-need scholarships 73 % **Athletic scholarships:** NA **FAF deadline:** Feb. 1
Off-campus part-time employment: Good **CO-OP program:** No
ROTC: at RPI **NROTC:** at RPI **AFROTC:** at RPI

Endowment

Total: $39 Million **Per student (including graduate students):** $16,000

Location

Acres: 800 **Setting:** Surburban
184 **Miles from** NYC **(Pop.** 7 Mil. **)**
Miles from town center: 1 **(Pop.** 30,000**)**
180 **Miles from** Boston **(Pop.** 600,000**)**

Class Composition

Asian: 3 % **Black:** 3 % **Hispanic:** 2 % **White:** 92 % **Other:** NA %
Total minority : 8 % **Foreign countries:** 2 % (40 students)
From public schools: 56 % **Students from in state:** 31 %

Housing (on campus)

Freshmen required to live on campus: Yes
Available for all students: 83 %
On-campus married student housing: No
Guaranteed for: NA
Fraternity / Sorority housing: No / No
Women-only dorms available: NA

Campus Life

Students living on campus: 83 % **Remain weekends:** NA % **Handicap access:** 50 %
Car regulations: All 4 years
Number with cars: 45 %
Adequacy of on-campus parking: Good
Number of fraternities: 0 **Chapter houses:** 0
Number of sororities: 0 **Chapter houses:** 0
Students belonging to fraternities: 0 %
Students belonging to sororities: 0 %

Libraries and Computers

Books: 373,000 **Periodicals:** 1,540 **Microform items:** 145,000
Microcomputers available: Yes **Microcomputers networked:** NA

Classes

Faculty / Student Ratio: 1/11 **Classes taught by teacher assistants:** 0 %
Most popular majors: Business, Psychology **Classes begin:** Mid Sept.
Baccalaureate degrees offered: BA, BS

Sports

Division: III **Except:** Skiing II **Physical ed requirements:** NA
Students participating in intercollegiate sports: 24 % **In intramural sports:** 80 %
Additional intercollegiate and/or intramural sports: (not found at all colleges)

Crew: Yes **Ice Hockey:** Yes **Lacrosse:** Yes **Wrestling:** No
Rugby: No **Sailing:** No **Skiing:** Yes
Squash: Yes **Ultimate Frisbee:** No **Water Polo:** No

Alumni

Number living: 17,000 **Annual giving:** $ 3.5 Mil. **Participation:** 42 %
Average annual gift: $ 470 **Average per student:** $1,400

3-2 Programs (2 degrees in 5 years)

Engineering with Clarkson U and Dartmouth
4-1 MBA with Clarkson U

Observation and Opinion of:

Undergraduates and graduates ____________________

____

College counselor ____________________

____

SMITH COLLEGE (Private)

Northampton, MA 01063

HIGHLY SELECTIVE
(Composite rating of guide books)

Main tel.: 413-584-2700
Admissions tel.: 413-585-2500
Financial aid tel.: 413-585-2330
Scheduled Airline Service: Hartford
Miles to airport: 40

Founded: 1871
Nickname: Pioneers
Religious affiliation: None
(Coed since 1871)

Student Body

Undergraduates: 2,550 **Men:** 0 % **Women:** 100 %
Graduate students: 100 **Freshman class:** 625

Academics

SAT Averages: 1190 **Verbal:** 580 **Math:** 610 **(Taking SATs:** NA %)
700-800: V 7 % **M** 8 % **500-600: V** 41 % **M** 41 %
600-700: V 33 % **M** 41 % **400-500: V** 17 % **M** 24 % **300-400: V** NA % **M** NA %
High school class rank: Top fifth 83 % **2nd fifth** 14 % **3rd fifth** 3 %

Admissions

Applied: 2,250 **Accepted:** 63 % **Matriculated:** 44 %
Deadline: Jan. 15 **Accept common application:** Yes
Interview recommended: Yes **Off-campus interview available:** No
Evaluative: No **Informational only:** No **LD program:** Yes
Night in dorm provided: NA **Non-refundable application fee:** $40
Early decision program: Yes **Applied:** 120 **Accepted:** 76 % **Deadline:** Nov. 15
Freshmen accepted other than Fall term: 0 % **SAT/FAF Code #** 3762

Transfers

Applied: 343 **Accepted:** 46 % **Application deadline for Fall:** Feb. 15 **Spring:** Nov. 15
Minimum grades recommended: C **All new students who were transfers into all classes:** 12 %

Class Experience

Return 2nd year: 92 % **Graduate after 4 years:** 84 % **To graduate school within 5 years:** NA %

Cost

Tuition deposit: $200 **Total cost (Including school's estimate on fees and books):** $23,300
Tuition: $16,200 **(In state:** $) **Room and board:** $6,300
Annual giving by parents: $534,000 **Average per student:** $220

Financial Aid

Average total package per student: $16,000 **Number receiving aid:** 45 %
Average scholarships and grants: $14,000 **Average loans:** $2,000 **Work-study program:** Yes
Undergraduates working on campus: 60 % **Average earnings:** $600
Non-need scholarships 0 % **Athletic scholarships:** NA **FAF deadline:** Feb. 1
Off-campus part-time employment: Excellent **CO-OP program:** No
ROTC: at U of Mass **NROTC:** No **AFROTC:** at U of Mass

Endowment

Total: $343 Million **Per student (including graduate students):** $135,000

Location

Acres: 125 **Setting:** Small city **Miles from town center:** 0 **(Pop.** 35,000**)**
20 **Miles from** Springfield **(Pop.** 160,000**)** **Miles from (Pop.)**

Class Composition

Asian: 10 % **Black:** 4 % **Hispanic:** 3 % **White:** 83 % **Other:** NA %
Total minority : 17 % **Foreign countries:** 6 % (150 students)
From public schools: 70 % **Students from in state:** 14 %

Housing (on campus)

Freshmen required to live on campus: Yes **Guaranteed for:** 4 years
Available for all students: 100 % **Fraternity / Sorority housing:** No / No
On-campus married student housing: Yes **Women-only dorms available:** NA

Campus Life

Students living on campus: 95 % **Remain weekends:** NA % **Handicap access:** NA %
Car regulations: Seniors only
Number with cars: 1 % **Adequacy of on-campus parking:** Poor
Number of fraternities: 0 **Chapter houses:** 0 **Number of sororities:** 0 **Chapter houses:** 0
Students belonging to fraternities: 0 % **Students belonging to sororities:** 0 %

Libraries and Computers

Books: 1 Million **Periodicals:** 3,150 **Microform items:** 60,000
Microcomputers available: Yes **Microcomputers networked:** Yes

Classes

Faculty / Student Ratio: 1/10 **Classes taught by teacher assistants:** 0 %
Most popular majors: Government, Economics **Classes begin:** Early Sept.
Baccalaureate degrees offered: AB

Sports

Division: III **Except:** **Physical ed requirements:** None
Students participating in intercollegiate sports: 18 % **In intramural sports:** 70 %
Additional intercollegiate and/or intramural sports: (not found at all colleges)

Crew: Yes **Ice Hockey:** No **Lacrosse:** Yes **Wrestling:** No
Rugby: Yes **Sailing:** No **Skiing:** Yes
Squash: Yes **Ultimate Frisbee:** Yes **Water Polo:** Yes

Alumni

Number living: 43,000 **Annual giving:** $2.5 Mil. **Participation:** 45 %
Average annual gift: $ 1,300 **Average per student:** $10,000

3-2 Programs (2 degrees in 5 years)

Engineering with U of Massachusetts

Observation and Opinion of:

Undergraduates and graduates ______________________

____

College counselor ______________________

____

UNIVERSITY OF SOUTHERN CALIFORNIA (Private)

University Park
Los Angeles, CA 90089-5012

SELECTIVE
(Composite rating of guide books)

Main tel.: 213-740-2311
Admissions tel.: 213-740-1111
Financial aid tel.: 213-740-1111
Scheduled Airline Service: Los Angeles
Miles to airport: 6

Founded: 1880
Nickname: Trojans
Religious affiliation: None
(Coed since 1880)

Student Body

Undergraduates: 16,000 **Men:** 55 % **Women:** 45 %
Graduate students: 14,000 **Freshman class:** 2,500

Academics

SAT Averages: 1085 **Verbal:** 500 **Math:** 585 **(Taking SATs:** NA %)
700-800: V NA % **M** NA % **500-600: V** NA % **M** NA %
600-700: V NA % **M** NA % **400-500: V** NA % **M** NA % **300-400: V** NA % **M** NA %
High school class rank: Top fifth 68 % **2nd fifth** 20 % **3rd fifth** NA %

Admissions

Applied: NA **Accepted:** 75 % **Matriculated:** NA %
Deadline: Mar. 1 **Accept common application:** No
Interview recommended: Yes **Off-campus interview available:** Yes
Evaluative: No **Informational only:** Yes **LD program:** Yes
Night in dorm provided: No **Non-refundable application fee:** $50
Early decision program: Yes **Applied:** NA **Accepted:** NA % **Deadline:** NA
Freshmen accepted other than Fall term: 5 % **SAT/FAF Code #** 4852

Transfers

Applied: NA **Accepted:** NA % **Application deadline for Fall:** Jun. 1 **Spring:** NA
Minimum grades recommended: NA **All new students who were transfers into all classes:** NA %

Class Experience

Return 2nd year: 94 % **Graduate after 4 years:** 63% **To graduate school within 5 years:** NA %

Cost

Tuition deposit: $250 **Total cost (Including school's estimate on fees and books):** $22,000
Tuition: $15,020 **(In state:** $) **Room and board:** $6,260
Annual giving by parents: $757,000 **Average per student:** $NA

Financial Aid

Average total package per student: $NA **Number receiving aid:** 55 %
Average scholarships and grants: $NA **Average loans:** $NA **Work-study program:** Yes
Undergraduates working on campus: NA % **Average earnings:** $NA
Non-need scholarships 4 % **Athletic scholarships:** Yes **FAF deadline:** Mar. 2
Off-campus part-time employment: Good **CO-OP program:** No
ROTC: Yes **NROTC:** Yes **AFROTC:** Yes

Endowment

Total: $523 Million **Per student (including graduate students):** $19,000

Location

Acres: 165 **Setting:** City **Miles from town center:** 0 **(Pop.** 3 Million**)**
Miles from **(Pop.** **)** **Miles from** **(Pop.** **)**

Class Composition

Asian: 20 % **Black:** 5 % **Hispanic:** 10 % **White:** 65 % **Other:** NA %
Total minority : NA % **Foreign countries:** 9 % (1400 students)
From public schools: NA % **Students from in state:** 55 %

Housing (on campus)

Freshmen required to live on campus: No **Guaranteed for:** 1 year
Available for all students: 31 % **Fraternity / Sorority housing:** Yes / Yes
On-campus married student housing: Yes **Women-only dorms available:** Yes

Campus Life

Students living on campus: 31 % **Remain weekends:** NA % **Handicap access:** 88 %
Car regulations: All may have
Number with cars: NA % **Adequacy of on-campus parking:** Poor
Number of fraternities: 28 **Chapter houses:** 28 **Number of sororities:** 15 **Chapter houses:** 15
Students belonging to fraternities: 25 % **Students belonging to sororities:** 25 %

Libraries and Computers

Books: 2.4 Million **Periodicals:** 33,000 **Microform items:** 1.9 Million
Microcomputers available: Yes **Microcomputers networked:** Yes

Classes

Faculty / Student Ratio: NA **Classes taught by teacher assistants:** 0 %
Most popular majors: Business, Communications **Classes begin:** Early Sept.
Baccalaureate degrees offered: BA, BS, B ARCH, BFA, B MUS, BS DENT HYG, BSN, BS PUB ADMIN, BS GERONTOLOGY

Sports

Division: I **Except:** **Physical ed requirements:** None
Students participating in intercollegiate sports: 5 % **In intramural sports:** 40 %
Additional intercollegiate and/or intramural sports: (not found at all colleges)

Crew: Yes **Ice Hockey:** No **Lacrosse:** Yes **Wrestling:** No
Rugby: Yes **Sailing:** Yes **Skiing:** Yes
Squash: Yes **Ultimate Frisbee:** No **Water Polo:** Yes

Alumni

Number living: 200,000 **Annual giving:** $ 22.5 Mil. **Participation:** 11 %
Average annual gift: $ 400 **Average per student:** $700

3-2 Programs (2 degrees in 5 years)

Engineering with USC and others

Observation and Opinion of:

Undergraduates and graduates ____________________

____

College counselor ____________________

____

SOUTHERN METHODIST UNIVERSITY (Private)

Dallas, TX 75275

SELECTIVE
(Composite rating of guide books)

Main tel.: 214-692-2000
Admissions tel.: 800-323-0672
Financial aid tel.: 214-692-3417
Scheduled Airline Service: Dallas
Miles to airport: 15

Founded: 1911
Nickname: Mustangs
Religious affiliation: Methodist
(Coed since 1911)

Student Body

Undergraduates: 5,000 **Men:** 48 % **Women:** 52 %
Graduate students: 3,400 **Freshman class:** 1,100

Academics

SAT Averages: 1085 **Verbal:** 510 **Math:** 575 **(Taking SATs:** NA %)
700-800: V 1 % M 8 % **500-600:** V 42 % M 40 %
600-700: V 17 % M 30 % **400-500:** V 40 % M 20 % **300-400:** V NA % M NA %
High school class rank: Top fifth 65 % **2nd fifth** 24 % **3rd fifth** 9 %

Admissions

Applied: 3,965 **Accepted:** 60 % **Matriculated:** 30 %
Deadline: Apr. 1 **Accept common application:** Yes
Interview recommended: Yes **Off-campus interview available:** Yes
Evaluative: No **Informational only:** Yes **LD program:** No
Night in dorm provided: No **Non-refundable application fee:** $35
Early decision program: Yes **Applied:** NA **Accepted:** NA % **Deadline:** Nov. 1
Freshmen accepted other than Fall term: 1 % **SAT/FAF Code #** 6660

Transfers

Applied: NA **Accepted:** NA % **Application deadline for Fall:** Jul. 1 **Spring:** NA
Minimum grades recommended: 2.5 **All new students who were transfers into all classes:** 20 %

Class Experience

Return 2nd year: 86 % **Graduate after 4 years:** 77 % **To graduate school within 5 years:** NA %

Cost

Tuition deposit: $200 **Total cost (Including school's estimate on fees and books):** $17,520
Tuition: $11,900 **(In state:** $) **Room and board:** $4,832
Annual giving by parents: $207,000 **Average per student:** $40

Financial Aid

Average total package per student: $NA **Number receiving aid:** 50 %
Average scholarships and grants: $NA **Average loans:** $NA **Work-study program:** Yes
Undergraduates working on campus: 40 % **Average earnings:** $NA
Non-need scholarships 5 % **Athletic scholarships:** Yes **FAF deadline:** Mar. 1
Off-campus part-time employment: Good **CO-OP program:** Yes
ROTC: at U of Texas **NROTC:** No **AFROTC:** at U of N Texas

Endowment

Total: $367 Million **Per student (including graduate students):** $40,000

Location

Acres: 165 **Setting:** Surburban **Miles from town center:** 5 (Pop. 1.1 Mil.)
Miles from (Pop.) **Miles from** (Pop.)

Class Composition

Asian: 4 % **Black:** 4 % **Hispanic:** 5 % **White:** 85 % **Other:** 2 %
Total minority : 15 % **Foreign countries:** 4 % (200 students)
From public schools: 73 % **Students from in state:** 52 %

Housing (on campus)

Freshmen required to live on campus: Yes **Guaranteed for:** 1 year
Available for all students: 38 % **Fraternity / Sorority housing:** Yes / Yes
On-campus married student housing: Yes **Women-only dorms available:** Yes

Campus Life

Students living on campus: NA % **Remain weekends:** NA % **Handicap access:** 90 %
Car regulations: All may have
Number with cars: NA % **Adequacy of on-campus parking:** Fair
Number of fraternities: 15 **Chapter houses:** 15 **Number of sororities:** 12 **Chapter houses:** 12
Students belonging to fraternities: 45 % **Students belonging to sororities:** 50 %

Libraries and Computers

Books: 2 Million **Periodicals:** 6,500 **Microform items:** 490,000
Microcomputers available: Yes **Microcomputers networked:** NA

Classes

Faculty / Student Ratio: 1/14 **Classes taught by teacher assistants:** 20 %
Most popular majors: Advertising, Finance **Classes begin:** Late Aug.
Baccalaureate degrees offered: BA, BBA, BPA, B MUS, BS

Sports

Division: I **Except:** **Physical ed requirements:** 2 hours credit
Students participating in intercollegiate sports: 5 % **In intramural sports:** 40 %
Additional intercollegiate and/or intramural sports: (not found at all colleges)

Crew: Yes **Ice Hockey:** Yes/M **Lacrosse:** Yes **Wrestling:** No
Rugby: Yes **Sailing:** Yes **Skiing:** No
Squash: No **Ultimate Frisbee:** No **Water Polo:** No

Alumni

Number living: 61,000 **Annual giving:** $ 5 Million **Participation:** 20 %
Average annual gift: $ NA **Average per student:** $NA

3-2 Programs (2 degrees in 5 years)

Business Administration Program

Observation and Opinion of:

Undergraduates and graduates ______________________________

____

College counselor ______________________________

____

STANFORD UNIVERSITY (Private)

Stanford, CA 94305

MOST SELECTIVE
(Composite rating of guide books)

Main tel.: 415-723-2300
Admissions tel.: 415-723-2091
Financial aid tel.: 415-723-3058
Scheduled Airline Service: San Francisco
Miles to airport: 30

Founded: 1891
Nickname: Cardinal
Religious affiliation: None
(Coed since 1921)

Student Body

Undergraduates: 6,500 **Men:** 57 % **Women:** 43 %
Graduate students: 6,850 **Freshman class:** 1,600

Academics

SAT Averages: 1340 **Verbal:** 640 **Math:** 700 **(Taking SATs:** 90 %**)**
700-800: V 23 % **M** 61 % **500-600: V** 22 % **M** 8 %
600-700: V 52 % **M** 30 % **400-500: V** 3 % **M** 1 % **300-400: V** NA % **M** NA %
High school class rank: Top fifth 96 % **2nd fifth** 2 % **3rd fifth** NA %

Admissions

Applied: 12,950 **Accepted:** 22 % **Matriculated:** 56 %
Deadline: Dec. 15 **Accept common application:** No
Interview recommended: No **Off-campus interview available:** No
Evaluative: NA **Informational only:** NA **LD program:** Yes
Night in dorm provided: Yes **Non-refundable application fee:** $50
Early decision program: No **Applied:** NA **Accepted:** NA % **Deadline:** NA
Freshmen accepted other than Fall term: 0 % **SAT/FAF Code #** 4704

Transfers

Applied: 1,160 **Accepted:** 16 % **Application deadline for Fall:** Mar. 15 **Spring:** NA
Minimum grades recommended: NA **All new students who were transfers into all classes:** 8 %

Class Experience

Return 2nd year: 97 % **Graduate after 4 years:** 91 % **To graduate school within 5 years:** NA %

Cost

Tuition deposit: $NA **Total cost (Including school's estimate on fees and books):** $24,000
Tuition: $16,535 **(In state:** $ **)** **Room and board:** $6,500
Annual giving by parents: $1.2 Million **Average per student:** $180

Financial Aid

Average total package per student: $NA **Number receiving aid:** 60 %
Average scholarships and grants: $7,644 **Average loans:** $NA **Work-study program:** Yes
Undergraduates working on campus: 40 % **Average earnings:** $NA
Non-need scholarships NA % **Athletic scholarships:** Yes **FAF deadline:** Feb. 1
Off-campus part-time employment: Excellent **CO-OP program:** No
ROTC: at Santa Clara **NROTC:** at Berkeley **AFROTC:** at San Jose

Endowment

Total: $2 Billion **Per student (including graduate students):** $150,000

Location

Acres: 8,200 **Setting:** Surburban
Miles from town center: 2 **(Pop.** 80,000)
30 **Miles from** San Francisco **(Pop.** 700,000)
20 **Miles from** San Jose **(Pop.** 630,000)

Class Composition

Asian: 18 % **Black:** 8 % **Hispanic:** 10 % **White:** 60 % **Other:** 4 %
Total minority : 40 % **Foreign countries:** 3 % (40 students)
From public schools: 37 % **Students from in state:** 37 %

Housing (on campus)

Freshmen required to live on campus: Yes
Available for all students: 91 %
On-campus married student housing: Yes
Guaranteed for: 1 year
Fraternity / Sorority housing: Yes/ No
Women-only dorms available: Yes

Campus Life

Students living on campus: 91 % **Remain weekends:** 90 % **Handicap access:** 85 %
Car regulations: All may have
Number with cars: 50 %
Adequacy of on-campus parking: Fair
Number of fraternities: 17 **Chapter houses:** 9
Students belonging to fraternities: 10 %
Number of sororities: 8 **Chapter houses:** 0
Students belonging to sororities: 10 %

Libraries and Computers

Books: 5.3 Million **Periodicals:** 50,000 **Microform items:** 2.6 Million
Microcomputers available: Yes **Microcomputers networked:** Yes

Classes

Faculty / Student Ratio: 1/10 **Classes taught by teacher assistants:** 10 %
Most popular majors: Economics, Engineering **Classes begin:** Late Sept.
Baccalaureate degrees offered: AB, BAS, BS

Sports

Division: I **Except:** **Physical ed requirements:** None
Students participating in intercollegiate sports: 12 % **In intramural sports:** 50 %
Additional intercollegiate and/or intramural sports: (not found at all colleges)

Crew: Yes **Ice Hockey:** Yes **Lacrosse:** Yes **Wrestling:** Yes
Rugby: Yes **Sailing:** Yes **Skiing:** NA
Squash: Yes **Ultimate Frisbee:** Yes **Water Polo:** Yes/M

Alumni

Number living: 157,000 **Annual giving:** $68 Million **Participation:** 21 %
Average annual gift: $ 2,200 **Average per student:** $2,200

3-2 Programs (2 degrees in 5 years)

Engineering with Claremont College and others
In-house bachelor's/master's degree programs

Observation and Opinion of:

Undergraduates and graduates ______________________________

____

College counselor ______________________________

____

SWARTHMORE COLLEGE (Private)

Swarthmore, PA 19081

MOST SELECTIVE
(Composite rating of guide books)

Main tel.: 215-328-8000
Admissions tel.: 215-328-8300
Financial aid tel.: 215-328-8358
Scheduled Airline Service: Philadelphia
Miles to airport: 15

Founded: 1864
Nickname: Little Quakers
Religious affiliation: None
(Coed since 1864)

Student Body

Undergraduates: 1,300 **Men:** 53 % **Women:** 47 %
Graduate students: 0 **Freshman class:** 360

Academics

SAT Averages: 1330 **Verbal:** 650 **Math:** 680 (Taking SATs: 100 %)
700-800: V 26 % M 42 % **500-600:** V 18 % M 9 %
600-700: V 51 % M 49 % **400-500:** V 5% M 0 % **300-400:** V NA % M NA%
High school class rank: Top fifth 92 % **2nd fifth** 5 % **3rd fifth** 3 %

Admissions

Applied: 3,240 **Accepted:** 31 % **Matriculated:** 31 %
Deadline: Feb. 1 **Accept common application:** Yes
Interview recommended: Yes **Off-campus interview available:** Yes
Evaluative: Yes **Informational only:** No **LD program:** No
Night in dorm provided: NA **Non-refundable application fee:** $40
Early decision program: Yes **Applied:** 200 **Accepted:** 45 % **Deadline:** Jan. 1
Freshmen accepted other than Fall term: 0 % **SAT/FAF Code #** 2821

Transfers

Applied: 300 **Accepted:** 7 % **Application deadline for Fall:** Apr. 15 **Spring:** Nov. 15
Minimum grades recommended: 3.0 **All new students who were transfers into all classes:** 5 %

Class Experience

Return 2nd year: 99 % **Graduate after 4 years:** 80 % **To graduate school within 5 years:** 40 %

Cost

Tuition deposit: $100 **Total cost (Including school's estimate on fees and books):** $23,500
Tuition: $17,460 **(In state: $)** **Room and board:** $5,844
Annual giving by parents: $192,000 **Average per student:** $150

Financial Aid

Average total package per student: $11,500 **Number receiving aid:** 60 %
Average scholarships and grants: $9,500 **Average loans:** $2,000 **Work-study program:** Yes
Undergraduates working on campus: 75 % **Average earnings:** $1,500
Non-need scholarships 0 % **Athletic scholarships:** 0 **FAF deadline:** Feb. 15
Off-campus part-time employment: Fair **CO-OP program:** NA
ROTC: No **NROTC:** at U of PA **AFROTC:** No

Endowment

Total: $342 Million **Per student (including graduate students):** $260,000

Location

Acres: 300 **Setting:** Surburban
Miles from town center: 1 (Pop. 6,000)
15 Miles from Phila (Pop. 1.7 Mil.)
Miles from (Pop.)

Class Composition

Asian: 9 % **Black:** 8 % **Hispanic:** 3 % **White:** 80 % **Other:** NA %
Total minority : 20 % **Foreign countries:** 10 % (130 students)
From public schools: 68% **Students from in state:** 10 %

Housing (on campus)

Freshmen required to live on campus: Yes
Guaranteed for: 4 years
Available for all students: 92 %
Fraternity / Sorority housing: Yes / No
On-campus married student housing: No
Women-only dorms available: Yes

Campus Life

Students living on campus: 92 % **Remain weekends:** 90 % **Handicap access:** 50 %
Car regulations: No freshmen, others with permission from dean
Number with cars: 10%
Adequacy of on-campus parking: NA
Number of fraternities: 3 **Chapter houses:** 3
Number of sororities: 0 **Chapter houses:** 0
Students belonging to fraternities: 15 %
Students belonging to sororities: 0 %

Libraries and Computers

Books: 678,000 **Periodicals:** 2,300 **Microform items:** 6,800
Microcomputers available: Yes **Microcomputers networked:** NA

Classes

Faculty / Student Ratio: 1/9 **Classes taught by teacher assistants:** NA %
Most popular majors: Economics, Engineering **Classes begin:** Early Sept.
Baccalaureate degrees offered: AB, BS Engineering

Sports

Division: III **Except:** **Physical ed requirements:** 2 semesters
Students participating in intercollegiate sports: 33 % **In intramural sports:** 55 %
Additional intercollegiate and/or intramural sports: (not found at all colleges)

Crew: No **Ice Hockey:** Yes **Lacrosse:** Yes **Wrestling:** Yes/M
Rugby: Yes **Sailing:** Yes **Skiing:** No
Squash: Yes **Ultimate Frisbee:** Yes **Water Polo:** No

Alumni

Number living: 15,000 **Annual giving:** $ 11.5 Mil. **Participation:** 61 %
Average annual gift: $ 1,200 **Average per student:** $8,800

3-2 Programs (2 degrees in 5 years)

Course interchange with Bryn Mawr, Haverford and U of Pennsylvania

Observation and Opinion of:

Undergraduates and graduates ______________________________

____

College counselor ______________________________

____

SYRACUSE UNIVERSITY (Private)

201 Administration Building
Syracuse, NY 13244

VERY SELECTIVE
(Composite rating of guide books)

Main tel.: 315-443-1870
Admissions tel.: 315-443-3611
Financial aid tel.: 315-443-1513
Scheduled Airline Service: Syracuse
Miles to airport: 10

Founded: 1870
Nickname: Orangemen
Religious affiliation: None
(Coed since 1870)

Student Body

Undergraduates: 12,000 **Men:** 48 % **Women:** 52 %
Graduate students: 4,500 **Freshman class:** 2,770

Academics

SAT Averages: 1120 **Verbal:** 520 **Math:** 600 **(Taking SATs:** 95 %**)**
700-800: V 2 % **M** 7 % **500-600: V** 54 % **M** 51 %
600-700: V 12 % **M** 29 % **400-500: V** 31 % **M** 12 % **300-400: V** 1 % **M** 1 %
High school class rank: Top fifth 63 % **2nd fifth** 23 % **3rd fifth** 12 %

Admissions

Applied: 13,555 **Accepted:** 64 % **Matriculated:** 32 %
Deadline: Feb. 1 **Accept common application:** No
Interview recommended: Yes **Off-campus interview available:** No
Evaluative: Yes **Informational only:** No **LD program:** Yes
Night in dorm provided: No **Non-refundable application fee:** $40
Early decision program: Yes **Applied:** 468 **Accepted:** 90 % **Deadline:** Dec. 1
Freshmen accepted other than Fall term: 1 % **SAT/FAF Code #** 2823

Transfers

Applied: 1,677 **Accepted:** 60 % **Application deadline for Fall:** Jun. 1 **Spring:** Nov. 15
Minimum grades recommended: 2.5 **All new students who were transfers into all classes:** 16 %

Class Experience

Return 2nd year: 91 % **Graduate after 4 years:** 70 % **To graduate school within 1 year:** 30 %

Cost

Tuition deposit: $200 **Total cost (Including school's estimate on fees and books):** $21,140
Tuition: $13,480 **(In state:** $ **)** **Room and board:** $6,000
Annual giving by parents: $525,000 **Average per student:** $45

Financial Aid

Average total package per student: $NA **Number receiving aid:** 49 %
Average scholarships and grants: $NA **Average loans:** $NA **Work-study program:** Yes
Undergraduates working on campus: 53 % **Average earnings:** $1,200
Non-need scholarships 0 % **Athletic scholarships:** 0 **FAF deadline:** Jan. 31
Off-campus part-time employment: Good **CO-OP program:** Yes
ROTC: Yes **NROTC:** No **AFROTC:** Yes

Endowment

Total: $172 Million **Per student (including graduate students):** $10,000

Location

Acres: 200 **Setting:** City **Miles from town center:** 2 **(Pop.** 250,000**)**
210 **Miles from** NYC **(Pop.** 7 Mil **)** **Miles from** **(Pop.** **)**

Class Composition

Asian: 3 % **Black:** 9 % **Hispanic:** 4 % **White:** 83 % **Other:** 1 %
Total minority : 17 % **Foreign countries:** 2 % (240 students)
From public schools: 80 % **Students from in state:** 35 %

Housing (on campus)

Freshmen required to live on campus: Yes **Guaranteed for:** 1 year
Available for all students: 75 % **Fraternity / Sorority housing:** Yes / Yes
On-campus married student housing: Yes **Women-only dorms available:** Yes

Campus Life

Students living on campus: 75 % **Remain weekends:** 85 % **Handicap access:** 85 %
Car regulations: No freshmen or sophomores
Number with cars: NA % **Adequacy of on-campus parking:** NA
Number of fraternities: 25 **Chapter houses:** 22 **Number of sororities:** 16 **Chapter houses:** 15
Students belonging to fraternities: 20 % **Students belonging to sororities:** 28 %

Libraries and Computers

Books: 2.3 Million **Periodicals:** 18,000 **Microform items:** 3.6 Million
Microcomputers available: Yes **Microcomputers networked:** Yes

Classes

Faculty / Student Ratio: 1/11 **Classes taught by teacher assistants:** 20 %
Most popular majors: Social Science, Communications **Classes begin:** Late Aug.
Baccalaureate degrees offered: BA, B ARCH, BPA, B IND DESIGN, B MUS, BS, BSW

Sports

Division: I **Except:** **Physical ed requirements:** NA
Students participating in intercollegiate sports: 3 % **In intramural sports:** 50 %
Additional intercollegiate and/or intramural sports: (not found at all colleges)

Crew: Yes	**Ice Hockey:** No	**Lacrosse:** Yes/M	**Wrestling:** Yes/M
Rugby: Yes	**Sailing:** No	**Skiing:** Yes	
Squash: Yes	**Ultimate Frisbee:** No	**Water Polo:** No	

Alumni

Number living: 133,000 **Annual giving:** $ 9.5 Mil. **Participation:** 19 %
Average annual gift: $ 400 **Average per student:** $550

3-2 Programs (2 degrees in 5 years)

Engineering, Law, MBA programs with accredited schools

Observation and Opinion of:

Undergraduates and graduates ______________________________

____

College counselor ______________________________

____

UNIVERSITY OF TEXAS (Austin) (Private)

Austin, TX 78712-1159

HIGHLY SELECTIVE
(Composite rating of guide books)

Main tel.: 512-471-3434
Admissions tel.: 512-471-1711
Financial aid tel.: 512-471-4001
Scheduled Airline Service: Austin
Miles to airport: 10

Founded: 1883
Nickname: Longhorns
Religious affiliation: None
(Coed since 1883)

Student Body

Undergraduates: 37,000 **Men:** 58 % **Women:** 42 %
Graduate students: 12,000 **Freshman class:** 7,780

Academics

SAT Averages: 1105 **Verbal:** 515 **Math:** 590 **(Taking SATs:** 65 %**)**
700-800: V 3 % **M** 13 % **500-600: V** 40 % **M** 40 %
600-700: V 16 % **M** 33 % **400-500: V** 41 % **M** 14 % **300-400: V** NA % **M** NA %
High school class rank: Top fifth 78 % **2nd fifth** 17 % **3rd fifth** 4 %

Admissions

Applied: 16,000 **Accepted:** 73 % **Matriculated:** 60 %
Deadline: Mar. 1 **Accept common application:** No
Interview recommended: No **Off-campus interview available:** No
Evaluative: No **Informational only:** NA **LD program:** Yes
Night in dorm provided: No **Non-refundable application fee:** $25
Early decision program: No **Applied:** NA **Accepted:** NA % **Deadline:** NA
Freshmen accepted other than Fall term: 20 % **SAT/FAF Code #** 6882

Transfers

Applied: 5,743 **Accepted:** 50 % **Application deadline for Fall:** Mar. 1 **Spring:** Oct. 1
Minimum grades recommended: 2.5 **All new students who were transfers into all classes:** 30 %

Class Experience

Return 2nd year: 83 % **Graduate after 4 years:** 52 % **To graduate school within 5 years:** NA %

Cost

Tuition deposit: $0 **Total cost (Including school's estimate on fees and books):** $9,500
Tuition: $5,000 **(In state:** $ **)** **Room and board:** $3,500
Annual giving by parents: $NA **Average per student:** $NA

Financial Aid

Average total package per student: $5,800 **Number receiving aid:** 33 %
Average scholarships and grants: $3,870 **Average loans:** $1,900 **Work-study program:** Yes
Undergraduates working on campus: 20 % **Average earnings:** $1,400
Non-need scholarships 50 % **Athletic scholarships:** Yes **FAF deadline:** Mar. 1
Off-campus part-time employment: Good **CO-OP program:** Yes
ROTC: Yes **NROTC:** Yes **AFROTC:** Yes

Endowment

Total: $355 Million **Per student (including graduate students):** $7,000

Location

Acres: 300 **Setting:** Urban **Miles from town center:** 2 **(Pop.** 495,000**)**
Miles from **(Pop.** **)** **Miles from** **(Pop.** **)**

Class Composition

Asian: 6 % **Black:** 4 % **Hispanic:** 11 % **White:** 71 % **Other:** 8 %
Total minority : 29 % **Foreign countries:** 4 % (1,400 students)
From public schools: NA % **Students from in state:** 94 %

Housing (on campus)

Freshmen required to live on campus: No **Guaranteed for:** 0 year
Available for all students: 13 % **Fraternity / Sorority housing:** Yes / Yes
On-campus married student housing: Yes **Women-only dorms available:** Yes

Campus Life

Students living on campus: 13 % **Remain weekends:** NA % **Handicap access:** 85 %
Car regulations: All may have
Number with cars: 50 % **Adequacy of on-campus parking:** Poor
Number of fraternities: 33 **Chapter houses:** 29 **Number of sororities:** 18 **Chapter houses:** 16
Students belonging to fraternities: 14 % **Students belonging to sororities:** 14 %

Libraries and Computers

Books: 6 Million **Periodicals:** 80,000 **Microform items:** 4 Million
Microcomputers available: Yes **Microcomputers networked:** Yes

Classes

Faculty / Student Ratio: 1/20 **Classes taught by teacher assistants:** 30 %
Most popular majors: Business, Accounting **Classes begin:** Late Aug.
Baccalaureate degrees offered: BA, B ARCH, BBA, BPA, B JOURNALISM, B MUS, BS, BSW

Sports

Division: I **Except:** **Physical ed requirements:** None
Students participating in intercollegiate sports: 1 % **In intramural sports:** 78 %
Additional intercollegiate and/or intramural sports: (not found at all colleges)
Crew: Yes **Ice Hockey:** No **Lacrosse:** Yes **Wrestling:** Yes/M
Rugby: No **Sailing:** Yes **Skiing:** Yes
Squash: Yes **Ultimate Frisbee:** Yes **Water Polo:** Yes

Alumni

Number living: 225,000 **Annual giving:** $ 6.2 Mil. **Participation:** 11 %
Average annual gift: $ 250 **Average per student:** $120

3-2 Programs (2 degrees in 5 years)

Business Administration, Engineering and Architecture

Observation and Opinion of:

Undergraduates and graduates ______________________________

____

College counselor ______________________________

____

TRINITY COLLEGE (Connecticut) (Private)

Summit Street
Hartford, CT 06016

HIGHLY SELECTIVE
(Composite rating of guide books)

Main tel.: 203-297-2000
Admissions tel.: 203-297-2180
Financial aid tel.: 203-297-2046
Scheduled Airline Service: Hartford
Miles to airport: 12

Founded: 1823
Nickname: Bantams
Religious affiliation: None
(Coed since 1969)

Student Body

Undergraduates: 1,750 **Men:** 55 % **Women:** 45 %
Graduate students: 180 **Freshman class:** 427

Academics

SAT Averages: 1180 **Verbal:** 560 **Math:** 620 **(Taking SATs:** 92 %**)**
700-800: V 4 % M 13 % **500-600:** V 50 % M 27 %
600-700: V 30 % M 57 % **400-500:** V 16 % M 3 % **300-400:** V NA % M NA %
High school class rank: Top fifth 40 % **2nd fifth** 13 % **3rd fifth** 3 %

Admissions

Applied: 2,900 **Accepted:** 50 % **Matriculated:** 29 %
Deadline: Jan. 15 **Accept common application:** Yes
Interview recommended: Yes **Off-campus interview available:** No
Evaluative: Yes **Informational only:** No **LD program:** No
Night in dorm provided: Yes **Non-refundable application fee:** $35
Early decision program: Yes **Applied:** 180 **Accepted:** 48 % **Deadline:** Dec. 1
Freshmen accepted other than Fall term: NA % **SAT/FAF Code #** 3899

Transfers

Applied: 175 **Accepted:** 58 % **Application deadline for Fall:** Mar. 15 **Spring:** Nov. 15
Minimum grades recommended: 3.2 **All new students who were transfers into all classes:** 9 %

Class Experience

Return 2nd year: 95 % **Graduate after 4 years:** 88 % **To graduate school within 5 years:** 60 %

Cost

Tuition deposit: $200 **Total cost (Including school's estimate on fees and books):** $23,200
Tuition: $17,090 **(In state:** $ **)** **Room and board:** $4,800
Annual giving by parents: $315,000 **Average per student:** $185

Financial Aid

Average total package per student: $16,700 **Number receiving aid:** 38 %
Average scholarships and grants: $14,100 **Average loans:** $2,625 **Work-study program:** NA
Undergraduates working on campus: 30 % **Average earnings:** $1,300
Non-need scholarships 0 % **Athletic scholarships:** NA **FAF deadline:** Feb. 15
Off-campus part-time employment: Excellent **CO-OP program:** NA
ROTC: at U of Conn **NROTC:** No **AFROTC:** No

Endowment

Total: $137 Million **Per student (including graduate students):** $65,000

Location

Acres: 90 **Setting:** Urban **Miles from town center:** 3 **(Pop.** 700,000)
Miles from **(Pop.**) **Miles from** **(Pop.**)

Class Composition

Asian: 6 % **Black:** 7 % **Hispanic:** 4 % **White:** 81 % **Other:** 2 %
Total minority : 19 % **Foreign countries:** 3 % (50 students)
From public schools: 59 % **Students from in state:** 34 %

Housing (on campus)

Freshmen required to live on campus: No **Guaranteed for:** 1 year
Available for all students: 90 % **Fraternity / Sorority housing:** No / No
On-campus married student housing: Yes **Women-only dorms available:** Yes

Campus Life

Students living on campus: 90 % **Remain weekends:** 80 % **Handicap access:** 85 %
Car regulations: No freshmen
Number with cars: NA % **Adequacy of on-campus parking:** Poor
Number of fraternities: 7 **Chapter houses:** 0 **Number of sororities:** 2 **Chapter houses:** 0
Students belonging to fraternities: 20 % **Students belonging to sororities:** 10 %

Libraries and Computers

Books: 811,000 **Periodicals:** 2,150 **Microform items:** 200,000
Microcomputers available: NA **Microcomputers networked:** NA

Classes

Faculty / Student Ratio: 1/12 **Classes taught by teacher assistants:** 0 %
Most popular majors: History, Economics **Classes begin:** Late Aug.
Baccalaureate degrees offered: BA, BS

Sports

Division: III **Except:** **Physical ed requirements:** None
Students participating in intercollegiate sports: 50 % **In intramural sports:** 40 %
Additional intercollegiate and/or intramural sports: (not found at all colleges)
Crew: Yes **Ice Hockey:** Yes **Lacrosse:** Yes **Wrestling:** Yes/M
Rugby: Yes **Sailing:** No **Skiing:** Yes
Squash: Yes **Ultimate Frisbee:** No **Water Polo:** Yes

Alumni

Number living: 17,200 **Annual giving:** $ 4.5 Mil. **Participation:** 45 %
Average annual gift: $ 600 **Average per student:** $2,400

3-2 Programs (2 degrees in 5 years)

Engineering/MS program
Member of 12-college exchange program

Observation and Opinion of:

Undergraduates and graduates ______________________________

____

College counselor ______________________________

____

TRINITY UNIVERSITY (Private)

715 Stadium Drive
San Antonia, TX 78212

HIGHLY SELECTIVE
(Composite rating of guide books)

Main tel.: 512-736-7011
Admissions tel.: 512-736-7207
Financial aid tel.: 512-736-8315
Scheduled Airline Service: San Antonio
Miles to airport: 5

Founded: 1869
Nickname: Tigers
Religious affiliation: Presbyterian
(Coed since 1869)

Student Body

Undergraduates: 2,250 **Men:** 46 % **Women:** 54 %
Graduate students: 200 **Freshman class:** 600

Academics

SAT Averages: 1210 **Verbal:** 585 **Math:** 625 **(Taking SATs:** 95 %)
700-800: V 4 % **M** 14 % **500-600: V** 46 % **M** 34 %
600-700: V 31 % **M** 47 % **400-500: V** 18 % **M** 5 % **300-400: V** 1 % **M** 0 %
High school class rank: Top fifth 83 % **2nd fifth** 17 % **3rd fifth** NA %

Admissions

Applied: 2,235 **Accepted:** 75 % **Matriculated:** 36 %
Deadline: Feb. 1 **Accept common application:** Yes
Interview recommended: Yes **Off-campus interview available:** No
Evaluative: Yes **Informational only:** NA **LD program:** No
Night in dorm provided: Yes **Non-refundable application fee:** $25
Early decision program: Yes **Applied:** 115 **Accepted:** 90 % **Deadline:** Dec. 15
Freshmen accepted other than Fall term: 1 % **SAT/FAF Code #** 6831

Transfers

Applied: 132 **Accepted:** 30 % **Application deadline for Fall:** Feb. 1 **Spring:** Dec. 1
Minimum grades recommended: 2.0 **All new students who were transfers into all classes:** 2 %

Class Experience

Return 2nd year: 90 % **Graduate after 4 years:** 69 % **To graduate school within 5 years:** 60 %

Cost

Tuition deposit: $100 **Total cost (Including school's estimate on fees and books):** $16,500
Tuition: $10,950 **(In state:** $) **Room and board:** $3,850
Annual giving by parents: $182,000 **Average per student:** $80

Financial Aid

Average total package per student: $NA **Number receiving aid:** 69 %
Average scholarships and grants: $8,136 **Average loans:** $NA **Work-study program:** Yes
Undergraduates working on campus: 10 % **Average earnings:** $1,050
Non-need scholarships 26 % **Athletic scholarships:** NA **FAF deadline:** Feb. 1
Off-campus part-time employment: Good **CO-OP program:** No
ROTC: at U of Texas **NROTC:** No **AFROTC:** at U of Texas

Endowment

Total: $285 Million **Per student (including graduate students):** $115,000

Location

Acres: 113 **Setting:** Surburban **Miles from town center:** 3 **(Pop.** 914,000**)**
Miles from **(Pop.** **)** **Miles from** **(Pop.** **)**

Class Composition

Asian: 5 % **Black:** 1 % **Hispanic:** 9 % **White:** 81 % **Other:** 4 %
Total minority : 94 % **Foreign countries:** 1 % (30 students)
From public schools: 80 % **Students from in state:** 60 %

Housing (on campus)

Freshmen required to live on campus: Yes **Guaranteed for:** 4 years
Available for all students: 80 % **Fraternity / Sorority housing:** 0 / 0
On-campus married student housing: NA **Women-only dorms available:** Yes

Campus Life

Students living on campus: 75 % **Remain weekends:** NA % **Handicap access:** 90 %
Car regulations: All may have
Number with cars: 50 % **Adequacy of on-campus parking:** Good
Number of fraternities: 6 **Chapter houses:** 0 **Number of sororities:** 6 **Chapter houses:** 0
Students belonging to fraternities: 29 % **Students belonging to sororities:** 29 %

Libraries and Computers

Books: 675,000 **Periodicals:** 2,500 **Microform items:** 225,000
Microcomputers available: Yes **Microcomputers networked:** Yes

Classes

Faculty / Student Ratio: 1/11 **Classes taught by teacher assistants:** 0 %
Most popular majors: Business, Economics **Classes begin:** Early Sept.
Baccalaureate degrees offered: BA, B MUS, BS

Sports

Division: III **Except:** **Physical ed requirements:** None
Students participating in intercollegiate sports: 10 % **In intramural sports:** 75 %
Additional intercollegiate and/or intramural sports: (not found at all colleges)
Crew: No **Ice Hockey:** No **Lacrosse:** No **Wrestling:** No
Rugby: No **Sailing:** No **Skiing:** No
Squash: No **Ultimate Frisbee:** Yes **Water Polo:** Yes

Alumni

Number living: 19,000 **Annual giving:** $ 450,000 **Participation:** 24 %
Average annual gift: $ 100 **Average per student:** $180

3-2 Programs (2 degrees in 5 years)

Bachelor's degree offered if entering professional school after completing junior year
MAT program for education majors

Observation and Opinion of:

Undergraduates and graduates ______________________________

____

College counselor ______________________________

____

TUFTS UNIVERSITY (Private)

Medford, MA 02155

MOST SELECTIVE
(Composite rating of guide books)

Main tel.: 617-628-5060
Admissions tel.: 617-381-3170
Financial aid tel.: 617-381-3528
Scheduled Airline Service: Boston
Miles to airport: 10

Founded: 1852
Nickname: Jumbos
Religious affiliation: None
(Coed since 1890)

Student Body

Undergraduates: 4,700 **Men:** 52 % **Women:** 48 %
Graduate students: 3,050 **Freshman class:** 1,115

Academics

SAT Averages: 1250 **Verbal:** 595 **Math:** 655 **(Taking SATs:** 95 %**)**
700-800: V 5 % **M** 30 % **500-600: V** 43 % **M** 15 %
600-700: V 45 % **M** 53 % **400-500: V** 7 % **M** 2 % **300-400: V** NA % **M** NA %
High school class rank: Top fifth 86 % **2nd fifth** 10 % **3rd fifth** 3 %

Admissions

Applied: 7,200 **Accepted:** 46 % **Matriculated:** 34 %
Deadline: Jan. 1 **Accept common application:** NA
Interview recommended: Yes **Off-campus interview available:** No
Evaluative: Yes **Informational only:** NA **LD program:** NA
Night in dorm provided: No **Non-refundable application fee:** $45
Early decision program: Yes **Applied:** 532 **Accepted:** 43 % **Deadline:** Jan. 1
Freshmen accepted other than Fall term: 0 % **SAT/FAF Code #** 3901

Transfers

Applied: 534 **Accepted:** 27 % **Application deadline for Fall:** Mar. 1 **Spring:** Nov. 15
Minimum grades recommended: C **All new students who were transfers into all classes:** 6 %

Class Experience

Return 2nd year: 99 % **Graduate after 4 years:** 90 % **To graduate school within 5 years:** NA %

Cost

Tuition deposit: $600 **Total cost (Including school's estimate on fees and books):** $23,500
Tuition: $17,897 **(In state: $)** **Room and board:** $5,400
Annual giving by parents: $757,000 **Average per student:** $200

Financial Aid

Average total package per student: $12,300 **Number receiving aid:** 51 %
Average scholarships and grants: $9,900 **Average loans:** $2,377 **Work-study program:** NA
Undergraduates working on campus: 46 % **Average earnings:** $1,300
Non-need scholarships 1 % **Athletic scholarships:** NA **FAF deadline:** Feb. 1
Off-campus part-time employment: Excellent **CO-OP program:** NA
ROTC: at MIT **NROTC:** at MIT **AFROTC:** at MIT

Endowment

Total: $156 Million **Per student (including graduate students):** $21,000

Location

Acres: 150 **Setting:** Surburban
Miles from town center: 1 **(Pop.** 65,000**)**
5 **Miles from** Boston **(Pop.** 700,000 **)**
Miles from (Pop.)

Class Composition

Asian: 8 % **Black:** 4 % **Hispanic:** 3% **White:** 79 % **Other:** 6 %
Total minority : 21 % **Foreign countries:** 6 % (250 students)
From public schools: 64 % **Students from in state:** 74 %

Housing (on campus)

Freshmen required to live on campus: Yes
Guaranteed for: 1 year
Available for all students: 80 %
Fraternity / Sorority housing: Yes / Yes
On-campus married student housing: NA
Women-only dorms available: Yes

Campus Life

Students living on campus: 80 % **Remain weekends:** 95 % **Handicap access:** 85 %
Car regulations: No freshmen
Number with cars: 30 %
Adequacy of on-campus parking: Poor
Number of fraternities: 11 **Chapter houses:** 9
Number of sororities: 3 **Chapter houses:** 2
Students belonging to fraternities: 15 %
Students belonging to sororities: 4 %

Libraries and Computers

Books: 717,000 **Periodicals:** 5,000 **Microform items:** 802,000
Microcomputers available: Yes **Microcomputers networked:** Yes

Classes

Faculty / Student Ratio: NA **Classes taught by teacher assistants:** 10 %
Most popular majors: Political Science, Economics **Classes begin:** Early Sept.
Baccalaureate degrees offered: BA, BS, BSCE, BSCHE, BSCOE, BSED, BSEE, BS ENG SCI, BS ME,

Sports

Division: III **Except:** **Physical ed requirements:** None
Students participating in intercollegiate sports: 20 % **In intramural sports:** 75 %
Additional intercollegiate and/or intramural sports: (not found at all colleges)

Crew: Yes	**Ice Hockey:** Yes	**Lacrosse:** Yes	**Wrestling:** No
Rugby: Yes	**Sailing:** Yes	**Skiing:** Yes	
Squash: Yes	**Ultimate Frisbee:** Yes	**Water Polo:** No	

Alumni

Number living: 66,000 **Annual giving:** $ 14.3 Mil. **Participation:** 42 %
Average annual gift: $ 870 **Average per student:** $2,000

3-2 Programs (2 degrees in 5 years)

Engineering/Liberal Arts program
Cross registration with Boston Coll, Boston U, and Brandeis

Observation and Opinion of:

Undergraduates and graduates ______________________________

____

College counselor ______________________________

____

TULANE UNIVERSITY (Private)

6823 St. Charles Avenue
New Orleans, LA 70118

HIGHLY SELECTIVE
(Composite rating of guide books)

Main tel.: 504-865-5000
Admissions tel.: 504-865-5731
Financial aid tel.: 504-865-5723
Scheduled Airline Service: New Orleans
Miles to airport: 8

Founded: 1834
Nickname: Green Wave
Religious affiliation: None
(Coed since 1886)

Student Body

Undergraduates: 5,600 **Men:** 53 % **Women:** 47 %
Graduate students: 4,000 **Freshman class:** 1,330

Academics

SAT Averages: 1175 **Verbal:** 565 **Math:** 610 **(Taking SATs:** NA **%)**
700-800: V 5 % **M** 12 % **500-600: V** 42 % **M** 40 %
600-700: V 25 % **M** 36 % **400-500: V** 26 % **M** 11 % **300-400: V** 2 % **M** 1 %
High school class rank: Top fifth 57 % **2nd fifth** 30 % **3rd fifth** 11 %

Admissions

Applied: 6,884 **Accepted:** 72 % **Matriculated:** 27 %
Deadline: Jan. 15 **Accept common application:** Yes
Interview recommended: Yes **Off-campus interview available:** No
Evaluative: No **Informational only:** Yes **LD program:** No
Night in dorm provided: Yes **Non-refundable application fee:** $35
Early decision program: Yes **Applied:** NA **Accepted:** NA % **Deadline:** NA
Freshmen accepted other than Fall term: Yes % **SAT/FAF Code #** 6832

Transfers

Applied: NA **Accepted:** 100 % **Application deadline for Fall:** NA **Spring:** NA
Minimum grades recommended: 3.0 **All new students who were transfers into all classes:** 7 %

Class Experience

Return 2nd year: 90 % **Graduate after 4 years:** 75% **To graduate school within 5 years:** 80 %

Cost

Tuition deposit: $150 **Total cost (Including school's estimate on fees and books):** $22,900
Tuition: $16,925 **(In state:** $ **)** **Room and board:** $5,600
Annual giving by parents: $554,000 **Average per student:** $100

Financial Aid

Average total package per student: $10,000 **Number receiving aid:** 48 %
Average scholarships and grants: $NA **Average loans:** $2,470 **Work-study program:** NA
Undergraduates working on campus: 30 % **Average earnings:** $900
Non-need scholarships 73 % **Athletic scholarships:** Yes **FAF deadline:** Feb. 1
Off-campus part-time employment: Good **CO-OP program:** No
ROTC: Yes **NROTC:** Yes **AFROTC:** Yes

Endowment

Total: $235 Million **Per student (including graduate students):** $20,000

Location

Acres: 110 **Setting:** City **Miles from town center:** 5 **(Pop.** 1.3 Million**)**
Miles from **(Pop.** **)** **Miles from** **(Pop.** **)**

Class Composition

Asian: 3 % **Black:** 8 % **Hispanic:** 4 % **White:** 84 % **Other:** 1 %
Total minority : 6 % **Foreign countries:** NA % (NA)
From public schools: 47 % **Students from in state:** 19 %

Housing (on campus)

Freshmen required to live on campus: Yes **Guaranteed for:** 1 year
Available for all students: 50 % **Fraternity / Sorority housing:** No / No
On-campus married student housing: Yes **Women-only dorms available:** Yes

Campus Life

Students living on campus: 50 % **Remain weekends:** NA % **Handicap access:** 85 %
Car regulations: All may have
Number with cars: 30% **Adequacy of on-campus parking:** Very poor
Number of fraternities: 19 **Chapter houses:** 0 **Number of sororities:** 10 **Chapter houses:** 0
Students belonging to fraternities: 34 % **Students belonging to sororities:** 38 %

Libraries and Computers

Books: 1.8 Million **Periodicals:** 16,700 **Microform items:** 1.9 Million
Microcomputers available: Yes **Microcomputers networked:** Yes

Classes

Faculty / Student Ratio: 1/14 **Classes taught by teacher assistants:** 30 %
Most popular majors: History, Psychology **Classes begin:** Sept.
Baccalaureate degrees offered: BA, B ARCH, BFA, BS, BSM

Sports

Division: I **Except:** **Physical ed requirements:** 1 to 2 years
Students participating in intercollegiate sports: 7 % **In intramural sports:** 85 %
Additional intercollegiate and/or intramural sports: (not found at all colleges)
Crew: Yes **Ice Hockey:** No **Lacrosse:** Yes **Wrestling:** Yes/M
Rugby: Yes **Sailing:** Yes **Skiing:** No
Squash: No **Ultimate Frisbee:** Yes **Water Polo:** No

Alumni

Number living: 64,000 **Annual giving:** $ 8.2 Mil. **Participation:** 23 %
Average annual gift: $ 570 **Average per student:** $850

3-2 Programs (2 degrees in 5 years)

BS/MBA with Tulane's Freeman School of Business

Observation and Opinion of:

Undergraduates and graduates ____________________

College counselor ____________________

UNIVERSITY OF TULSA (Private)

600 South College Avenue
Tulsa, OK 74104

HIGHLY SELECTIVE
(Composite rating of guide books)

Main tel.: 918-631-2000
Admissions tel.: 800-331-3050
Financial aid tel.: 918-631-2526
Scheduled Airline Service: Tulsa
Miles to airport: 7

Founded: 1894
Nickname: Hurricanes
Religious affiliation: Presbyterian
(Coed since 1894)

Student Body

Undergraduates: 2,600 **Men:** 53 % **Women:** 47 %
Graduate students: 1,350 **Freshman class:** 722

Academics

SAT Averages: 1100 **Verbal:** 525 **Math:** 575 **(Taking SATs:** 65 %**)**
700-800: V 2 % **M** 16 % **500-600: V** 48 % **M** 42 %
600-700: V 18 % **M** 31 % **400-500: V** 32 % **M** 14 % **300-400: V** 2 % **M** 3 %
High school class rank: Top fifth 47 % **2nd fifth** 19 % **3rd fifth** 10 %

Admissions

Applied: 1,635 **Accepted:** 92 % **Matriculated:** 48 %
Deadline: Rolling **Accept common application:** Yes
Interview recommended: NA **Off-campus interview available:** NA
Evaluative: NA **Informational only:** NA **LD program:** NA
Night in dorm provided: NA **Non-refundable application fee:** $35
Early decision program: No **Applied:** NA **Accepted:** NA % **Deadline:** NA
Freshmen accepted other than Fall term: 2 % **SAT/FAF Code #** 6883

Transfers

Applied: 582 **Accepted:** 78 % **Application deadline for Fall:** NA **Spring:** NA
Minimum grades recommended: 2.5 **All new students who were transfers into all classes:** 28 %

Class Experience

Return 2nd year: 85 % **Graduate after 4 years:** 65 % **To graduate school within 5 years:** 35 %

Cost

Tuition deposit: $100 **Total cost (Including school's estimate on fees and books):** $12,000
Tuition: $9,380 **(In state:** $ **)** **Room and board:** $3,650
Annual giving by parents: $404,000 **Average per student:** $100

Financial Aid

Average total package per student: $NA **Number receiving aid:** 60 %
Average scholarships and grants: $3,500 **Average loans:** $NA **Work-study program:** NA
Undergraduates working on campus: 35 % **Average earnings:** $1,500
Non-need scholarships 50 % **Athletic scholarships:** Yes **FAF deadline:** Mar. 1
Off-campus part-time employment: Excellent **CO-OP program:** No
ROTC: Yes **NROTC:** No **AFROTC:** No

Endowment

Total: $60 Million **Per student (including graduate students):** $14,000

Location

Acres: 100 **Setting:** Urban **Miles from town center:** 2 **(Pop.** 725,000**)**
100 **Miles from** Oklahoma City **(Pop.)** **Miles from (Pop.)**

Class Composition

Asian: 2 % **Black:** 5 % **Hispanic:** 1 % **White:** 81 % **Other:** 11 %
Total minority : 19 % **Foreign countries:** 10 % (260 students)
From public schools: 85 % **Students from in state:** 61 %

Housing (on campus)

Freshmen required to live on campus: Yes **Guaranteed for:** 1 year
Available for all students: 51 % **Fraternity / Sorority housing:** Yes / Yes
On-campus married student housing: Yes **Women-only dorms available:** Yes

Campus Life

Students living on campus: 51 % **Remain weekends:** NA % **Handicap access:** NA %
Car regulations: All may have
Number with cars: 60 % **Adequacy of on-campus parking:** Fair
Number of fraternities: 7 **Chapter houses:** 7 **Number of sororities:** 6 **Chapter houses:** 6
Students belonging to fraternities: 21 % **Students belonging to sororities:** 22 %

Libraries and Computers

Books: 2 Million **Periodicals:** 4,500 **Microform items:** 716,000
Microcomputers available: Yes **Microcomputers networked:** Yes

Classes

Faculty / Student Ratio: 1/12 **Classes taught by teacher assistants:** 20 %
Most popular majors: Communications, Engineering **Classes begin:** Late Aug.
Baccalaureate degrees offered: BA, BPA, B MUS ED, BS, BSBA, BSN

Sports

Division: I **Except:** **Physical ed requirements:** 4 semesters
Students participating in intercollegiate sports: 15 % **In intramural sports:** 15 %
Additional intercollegiate and/or intramural sports: (not found at all colleges)

Crew: No **Ice Hockey:** No **Lacrosse:** No **Wrestling:** No
Rugby: No **Sailing:** No **Skiing:** No
Squash: Yes **Ultimate Frisbee:** Yes **Water Polo:** Yes

Alumni

Number living: 26,500 **Annual giving:** $ 1.5 Mil. **Participation:** 12 %
Average annual gift: $ 450 **Average per student:** $400

3-2 Programs (2 degrees in 5 years)

5-year MBA program

Observation and Opinion of:

Undergraduates and graduates ______________________________

____

College counselor ______________________________

____

UNION COLLEGE (Private)

Schenectady, NY 12308

HIGHLY SELECTIVE
(Composite rating of guide books)

Main tel.: 518-370-6000
Admissions tel.: 518-370-6112
Financial aid tel.: 518-370-6123
Scheduled Airline Service: Albany
Miles to airport: 16

Founded: 1795
Nickname: Dutchmen
Religious affiliation: None
(Coed since 1970)

Student Body

Undergraduates: 2,000 **Men:** 57 % **Women:** 43 %
Graduate students: 250 **Freshman class:** 443

Academics

SAT Averages: 1170 **Verbal:** NA **Math:** NA **(Taking SATs:** NA %**)**
700-800: V NA % **M** NA % **500-600: V** NA % **M** NA %
600-700: V NA% **M** NA% **400-500: V** NA % **M** NA % **300-400: V** NA % **M** NA %
High school class rank: Top fifth 70 % **2nd fifth** 20 % **3rd fifth** NA %

Admissions

Applied: 2,750 **Accepted:** 52 % **Matriculated:** 31 %
Deadline: Feb. 1 **Accept common application:** Yes
Interview recommended: Yes **Off-campus interview available:** Yes
Evaluative: Yes **Informational only:** No **LD program:** NA
Night in dorm provided: Yes **Non-refundable application fee:** $35
Early decision program: Yes **Applied:** 217 **Accepted:** 77 % **Deadline:** Feb. 1
Freshmen accepted other than Fall term: 0 % **SAT/FAF Code #** 2920

Transfers

Applied: 113 **Accepted:** 65 % **Application deadline for Fall:** Feb. 1 **Spring:** Nov. 1
Minimum grades recommended: C **All new students who were transfers into all classes:** 11 %

Class Experience

Return 2nd year: 94 % **Graduate after 4 years:** 76 % **To graduate school within 1 year:** 35 %

Cost

Tuition deposit: $200 **Total cost (Including school's estimate on fees and books):** $23,900
Tuition: $16,600 **(In state:** $ **)** **Room and board:** $5,725
Annual giving by parents: $399,000 **Average per student:** $160

Financial Aid

Average total package per student: $NA **Number receiving aid:** 37 %
Average scholarships and grants: $8,800 **Average loans:** $2,200 **Work-study program:** NA
Undergraduates working on campus: 30 % **Average earnings:** $NA
Non-need scholarships 0 % **Athletic scholarships:** NA **FAF deadline:** Feb. 1
Off-campus part-time employment: NA **CO-OP program:** No
ROTC: at Siena **NROTC:** at RPI **AFROTC:** at RPI

Endowment

Total: $102 Million **Per student (including graduate students):** $34,000

Location

Acres: 100 **Setting:** Urban **Miles from town center:** 2 **(Pop.** 65,000**)**
15 **Miles from** Albany **(Pop.)** **Miles from** **(Pop.)**

Class Composition

Asian: 5 % **Black:** 3 % **Hispanic:** 3 % **White:** 88 % **Other:** 1 %
Total minority : 12 % **Foreign countries:** 2 % (400 students)
From public schools: 71 % **Students from in state:** 55 %

Housing (on campus)

Freshmen required to live on campus: Yes **Guaranteed for:** 3 years
Available for all students: 76 % **Fraternity / Sorority housing:** Yes / Yes
On-campus married student housing: Yes **Women-only dorms available:** Yes

Campus Life

Students living on campus: 76% **Remain weekends:** NA % **Handicap access:** NA %
Car regulations: All may have
Number with cars: 27 % **Adequacy of on-campus parking:** Fair
Number of fraternities: 18 **Chapter houses:** 13 **Number of sororities:** 4 **Chapter houses:** 3
Students belonging to fraternities: 45 % **Students belonging to sororities:** 25 %

Libraries and Computers

Books: 473,000 **Periodicals:** 2,300 **Microform items:** 460,000
Microcomputers available: Yes **Microcomputers networked:** Yes

Classes

Faculty / Student Ratio: 1/12 **Classes taught by teacher assistants:** 0 %
Most popular majors: Electrical Engineering, Political Science **Classes begin:** Early Sept.
Baccalaureate degrees offered: BA, BS, BSCE, BSEE, BSME

Sports

Division: III **Except:** **Physical ed requirements:** None
Students participating in intercollegiate sports: 35 % **In intramural sports:** 70 %
Additional intercollegiate and/or intramural sports: (not found at all colleges)
Crew: Yes **Ice Hockey:** Yes **Lacrosse:** Yes **Wrestling:** No
Rugby: Yes **Sailing:** Yes **Skiing:** Yes
Squash: Yes **Ultimate Frisbee:** Yes **Water Polo:** Yes

Alumni

Number living: 17,500 **Annual giving:** $ 4.9 Mil. **Participation:** 60 %
Average annual gift: $ 500 **Average per student:** $2,300

3-2 Programs (2 degrees in 5 years)

5-year BA/MBA and BS/MBA program
Cross registration with RPI and Skidmore

Observation and Opinion of:

Undergraduates and graduates ____________________

____

College counselor ____________________

____

UNITED STATES AIR FORCE ACADEMY (Public)

Colorado Springs, CO 80840

HIGHLY SELECTIVE
(Composite rating of guide books)

Main tel.: 719-472-1818
Admissions tel.: 719-472-2520
Financial aid tel.:
Scheduled Airline Service: Denver
Miles to airport: 45

Founded: 1955
Nickname: Falcons
Religious affiliation: None
(Coed since 1976)

Student Body

Undergraduates: 4,300 **Men:** 89 % **Women:** 11 %
Graduate students: 0 **Freshman class:** 1,390

Academics

SAT Averages: 1220 **Verbal:** 565 **Math:** 655 **(Taking SATs:** 54 %)
700-800: V 2 % **M** 26 % **500-600: V** 66 % **M** 17 %
600-700: V 27 % **M** 57 % **400-500: V** 5 % **M** 0 % **300-400: V** NA % **M** NA %
High school class rank: Top fifth 92 % **2nd fifth** 99 % **3rd fifth** NA %

Admissions

Applied: 12,672 **Accepted:** 15 % **Matriculated:** 74 %
Deadline: Jan. 15 **Accept common application:** NA
Interview recommended: Yes **Off-campus interview available:** Yes
Evaluative: Yes **Informational only:** No **LD program:** No
Night in dorm provided: No **Non-refundable application fee:** $0
Early decision program: NA **Applied:** NA **Accepted:** NA % **Deadline:** NA
Freshmen accepted other than Fall term: 0 % **SAT/FAF Code #** 4380

Transfers

Applied: NA **Accepted:** NA % **Application deadline for Fall:** Jan. 31 **Spring:** NA
Minimum grades recommended: NA **All new students who were transfers into all classes:** NA %

Class Experience

Return 2nd year: 83 % **Graduate after 4 years:** 74 % **To graduate school within 5 years:** NA %

Cost

Tuition deposit: $0 **Total cost (Including school's estimate on fees and books):** $0
Tuition: $0 **(In state:** $) **Room and board:** $0
Annual giving by parents: NA **Average per student:** $NA

Financial Aid

Average total package per student: $NA **Number receiving aid:** NA %
Average scholarships and grants: $NA **Average loans:** $NA **Work-study program:** NA
Undergraduates working on campus: NA % **Average earnings:** $NA
Non-need scholarships NA % **Athletic scholarships:** NA **FAF deadline:** NA
Off-campus part-time employment: NA **CO-OP program:** NA
ROTC: NA **NROTC:** NA **AFROTC:** NA

Endowment

Total: $NA **Per student (including graduate students):** $NA

Location

Acres: 18,000 **Setting:** Rural
Miles from town center: 6 **(Pop.** 273,000**)**
50 **Miles from** Denver **(Pop.)**
Miles from (Pop.)

Class Composition

Asian: 3 % **Black:** 6 % **Hispanic:** 5 % **White:** 85 % **Other:** 1 %
Total minority : 15 % **Foreign countries:** 1 % (40 students)
From public schools: NA % **Students from in state:** 2 %

Housing (on campus)

Freshmen required to live on campus: Yes
Guaranteed for: 4 years
Available for all students: 100 %
Fraternity / Sorority housing: 0 / 0
On-campus married student housing: No
Women-only dorms available: No

Campus Life

Students living on campus: 100 % **Remain weekends:** NA % **Handicap access:** NA %
Car regulations: Upper classmen may have cars
Number with cars: 40%
Adequacy of on-campus parking: NA
Number of fraternities: 0 **Chapter houses:** 0
Number of sororities: 0 **Chapter houses:** 0
Students belonging to fraternities: 0 %
Students belonging to sororities: 0 %

Libraries and Computers

Books: 580,000 **Periodicals:** 3,570 **Microform items:** 15,000
Microcomputers available: Yes **Microcomputers networked:** Yes

Classes

Faculty / Student Ratio: 1/8 **Classes taught by teacher assistants:** 0 %
Most popular majors: Behavorial Science, International Affairs **Classes begin:** Aug.
Baccalaureate degrees offered: BS

Sports

Division: I **Except:** Women II **Physical ed requirements:** 14 hours
Students participating in intercollegiate sports: 35 % **In intramural sports:** 65 %
Additional intercollegiate and/or intramural sports: (not found at all colleges)

Crew: No	**Ice Hockey:** Yes	**Lacrosse:** Yes	**Wrestling:** Yes/M
Rugby: Yes	**Sailing:** No	**Skiing:** Yes	
Squash: Yes	**Ultimate Frisbee:** Yes	**Water Polo:** Yes	

Alumni

Number living: NA **Annual giving:** $ NA **Participation:** NA %
Average annual gift: $ NA **Average per student:** $NA

3-2 Programs (2 degrees in 5 years)

Exchange programs with the 3 other Service Academies

Observation and Opinion of:

Undergraduates and graduates ______________________________

____

College counselor ______________________________

____

UNITED STATES MILITARY ACADEMY (Public)

West Point, NY10996-1797

HIGHLY SELECTIVE
(Composite rating of guide books)

Main tel.: 914-938-1110
Admissions tel.: 914-938-4041
Financial aid tel.: NA
Scheduled Airline Service: NYC
Miles to airport: 55

Founded: 1802
Nickname: NA
Religious affiliation: None
(Coed since 1976)

Student Body

Undergraduates: 4,400 **Men:** 88 % **Women:** 12 %
Graduate students: 0 **Freshman class:** 1,340

Academics

SAT Averages: 1215 **Verbal:** 575 **Math:** 640 **(Taking SATs:** 65 %)
700-800: V 4 % **M** 22 % **500-600: V** 49 % **M** 21 %
600-700: V 31 % **M** 57 % **400-500: V** 16 % **M** 0 % **300-400: V** NA % **M** NA %
High school class rank: Top fifth 86 % **2nd fifth** 13 % **3rd fifth** NA %

Admissions

Applied: 12,757 **Accepted:** 14 % **Matriculated:** 74 %
Deadline: Jan. 15 **Accept common application:** No
Interview recommended: Yes **Off-campus interview available:** No
Evaluative: Yes **Informational only:** No **LD program:** No
Night in dorm provided: No **Non-refundable application fee:** $05
Early decision program: NA **Applied:** NA **Accepted:** NA % **Deadline:** NA
Freshmen accepted other than Fall term: 0 % **SAT/FAF Code #** 2924

Transfers

Applied: NA **Accepted:** NA % **Application deadline for Fall:** Mar. 21 **Spring:** NA
Minimum grades recommended: NA **All new students who were transfers into all classes:** NA %

Class Experience

Return 2nd year: 85 % **Graduate after 4 years:** 76 % **To graduate school within 5 years:** NA %

Cost

Tuition deposit: $1,500 **Total cost (Including school's estimate on fees and books):** $0
Tuition: $0 **(In state:** $) **Room and board:** $0
Annual giving by parents: $0 **Average per student:** $0

Financial Aid

Average total package per student: $NA **Number receiving aid:** 52 %
Average scholarships and grants: $0 **Average loans:** $NA **Work-study program:** NA
Undergraduates working on campus: NA % **Average earnings:** $NA
Non-need scholarships NA % **Athletic scholarships:** NA **FAF deadline:** NA
Off-campus part-time employment: NA **CO-OP program:** NA
ROTC: NA **NROTC:** NA **AFROTC:** NA

Endowment

Total: $NA **Per student (including graduate students):** $NA

Location

Acres: 16,000 **Setting:** Rural
Miles from town center: 2 **(Pop.** 5,000**)**
50 **Miles from** NYC **(Pop.** 7 Mil. **)**
Miles from (Pop.)

Class Composition

Asian: 5 % **Black:** 7 % **Hispanic:** 4 % **White:** 83 % **Other:** 1 %
Total minority : 17 % **Foreign countries:** 1 % (45 students)
From public schools: NA % **Students from in state:** 13 %

Housing (on campus)

Freshmen required to live on campus: Yes
Guaranteed for: 4 years
Available for all students: 100 %
Fraternity / Sorority housing: 0 / 0
On-campus married student housing: No
Women-only dorms available: No

Campus Life

Students living on campus: 100 % **Remain weekends:** NA% **Handicap access:** 0 %
Car regulations: Seniors only
Number with cars: NA %
Adequacy of on-campus parking: NA
Number of fraternities: 0 **Chapter houses:** 0
Number of sororities: 0 **Chapter houses:** 0
Students belonging to fraternities: 0 %
Students belonging to sororities: 0 %

Libraries and Computers

Books: 407,000 **Periodicals:** 2,500 **Microform items:** 214,000
Microcomputers available: Yes **Microcomputers networked:** Yes

Classes

Faculty / Student Ratio: 1/8 **Classes taught by teacher assistants:** 0 %
Most popular majors: Engineering
Classes begin: Mid Aug.
Baccalaureate degrees offered: BS

Sports

Division: I **Except:** **Physical ed requirements:** 8 semesters
Students participating in intercollegiate sports: 25 % **In intramural sports:** 100 %
Additional intercollegiate and/or intramural sports: (not found at all colleges)

Crew: Yes **Ice Hockey:** Yes **Lacrosse:** Yes **Wrestling:** Yes
Rugby: Yes **Sailing:** No **Skiing:** Yes
Squash: Yes **Ultimate Frisbee:** No **Water Polo:** Yes

Alumni

Number living: NA **Annual giving:** $ NA **Participation:** NA %
Average annual gift: $ NA **Average per student:** $NA

3-2 Programs (2 degrees in 5 years)

Exchange programs with the 3 other Service Academies

Observation and Opinion of:

Undergraduates and graduates ______________________

____

College counselor ______________________

____

UNITED STATES NAVAL ACADEMY (Public)

Annapolis, MD 21402-5018

HIGHLY SELECTIVE
(Composite rating of guide books)

Main tel.: 301-267-6100
Admissions tel.: 301-267-4361
Financial aid tel.: NA
Scheduled Airline Service: Baltimore
Miles to airport: 25

Founded: 1845
Nickname: Middies
Religious affiliation: None
(Coed since 1976)

Student Body

Undergraduates: 4,300 **Men:** 90 % **Women:** 10 %
Graduate students: 0 **Freshman class:** 1,232

Academics

SAT Averages: 1240 **Verbal:** 575 **Math:** 640 **(Taking SATs:** 65 %)
700-800: V 5 % **M** 30 % **500-600: V** 48 % **M** 16 %
600-700: V 33 % **M** 53 % **400-500: V** 14 % **M** 1 % **300-400: V** NA % **M** NA %
High school class rank: Top fifth 81 % **2nd fifth** 14 % **3rd fifth** 4 %

Admissions

Applied: 12,476 **Accepted:** 12 % **Matriculated:** 83 %
Deadline: Dec. 15 **Accept common application:** NA
Interview recommended: Yes **Off-campus interview available:** No
Evaluative: Yes **Informational only:** No **LD program:** No
Night in dorm provided: No **Non-refundable application fee:** $0
Early decision program: NA **Applied:** NA **Accepted:** NA % **Deadline:** NA
Freshmen accepted other than Fall term: 0 % **SAT/FAF Code #** 5809

Transfers

Applied: NA **Accepted:** NA % **Application deadline for Fall:** Mar. 1 **Spring:** NA
Minimum grades recommended: NA **All new students who were transfers into all classes:** 8 %

Class Experience

Return 2nd year: 86 % **Graduate after 4 years:** 74% **To graduate school within 5 years:** NA %

Cost

Tuition deposit: $1,500 **Total cost (Including school's estimate on fees and books):** $NA
Tuition: $NA (In state: $) **Room and board:** $NA
Annual giving by parents: $NA **Average per student:** $NA

Financial Aid

Average total package per student: $NA **Number receiving aid:** NA %
Average scholarships and grants: $NA **Average loans:** $NA **Work-study program:** NA
Undergraduates working on campus: NA % **Average earnings:** $NA
Non-need scholarships NA % **Athletic scholarships:** NA **FAF deadline:** NA
Off-campus part-time employment: NA **CO-OP program:** NA
ROTC: NA **NROTC:** NA **AFROTC:** NA

Endowment

Total: $NA **Per student (including graduate students):** $NA

Location

Acres: 338 **Setting:** City **Miles from town center:** 1 **(Pop.** 35,000 **)**
25 **Miles from** Baltimore **(Pop.** **)** 32 **Miles from** Wash DC **(Pop.** 700,000 **)**

Class Composition

Asian: 6 **%** **Black:** 6 **%** **Hispanic:** 4 **%** **White:** 84 **%** **Other:** NA **%**
Total minority : 16 **%** **Foreign countries:** 1 **%** **(** 40 **students)**
From public schools: NA **%** **Students from in state:** 5 **%**

Housing (on campus)

Freshmen required to live on campus: Yes **Guaranteed for:** 4 years
Available for all students: 100 **%** **Fraternity / Sorority housing:** No / No
On-campus married student housing: No **Women-only dorms available:** No

Campus Life

Students living on campus: 100 **%** **Remain weekends:** NA **%** **Handicap access:** NA **%**
Car regulations: Seniors only
Number with cars: 23 **%** **Adequacy of on-campus parking:** NA
Number of fraternities: 0 **Chapter houses:** 0 **Number of sororities:** 0 **Chapter houses:** 0
Students belonging to fraternities: 55 **%** **Students belonging to sororities:** 60 **%**

Libraries and Computers

Books: 750,000 **Periodicals:** 2,000 **Microform items:** 75,000
Microcomputers available: Yes **Microcomputers networked:** Yes

Classes

Faculty / Student Ratio: 1/8 **Classes taught by teacher assistants:** 0 **%**
Most popular majors: NA **Classes begin:** Late Aug.
Baccalaureate degrees offered: BS, BSE

Sports

Division: I **Except:** **Physical ed requirements:** 8 semesters
Students participating in intercollegiate sports: 40 **%** **In intramural sports:** 100 **%**
Additional intercollegiate and/or intramural sports: (not found at all colleges)

Crew: Yes **Ice Hockey:** Yes **Lacrosse:** Yes **Wrestling:** Yes/M
Rugby: Yes **Sailing:** Yes **Skiing:** No
Squash: Yes **Ultimate Frisbee:** Yes **Water Polo:** Yes

Alumni

Number living: NA **Annual giving:** $ NA **Participation:** NA **%**
Average annual gift: $ NA **Average per student:** $NA

3-2 Programs (2 degrees in 5 years)

Exchange program with other Service Academies

Observation and Opinion of:

Undergraduates and graduates ______________________________

____

College counselor ______________________________

____

UNIVERSITY OF NORTH CAROLINA (Public)

Chapel Hill, NC 27599-2200

HIGHLY SELECTIVE
(Composite rating of guide books)

Main tel.: 919-962-2211
Admissions tel.: 919-962-3621
Financial aid tel.: 919-962-8396
Scheduled Airline Service: Raleigh-Durham
Miles to airport: 22

Founded: 1789
Nickname: Tar Heels
Religious affiliation: None
(Coed since 1789)

Student Body

Undergraduates: 15,000 **Men:** 39 % **Women:** 61 %
Graduate students: 6,200 **Freshman class:** 3252

Academics

SAT Averages: 1110 **Verbal:** 525 **Math:** 585 **(Taking SATs:** NA %**)**
700-800: V 3 % **M** 11 % **500-600: V** 39 % **M** 38 %
600-700: V 20 % **M** 35 % **400-500: V** 31 % **M** 15 % **300-400: V** 2 % **M** 1 %
High school class rank: Top fifth 93 % **2nd fifth** 6 % **3rd fifth** 1 %

Admissions

Applied: 15,172 **Accepted:** 32 % **Matriculated:** 67 %
Deadline: Jan. 15 **Accept common application:** No
Interview recommended: No **Off-campus interview available:** Yes
Evaluative: No **Informational only:** Yes **LD program:** Yes
Night in dorm provided: No **Non-refundable application fee:** $35
Early decision program: No **Applied:** NA **Accepted:** NA % **Deadline:** NA
Freshmen accepted other than Fall term: 0 % **SAT/FAF Code #** 5816

Transfers

Applied: NA **Accepted:** NA % **Application deadline for Fall:** Mar. 1 **Spring:** NA
Minimum grades recommended: 3.5 **All new students who were transfers into all classes:** 22 %

Class Experience

Return 2nd year: 92 % **Graduate after 4 years:** 77 % **To graduate school within 5 years:** 16 %

Cost

Tuition deposit: $25 **Total cost (Including school's estimate on fees and books):** $13,025
Tuition: $7,120 (In state: $1,250) **Room and board:** $3,950
Annual giving by parents: $275,000 **Average per student:** $180

Financial Aid

Average total package per student: $NA **Number receiving aid:** 52 %
Average scholarships and grants: $2,200 **Average loans:** $NA **Work-study program:** Yes
Undergraduates working on campus: 3 % **Average earnings:** $900
Non-need scholarships 73 % **Athletic scholarships:** Yes **FAF deadline:** Mar. 1
Off-campus part-time employment: Good **CO-OP program:** No
ROTC: at NC State **NROTC:** Yes **AFROTC:** Yes

Endowment

Total: $200 Million **Per student (including graduate students):** $9,000

Location

Acres: 640 **Setting:** Surburban **Miles from town center:** 0 **(Pop.** 30,000**)**
15 **Miles from** Durham **(Pop.)** **Miles from (Pop.)**

Class Composition

Asian: 2 % **Black:** 10 % **Hispanic:** 1 % **White:** 86 % **Other:** 1 %
Total minority : 14 % **Foreign countries:** NA % (NA students)
From public schools: NA % **Students from in state:** 82 %

Housing (on campus)

Freshmen required to live on campus: No **Guaranteed for:** 0 year
Available for all students: 40 % **Fraternity / Sorority housing:** Yes / Yes
On-campus married student housing: Yes **Women-only dorms available:** Yes

Campus Life

Students living on campus: 80 % **Remain weekends:** NA % **Handicap access:** 50 %
Car regulations: No freshmen
Number with cars: NA % **Adequacy of on-campus parking:** Poor
Number of fraternities: 27 **Chapter houses:** 23 **Number of sororities:** 16 **Chapter houses:** 13
Students belonging to fraternities: NA % **Students belonging to sororities:** NA %

Libraries and Computers

Books: 3.3 Million **Periodicals:** 23,000 **Microform items:** 5.5 Million
Microcomputers available: Yes **Microcomputers networked:** Yes

Classes

Faculty / Student Ratio: 1/16 **Classes taught by teacher assistants:** 15 %
Most popular majors: Business, Poly Science **Classes begin:** Early Sept.
Baccalaureate degrees offered: BA, BS

Sports

Division: I **Except:** **Physical ed requirements:** 2 semesters
Students participating in intercollegiate sports: 5 % **In intramural sports:** 51 %
Additional intercollegiate and/or intramural sports: (not found at all colleges)

Crew: Yes **Ice Hockey:** No **Lacrosse:** Yes **Wrestling:** Yes
Rugby: Yes **Sailing:** Yes **Skiing:** Yes
Squash: No **Ultimate Frisbee:** Yes **Water Polo:** Yes

Alumni

Number living: 161,000 **Annual giving:** $ 19.3 Mil. **Participation:** 23 %
Average annual gift: $ 550 **Average per student:** $900

3-2 Programs (2 degrees in 5 years)

Exchange programs with universities in Germany, Columbia, SA, France and Puerto Rico

Observation and Opinion of:

Undergraduates and graduates ______________________________

____

College counselor ______________________________

____

UNIVERSITY OF THE SOUTH (Private)

Sewanee, TN 37375-4004

HIGHLY SELECTIVE
(Composite rating of guide books)

Main tel.: 615-598-1000
Admissions tel.: 615-598-1238
Financial aid tel.: 615-598-1312
Scheduled Airline Service: Chattanooga
Miles to airport: 47

Founded: 1857
Nickname: Tigers
Religious affiliation: Episcopal
(Coed since 1969)

Student Body

Undergraduates: 1,051 **Men:** 52 % **Women:** 48 %
Graduate students: 75 **Freshman class:** 288

Academics

SAT Averages: 1155 **Verbal:** 575 **Math:** 640 **(Taking SATs:** 65 %**)**
700-800: V 4 % **M** 7 % **500-600: V** 49 % **M** 42 %
600-700: V 22 % **M** 44 % **400-500: V** 25 % **M** 10 % **300-400: V** NA % **M** NA %
High school class rank: Top fifth 75 % **2nd fifth** 21 % **3rd fifth** 4 %

Admissions

Applied: 1,124 **Accepted:** 69 % **Matriculated:** 37 %
Deadline: Feb. 1 **Accept common application:** Yes
Interview recommended: Yes **Off-campus interview available:** No
Evaluative: No **Informational only:** NA **LD program:** No
Night in dorm provided: Yes **Non-refundable application fee:** $30
Early decision program: Yes **Applied:** 83 **Accepted:** 90 % **Deadline:** Nov. 15
Freshmen accepted other than Fall term: 1 % **SAT/FAF Code #** 1842

Transfers

Applied: 59 **Accepted:** 60 % **Application deadline for Fall:** Apr. 1 **Spring:** Dec. 1
Minimum grades recommended: 3.0 **All new students who were transfers into all classes:** 7 %

Class Experience

Return 2nd year: 87 % **Graduate after 4 years:** 77 % **To graduate school within 1 year:** 37 %

Cost

Tuition deposit: $300 **Total cost (Including school's estimate on fees and books):** $18,200
Tuition: $13,700 **(In state:** $ **)** **Room and board:** $3,700
Annual giving by parents: $527,000 **Average per student:** $500

Financial Aid

Average total package per student: $13,650 **Number receiving aid:** 45%
Average scholarships and grants: $11,876 **Average loans:** $1,764 **Work-study program:** NA
Undergraduates working on campus: 43 % **Average earnings:** $1,000
Non-need scholarships 4 % **Athletic scholarships:** NA **FAF deadline:** Mar. 1
Off-campus part-time employment: Fair **CO-OP program:** No
ROTC: No **NROTC:** No **AFROTC:** No

Endowment

Total: $96 Million **Per student (including graduate students):** $90,000

Location

Acres: 10,000 **Setting:** Rural **Miles from town center:** 0 **(Pop.** 3,200)
45 **Miles from** Chattanooga **(Pop.**) 90 **Miles from** Nashville **(Pop.**)

Class Composition

Asian: 1 % **Black:** 1 % **Hispanic:** 1 % **White:** 97 % **Other:** NA %
Total minority : 3 % **Foreign countries:**2 % (20 students)
From public schools: 54 % **Students from in state:** 22 %

Housing (on campus)

Freshmen required to live on campus: Yes **Guaranteed for:** 4 years
Available for all students: 95 % **Fraternity / Sorority housing:** Yes / No
On-campus married student housing: Yes **Women-only dorms available:** Yes

Campus Life

Students living on campus: 93 % **Remain weekends:** 96 % **Handicap access:** 85 %
Car regulations: All may have
Number with cars: 75 % **Adequacy of on-campus parking:** Good
Number of fraternities: 11 **Chapter houses:** 11 **Number of sororities:** 6 **Chapter houses:** 0
Students belonging to fraternities: 70 % **Students belonging to sororities:** 74 %

Libraries and Computers

Books: 405,000 **Periodicals:** 2,640 **Microform items:** 145,000
Microcomputers available: Yes **Microcomputers networked:** Yes

Classes

Faculty / Student Ratio: 1/10 **Classes taught by teacher assistants:** 0 %
Most popular majors: Poly Science, Economics **Classes begin:** Late Aug.
Baccalaureate degrees offered: BA, BS

Sports

Division: III **Except:** **Physical ed requirements:** 2 semesters
Students participating in intercollegiate sports: 40 % **In intramural sports:** 80 %
Additional intercollegiate and/or intramural sports: (not found at all colleges)

Crew: Yes **Ice Hockey:** No **Lacrosse:** Yes **Wrestling:** Yes/M
Rugby: Yes **Sailing:** No **Skiing:** No
Squash: No **Ultimate Frisbee:** Yes **Water Polo:** No

Alumni

Number living: 11,400 **Annual giving:** $ 1.5 Mil. **Participation:** 53 %
Average annual gift: $ 280 **Average per student:** $1,300

3-2 Programs (2 degrees in 5 years)

Engineering with Columbia, GA Tech, NYU, RPI, Vanderbilt, Washington U
Forestry with Duke and Yale

Observation and Opinion of:

Undergraduates and graduates ______________________________

____

College counselor ______________________________

____

VANDERBILT UNIVERSITY (Private)

Nashville, TN

HIGHLY SELECTIVE
(Composite rating of guide books)

Main tel.: 615-322-7511
Admissions tel.: 615-322-2561
Financial aid tel.: 615-322-3591
Scheduled Airline Service: Nashville
Miles to airport: 9

Founded: 1873
Nickname: Commodores
Religious affiliation: None
(Coed since 1873)

Student Body

Undergraduates: 5,200 **Men:** 53 % **Women:** 47 %
Graduate students: 3,800 **Freshman class:** 1,397

Academics

SAT Averages: 1195 **Verbal:** 555 **Math:** 640 **(Taking SATs:** 94 %**)**
700-800: V 3 % **M** 17 % **500-600: V** 52 % **M** 28 %
600-700: V 29 % **M** 52 % **400-500: V** 15 % **M** 3 % **300-400: V** 1 % **M** 0 %
High school class rank: Top fifth 54 % **2nd fifth** 12 % **3rd fifth** NA %

Admissions

Applied: 7,047 **Accepted:** 59 % **Matriculated:** 34 %
Deadline: Jan. 15 **Accept common application:** Yes
Interview recommended: No **Off-campus interview available:** Yes
Evaluative: No **Informational only:** Yes **LD program:** Yes
Night in dorm provided: Yes **Non-refundable application fee:** $35
Early decision program: Yes **Applied:** 347 **Accepted:** 42 % **Deadline:** Nov. 1
Freshmen accepted other than Fall term: 1 % **SAT/FAF Code #** 1871

Transfers

Applied: 336 **Accepted:** 51 % **Application deadline for Fall:** Feb. 1 **Spring:** Nov. 15
Minimum grades recommended: C **All new students who were transfers into all classes:** 5 %

Class Experience

Return 2nd year: 90 % **Graduate after 4 years:** 79 % **To graduate school within 2 years:** 46 %

Cost

Tuition deposit: $200 **Total cost (Including school's estimate on fees and books):** $23,760
Tuition: $15,975 **(In state:** $ **)** **Room and board:** $5,750
Annual giving by parents: $404,000 **Average per student:** $45

Financial Aid

Average total package per student: $10,700 **Number receiving aid:** 39 %
Average scholarships and grants: $7,576 **Average loans:** $3,100 **Work-study program:** Yes
Undergraduates working on campus: 55 % **Average earnings:** $1,500
Non-need scholarships 21 % **Athletic scholarships:** Yes **FAF deadline:** Feb. 15
Off-campus part-time employment: Excellent **CO-OP program:** No
ROTC: Yes **NROTC:** No **AFROTC:** at TN State

Endowment

Total: $604Million **Per student (including graduate students):** $65,000

Location

Acres: 330 **Setting:** City **Miles from town center:** 2 (**Pop.** 520,000)
Miles from (**Pop.**) **Miles from** (**Pop.**)

Class Composition

Asian: 4 % **Black:** 4 % **Hispanic:** 1 % **White:** 90 % **Other:** NA %
Total minority : 10 % **Foreign countries:** 2 % (100 students)
From public schools: 60 % **Students from in state:** 18 %

Housing (on campus)

Freshmen required to live on campus: Yes **Guaranteed for:** 1 year
Available for all students: 95 % **Fraternity / Sorority housing:** Yes / Yes
On-campus married student housing: Yes **Women-only dorms available:** Yes

Campus Life

Students living on campus: 91 % **Remain weekends:** 90 % **Handicap access:** 80 %
Car regulations: No freshmen
Number with cars: 95 % **Adequacy of on-campus parking:** Fair
Number of fraternities: 16 **Chapter houses:** 15 **Number of sororities:** 12 **Chapter houses:** 10
Students belonging to fraternities: 47 % **Students belonging to sororities:** 51 %

Libraries and Computers

Books: 1.9 Million **Periodicals:** 16,500 **Microform items:** 1.7 Million
Microcomputers available: Yes **Microcomputers networked:** Yes

Classes

Faculty / Student Ratio: 1/8 **Classes taught by teacher assistants:** 20 %
Most popular majors: Human Development, Elect Engineering **Classes begin:** Late Aug.
Baccalaureate degrees offered: BA, BE, B MUS, BS

Sports

Division: I **Except:** **Physical ed requirements:** 4 semesters
Students participating in intercollegiate sports: 4 % **In intramural sports:** 15 %
Additional intercollegiate and/or intramural sports: (not found at all colleges)

Crew: Yes **Ice Hockey:** Yes **Lacrosse:** Yes **Wrestling:** Yes/M
Rugby: Yes **Sailing:** Yes **Skiing:** Yes
Squash: Yes **Ultimate Frisbee:** Yes **Water Polo:** Yes

Alumni

Number living: 80,000 **Annual giving:** $ 13 Mil. **Participation:** 28 %
Average annual gift: $ NA **Average per student:** $1,300

3-2 Programs (2 degrees in 5 years)

Engineering/Liberal Arts program
Also, BS/MBA and BA or BS/MD programs

Observation and Opinion of:

Undergraduates and graduates ____________________

____

College counselor ____________________

____

VASSAR COLLEGE (Private)

Raymond Avenue
Poughkeepsie, NY 12601

HIGHLY SELECTIVE
(Composite rating of guide books)

Main tel.: 914-437-7000
Admissions tel.: 914-437-7300
Financial aid tel.: 914-437-5320
Scheduled Airline Service: Newburgh
Miles to airport: 60

Founded: 1861
Nickname: Brewers
Religious affiliation: None
(Coed since 1969)

Student Body

Undergraduates: 2,450 **Men:** 40 % **Women:** 60 %
Graduate students: NA **Freshman class:** 571

Academics

SAT Averages: 1240 **Verbal:** 610 **Math:** 630 **(Taking SATs:** 90 %**)**
700-800: V 10 % **M** 22 % **500-600: V** 24 % **M** 20 %
600-700: V 55 % **M** 53 % **400-500: V** 10 % **M** 5 % **300-400: V** NA % **M** NA %
High school class rank: Top fifth 76 % **2nd fifth** 20 % **3rd fifth** NA %

Admissions

Applied: 3,975 **Accepted:** 43 % **Matriculated:** 33 %
Deadline: Jan. 15 **Accept common application:** Yes
Interview recommended: NA **Off-campus interview available:** NA
Evaluative: NA **Informational only:** NA **LD program:** NA
Night in dorm provided: Yes **Non-refundable application fee:** $50
Early decision program: Yes **Applied:** 299 **Accepted:** 54 % **Deadline:** Jan. 15
Freshmen accepted other than Fall term: 0 % **SAT/FAF Code #** 2956

Transfers

Applied: 233 **Accepted:** 49 % **Application deadline for Fall:** Mar. 1 **Spring:** Nov. 15
Minimum grades recommended: 3.0 **All new students who were transfers into all classes:** 10 %

Class Experience

Return 2nd year: 93% **Graduate after 4 years:** 76 % **To graduate school within 5 years:** NA %

Cost

Tuition deposit: $500 **Total cost (Including school's estimate on fees and books):** $23,200
Tuition: $17,210 **(In state:** $ **)** **Room and board:** $5,500
Annual giving by parents: $484,000 **Average per student:** $200

Financial Aid

Average total package per student: $11,575 **Number receiving aid:** 60 %
Average scholarships and grants: $9,275 **Average loans:** $2,300 **Work-study program:** Yes
Undergraduates working on campus: 62 % **Average earnings:** $1,000
Non-need scholarships 0 % **Athletic scholarships:** NA **FAF deadline:** Feb. 15
Off-campus part-time employment: Fair **CO-OP program:** No
On Campus: ROTC: Yes **NROTC:** No **AFROTC:** No

Endowment

Total: $242 Million **Per student (including graduate students):** $120,000

Location

Acres: 1,000 **Setting:** Urban
75 **Miles from** NYC **(Pop.** 7 Mil. **)**
Miles from town center: 2 **(Pop.** 70,000**)**
Miles from (Pop.)

Class Composition

Asian: 9 % **Black:** 8 % **Hispanic:** 4 % **White:** 79 % **Other:** NA %
Total minority : 21 % **Foreign countries:** 7 % (160 students)
From public schools: NA % **Students from in state:** 41 %

Housing (on campus)

Freshmen required to live on campus: Yes **Guaranteed for:** 4 years
Available for all students: 95 % **Fraternity / Sorority housing:** 0 / 0
On-campus married student housing: Yes **Women-only dorms available:** Yes

Campus Life

Students living on campus: 95 % **Remain weekends:** 90 % **Handicap access:** NA %
Car regulations: NA
Number with cars: NA % **Adequacy of on-campus parking:** Poor
Number of fraternities: 0 **Chapter houses:** 0 **Number of sororities:** 0 **Chapter houses:** 0
Students belonging to fraternities: 0 % **Students belonging to sororities:** 0 %

Libraries and Computers

Books: 700,000 **Periodicals:** 3,900 **Microform items:** 350,000
Microcomputers available: Yes **Microcomputers networked:** NA

Classes

Faculty / Student Ratio: 1/11 **Classes taught by teacher assistants:** 0 %
Most popular majors: English, Poly Science **Classes begin:** Early Sept.
Baccalaureate degrees offered: AB

Sports

Division: III **Except:** **Physical ed requirements:** None
Students participating in intercollegiate sports: 25 % **In intramural sports:** 50 %
Additional intercollegiate and/or intramural sports: (not found at all colleges)

Crew: Yes **Ice Hockey:** No **Lacrosse:** Yes **Wrestling:** No
Rugby: Yes **Sailing:** Yes **Skiing:** Yes
Squash: Yes **Ultimate Frisbee:** Yes **Water Polo:** Yes

Alumni

Number living: 28,000 **Annual giving:** $ 9 Million **Participation:** 55 %
Average annual gift: $ 700 **Average per student:** $4,000

3-2 Programs (2 degrees in 5 years)

Engineering with Dartmouth
Member of 12-college exchange program

Observation and Opinion of:

Undergraduates and graduates ______________________________

____

College counselor ______________________________

____

UNIVERSITY OF VERMONT (Private)

Burlington, VT 05405-3596

VERY SELECTIVE
(Composite rating of guide books)

Main tel.: 802-656-3480
Admissions tel.: 802-656-3370
Financial aid tel.: 802-656-3156
Scheduled Airline Service: Burlington
Miles to airport: 6

Founded: 1791
Nickname: Cats
Religious affiliation: None
(Coed since 1871)

Student Body

Undergraduates: 8,500 **Men:** 45 % **Women:** 55 %
Graduate students: 1,450 **Freshman class:** NA

Academics

SAT Averages: 1085 **Verbal:** 510 **Math:** 575 **(Taking SATs:** NA **%)**
700-800: V 2 % **M** 6 % **500-600: V** 42 % **M** 41 %
600-700: V 11 % **M** 33 % **400-500: V** 45 % **M** 20 % **300-400: V** NA **%** **M** NA **%**
High school class rank: Top fifth 68 % **2nd fifth** NA % **3rd fifth** NA %

Admissions

Applied: 8,500 **Accepted:** 55 % **Matriculated:** 37 %
Deadline: Feb. 1 **Accept common application:** Yes
Interview recommended: Yes **Off-campus interview available: Yes**
Evaluative: Yes **Informational only:** No **LD program:** Yes
Night in dorm provided: Yes **Non-refundable application fee:** $45
Early decision program: Yes **Applied:** 360 **Accepted:** 21 % **Deadline:** NA
Freshmen accepted other than Fall term: 2 % **SAT/FAF Code #** 3920

Transfers

Applied: 1,062 **Accepted:** 34 % **Application deadline for Fall:** NA **Spring:** NA
Minimum grades recommended: NA **All new students who were transfers into all classes:** 11 %

Class Experience

Return 2nd year: 86 % **Graduate after 4 years:** 71 % **To graduate school within 5 years:** NA %

Cost

Tuition deposit: $225 **Total cost (Including school's estimate on fees and books):** $18,600
Tuition: $14,340 **(In state:** $ 5,740 **)** **Room and board:** $4,026
Annual giving by parents: $933,000 **Average per student:** $90

Financial Aid

Average total package per student: $NA **Number receiving aid:** NA %
Average scholarships and grants: $NA **Average loans:** $NA **Work-study program:** Yes
Undergraduates working on campus: 14 % **Average earnings:** $NA
Non-need scholarships NA % **Athletic scholarships:** Yes **FAF deadline:** Mar. 1
Off-campus part-time employment: Excellent **CO-OP program:** Yes
ROTC: Yes **NROTC:** No **AFROTC:** No

Endowment

Total: $84 Million **Per student (including graduate students):** $7,500

Location

Acres: 715 **Setting:** Urban **Miles from town center:** 2 **(Pop.** 40,000 **)**
95 **Miles from** Montreal **(Pop.** **)** **Miles from** **(Pop.** **)**

Class Composition

Asian: 3 **%** **Black:** 1 **%** **Hispanic:** 1 **%** **White:** 94 **%** **Other:** 1 **%**
Total minority : 6 **%** **Foreign countries:** 1 **%** (85 students)
From public schools: NA **%** **Students from in state:** 49 **%**

Housing (on campus)

Freshmen required to live on campus: Yes **Guaranteed for:** 4 years
Available for all students: 46 **%** **Fraternity / Sorority housing:** Yes / Yes
On-campus married student housing: No **Women-only dorms available:** Yes

Campus Life

Students living on campus: 46 **%** **Remain weekends:** NA **%** **Handicap access:** 85 **%**
Car regulations: No freshmen
Number with cars: 20 **%** **Adequacy of on-campus parking:** NA
Number of fraternities: 14 **Chapter houses:** 14 **Number of sororities:** 6 **Chapter houses:** 6
Students belonging to fraternities: 11 **%** **Students belonging to sororities:** 21 **%**

Libraries and Computers

Books: 970,000 **Periodicals:** 10,450 **Microform items:** 873,000
Microcomputers available: Yes **Microcomputers networked:** Yes

Classes

Faculty / Student Ratio: 1/16 **Classes taught by teacher assistants:** 15 **%**
Most popular majors: Poly Science, Business **Classes begin:** Late Aug.
Baccalaureate degrees offered: BA, B MUS, BS

Sports

Division: I **Except:** **Physical ed requirements:** 1 year
Students participating in intercollegiate sports: 11 **%** **In intramural sports:** 21 **%**
Additional intercollegiate and/or intramural sports: (not found at all colleges)

Crew: Yes **Ice Hockey:** Yes **Lacrosse:** Yes **Wrestling:** Yes/M
Rugby: Yes **Sailing:** No **Skiing:** Yes
Squash: Yes **Ultimate Frisbee:** Yes **Water Polo:** No

Alumni

Number living: 47,000 **Annual giving:** $ 28 Million **Participation:** 29 **%**
Average annual gift: $ 210 **Average per student:** $350

3-2 Programs (2 degrees in 5 years)

Member of consortium of Vermont colleges

Observation and Opinion of:

Undergraduates and graduates ______________________________

____

College counselor ______________________________

____

VILLANOVA UNIVERSITY (Private)

Villanova, PA 19085

VERY SELECTIVE
(Composite rating of guide books)

Main tel.: 215-645-4500
Admissions tel.: 800-338-7927
Financial aid tel.: 215-645-4010
Scheduled Airline Service: Philadelphia
Miles to airport: 14

Founded: 1842
Nickname: Wildcats
Religious affiliation: Catholic
(Coed since 1953)

Student Body

Undergraduates: 6,400 **Men:** 53 % **Women:** 47 %
Graduate students: 2,300 **Freshman class:** 1,608

Academics

SAT Averages: 1110 **Verbal:** 515 **Math:** 590 **(Taking SATs:** NA **%)**
700-800: V 1 % **M** 7 % **500-600: V** 48 % **M** 39 %
600-700: V 12 % **M** 43 % **400-500: V** 35 % **M** 9 % **300-400: V** 3 % **M** 1 %
High school class rank: Top fifth 51 % **2nd fifth** 23 % **3rd fifth** 4 %

Admissions

Applied: 8,060 **Accepted:** 65 % **Matriculated:** 31 %
Deadline: Jan. 15 **Accept common application:** NA
Interview recommended: No **Off-campus interview available:** No
Evaluative: No **Informational only:** Yes **LD program:** NA
Night in dorm provided: Yes **Non-refundable application fee:** $40
Early decision program: Yes **Applied:** NA **Accepted:** NA % **Deadline:** NA
Freshmen accepted other than Fall term: 1 % **SAT/FAF Code #** 2959

Transfers

Applied: 406 **Accepted:** 60 % **Application deadline for Fall:** Jun. 15 **Spring:** Nov. 15
Minimum grades recommended: 3.0 **All new students who were transfers into all classes:** 9 %

Class Experience

Return 2nd year: 91 % **Graduate after 4 years:** 82 % **To graduate school within 5 years:** 25 %

Cost

Tuition deposit: $400 **Total cost (Including school's estimate on fees and books):** $21,000
Tuition: $13,200 (In state: $) **Room and board:** $5,800
Annual giving by parents: $324,000 **Average per student:** $NA

Financial Aid

Average total package per student: $10,225 **Number receiving aid:** 38 %
Average scholarships and grants: $7,600 **Average loans:** $2,625 **Work-study program:** NA
Undergraduates working on campus: 25 % **Average earnings:** $1,300
Non-need scholarships 43 % **Athletic scholarships:** Yes **FAF deadline:** Feb. 15
Off-campus part-time employment: Good **CO-OP program:** NA
ROTC: Yes **NROTC:** No **AFROTC:** at St Joe's

Endowment

Total: $28 Million **Per student (including graduate students):** $2,500

Location

Acres: 240 **Setting:** Rural
12 **Miles from** Philadelphia **(Pop.** 1.7 Mil.)
Miles from town center: 0 **(Pop.** 6,000**)**
Miles from **(Pop.** **)**

Class Composition

Asian: 3 % **Black:** 2 % **Hispanic:** 2 % **White:** 92 % **Other:** 1 %
Total minority : 8 % **Foreign countries:** 2 % (130 students)
From public schools: 52 % **Students from in state:** 32 %

Housing (on campus)

Freshmen required to live on campus: No
Available for all students: 80 %
On-campus married student housing: No
Guaranteed for: 1 year
Fraternity / Sorority housing: No / No
Women-only dorms available: Yes

Campus Life

Students living on campus: 50 % **Remain weekends:** 90 % **Handicap access:** 100 %
Car regulations: No freshmen or sophomores
Number with cars: 30 %
Number of fraternities: 12 **Chapter houses:** 0
Students belonging to fraternities: 30 %
Adequacy of on-campus parking: Poor
Number of sororities: 8 **Chapter houses:** 0
Students belonging to sororities: 30 %

Libraries and Computers

Books: 571,000 **Periodicals:** 2,900 **Microform items:** 1 Million
Microcomputers available: Yes **Microcomputers networked:** Yes

Classes

Faculty / Student Ratio: 1/14 **Classes taught by teacher assistants:** 0 %
Most popular majors: Political Science **Classes begin:** Late Aug.
Baccalaureate degrees offered: BA, BCE, BCHE, BEE, BME, BS, BSBA, BSN

Sports

Division: I **Except:** Hockey III **Physical ed requirements:** None
Students participating in intercollegiate sports: 10 % **In intramural sports:** 70 %
Additional intercollegiate and/or intramural sports: (not found at all colleges)

Crew: Yes **Ice Hockey:** Yes **Lacrosse:** Yes **Wrestling:** No
Rugby: Yes **Sailing:** Yes **Skiing:** Yes
Squash: No **Ultimate Frisbee:** No **Water Polo:** Yes

Alumni

Number living: 57,000 **Annual giving:** $ 3.4 Million **Participation:** 23 %
Average annual gift: $ 250 **Average per student:** $250

3-2 Programs (2 degrees in 5 years)

3-4 MD with Medical College of PA
Exchange programs with Fordham, Notre Dame, Georgetown

Observation and Opinion of:

Undergraduates and graduates ______________________________

____

College counselor ______________________________

____

UNIVERSITY OF VIRGINIA (Public)

Charlottesville, VA 22903

MOST SELECTIVE
(Composite rating of guide books)

Main tel.: 804-924-0311
Admissions tel.: 804-982-3000
Financial aid tel.: 804-924-3725
Scheduled Airline Service:
Miles to airport: 12

Founded: 1819
Nickname: Cavaliers
Religious affiliation: None
(Coed since 1970)

Student Body

Undergraduates: 11,100 **Men:** 50 % **Women:** 50 %
Graduate students: 6,200 **Freshman class:** 2,566

Academics

SAT Averages: 1210 **Verbal:** 570 **Math:** 640 **(Taking SATs:** 100 %**)**
700-800: V 6 % **M** 26 % **500-600: V** 41 % **M** 22 %
600-700: V 33 % **M** 46 % **400-500: V** 17 % **M** 6 % **300-400: V** 3 % **M** 0 %
High school class rank: Top fifth 68 % **2nd fifth** 5 % **3rd fifth** 1 %

Admissions

Applied: 12,862 **Accepted:** 38 % **Matriculated:** 52 %
Deadline: Jan. 2 **Accept common application:** No
Interview recommended: NA **Off-campus interview available:** NA
Evaluative: NA **Informational only:** NA **LD program:** Yes
Night in dorm provided: NA **Non-refundable application fee:** $40
Early decision program: Yes **Applied:** 1,205 **Accepted:** 40 % **Deadline:** Nov. 1
Freshmen accepted other than Fall term: 0 % **SAT/FAF Code #** 5820

Transfers

Applied: 2,109 **Accepted:** 39 % **Application deadline for Fall:** Mar. 1 **Spring:** NA
Minimum grades recommended: C **All new students who were transfers into all classes:** 18 %

Class Experience

Return 2nd year: 97 % **Graduate after 4 years:** 78 % **To graduate school within 5 years:** 64 %

Cost

Tuition deposit: $250 **Total cost (Including school's estimate on fees and books):** $15,850
Tuition: $10,826 **(In state:** $3,890**)** **Room and board:** $3,500
Annual giving by parents: $918,000 **Average per student:** $85

Financial Aid

Average total package per student: $5,700 **Number receiving aid:** 28 %
Average scholarships and grants: $3,500 **Average loans:** $2,200 **Work-study program:** Yes
Undergraduates working on campus: 27 % **Average earnings:** $1,500
Non-need scholarships 37 % **Athletic scholarships:** Yes **FAF deadline:** Mar. 31
Off-campus part-time employment: Good **CO-OP program:** No
ROTC: Yes **NROTC:** Yes **AFROTC:** Yes

Endowment

Total: $487 Million **Per student (including graduate students):** $28,000

Location

Acres: 2,440 **Setting:** Surburban **Miles from town center:** 3 **(Pop.** 100,000**)**
110 **Miles from** Richmond **(Pop.)** **Miles from (Pop.)**

Class Composition

Asian: 7 % **Black:** 11 % **Hispanic:** 1 % **White:** 79 % **Other:** 2 %
Total minority : 21 % **Foreign countries:** 2 % (220 students)
From public schools: 77 % **Students from in state:** 65 %

Housing (on campus)

Freshmen required to live on campus: Yes **Guaranteed for:** 1 year
Available for all students: 51 % **Fraternity / Sorority housing:** Yes / Yes
On-campus married student housing: No **Women-only dorms available:** No

Campus Life

Students living on campus: 51 % **Remain weekends:** NA % **Handicap access:** 50 %
Car regulations: No freshmen 1st semester
Number with cars: 26% **Adequacy of on-campus parking:** Poor
Number of fraternities: 39 **Chapter houses:** 33 **Number of sororities:** 22 **Chapter houses:** 18
Students belonging to fraternities: 28 % **Students belonging to sororities:** 30 %

Libraries and Computers

Books: 3.2 Million **Periodicals:** 21,600 **Microform items:** 4.3 Million
Microcomputers available: Yes **Microcomputers networked:** Yes

Classes

Faculty / Student Ratio: 1/11 **Classes taught by teacher assistants:** 25 %
Most popular majors: Commerce, Psychology **Classes begin:** Late Aug.
Baccalaureate degrees offered: BA, B ARCH/HIST, B CITY PLAN, BS, BS COM, BSE, BSED, BSN

Sports

Division: I **Except:** **Physical ed requirements:** None
Students participating in intercollegiate sports: 50 % **In intramural sports:** 85 %
Additional intercollegiate and/or intramural sports: (not found at all colleges)

Crew: Yes **Ice Hockey:** No **Lacrosse:** Yes **Wrestling:** Yes/M
Rugby: Yes **Sailing:** Yes **Skiing:** Yes
Squash: No **Ultimate Frisbee:** No **Water Polo:** Yes

Alumni

Number living: 107,000 **Annual giving:** $ 14.8 Mil. **Participation:** 35 %
Average annual gift: $ 400 **Average per student:** $800

3-2 Programs (2 degrees in 5 years)

BA/MT program in Education
BS/MS program in Engineering

Observation and Opinion of:

Undergraduates and graduates ____________________

____

College counselor ____________________

____

VIRGINIA POLYTECHNIC INSTITUTE (Public)

Blacksburg, VA 24061

SELECTIVE
(Composite rating of guide books)

Main tel.: 703-231-6000
Admissions tel.: 703-231-6267
Financial aid tel.: 703-231-5179
Scheduled Airline Service: Roanoke
Miles to airport: 38

Founded: 1872
Nickname: Gobblers
Religious affiliation: None
(Coed since 1963)

Student Body

Undergraduates: 18,200 **Men:** 59 % **Women:** 41 %
Graduate students: 4,100 **Freshman class:** 4,213

Academics

SAT Averages: 1100 **Verbal:** NA **Math:** NA **(Taking SATs:** NA **%)**
700-800: V 2 % **M** 11 % **500-600: V** 38 % **M** 38 %
600-700: V 11 % **M** 35 % **400-500: V** 41 % **M** 15 % **300-400: V** 8 % **M** 1 %
High school class rank: Top fifth 61 % **2nd fifth** 25 % **3rd fifth** NA %

Admissions

Applied: 15,160 **Accepted:** 68 % **Matriculated:** 41 %
Deadline: Feb. 1 **Accept common application:** Yes
Interview recommended: Yes **Off-campus interview available:** No
Evaluative: No **Informational only:** Yes **LD program:** Yes
Night in dorm provided: NA **Non-refundable application fee:** $20
Early decision program: Yes **Applied:** 1,669 **Accepted:** 46 % **Deadline:** Nov. 1
Freshmen accepted other than Fall term: 5 % **SAT/FAF Code #** 5859

Transfers

Applied: 2,464 **Accepted:** 50 % **Application deadline for Fall:** Mar. 1 **Spring:** Oct. 1
Minimum grades recommended: 2.0 **All new students who were transfers into all classes:** 4 %

Class Experience

Return 2nd year: 89 % **Graduate after 4 years:** 71 % **To graduate school within 1 year:** 15 %

Cost

Tuition deposit: $250 **Total cost (Including school's estimate on fees and books):** $12,400
Tuition: $8,520 **(In state:** $ 3,300**)** **Room and board:** $2,875
Annual giving by parents: $43,000 **Average per student:** $NA

Financial Aid

Average total package per student: $3,300 **Number receiving aid:** 45 %
Average scholarships and grants: $1,000 **Average loans:** $2,200 **Work-study program:** Yes
Undergraduates working on campus: 25 % **Average earnings:** $800
Non-need scholarships NA % **Athletic scholarships:** Yes **FAF deadline:** Feb. 1
Off-campus part-time employment: Good **CO-OP program:** Yes
ROTC: Yes **NROTC:** Yes **AFROTC:** Yes

Endowment

Total: $120 Million **Per student (including graduate students):** $5,000

Location

Acres: 2,600 **Setting:** Urban
Miles from town center: 2 **(Pop.** 32,000**)**
38 **Miles from** Roanoke **(Pop.** 100,000**)**
Miles from (Pop.)

Class Composition

Asian: 6 % **Black:** 5 % **Hispanic:** 1 % **White:** 87 % **Other:** 1 %
Total minority : NA % **Foreign countries:** 1 % (180 students)
From public schools: 99 % **Students from in state:** 75 %

Housing (on campus)

Freshmen required to live on campus: Yes
Guaranteed for: 1 year
Available for all students: 15 %
Fraternity / Sorority housing: Yes / Yes
On-campus married student housing: No
Women-only dorms available: Yes

Campus Life

Students living on campus: 45 % **Remain weekends:** NA % **Handicap access:** 60 %
Car regulations: All may have
Number with cars: 65 %
Adequacy of on-campus parking: NA
Number of fraternities: 33 **Chapter houses:** 21
Number of sororities: 16 **Chapter houses:** 10
Students belonging to fraternities: 17 %
Students belonging to sororities: 18 %

Libraries and Computers

Books: 1.7 Million **Periodicals:** 17,750 **Microform items:** 5 Million
Microcomputers available: Yes **Microcomputers networked:** Yes

Classes

Faculty / Student Ratio: 1/17 **Classes taught by teacher assistants:** 20 %
Most popular majors: Marketing, Finance **Classes begin:** Late Aug.
Baccalaureate degrees offered: BA, B ARCH, BLA, BS

Sports

Division: I **Except:** **Physical ed requirements:** None
Students participating in intercollegiate sports: NA % **In intramural sports:** NA %
Additional intercollegiate and/or intramural sports: (not found at all colleges)

Crew: No **Ice Hockey:** No **Lacrosse:** Yes **Wrestling:** Yes
Rugby: Yes **Sailing:** No **Skiing:** No
Squash: No **Ultimate Frisbee:** Yes **Water Polo:** No

Alumni

Number living: 101,000 **Annual giving:** $ 4.1 Million **Participation:** 24 %
Average annual gift: $ 180 **Average per student:** $170

3-2 Programs (2 degrees in 5 years)

Member of architecture consortium with Miami U, Oxford and California Poly Institute

Observation and Opinion of:

Undergraduates and graduates ______________________

____

College counselor ______________________

____

WAKE FOREST UNIVERSITY (Private)

Winston-Salem, NC 27109

HIGHLY SELECTIVE
(Composite rating of guide books)

Main tel.: 919-759-5000
Admissions tel.: 919-759-5201
Financial aid tel.: 919-759-5176
Scheduled Airline Service: Greensboro
Miles to airport: 30

Founded: 1834
Nickname: Blue Devils
Religious affiliation: Baptist
(Coed since 1942)

Student Body

Undergraduates: 3,400 **Men:** 55 % **Women:** 45 %
Graduate students: 1,950 **Freshman class:** 869

Academics

SAT Averages: 1250 **Verbal:** 575 **Math:** 675 **(Taking SATs:** 100 %**)**
700-800: V 3 % **M** 15 % **500-600: V** 50 % **M** 30 %
600-700: V 32 % **M** 50 % **400-500: V** 15 % **M** 5 % **300-400: V** NA % **M** NA %
High school class rank: Top fifth 59 % **2nd fifth** 18 % **3rd fifth** NA %

Admissions

Applied: 5,430 **Accepted:** 37 % **Matriculated:** 43 %
Deadline: Jan. 15 **Accept common application:** Yes
Interview recommended: Yes **Off-campus interview available:** No
Evaluative: No **Informational only:** Yes **LD program:** No
Night in dorm provided: Yes **Non-refundable application fee:** $25
Early decision program: Yes **Applied:** 422 **Accepted:** 50 % **Deadline:** Nov. 15
Freshmen accepted other than Fall term: 3 % **SAT/FAF Code #** 5885

Transfers

Applied: 377 **Accepted:** 57 % **Application deadline for Fall:** Feb. 15 **Spring:** Nov. 15
Minimum grades recommended: 2.0 **All new students who were transfers into all classes:** 3 %

Class Experience

Return 2nd year: 92 % **Graduate after 4 years:** 72 % **To graduate school within 1 year:** 29 %

Cost

Tuition deposit: $200 **Total cost (Including school's estimate on fees and books):** $16,200
Tuition: $12,000 **(In state:** $ **)** **Room and board:** $4,100
Annual giving by parents: $391,000 **Average per student:** $75

Financial Aid

Average total package per student: $7,800 **Number receiving aid:** 55 %
Average scholarships and grants: $5,000 **Average loans:** $2,800 **Work-study program:** Yes
Undergraduates working on campus: 31 % **Average earnings:** $1,250
Non-need scholarships 53 % **Athletic scholarships:** Yes **FAF deadline:** Mar. 1
Off-campus part-time employment: Good **CO-OP program:** No
ROTC: Yes **NROTC:** Yes **AFROTC:** Yes

Endowment

Total: $318 Million **Per student (including graduate students):** $60,000

Location

Acres: 490 **Setting:** Surburban
Miles from town center: 3 **(Pop.** 150,000**)**
30 **Miles from** Greensboro **(Pop.** **)**
Miles from **(Pop.** **)**

Class Composition

Asian: 1 % **Black:** 7 % **Hispanic:** 1 % **White:** 90 % **Other:** 1 %
Total minority : 10 % **Foreign countries:** 2 % (70 students)
From public schools: 74 % **Students from in state:** 39 %

Housing (on campus)

Freshmen required to live on campus: Yes
Available for all students: 84 %
On-campus married student housing: Yes
Guaranteed for: 1 year
Fraternity / Sorority housing: No / No
Women-only dorms available: Yes

Campus Life

Students living on campus: 84 % **Remain weekends:** 80 % **Handicap access:** 50 %
Car regulations: All may have
Number with cars: 63 %
Adequacy of on-campus parking: Fair
Number of fraternities: 13 **Chapter houses:** 0
Students belonging to fraternities: 40 %
Number of sororities: 10 **Chapter houses:** 0
Students belonging to sororities: 44 %

Libraries and Computers

Books: 1.1 Million **Periodicals:** 18,800 **Microform items:** 605,000
Microcomputers available: Yes **Microcomputers networked:** Yes

Classes

Faculty / Student Ratio: 1/13 **Classes taught by teacher assistants:** 0 %
Most popular majors: Business, History **Classes begin:** Late Aug.
Baccalaureate degrees offered: BA, BS

Sports

Division: I **Except:** **Physical ed requirements:** 2 semesters
Students participating in intercollegiate sports: 10 % **In intramural sports:** 55 %
Additional intercollegiate and/or intramural sports: (not found at all colleges)

Crew: No	**Ice Hockey:** No	**Lacrosse:** Yes	**Wrestling:** Yes/M
Rugby: Yes	**Sailing:** No	**Skiing:** Yes	
Squash: No	**Ultimate Frisbee:** No	**Water Polo:** Yes	

Alumni

Number living: 35,000 **Annual giving:** $ 4.8 Mil. **Participation:** 31 %
Average annual gift: $ 410 **Average per student:** $950

3-2 Programs (2 degrees in 5 years)

Engineering with North Carolina State
Forestry with Duke

Observation and Opinion of:

Undergraduates and graduates ____________________

____

College counselor ____________________

____

WASHINGTON AND LEE UNIVERSITY (Private)

Lexington, VA 24450

MOST SELECTIVE
(Composite rating of guide books)

Founded: 1749
Nickname: Generals
Religious affiliation: None
(Coed since 1985)

Main tel.: 703-463-8400
Admissions tel.: 703-463-8710
Financial aid tel.: 703-463-8715
Scheduled Airline Service: Roanoke
Miles to airport: 50

Student Body

Undergraduates: 1,600 **Men:** 65 % **Women:** 35 %
Graduate students: 400 **Freshman class:** 391

Academics

SAT Averages: 1250 **Verbal:** 610 **Math:** 640 **(Taking SATs:** 89 %**)**
700-800: V 5 % **M** 23 % **500-600: V** 42 % **M** 19 %
600-700: V 49 % **M** 58 % **400-500: V** 1 % **M** 0 % **300-400: V** NA % **M** NA %
High school class rank: Top fifth 83 % **2nd fifth** 16 % **3rd fifth** 1 %

Admissions

Applied: 3,067 **Accepted:** 31 % **Matriculated:** 41 %
Deadline: Feb. 1 **Accept common application:** Yes
Interview recommended: Yes **Off-campus interview available:** Yes
Evaluative: No **Informational only:** Yes **LD program:** NA
Night in dorm provided: No **Non-refundable application fee:** $30
Early decision program: Yes **Applied:** 310 **Accepted:** 33 % **Deadline:** Dec. 1
Freshmen accepted other than Fall term: 0 % **SAT/FAF Code #** 5887

Transfers

Applied: 128 **Accepted:** 10 % **Application deadline for Fall:** Apr. 1 **Spring:** Nov. 1
Minimum grades recommended: 3.0 **All new students who were transfers into all classes:** 1 %

Class Experience

Return 2nd year: 95 % **Graduate after 4 years:** 85% **To graduate school within 5 years:** NA %

Cost

Tuition deposit: $150 **Total cost (Including school's estimate on fees and books):** $16,500
Tuition: $11,575 **(In state:** $ **)** **Room and board:** $4,068
Annual giving by parents: $265,000 **Average per student:** $130

Financial Aid

Average total package per student: $9,000 **Number receiving aid:** 54 %
Average scholarships and grants: $6,750 **Average loans:** $2,200 **Work-study program:** Yes
Undergraduates working on campus: 15 % **Average earnings:** $875
Non-need scholarships 23 % **Athletic scholarships:** NA **FAF deadline:** Feb. 1
Off-campus part-time employment: Poor **CO-OP program:** NA
ROTC: No **NROTC:** No **AFROTC:** No

Endowment

Total: $100 Million **Per student (including graduate students):** $50,000

Location

Acres: 300 **Setting:** Rural **Miles from town center:** 0 (**Pop.** 7,000)
50 **Miles from** Roanoke (**Pop.**) 50 **Miles from** Lynchburg (**Pop.**)

Class Composition

Asian: 1 % **Black:** 4 % **Hispanic:** 1 % **White:** 93 % **Other:** 1 %
Total minority : 7 % **Foreign countries:** 1 % (16 students)
From public schools: 67 % **Students from in state:** 11 %

Housing (on campus)

Freshmen required to live on campus: Yes **Guaranteed for:** 4 years
Available for all students: 67 % **Fraternity / Sorority housing:** Yes / No
On-campus married student housing: No **Women-only dorms available:** No

Campus Life

Students living on campus: 67 % **Remain weekends:** 80 % **Handicap access:** 60 %
Car regulations: All may have
Number with cars: 33 % **Adequacy of on-campus parking:** Good
Number of fraternities: 16 **Chapter houses:** 16 **Number of sororities:** 4 **Chapter houses:** 0
Students belonging to fraternities: 70 % **Students belonging to sororities:** 53 %

Libraries and Computers

Books: 377,000 **Periodicals:** 2,633 **Microform items:** 113,000
Microcomputers available: Yes **Microcomputers networked:** Yes

Classes

Faculty / Student Ratio: 1/13 **Classes taught by teacher assistants:** 0 %
Most popular majors: Journalism, Economics **Classes begin:** Mid Sept.
Baccalaureate degrees offered: BA, BS

Sports

Division: III **Except:** **Physical ed requirements:** NA
Students participating in intercollegiate sports: 40 % **In intramural sports:** 75 %
Additional intercollegiate and/or intramural sports: (not found at all colleges)

Crew: No **Ice Hockey:** Yes **Lacrosse:** Yes **Wrestling:** Yes/M
Rugby: Yes **Sailing:** No **Skiing:** Yes
Squash: No **Ultimate Frisbee:** No **Water Polo:** Yes

Alumni

Number living: 17,000 **Annual giving:** $ 8 Mil. **Participation:** 37 %
Average annual gift: $ 1,200 **Average per student:** $4,000

3-2 Programs (2 degrees in 5 years)

Engineering with RPI, U VA, Va Tech, Duke, Penn State, Johns Hopkins, Columbia
3-1 Forestry with Duke

Observation and Opinion of:

Undergraduates and graduates ____________________

____

College counselor ____________________

____

WASHINGTON UNIVERSITY (Private)

One Brookings Drive, WA
St. Louis, MO 63130

HIGHLY SELECTIVE
(Composite rating of guide books)

Main tel.: 314-935-5000
Admissions tel.: 314-935-6000
Financial aid tel.: 314-935-5900
Scheduled Airline Service: St. Louis
Miles to airport: 10

Founded: 1853
Nickname: Bears
Religious affiliation: None
(Coed since 1853)

Student Body

Undergraduates: 5,000 **Men:** 47 % **Women:** 53 %
Graduate students: 5,300 **Freshman class:** 1,227

Academics

SAT Averages: 1210 **Verbal:** 560 **Math:** 650 **(Taking SATs: 95 %)**
700-800: V 4 % **M** 28 % **500-600: V** 46 % **M** 22 %
600-700: V 29 % **M** 46 % **400-500: V** 18 % **M** 3 % **300-400: V** 2 % **M** 0 %
High school class rank: Top fifth 87 % **2nd fifth** 11 % **3rd fifth** 2 %

Admissions

Applied: 8,000 **Accepted:** 58 % **Matriculated:** 26 %
Deadline: Feb. 1 **Accept common application:** No
Interview recommended: Yes **Off-campus interview available:** No
Evaluative: No **Informational only:** Yes **LD program:** Yes
Night in dorm provided: Yes **Non-refundable application fee:** $40
Early decision program: Yes **Applied:** 389 **Accepted:** 60 % **Deadline:** Dec. 1
Freshmen accepted other than Fall term: 1 % **SAT/FAF Code #** 6929

Transfers

Applied: 592 **Accepted:** 64 % **Application deadline for Fall:** Nov. 15 **Spring:** Apr. 1
Minimum grades recommended: 3.0 **All new students who were transfers into all classes:** 13 %

Class Experience

Return 2nd year: 92 % **Graduate after 4 years:** 84 % **To graduate school within 5 years:** 61 %

Cost

Tuition deposit: $200 **Total cost (Including school's estimate on fees and books):** $23,500
Tuition: $15,950 **(In state: $)** **Room and board:** $6,206
Annual giving by parents: $405,000 **Average per student:** $80

Financial Aid

Average total package per student: $11,400 **Number receiving aid:** 54 %
Average scholarships and grants: $9,000 **Average loans:** $2,400 **Work-study program:** NA
Undergraduates working on campus: 24 % **Average earnings:** $1,400
Non-need scholarships 14 % **Athletic scholarships:** NA **FAF deadline:** Feb. 15
Off-campus part-time employment: Excellent **CO-OP program:** Yes
ROTC: Yes **NROTC:** No **AFROTC:** at Parks Coll

Endowment

Total: $1.37 Billion **Per student (including graduate students):** $137,000

Location

Acres: 169 **Setting:** Surburban **Miles from town center:** 5 **(Pop.** 426,000)
Miles from (Pop.) **Miles from** (Pop.)

Class Composition

Asian: 9 % **Black:** 6 % **Hispanic:** 2 % **White:** 80 % **Other:** 3 %
Total minority : 20% **Foreign countries:** 4 % (200 students)
From public schools: 71 % **Students from in state:** 85 %

Housing (on campus)

Freshmen required to live on campus: Yes **Guaranteed for:** 4 years
Available for all students: 60 % **Fraternity / Sorority housing:** Yes / No
On-campus married student housing: No **Women-only dorms available:** No

Campus Life

Students living on campus: 60 % **Remain weekends:** 80 % **Handicap access:** 85 %
Car regulations: No freshmen
Number with cars: 36 % **Adequacy of on-campus parking:** Poor
Number of fraternities: 12 **Chapter houses:** 12 **Number of sororities:** 7 **Chapter houses:** 0
Students belonging to fraternities: 32 % **Students belonging to sororities:** 35 %

Libraries and Computers

Books: 2.3 Million **Periodicals:** 18,000 **Microform items:** 1.8 Mil.
Microcomputers available: Yes **Microcomputers networked:** Yes

Classes

Faculty / Student Ratio: 1/9 **Classes taught by teacher assistants:** 10 %
Most popular majors: NA **Classes begin:** Late Aug.
Baccalaureate degrees offered: BA, BFA, BS, BSBA, BSOT, BTECH

Sports

Division: III **Except:** **Physical ed requirements:** NA
Students participating in intercollegiate sports: 15 % **In intramural sports:** 75 %
Additional intercollegiate and/or intramural sports: (not found at all colleges)
Crew: Yes **Ice Hockey:** Yes **Lacrosse:** Yes **Wrestling:** Yes/M
Rugby: Yes **Sailing:** No **Skiing:** No
Squash: No **Ultimate Frisbee:** Yes **Water Polo:** No

Alumni

Number living: 78,000 **Annual giving:** $ 13 Mil. **Participation:** 32 %
Average annual gift: $ 600 **Average per student:** $1,300

3-2 Programs (2 degrees in 5 years)

In-house business and engineering programs
4-3 BS/M ARCH program

Observation and Opinion of:

Undergraduates and graduates ______________________________

____

College counselor ______________________________

____

UNIVERSITY OF WASHINGTON (Public)

1400 NE Campus Parkway
Seattle, WA 98195

SELECTIVE
(Composite rating of guide books)

Main tel.: 206-543-2100
Admissions tel.: 206-543-9686
Financial aid tel.: 206-543-6301
Scheduled Airline Service: Seattle
Miles to airport: 15

Founded: 1861
Nickname: Huskies
Religious affiliation: None
(Coed since 1861)

Student Body

Undergraduates: 20,000 **Men:** 52 % **Women:** 48 %
Graduate students: 9,000 **Freshman class:** 3,580

Academics

SAT Averages: 1090 **Verbal:** 480 **Math:** 610 **(Taking SATs:** 85 %)
700-800: V 1 % **M** 8 % **500-600: V** 30 % **M** 37 %
600-700: V 9 % **M** 27 % **400-500: V** 40 % **M** 21 % **300-400: V** 16 % **M** 7 %
High school class rank: Top fifth 70 % **2nd fifth** NA % **3rd fifth** NA %

Admissions

Applied: 9,992 **Accepted:** 75 % **Matriculated:** 48 %
Deadline: Feb. 1 **Accept common application:** No
Interview recommended: Yes **Off-campus interview available:** No
Evaluative: No **Informational only:** Yes **LD program:** No
Night in dorm provided: Yes **Non-refundable application fee:** $25
Early decision program: Yes **Applied:** NA **Accepted:** NA % **Deadline:** NA
Freshmen accepted other than Fall term: 2 % **SAT/FAF Code #** 4854

Transfers

Applied: 6,000 **Accepted:** 50 % **Application deadline for Fall:** Jul. 1 **Spring:** Feb. 1
Minimum grades recommended: 2.0 **All new students who were transfers into all classes:** 33 %

Class Experience

Return 2nd year: 89 % **Graduate after 4 years:** 51 % **To graduate school within 5 years:** NA %

Cost

Tuition deposit: $50 **Total cost (Including school's estimate on fees and books):** $10,800
Tuition: $6,300 (In state: $ 2,178) **Room and board:** $3,900
Annual giving by parents: $NA **Average per student:** $NA

Financial Aid

Average total package per student: $4,550 **Number receiving aid:** NA %
Average scholarships and grants: $2,300 **Average loans:** $2,250 **Work-study program:** Yes
Undergraduates working on campus: NA % **Average earnings:** $NA
Non-need scholarships 2 % **Athletic scholarships:** Yes **FAF deadline:** Mar. 1
Off-campus part-time employment: Good **CO-OP program:** Yes
ROTC: Yes **NROTC:** Yes **AFROTC:** Yes

Endowment

Total: $170 Million **Per student (including graduate students):** $5,100

Location

Acres: 680 **Setting:** Surburban **Miles from town center:** 3 **(Pop.** 505,000**)**
Miles from **(Pop.** **)** **Miles from** **(Pop.** **)**

Class Composition

Asian: 17 % **Black:** 4 % **Hispanic:** 3 % **White:** 64 % **Other:** 12 %
Total minority : 36 % **Foreign countries:** 2 % (400 students)
From public schools: NA % **Students from in state:** 90 %

Housing (on campus)

Freshmen required to live on campus: No
Available for all students: 15 %
On-campus married student housing: No
Guaranteed for: 0 year
Fraternity / Sorority housing: Yes / Yes
Women-only dorms available: No

Campus Life

Students living on campus: 15 % **Remain weekends:** NA % **Handicap access:** 85 %
Car regulations: Cars discouraged
Number with cars: 4 % **Adequacy of on-campus parking:** Poor
Number of fraternities: 32 **Chapter houses:** 32 **Number of sororities:** 18 **Chapter houses:** 18
Students belonging to fraternities: 18 % **Students belonging to sororities:** 16 %

Libraries and Computers

Books: 4.8 Million **Periodicals:** 50,000 **Microform items:** 5.3 Mil.
Microcomputers available: Yes **Microcomputers networked:** Yes

Classes

Faculty / Student Ratio: 1/12 **Classes taught by teacher assistants:** 25 %
Most popular majors: Business Administration, Psychology **Classes begin:** LateSept.
Baccalaureate degrees offered: BA, BEA, B.MUS, BS, BS ENGR, BS FOOD, BS MED TECH, BSN, BS PHARM, BS PHYS THER

Sports

Division: I **Except:** **Physical ed requirements:** None
Students participating in intercollegiate sports: NA % **In intramural sports:** NA %
Additional intercollegiate and/or intramural sports: (not found at all colleges)

Crew: Yes **Ice Hockey:** Yes **Lacrosse:** Yes **Wrestling:** Yes/M
Rugby: Yes **Sailing:** Yes **Skiing:** Yes
Squash: Yes **Ultimate Frisbee:** Yes **Water Polo:** Yes

Alumni

Number living: 166,000 **Annual giving:** $ 12.8 Mil. **Participation:** 24 %
Average annual gift: $ 550 **Average per student:** $400

3-2 Programs (2 degrees in 5 years)

Cooperative education programs in business and engineering

Observation and Opinion of:

Undergraduates and graduates ______________________________

____

College counselor ______________________________

____

WELLESLEY COLLEGE (Private)

Wellesley, MA 02181

MOST SELECTIVE
(Composite rating of guide books)

Main tel.: 617-235-0320
Admissions tel.: 617-235-2270
Financial aid tel.: 617-235-0320, Ext. 2360
Scheduled Airline Service: NA
Miles to airport: NA

Founded: 1870
Nickname: NA
Religious affiliation: None
(Coed since 1870)

Student Body

Undergraduates: 2,300 **Men:** 0 % **Women:** 100 %
Graduate students: 0 **Freshman class:** 584

Academics

SAT Averages: 1250 **Verbal:** NA **Math:** NA **(Taking SATs:** 99 %)
700-800: V NA % **M** NA % **500-600: V** NA % **M** NA %
600-700: V NA % **M** NA % **400-500: V** NA % **M** NA % **300-400: V** NA % **M** NA %
High school class rank: Top fifth 92 % **2nd fifth** NA % **3rd fifth** NA%

Admissions

Applied: 2,594 **Accepted:** 49 % **Matriculated:** 46 %
Deadline: Feb. 1 **Accept common application:** No
Interview recommended: Yes **Off-campus interview available:** Yes
Evaluative: No **Informational only:** Yes **LD program:** Yes
Night in dorm provided: NA **Non-refundable application fee:** $40
Early decision program: Yes **Applied:** 127 **Accepted:** 80 % **Deadline:** Nov. 1
Freshmen accepted other than Fall term: 0 % **SAT/FAF Code #** 3957

Transfers

Applied: 130 **Accepted:** 32 % **Application deadline for Fall:** Feb. 1 **Spring:** Nov. 15
Minimum grades recommended: C **All new students who were transfers into all classes:** 6 %

Class Experience

Return 2nd year: 98 % **Graduate after 4 years:** 84 % **To graduate school within 5 years:** 35 %

Cost

Tuition deposit: $350 **Total cost (Including school's estimate on fees and books):** $23,000
Tuition: $15,966 **(In state:** $) **Room and board:** $5,657
Annual giving by parents: $266,000 **Average per student:** $115

Financial Aid

Average total package per student: $12,750 **Number receiving aid:** 43 %
Average scholarships and grants: $10,172 **Average loans:** $2,486 **Work-study program:** Yes
Undergraduates working on campus: 46 % **Average earnings:** $1,400
Non-need scholarships NA % **Athletic scholarships:** NA **FAF deadline:** Feb.1
Off-campus part-time employment: Excellent **CO-OP program:** No
ROTC: at MIT **NROTC:** at MIT **AFROTC:** at MIT

Endowment

Total: $374 Million **Per student (including graduate students):** $165,000

Location

Acres: 500 **Setting:** Surburban **Miles from town center:** 2 **(Pop.** 30,000**)**
12 **Miles from** Boston **(Pop.** 700,000 **)** **Miles from (Pop.)**

Class Composition

Asian: 19 % **Black:** 7 % **Hispanic:** 4 % **White:** 69 % **Other:** 1 %
Total minority : 31 % **Foreign countries:** 6 % (150 students)
From public schools: 65 % **Students from in state:** 16 %

Housing (on campus)

Freshmen required to live on campus: Yes **Guaranteed for:** 4 years
Available for all students: 92 % **Fraternity / Sorority housing:** No/ No
On-campus married student housing: No **Women-only dorms available:** Yes

Campus Life

Students living on campus: 92 % **Remain weekends:** NA % **Handicap access:** 100 %
Car regulations: Freshmen with permission only
Number with cars: 23 % **Adequacy of on-campus parking:** Poor
Number of fraternities: 0 **Chapter houses:** 0 **Number of sororities:** 0 **Chapter houses:** 0
Students belonging to fraternities: NA % **Students belonging to sororities:** 0 %

Libraries and Computers

Books: 660,000 **Periodicals:** 2,760 **Microform items:** 53,600
Microcomputers available: Yes **Microcomputers networked:** Yes

Classes

Faculty / Student Ratio: 1/10 **Classes taught by teacher assistants:** 0 %
Most popular majors: Poly Science, Economics **Classes begin:** Sept.
Baccalaureate degrees offered: BA

Sports

Division: III **Except:** **Physical ed requirements:** 2 semesters
Students participating in intercollegiate sports: 8 % **In intramural sports:** 20 %
Additional intercollegiate and/or intramural sports: (not found at all colleges)

Crew: Yes **Ice Hockey:** Yes **Lacrosse:** Yes **Wrestling:** No
Rugby: Yes **Sailing:** Yes **Skiing:** Yes
Squash: Yes **Ultimate Frisbee:** No **Water Polo:** Yes

Alumni

Number living: 29,100 **Annual giving:** $ 23 Mil. **Participation:** 55 %
Average annual gift: $ 1,400 **Average per student:** $10,400

3-2 Programs (2 degrees in 5 years)

Double degrees program with MIT
Cross-registration with MIT

Observation and Opinion of:

Undergraduates and graduates ____________________

____

College counselor ____________________

____

WESLEYAN UNIVERSITY (Private)

Richmond, VA 23173

MOST SELECTIVE
(Composite rating of guide books)

Main tel.: 203-347-9411
Admissions tel.: 203-347-9411, Ext. 2900
Financial aid tel.: 203-347-9411, Ext. 2304
Scheduled Airline Service: Hartford
Miles to airport: 24

Founded: 1831
Nickname: Cardinals
Religious affiliation: None
(Coed since 1968)

Student Body

Undergraduates: 2,650 **Men:** 48 % **Women:** 52 %
Graduate students: 150 **Freshman class:** 700

Academics

SAT Averages: 1285 **Verbal:** 615 **Math:** 670 **(Taking SATs:** 99 %)
700-800: V 14 % **M** 39 % **500-600: V** 30 % **M** 12 %
600-700: V 50 % **M** 47 % **400-500: V** 7 % **M** 2 % **300-400: V** NA % **M** NA %
High school class rank: Top fifth 89 % **2nd fifth** 10 % **3rd fifth** 4 %

Admissions

Applied: 4,833 **Accepted:** 40 % **Matriculated:** 37 %
Deadline: Jan. 15 **Accept common application:** Yes
Interview recommended: Yes **Off-campus interview available:** Yes
Evaluative: Yes **Informational only:** No **LD program:** No
Night in dorm provided: NA **Non-refundable application fee:** $50
Early decision program: Yes **Applied:** 506 **Accepted:** 40 % **Deadline:** Nov. 15
Freshmen accepted other than Fall term: 5 % **SAT/FAF Code #** 3959

Transfers

Applied: 511 **Accepted:** 20 % **Application deadline for Fall:** Mar. 1 **Spring:** Nov. 1
Minimum grades recommended: 3.5 **All new students who were transfers into all classes:** 9 %

Class Experience

Return 2nd year: 97 % **Graduate after 4 years:** 92 % **To graduate school within 5 years:** 75 %

Cost

Tuition deposit: $200 **Total cost (Including school's estimate on fees and books):** $24,000
Tuition: $17,200 **(In state:** $) **Room and board:** $5,500
Annual giving by parents: $225,000 **Average per student:** $NA

Financial Aid

Average total package per student: $12,800 **Number receiving aid:** 35 %
Average scholarships and grants: $10,353 **Average loans:** $2,450 **Work-study program:** Yes
Undergraduates working on campus: 64 % **Average earnings:** $1,010
Non-need scholarships 0 % **Athletic scholarships:** NA **FAF deadline:** Jan. 15
Off-campus part-time employment: Good **CO-OP program:** No
ROTC: No **NROTC:** No **AFROTC:** No

Endowment

Total: $271 Million **Per student (including graduate students):** $100,000

Location

Acres: 120 **Setting:** Surburban **Miles from town center:** 1 **(Pop.** 50,000**)**
15 **Miles from** Hartford **(Pop.** 136,000 **)** 20 **Miles from** New Haven **(Pop.** 126,000**)**

Class Composition

Asian: 7 % **Black:** 8 % **Hispanic:** 4% **White:** 74 % **Other:** 7 %
Total minority : 26 % **Foreign countries:** 2 % (60 students)
From public schools: 63 % **Students from in state:** 10 %

Housing (on campus)

Freshmen required to live on campus: Yes **Guaranteed for:** 4 years
Available for all students: 92 % **Fraternity / Sorority housing:** Yes / No
On-campus married student housing: No **Women-only dorms available:** Yes

Campus Life

Students living on campus: 92 % **Remain weekends:** NA % **Handicap access:** 90 %
Car regulations: No financial aid students
Number with cars: 30 % **Adequacy of on-campus parking:** Good
Number of fraternities: 6 **Chapter houses:** 4 **Number of sororities:** 4 **Chapter houses:** 0
Students belonging to fraternities: 10 % **Students belonging to sororities:** 2 %

Libraries and Computers

Books: 1.2 Million **Periodicals:** 3,460 **Microform items:** 192,000
Microcomputers available: Yes **Microcomputers networked:** Yes

Classes

Faculty / Student Ratio: 1/11 **Classes taught by teacher assistants:** 0 %
Most popular majors: English, Government **Classes begin:** Early Sept.
Baccalaureate degrees offered: BA

Sports

Division: III **Except:** **Physical ed requirements:** None
Students participating in intercollegiate sports: 50 % **In intramural sports:** 45 %
Additional intercollegiate and/or intramural sports: (not found at all colleges)
Crew: Yes **Ice Hockey:** Yes **Lacrosse:** Yes **Wrestling:** Yes/M
Rugby: Yes **Sailing:** Yes **Skiing:** NA
Squash: Yes **Ultimate Frisbee:** Yes **Water Polo:** Yes

Alumni

Number living: 22,700 **Annual giving:** $ 8.2 Mil. **Participation:** 40 %
Average annual gift: $ 800 **Average per student:** $3,000

3-2 Programs (2 degrees in 5 years)

Engineering with Cal Tech and Columbia
Member of 12-college exchange program

Observation and Opinion of:

Undergraduates and graduates ______________________________

College counselor ______________________________

WHEATON COLLEGE (Private)

501 East College Avenue
Wheaton, IL 60187

HIGHLY SELECTIVE
(Composite rating of guide books)

Main tel.: 708-752-5000
Admissions tel.: 708-752-5005
Financial aid tel.: 708-752-5021
Scheduled Airline Service: Chicago
Miles to airport: 24

Founded: 1860
Nickname: Crusaders
Religious affiliation: None
(Coed since 1860)

Student Body

Undergraduates: 2,200 **Men:** 45 % **Women:** 55 %
Graduate students: 300 **Freshman class:** 508

Academics

SAT Averages: 1145 **Verbal:** 575 **Math:** 640 **(Taking SATs:** 65 %**)**
700-800: V 5 % **M** 11 % **500-600: V** 44 % **M** 38 %
600-700: V 22 % **M** 41 % **400-500: V** 26 % **M** 9 % **300-400: V** 3 % **M** 1 %
High school class rank: Top fifth 77 % **2nd fifth** 18 % **3rd fifth** 4 %

Admissions

Applied: 1,185 **Accepted:** 77 % **Matriculated:** 56 %
Deadline: Feb. 15 **Accept common application:** No
Interview recommended: NA **Off-campus interview available:** NA
Evaluative: NA **Informational only:** NA **LD program:** NA
Night in dorm provided: NA **Non-refundable application fee:** $30
Early decision program: Yes **Applied:** NA **Accepted:** NA % **Deadline:** Dec. 1
Freshmen accepted other than Fall term: 2 % **SAT/FAF Code #** 1905

Transfers

Applied: 262 **Accepted:** 58 % **Application deadline for Fall:** Mar. 1 **Spring:** Oct. 1
Minimum grades recommended: 3.0 **All new students who were transfers into all classes:** 15 %

Class Experience

Return 2nd year: 94 % **Graduate after 4 years:** 75 % **To graduate school within 5 years:** NA %

Cost

Tuition deposit: $200 **Total cost (Including school's estimate on fees and books):** $14,250
Tuition: $10,280 **(In state:** $ **)** **Room and board:** $3,970
Annual giving by parents: $858,000 **Average per student:** $370

Financial Aid

Average total package per student: $5,900 **Number receiving aid:** 7 %
Average scholarships and grants: $4,800 **Average loans:** $1,100 **Work-study program:** NA
Undergraduates working on campus: 43 % **Average earnings:** $600
Non-need scholarships 1 % **Athletic scholarships:** Yes **FAF deadline:** Mar. 15
Off-campus part-time employment: Good **CO-OP program:** NA
ROTC: Yes **NROTC:** No **AFROTC:** No

Endowment

Total: $87 Million **Per student (including graduate students):** $33,000

Location

Acres: 80 **Setting:** Surburban **Miles from town center:** 2 **(Pop.** 48,000 **)**
25 **Miles from** Chicago **(Pop.** 3 Mil. **)** **Miles from** **(Pop.** **)**

Class Composition

Asian: 5 % **Black:** 1 % **Hispanic:** 1 % **White:** 92 % **Other:** 1 %
Total minority : 8 % **Foreign countries:** 1 % (25 students)
From public schools: 70 % **Students from in state:** 24 %

Housing (on campus)

Freshmen required to live on campus: Yes **Guaranteed for:** 4 years
Available for all students: 85 % **Fraternity / Sorority housing:** 0 / 0
On-campus married student housing: No **Women-only dorms available:** Yes

Campus Life

Students living on campus: 85 % **Remain weekends:** NA % **Handicap access:** 50 %
Car regulations: No freshmen
Number with cars: 35 % **Adequacy of on-campus parking:** NA
Number of fraternities: 0 **Chapter houses:** 0 **Number of sororities:** 0 **Chapter houses:** 0
Students belonging to fraternities: 0 % **Students belonging to sororities:** 0 %

Libraries and Computers

Books: 350,000 **Periodicals:** 2,100 **Microform items:** 377,000
Microcomputers available: Yes **Microcomputers networked:** Yes

Classes

Faculty / Student Ratio: 1/15 **Classes taught by teacher assistants:** 0 %
Most popular majors: Economics, Literature **Classes begin:** Late Aug.
Baccalaureate degrees offered: BA, B MUS, B MUS ED, BS

Sports

Division: NA **Except:** **Physical ed requirements:** 3 credit hours
Students participating in intercollegiate sports: NA % **In intramural sports:** NA %
Additional intercollegiate and/or intramural sports: (not found at all colleges)

Crew:	**Ice Hockey:** Yes	**Lacrosse:** Yes	**Wrestling:** Yes/M
Rugby:	**Sailing:**	**Skiing:**	
Squash:	**Ultimate Frisbee:**	**Water Polo:** Yes	

Alumni

Number living: 29,800 **Annual giving:** $ 3.7 Mil. **Participation:** 33 %
Average annual gift: $ 380 **Average per student:** $1,500

3-2 Programs (2 degrees in 5 years)

Nursing and Engineering with Emory, U of Illinois, Western Reserve, Illinois Institute, and Washington U

Observation and Opinion of:

Undergraduates and graduates ______________________________

____

College counselor ______________________________

____

THE COLLEGE OF WILLIAM AND MARY (Public)

Williamsburg, VA 23185

MOST SELECTIVE
(Composite rating of guide books)

Main tel.: 804-221-4000
Admissions tel.: 804-221-3999
Financial aid tel.: 804-221-2420
Scheduled Airline Service: Richmond
Miles to airport: 48

Founded: 1693
Nickname: The Tribe
Religious affiliation: None
(Coed since 1918)

Student Body

Undergraduates: 5,250 **Men:** 47 % **Women:** 53 %
Graduate students: 1,600 **Freshman class:** 1,260

Academics

SAT Averages: 1225 **Verbal:** 590 **Math:** 635 **(Taking SATs:** 100 %)
700-800: V 9 % M 24 % **500-600:** V 34 % M 24 %
600-700: V 44 % M 47 % **400-500:** V 13 % M 5 % **300-400:** V NA % M NA %
High school class rank: Top fifth 91 % **2nd fifth** 7 % **3rd fifth** 2 %

Admissions

Applied: 9,500 **Accepted:** 27 % **Matriculated:** 50 %
Deadline: Jan. 15 **Accept common application:** No
Interview recommended: No **Off-campus interview available:** Yes
Evaluative: No **Informational only:** Yes **LD program:** No
Night in dorm provided: No **Non-refundable application fee:** $30
Early decision program: Yes **Applied:** 1,050 **Accepted:** 38 % **Deadline:** Nov. 1
Freshmen accepted other than Fall term: 1 % **SAT/FAF Code #** 5115

Transfers

Applied: 921 **Accepted:** 19 % **Application deadline for Fall:** Mar. 1 **Spring:** NA
Minimum grades recommended: 3.0 **All new students who were transfers into all classes:** 7 %

Class Experience

Return 2nd year: 95 % **Graduate after 4 years:** 80 % **To graduate school within 5 years:** NA %

Cost

Tuition deposit: $150 **Total cost (Including school's estimate on fees and books):** $15,470
Tuition: $11,428 **(In state:** $4,048) **Room and board:** $3,750
Annual giving by parents: $515,000 **Average per student:** $75

Financial Aid

Average total package per student: $NA **Number receiving aid:** 21 %
Average scholarships and grants: $NA **Average loans:** $1,918 **Work-study program:** NA
Undergraduates working on campus: 30 % **Average earnings:** $600
Non-need scholarships 0 % **Athletic scholarships:** Yes **FAF deadline:** Feb. 15
Off-campus part-time employment: Excellent **CO-OP program:** No
ROTC: Yes **NROTC:** No **AFROTC:** No

Endowment

Total: $88 Million **Per student (including graduate students):** $12,000

Location

Acres: 1,200 **Setting:** Rural **Miles from town center:** 0 **(Pop.** 12,000**)**
15 **Miles from** Newport News **(Pop.** 145,000**)** 50 **Miles from** Richmond **(Pop.** 220,000**)**

Class Composition

Asian: 4 % **Black:** 7 % **Hispanic:** 1 % **White:** 89 % **Other:** NA %
Total minority : 11 % **Foreign countries:** 3 % (155 students)
From public schools: NA % **Students from in state:** 65 %

Housing (on campus)

Freshmen required to live on campus: Yes **Guaranteed for:** NA
Available for all students: 80 % **Fraternity / Sorority housing:** Yes / Yes
On-campus married student housing: Yes **Women-only dorms available:** Yes

Campus Life

Students living on campus: 80 % **Remain weekends:** 95 % **Handicap access:** 50 %
Car regulations: Only after 4 regular semesters
Number with cars: 48 % **Adequacy of on-campus parking:** NA
Number of fraternities: 13 **Chapter houses:** 11 **Number of sororities:** 12 **Chapter houses:** 10
Students belonging to fraternities: 35 % **Students belonging to sororities:** 35 %

Libraries and Computers

Books: 900,000 **Periodicals:** 5,750 **Microform items:** 780,000
Microcomputers available: 500 **Microcomputers networked:** Yes

Classes

Faculty / Student Ratio: 1/14 **Classes taught by teacher assistants:** 0 %
Most popular majors: Business, Economics, Government **Classes begin:** Early Sept.
Baccalaureate degrees offered: AB, BBA, BS

Sports

Division: I **Except:** **Physical ed requirements:** 4 semesters
Students participating in intercollegiate sports: 13% **In intramural sports:** 80 %
Additional intercollegiate and/or intramural sports: (not found at all colleges)

Crew: Yes/M **Ice Hockey:** No **Lacrosse:** Yes/M **Wrestling:** Yes/M
Rugby: Yes **Sailing:** No **Skiing:** Yes
Squash: No **Ultimate Frisbee:** No **Water Polo:** No

Alumni

Number living: 50,500 **Annual giving:** $ 7.6 Million **Participation:** 22 %
Average annual gift: $ 700 **Average per student:** $1,000

3-2 Programs (2 degrees in 5 years)

Engineering with RPI, Case Western, Columbia U, Washington U, U of Virginia
Forestry with Duke

Observation and Opinion of:

Undergraduates and graduates ____________________

____

College counselor ____________________

____

WILLIAMS COLLEGE (Private)

Williamstown, MA 01267

MOST SELECTIVE
(Composite rating of guide books)

Main tel.: 413-597-3131
Admissions tel.: 413-597-2211
Financial aid tel.: 413-597-4181
Scheduled Airline Service: Albany or Hartford
Miles to airport: 38 or 90

Founded: 1793
Nickname: Ephs
Religious affiliation: None
(Coed since 1969)

Student Body

Undergraduates: 2,070 **Men:** 55 % **Women:** 45 %
Graduate students: 50 **Freshman class:** 500

Academics

SAT Averages: 1335 **Verbal:** NA **Math:** NA **(Taking SATs:** 98 %**)**
700-800: V 34 % **M** 48 % **500-600: V** 19 % **M** 11 %
600-700: V 40 % **M** 37 % **400-500: V** 6 % **M** 3 % **300-400: V** 1 % **M** 1 %
High school class rank: Top fifth 91 % **2nd fifth** 7 % **3rd fifth** 2 %

Admissions

Applied: 4,340 **Accepted:** 28 % **Matriculated:** 41 %
Deadline: Feb. 1 **Accept common application:** Yes
Interview recommended: No **Off-campus interview available:** Yes
Evaluative: No **Informational only:** Yes **LD program:** No
Night in dorm provided: Yes **Non-refundable application fee:** $50
Early decision program: Yes **Applied:** 370 **Accepted:** 39 % **Deadline:** Nov. 15
Freshmen accepted other than Fall term: 0 % **SAT/FAF Code #** 3965

Transfers

Applied: 193 **Accepted:** 17 % **Application deadline for Fall:** Mar. 1 **Spring:** Dec. 1
Minimum grades recommended: 3.5 **All new students who were transfers into all classes:** NA %

Class Experience

Return 2nd year: 98 % **Graduate after 4 years:** 90 % **To graduate school within 5 years:** NA %

Cost

Tuition deposit: $200 **Total cost (Including school's estimate on fees and books):** $23,250
Tuition: $17,685 **(In state:** $ **)** **Room and board:** $5,200
Annual giving by parents: $1.1 Million **Average per student:** $500

Financial Aid

Average total package per student: $15,950 **Number receiving aid:** 36 %
Average scholarships and grants: $13,900 **Average loans:** $2,050 **Work-study program:** NA
Undergraduates working on campus: 32 % **Average earnings:** $NA
Non-need scholarships 0 % **Athletic scholarships:** 0 **FAF deadline:** Feb.1
Off-campus part-time employment: Fair **CO-OP program:** No
ROTC: No **NROTC:** No **AFROTC:** No

Endowment

Total: $333 Million **Per student (including graduate students):** $160,000

Location

Acres: 450 **Setting:** Rural **Miles from town center:** 0 **(Pop.** 9,000 **)**
38 **Miles from** Albany **(Pop.** 285,000 **)** 140 **Miles from** Boston **(Pop.** 600,000**)**

Class Composition

Asian: 9 % **Black:** 8 % **Hispanic:** 5 % **White:** 78 % **Other:** NA %
Total minority : 22 % **Foreign countries:** 3 % (60 students)
From public schools: 54 % **Students from in state:** 12 %

Housing (on campus)

Freshmen required to live on campus: Yes **Guaranteed for:** 4 years
Available for all students: 100 % **Fraternity / Sorority housing:** 0 / 0
On-campus married student housing: No **Women-only dorms available:** No

Campus Life

Students living on campus: 98 % **Remain weekends:** 94 % **Handicap access:** 75 %
Car regulations: No freshmen
Number with cars: 28 % **Adequacy of on-campus parking:** Fair (fee)
Number of fraternities: 0 **Chapter houses:** 0 **Number of sororities:** 0 **Chapter houses:** 0
Students belonging to fraternities: 0 % **Students belonging to sororities:** 0 %

Libraries and Computers

Books: 665,000 **Periodicals:** 3,100 **Microform items:** 445,000
Microcomputers available: 100 **Microcomputers networked:** Yes

Classes

Faculty / Student Ratio: 1/11 **Classes taught by teacher assistants:** 0 %
Most popular majors: English, History, Poly Science **Classes begin:** Sept.
Baccalaureate degrees offered: BA

Sports

Division: III **Except:** I Skiing **Physical ed requirements:** 3 semesters
Students participating in intercollegiate sports: 50 % **In intramural sports:** 50 %
Additional intercollegiate and/or intramural sports: (not found at all colleges)

Crew: Yes	**Ice Hockey:** Yes	**Lacrosse:** Yes	**Wrestling:** Yes
Rugby: Yes	**Sailing:** Yes	**Skiing:** Yes	
Squash: Yes	**Ultimate Frisbee:** Yes	**Water Polo:** Yes	

Alumni

Number living: 18,900 **Annual giving:** $ 12.7 Million **Participation:** 62 %
Average annual gift: $ 1,050 **Average per student:** $6,000

3-2 Programs (2 degrees in 5 years)

Engineering with Columbia U and Washington U
Member of 12-college exchange program

Observation and Opinion of:

Undergraduates and graduates ______________________________

____

College counselor ______________________________

____

UNIVERSITY OF WISCONSIN (Madison) (Public)

750 University Avenue
Madison, WI 53706

VERY SELECTIVE
(Composite rating of guide books)

Main tel.: 608-262-1234
Admissions tel.: 608-262-3961
Financial aid tel.: 608-262-3060
Scheduled Airline Service: Madison
Miles to airport: 7

Founded: 1848
Nickname: Badgers
Religious affiliation: None
(Coed since 1848)

Student Body

Undergraduates: 27,000 **Men:** 50 % **Women:** 50 %
Graduate students: 11,600 **Freshman class:** 4,700

Academics

SAT Averages: 1080 **Verbal:** 500 **Math:** 590 (Taking SATs: 40 %)
700-800: V 1 % **M** 15 % **500-600: V** 35 % **M** 33 %
600-700: V 15 % **M** 35 % **400-500: V** 36 % **M** 14 % **300-400: V** 11 % **M** 3 %
High school class rank: Top fifth 62 % **2nd fifth** 34 % **3rd fifth** 3 %

Admissions

Applied: 14,200 **Accepted:** 72 % **Matriculated:** 46 %
Deadline: Feb. 1 **Accept common application:** No
Interview recommended: No **Off-campus interview available:** No
Evaluative: NA **Informational only:** NA **LD program:** Yes
Night in dorm provided: NA **Non-refundable application fee:** $10
Early decision program: No **Applied:** NA **Accepted:** NA % **Deadline:** NA
Freshmen accepted other than Fall term: 2 % **SAT/FAF Code #** 1846

Transfers

Applied: 4,800 **Accepted:** 53 % **Application deadline for Fall:** Mar. 1 **Spring:** Nov. 15
Minimum grades recommended: C **All new students who were transfers into all classes:** 27 %

Class Experience

Return 2nd year: 86 % **Graduate after 4 years:** 61 % **To graduate school within 5 years:** NA %

Cost

Tuition deposit: $NA **Total cost (Including school's estimate on fees and books):** $13,000
Tuition: $7,800 **(In state:** $ 2,400**)** **Room and board:** $3,715
Annual giving by parents: $0 **Average per student:** $0

Financial Aid

Average total package per student: $4,400 **Number receiving aid:** NA %
Average scholarships and grants: $1,900 **Average loans:** $2,600 **Work-study program:** NA
Undergraduates working on campus: 50 % **Average earnings:** $1,500
Non-need scholarships 24 % **Athletic scholarships:** NA **FAF deadline:** Mar. 15
Off-campus part-time employment: Excellent **CO-OP program:** Yes
ROTC: Yes **NROTC:** Yes **AFROTC:** Yes

Endowment

Total: $218 Million **Per student (including graduate students):** $5,000

Location

Acres: 900 **Setting:** City **Miles from town center:** 0 **(Pop.** 170,000**)**
75 **Miles from** Milwaukee **(Pop.** 835,000 **)** 140 **Miles from** Chicago **(Pop.** 3 **Mil.)**

Class Composition

Asian: 4 % **Black:** 2 % **Hispanic:** 1 % **White:** 93 % **Other:** NA %
Total minority : 7 % **Foreign countries:** 3 % (700 students)
From public schools: 75 % **Students from in state:** 70 %

Housing (on campus)

Freshmen required to live on campus: No **Guaranteed for:** 0 years
Available for all students: 25 % **Fraternity / Sorority housing:** Yes / Yes
On-campus married student housing: Yes **Women-only dorms available:** Yes

Campus Life

Students living on campus: 24 % **Remain weekends:** NA % **Handicap access:** 95 %
Car regulations: None
Number with cars: 9 % **Adequacy of on-campus parking:** NA
Number of fraternities: 34 **Chapter houses:** 26 **Number of sororities:** 9 **Chapter houses:** 8
Students belonging to fraternities: 14 % **Students belonging to sororities:** 10 %

Libraries and Computers

Books: 4.8 Million **Periodicals:** 51,000 **Microform items:** 2 Million
Microcomputers available: Yes **Microcomputers networked:** Yes

Classes

Faculty / Student Ratio: 1/14 **Classes taught by teacher assistants:** 20 %
Most popular majors: Engineering, Business, Economics **Classes begin:** Early Sept.
Baccalaureate degrees offered: BA, BBA, BFA, B MUS, BNS, BS

Sports

Division: I **Except:** **Physical ed requirements:** None
Students participating in intercollegiate sports: 4% **In intramural sports:** NA %
Additional intercollegiate and/or intramural sports: (not found at all colleges)

Crew: Yes **Ice Hockey:** Yes **Lacrosse:** NA **Wrestling:** Yes/M
Rugby: Yes **Sailing:** Yes **Skiing:** NA
Squash: NA **Ultimate Frisbee:** NA **Water Polo:** NA

Alumni

Number living: 232,000 **Annual giving:** $14 Million **Participation:** 18 %
Average annual gift: $ 370 **Average per student:** $380

3-2 Programs (2 degrees in 5 years)

Observation and Opinion of:

Undergraduates and graduates ______________________________

____

College counselor ______________________________

____

WORCESTER POLYTECHNIC INSTITUTE (Private)

100 Institute Road
Worcester, MA 01609

Main tel.: 508-831-5000
Admissions tel.: 508-831-5286
Financial aid tel.: 508-831-5469
Scheduled Airline Service: Boston
Miles to airport: 42

HIGHLY SELECTIVE
(Composite rating of guide books)

Founded: 1865
Nickname: Engineers
Religious affiliation: None
(Coed since 1968)

Student Body

Undergraduates: 2,700 **Men:** 82 % **Women:** 18 %
Graduate students: 1,000 **Freshman class:** 700

Academics

SAT Averages: 1210 **Verbal:** NA **Math:** NA (Taking SATs: 96 %)
700-800: V 2 % **M** 27 % **500-600: V** 46 % **M** 17 %
600-700: V 20 % **M** 55 % **400-500: V** 21 % **M** 1 % **300-400: V** 1 % **M** 0 %
High school class rank: Top fifth 85 % **2nd fifth** 13 % **3rd fifth** 2 %

Admissions

Applied: 2,700 **Accepted:** 79 % **Matriculated:** 33 %
Deadline: Feb. 15 **Accept common application:** Yes
Interview recommended: Yes **Off-campus interview available:** Yes
Evaluative: No **Informational only:** Yes **LD program:** Yes
Night in dorm provided: Yes **Non-refundable application fee:** $35
Early decision program: Yes **Applied:** 160 **Accepted:** 75 % **Deadline:** Dec. 1
Freshmen accepted other than Fall term: 2 % **SAT/FAF Code #** 3969

Transfers

Applied: 152 **Accepted:** 70 % **Application deadline for Fall:** Apr. 15 **Spring:** Nov. 15
Minimum grades recommended: C **All new students who were transfers into all classes:** 3 %

Class Experience

Return 2nd year: 89 % **Graduate after 4 years:** 65 % **To graduate school within 1 year:** 12 %

Cost

Tuition deposit: $200 **Total cost (Including school's estimate on fees and books):** $20,700
Tuition: $14,600 **(In state:** $ **)** **Room and board:** $4,900
Annual giving by parents: $21,000 **Average per student:** $NA

Financial Aid

Average total package per student: $9,350 **Number receiving aid:** 65 %
Average scholarships and grants: $6,350 **Average loans:** $3,000 **Work-study program:** Yes
Undergraduates working on campus: 31 % **Average earnings:** $800
Non-need scholarships 0 % **Athletic scholarships:** No **FAF deadline:** Mar. 1
Off-campus part-time employment: Excellent **CO-OP program:** No
ROTC: Yes **NROTC:** Off campus **AFROTC:** Yes

Endowment

Total: $98 Million **Per student (including graduate students):** $25,000

Location

Acres: 62 **Setting:** Surburban **Miles from town center:** 1 **(Pop.** 170,000 **)**
45 **Miles from** Boston **(Pop.** 600,000 **)** 70 **Miles from** Hartford **(Pop.** 137,000 **)**

Class Composition

Asian: 5 % **Black:** 1 % **Hispanic:** 1 % **White:** 92% **Other:** NA %
Total minority : 8 % **Foreign countries:** 5 % (35 students)
From public schools: 76 % **Students from in state:** 11 %

Housing (on campus)

Freshmen required to live on campus: No **Guaranteed for:** 1 year
Available for all students: 50 % **Fraternity / Sorority housing:** Yes / Yes
On-campus married student housing: Yes **Women-only dorms available:** Yes

Campus Life

Students living on campus: 50 % **Remain weekends:** 85 % **Handicap access:** 90 %
Car regulations: No freshmen
Number with cars: 25 % **Adequacy of on-campus parking:** NA
Number of fraternities: 11 **Chapter houses:** 11 **Number of sororities:** 3 **Chapter houses:** 1
Students belonging to fraternities: 40 % **Students belonging to sororities:** 40 %

Libraries and Computers

Books: 290,000 **Periodicals:** 1,420 **Microform items:** 780,000
Microcomputers available: Yes **Microcomputers networked:** Yes

Classes

Faculty / Student Ratio: 1/11 **Classes taught by teacher assistants:** 0 %
Most popular majors: Civil, Mechanical, Electrical Engineering **Classes begin:** Late Aug.
Baccalaureate degrees offered: BS

Sports

Division: III **Except:** **Physical ed requirements:** 2 semesters
Students participating in intercollegiate sports: 40 % **In intramural sports:** 55 %
Additional intercollegiate and/or intramural sports: (not found at all colleges)

Crew: Yes **Ice Hockey:** Yes **Lacrosse:** Yes **Wrestling:** Yes/M
Rugby: Yes **Sailing:** Yes **Skiing:** Yes
Squash: NA **Ultimate Frisbee:** Yes **Water Polo:** Yes

Alumni

Number living: 17,600 **Annual giving:** $3.4 Million **Participation:** 38 %
Average annual gift: $ 500 **Average per student:** $950

3-2 Programs (2 degrees in 5 years)

Engineering with St. Lawrence U and Emmanuel College

Observation and Opinion of:

Undergraduates and graduates ____________________

____

College counselor ____________________

____

YALE UNIVERSITY (Private)

1502A Yale Station
New Haven, CT 06520

MOST SELECTIVE
(Composite rating of guide books)

Main tel.: 203-432-4771
Admissions tel.: 203-432-1900
Financial aid tel.: 203-432-0360
Scheduled Airline Service: Hartford
Miles to airport: 50

Founded: 1701
Nickname: Bulldogs
Religious affiliation: None
(Coed since 1969)

Student Body

Undergraduates: 5,200 **Men:** 60 % **Women:** 40 %
Graduate students: 5,600 **Freshman class:** 1,360

Academics

SAT Averages: 1350 **Verbal:** NA **Math:** NA (Taking SATs: NA %)
700-800: V 30 % **M** 55 % **500-600: V** 18 % **M** 8 %
600-700: V 50 % **M** 35 % **400-500: V** 3 % **M** 1 % **300-400: V** NA % **M** NA %
High school class rank: Top fifth 95 % **2nd fifth** 5 % **3rd fifth** NA %

Admissions

Applied: 11,900 **Accepted:** 20 % **Matriculated:** 58 %
Deadline: Feb. 1 **Accept common application:** No
Interview recommended: No **Off-campus interview available:** Yes
Evaluative: No **Informational only:** Yes **LD program:** No
Night in dorm provided: Yes **Non-refundable application fee:** $505
Early decision program: Yes **Applied:** NA **Accepted:** NA % **Deadline:** Nov. 1
Freshmen accepted other than Fall term: 0 % **SAT/FAF Code #** 3987

Transfers

Applied: 716 **Accepted:** 3 % **Application deadline for Fall:** Mar. 11 **Spring:** NA
Minimum grades recommended: NA **All new students who were transfers into all classes:** 2 %

Class Experience

Return 2nd year: 98 % **Graduate after 4 years:** 95 % **To graduate school within 1 year:** 28 %

Cost

Tuition deposit: $NA **Total cost (Including school's estimate on fees and books):** $24,000
Tuition: $17,500 **(In state: $)** **Room and board:** $6,200
Annual giving by parents: $915,000 **Average per student:** $80

Financial Aid

Average total package per student: $11,900 **Number receiving aid:** 40 %
Average scholarships and grants: $9,300 **Average loans:** $2,600 **Work-study program:** Yes
Undergraduates working on campus: 60 % **Average earnings:** $1,700
Non-need scholarships 0 % **Athletic scholarships:** No **FAF deadline:** Feb. 1
Off-campus part-time employment: Good **CO-OP program:** No
ROTC: Off campus **NROTC:** No **AFROTC:** Off campus

Endowment

Total: $2.6 Million **Per student (including graduate students):** $230,000

Location

Acres: 175 **Setting:** City **Miles from town center:** 1/2 **(Pop.** 130,000 **)**
40 **Miles from** Hartford **(Pop.** 137,000 **)** 75 **Miles from** New York **(Pop.** 7.5 Mil. **)**

Class Composition

Asian: 13 % **Black:** 8 % **Hispanic:** 5 % **White:** 74 % **Other:** NA %
Total minority : 16 % **Foreign countries:** 4 % (55 students)
From public schools: 60 % **Students from in state:** 10 %

Housing (on campus)

Freshmen required to live on campus: Yes **Guaranteed for:** 1 year
Available for all students: 90 % **Fraternity / Sorority housing:** 0 / 0
On-campus married student housing: Yes **Women-only dorms available:** No

Campus Life

Students living on campus: 90 % **Remain weekends:** 85 % **Handicap access:** 80 %
Car regulations: All may have
Number with cars: NA % **Adequacy of on-campus parking:** Poor
Number of fraternities: 7 **Chapter houses:** 0 **Number of sororities:** 4 **Chapter houses:** 0
Students belonging to fraternities: 10 % **Students belonging to sororities:** 10 %

Libraries and Computers

Books: 9.8 Million **Periodicals:** 52,000 **Microform items:** 3.4 Million
Microcomputers available: Yes **Microcomputers networked:** Yes

Classes

Faculty / Student Ratio: 1/5 **Classes taught by teacher assistants:** 20 %
Most popular majors: History, English, Economics **Classes begin:** Early Sept.
Baccalaureate degrees offered: BA, BIS, BS

Sports

Division: I **Except:** **Physical ed requirements:** None
Students participating in intercollegiate sports: 30 % **In intramural sports:** 50 %
Additional intercollegiate and/or intramural sports: (not found at all colleges)

Crew: Yes **Ice Hockey:** Yes **Lacrosse:** Yes **Wrestling:** Yes/M
Rugby: Yes **Sailing:** Yes **Skiing:** Yes
Squash: Yes **Ultimate Frisbee:** Yes **Water Polo:** Yes

Alumni

Number living: 118,000 **Annual giving:** $ 50 Million **Participation:** 3 %
Average annual gift: $ 1,500 **Average per student:** $4,600

3-2 Programs (2 degrees in 5 years)

Double majors - dual degrees

Observation and Opinion of:

Undergraduates and graduates ______________________________

____

College counselor ______________________________

____

Summary of Other Helpful College Guides and Books

This COLLEGE COMPARISON GUIDE enables you to select 10 to 20 schools from the 2000 four-year colleges. This manageable number can then be investigated more thoroughly, including an actual visit to those selected. After that, you will have reduced the suitable choices to 5 or 10 to which you should apply.

Appropriate facts and figures needed to make such an intelligent preliminary decision are contained between this book's covers, including numerous invaluable comparison tables found in no other book.

However, once this initial selection process is completed, the author recommends that you look at certain detailed information found in other college guides and books that can be helpful. These are available in many libraries and bookstores.

You will find the three books set out below are very useful in furnishing additional background material.

> *The Fiske Guide to Colleges* by Edward B. Fiske (Times Books). "Must" reading, once the serious interest list is narrowed down to 10 to 20 schools. Excellent description of each school in 3 or 4 pages. The setting, facilities, student body, campus life, academics, etc.
>
> *The Insider's Guide to the Colleges* by the Yale Daily News (St. Martin's Press, NY). Another excellent insight into the flavor of the colleges. A similar 2 or 3 pages on each college written by the students themselves and furnishing different perspectives.
>
> *New and Improved College Book* by Lisa Birnbach (Prentice Hall, NYC). A unique, humorous summary of best places to eat, drink, play, study, etc., as well as personal observation of students about campus life, professors, food, etc.

Some of the six 750 to 2800 page college guides set out below can be useful as to the supplementary material shown in **bold type**, but, as a practical matter, only after preliminary selections have been made by the use of the COLLEGE COMPARISON GUIDE.

> *Arco's The Right College* (1300 pages). A review of 1500 schools. **Information on admission to graduate schools, job outlook, etc.**
>
> *Barron's Profile of American Colleges* (1310 pages). A similar review of 1500 schools in narrative form. **Valuable information for international students, editorial advice on taking entrance exams, finding aid, etc.**

The College Handbook, published by the College Board (2000 pages). Basic information on 3100 two and four colleges. **A voluminous listing of majors available.**

Comparative Guide To American Colleges by Cass & Birnbaum (850 pages). A shorter concise descriptive review of several thousand colleges. **Extensive listing of majors offered.**

Lovejoy's College Guide (750 pages). Description of 2500 colleges. **Comprehensive sports index and a unique sports activities table.**

Peterson's Four-year Colleges (2775 pages). Covers nearly 2000 schools. **Helpful advice as to admissions, aid, etc. Two page description written by 800 colleges about themselves.**

Some of the following very readable books also can be of help:

Looking Beyond the Ivy League by Loren Pope (Penguin, 1990). Makes a compelling case for considering the smaller and often less well known but equally fine colleges. Also, guidance on the admission process and the application itself.

How To Get Into The Right College by Edward B. Fiske (Times Books, 1988). Though mainly a well done "how to get in" book, it also contains some interesting tables on "most Rhodes Scholars," "colleges offering unusual majors," and others.

Insider's Guide to the top 25 Colleges by Tom Fischgrund (Longstreet Press, 1989). A thorough discussion of the 25, all of of which are included in those selected by this COLLEGE COMPARISON GUIDE as among the leading colleges.

Choosing A College by Thomas Sowell (Harper and Row, 1989). Advice as to admissions, visiting, campus life, etc.

The College Student's Guide To Transferring Schools by Jennifer and David Smith (Avon Books, 1990). A comprehensive insight into the "how's, where's and why's of switching."

The Common Sense Guide to American Colleges by Charles Horner (Madison Books, 1991) 5 to 8 page commentary on each of 57 colleges included in this COLLEGE COMPARISON GUIDE.

About the Author

Born in Garden City, Long Island, NY, the author attended the local public school, the Browning School in New York City and Trinity-Pawling, the boarding school in Pawling, NY.

He is a graduate of Williams College and the University of Virginia Law School. He also has a Certified Financial Planner degree and is a member of the Georgia Bar.

A developer and businessman in Atlanta as well as a Georgia state legislator for the last 27 years, the author retired from the corporate business world a decade ago and is now an Educational Consultant in Atlanta. He is a member of the Secondary School Admission Test Board and has visited a number of colleges covered in this book.

He has authored *The Boarding School Guide,* a book on 231 leading schools throughout the United States.

The author also has an additional personal knowledge of and insight into colleges and boarding schools. One son, a graduate of the Westminister School in Atlanta, Williams College and Middlebury's Breadloaf School, has taught at the Darlington School in Rome, Georgia and is now teaching at St. Mark's in Southborough, MA. He also taught a year at Radley College in Oxford.

The author's other son graduated from the Lovett Lower School in Atlanta, Eaglebrook Junior Boarding School in Massachusetts, and Deerfield Academy. He is now a student at the University of Virginia.

Kiliaen V. R. Townsend
Educational Consultant
56 Paces West Dr., N.W.
Atlanta, Georgia 30327
(404) 261-2682